THE
PUSHCART PRIZE, XXX

AN ANNUAL SMALL PRESS READER

THIRTIETH ANNIVERSARY EDITION

BEST OF
THE SMALL
PRESSES

# The
# PUSHCART
# PRIZE

2006

PUSHCART

XXX

Edited by
Bill Henderson
with the Pushcart
Prize editors

Note: nominations for this series are invited from any small, independent, literary book press or magazine in the world, print or online. Up to six nominations—tear sheets or copies, selected from work published, or about to be published, in the calendar year—are accepted by our December 1 deadline each year. Write to Pushcart Press, P.O. Box 380, Wainscott, N.Y. 11975 for more information or consult our website www.pushcartprize.com.

## Acknowledgments

Selections for The Pushcart Prize are reprinted with the permission of authors and presses cited. Copyright reverts to authors and presses immediately after publication.

*Distributed by W. W. Norton & Co.*
*500 Fifth Ave., New York, N.Y. 10110*

Library of Congress Card Number: 76–58675
ISBN: 1–888889–19–5
      1–888889–21–7 (paperback)
ISSN: 0149–7863

*For Frank Conroy (1936–2005),
with thanks to Anthony Brandt*

# INTRODUCTION

## by BILL HENDERSON

THE PERSISTENT MYTH ABOUT SMALL PRESSES is that they rise like spring flowers, bloom for a season or two, droop and fold up. Somehow, the myth goes, it is supposed to be that way. The small and the literary are doomed from the get go.

This myth makes the rest of the comfortable, and crazed, commercial world feel better. Why step out of line, quit the day job, burn the credit cards and do something truly stupid like write a poem or a novel or, god forbid, dump your savings into a publishing operation run from your attic, basement or broom closet? Even publishing internet-lit seems a waste of effort, lost in porn and massive drivel.

But the myth often proves to be a lie. Some small presses, thanks to the writers that support them, have survived. This year the Pushcart Prize series rounds its third decade of total independence— no government grants, no institutional support—all thanks to our hundreds of volunteer contributing editors over so many years and to individual donors to our new endowment, the Pushcart Prize Fellowships. You will find their names elsewhere in the book.

But we share our birthday with many other presses. To name but a few: Wendy Lesser's eclectic and often astonishing *Threepenny Review* published issue one hundred recently after twenty-five years of slugging it out. *Sonora Review*, the oldest student run literary journal in the country, also turned twenty-five. Richard Burgin's *Boulevard* hit the two-decade mark as did Consortium—the determined distributor for eighty presses (often distributors expire faster than the supposedly ephemeral presses they distribute), and the excellent *Ontario Review* turned thirty.

Poets & Writers, that marvelous information source for serious literary sorts, founded by Galen Williams in 1970, reached thirty-five this year as did the Feminist Press. *TriQuarterly* is forty, *Chelsea* reached forty-seven, City Lights Books—fifty, *Paris Review*—fifty-one, *Hudson Review*—fifty-five, *Chicago Review*—fifty-nine, *Kenyon Review*—sixty-six, and a granddaddy of them all, *Prairie Schooner*, celebrated its seventy-eighth anniversary recently, surpassed only by *Poetry* founded in 1912.

So, on the subject of longevity, *Pushcart* has little to crow about. At thirty (or XXX) it's still a youth—but a kid with memories of its infancy that somehow tie into the present.

Back in 1976 our first edition was almost universally hailed by the book pundits—several features and reviews in the *New York Times*, *Publishers Weekly*, *Kirkus*, *Booklist*, *Library Journal*, etc., even *Newsweek* chimed in. Back then the fear of conglomerates taking over the entire book and magazine industry was palpable. What if Mattel toys absorbed Random House? Whence the culture? Well, now in 2005 when all commercial publishing has been chewed up by giants that make Mattel toys seem like, well, a toy, too few of us seem to notice or care—except for the stalwart small press remnant, of course.

In 1976 the *Pushcart Prize* was saluted for its ringing defiance of commercial trends. But *Time* magazine pointedly refused to review our first edition (although they did come through for PPVI). *Time's* book reviewer growled, "that's not small press, there's Saul Bellow in it!" And sure enough we did run a self-interview with Bellow from *Ontario Review*. Noted Bellow then, "TV creates the exciting fiction . . . accepted by the great public and believed by almost everyone to be real. Is reading possible for a people with its mind in this state?" He also took a swipe at *Time* magazine "with its strangely artificial approach to the world".

Over thirty years later some things have changed, and ironies abound. The great Saul Bellow, who died in April, 2005, himself became a small press publisher in his later years with his *News From The Republic of Letters*, edited with Keith Botsford. Last year PPXXIX featured a debut short story from Bellow's magazine, "The Core" by Jack Herlihy, cited by *Publishers Weekly* as a highlight of that edition.

Said Bellow in his final issue ". . . there are in fact millions of literate Americans in a state of separation from others of their kind. They are, if you like, the readers of Cheever, a crowd of them too large to be hidden in the woods. Departments of literature across the country have not succeeded in alienating them from books, works old and new. My friend Keith Botsford and I felt strongly that if the woods were filled with readers gone astray, among those readers there were probably writers as well . . . We are a pair of utopian codgers who feel we have a duty to literature. I hope we are not like those humane do-gooders who, when the horse was vanishing, still donated troughs in City Hall Square for thirsty nags."

April 2005 was a doubly sad month for American literature: we lost Frank Conroy, author of the memoir *Stop-Time*, the novel *Body & Soul* and other books, director of the University of Iowa's Writers Workshop for eighteen years and former head of the Literature Panel for the National Endowment for the Arts. Frank was a friend and a supporter of this series for decades.

In his introduction to PPXII, he warned of the encroaching right-wing threat at the National Endowment—"Voluble conservatives with such a marked animus to contemporary American literature . . . that it would appear their agenda is not to support it but to change it."

As an example of far right nonsense, Frank's introduction included this tidbit, which I reprint in full from his PP intro. It's so delicious.

"During my time at the NEA a down-home congressman from Texas, hot on the trail of degeneracy, sent some clean-cut (and actually quite pleasant) young people from his staff to go through the files of poetry fellowship winners. 'This stuff don't rhyme', one of them remarked to me. When I asked what their instructions were another one answered 'we're supposed to find dirty words. Sex words, and like that.' Despite days of reading, and many pages carried back for the Congressman's perusal, they apparently couldn't find anything horrendous enough. The Congressman changed his tactics. Using a flashy, trashy article from a right-wing magazine as his source, he picked some controversial names from past winners of poetry fellowships, took lines and sections out of context from work done over their whole careers, (none of which work was ever part of the fellowship application, or was written dur-

9

ing the period of support) and waved his peculiar anthology around in the air during the vote on the NEA budget in the House of Representatives, claiming the taxpayers' money was going to support 'filth'. We can laugh, certainly, but the fact is this crude, dishonest tactic resulted in a substantial cut in the budget in the entire agency. Thousands of artists in many different genres were affected. (A pyrrhic victory for the Congressman, however, who went home to read the startling news in the local paper that the State of Texas had for years gotten much more money back from the NEA than it had contributed to it through taxes, and what on earth did he think he was doing, etc.)"

Frank was a personal model to countless writing students and an exacting teacher. Writer David Halberstam remarked in Frank's *New York Times* obituary on April 7, 2005, "I think what made him a great teacher was that he was so wounded himself; he had a very good sense for the wounds of other people. He knew what a frail business this being a writer is."

Frank was also a good enough pool player to have run the table twice, and, a good enough self-taught pianist to have jammed with Charles Mingus. Mingus recalled how Frank once apologized to him for being a klutz: "You are an authentic primitive," Mingus said. "That's true. But you also swing."

Years ago my wife Genie, daughter Lily and I visited Frank in his Nantucket summer home and took along a gift for his new son (a stuffed cloth toy that I think resembled a monkey). I say I think because a few years ago Frank sent us photos of that toy after years of use and misuse. "Thanks so much for your gift," said Frank. "My son is mostly grown up now. As you can see it was much appreciated." The photos of a lumpish tangle still hang on my office wall, a reminder of Frank's courtesy and humor.

For all of his students—including the many writers he influenced who have appeared in this series over three decades—goodbye Frank, and thank you. You swing.

Pushcart was honored this year by the poetry editing of co-editors David Baker and Linda Gregerson. Their job, sifting through thousands of poems, was of course impossible. For attempting the impossible and for coming up with such a terrific selection, I thank them profoundly.

David Baker is the author of eight books of poetry, including *Midwest Ecologue* (2005 W. W. Norton). His poems have appeared widely in journals such as *Atlantic Monthly*, *The Georgia Review*, *The Nation*, *The New Yorker*, *The Paris Review*, *Poetry* and *Yale Review* and his essays about poetry were published in *American Book Review*, *Gettysburg Review*, *New England Review*, *Southern Review* and elsewhere.

He has won awards and fellowships from among others the Guggenheim Foundation, the National Endowment for the Arts, the Ohio Arts Council and Poetry Society of America.

Baker is currently professor of English at Denison University and he serves regularly on the faculty of the MFA program for writers at Warren Wilson College and is poetry editor of *The Kenyon Review*. He is married to poet Ann Townsend and they live with their daughter Katherine "on small acreage" in rural Ohio.

Linda Gregerson is the author of three collections of poetry: *Fire in the Conservatory* (Dragon Gate 1982), *The Woman Who Died in Her Sleep* (Houghton Mifflin 1996), and *Waterborne* (Houghton Mifflin 2002). *The Woman Who Died in Her Sleep* was a finalist for the Lenore Marshall Prize and The Poets Prize; *Waterborne* won the 2003 Kingsley Tufts Poetry Award.

Gregerson is also the author of two volumes of criticism: *The Reformation of the Subject: Spenser, Milton, and the English Protestant Epic* (Cambridge University Press 1995), and *Negative Capability: Contemporary American Poetry* (University of Michigan Press 2001).

Gregerson has received awards from the American Academy of Arts and Letters, the Poetry Society of America, and the Modern Poetry Association, and fellowships from the Guggenheim Foundation, the Institute for Advanced Study, the National Humanities Center, and the National Endowment for the Arts. She has served on the faculties of the Bread Loaf Writers Conference, The Kenyon Review Writers Conference, and the Warren Wilson MFA Program for Writers. Gregerson is the Frederick G. L. Huetwell Professor of English Language and Literature at the University of Michigan, where she teaches creative writing and Renaissance literature.

PPXXX is extraordinary in many ways. Most important to me is the number of new presses featured here: a record for recent years. We honor reprints from *Dogwood, Bellevue Literary Review, National Poetry Review, Chautauqua Literary Journal, Speakeasy,* Perugia Press, *Great River Review, Literary Imagination, Bloom,* and *Blackbird*. As always we welcome online and print journals, and are pleased that so many new publications have emerged this year.

PPXXX is missing one important person—our essays editor Tony Brandt has retired. For almost two decades Tony turned a tough eye on the essays pile, and always produced a superb selection. A few years ago, Pushcart published a collection of his picks, *The Pushcart Book of Essays,* granted a rave review and a star by *Publishers Weekly*. Tony will devote his time to writing a history of Arctic exploration to be published by Knopf, "The Man Who Ate His Boots."

As a veteran of the small press scene, and the pittance paid (translation: copies) Tony is used to eating his boots, or, rather sneakers. Who can afford boots?

Enjoy this new Pushcart Prize. As I say every year, it is the best yet. After three decades, it only gets better and better, and for that we honor the indomitable heart and spirit of small press writers and editors.

# THE PEOPLE WHO
# HELPED

FOUNDING EDITORS—*Anaïs Nin (1903–1977), Buckminster Fuller (1895–1983), Charles Newman, Daniel Halpern, Gordon Lish, Harry Smith, Hugh Fox, Ishmael Reed, Joyce Carol Oates, Len Fulton, Leonard Randolph, Leslie Fiedler (1917–2003), Nona Balakian (1918–1991), Paul Bowles (1910–1999), Paul Engle (1908–1991), Ralph Ellison (1914–1994), Reynolds Price, Rhoda Schwartz, Richard Morris, Ted Wilentz (1915–2001), Tom Montag, William Phillips (1907–2002), Poetry editor: H. L. Van Brunt.*

CONTRIBUTING EDITORS FOR THIS EDITION—*Maureen Seaton, Nicola Mason, Martha Collins, Stephen Corey, Toi Derricotte, Mark Irwin, Dara Wier, Paul Maliszewski, Vern Rutsala, Tony Ardizzone, Bob Cording, Jana Harris, Ethan Bumas, Colette Inez, Lance Olsen, Erin McGraw, Sheila Schwartz, Dan Chaon, Patricia Staton, Edward Hoagland, R. T. Smith, Alice Fulton, Pinckney Benedict, Joshua Beckman, Molly Bendall, Tony Quagliano, Christine Zawadiwsky, Robert Boswell, Roger Weingarten, Andrew Feld, Antler, Claire Bateman, James Reiss, Kevin Prufer, Paul Zimmer, Michael Martone, Sydney Lea, Wes McNair, Joan Connor, Philip Appleman, Gerry Locklin, Kim Barnes, Mary Yukari Waters, Richard Burgin, Carl Phillips, Gary Gildner, Linda Bierds, Rachel Hadas, Debra Spark, Laura Kasischke, Carl Dennis, Melanie Rae Thon, Timothy Geiger, Chard deNiord, Kay Ryan, Claire Davis, Gary Fincke, Kathy Fagan, Andrew Hudgins, Christopher Buckley, Lee Upton, Len Roberts, Elizabeth Spires, C. E. Poverman, Grace Schulman, Floyd Skloot, Billy Collins, Kent Nelson, William Olsen, Ellen Bass, Donald Platt, Marianne Boruch, Kirk Nesset, Nancy McCabe, Marilyn*

13

Hacker, Fred Leebron, Katrina Roberts, Sharon Dilworth, Jim Moore, Gibbons Ruark, Jennifer Atkinson, Bob Hicok, Eric Puchner, Matt Yurdana, Reginald Gibbons, Charles Harper Webb, Michael Collier, Robert Wrigley, Tom Filer, Kathleen Hill, Christopher Howell, Alan Michael Parker, Rita Dove, Richard Jackson, Daniel Hoffman, Brigit Kelly, Susan Hahn, Marvin Bell, Judith Kitchen, Jack Marshall, S. L. Wisenberg, Daniel Libman, Gerald Stern, Jim Barnes, Dorianne Laux, Thomas Kennedy, Maura Stanton, David Jauss, William Heyen, Arthur Smith, Jeffrey Harrison, Brenda Miller, Terrance Hayes, Deb Olin Unferth, Gerald Shapiro, Joyce Carol Oates, Pamela Stewart, Andrea Hollander Budy, Dan Masterson, Sherod Santos, Bruce Beasley, John Drury, Jane Hirshfield, Ed Ochester, Steve Kowit, Ted Deppe, Michael Waters, Edward Hirsch, Cyrus Cassells, Reginald Shepherd, Carolyn Alessio, Dick Allen, Henry Carlile, Suzanne Cleary, Nadine Meyer, Robert Thomas, Rachel Loden, Ed Falco, Stephen Dunn, John Allman, Katherine Taylor, Kim Addonizio, Renée Ashley, Dana Levin, Margaret Luongo, Joseph Hurka, Richard Garcia, Alice Mattison, Kenneth Gangemi, Eleanor Wilner, Catherine Barnett, Stuart Dischell, David Rivard, Robin Hemley, Michael Heffernan, Sharon Solwitz, BJ Ward, Sylvia Watanabe, Joan Murray, Ralph Angel, Kathy Callaway, Judith Hall, Jean Thompson, Jane Brox, David Wojahn, David St. John, Mike Newirth, Jeffrey Hammond, Valerie Laken, Yiyun Li, Cleopatra Mathis, Marianna Cherry, M. D. Elevitch, Elizabeth Graver, Robert McBrearty, Nancy Richard, Daniel Henry, Stacey Richter, Michael Bowden, Kristin King, Elizabeth McKenzie, Alice Schell, Donald Revell, DeWitt Henry, Eamon Grennan, George Keithley, T. Coraghessan Boyle, Wally Lamb, John Kistner, Jim Simmerman, Jessica Roeder, Tracy Mayor, Karl Elder, Katherine Min, Salvatore Scibona, Jewel Mogan, Rosellen Brown, Caroline Langston, Philip Levine, Julia Kasdorf, Lucia Perillo, Maxine Kumin, Marie S. Williams, Ron Tanner, Terese Svoboda, Bonnie Jo Campbell, Malinda McCollum, H. E. Francis, Tom Lux, R. C. Hildebrandt, John Kister, Eugene Stein, Joe Ashby Porter, Mark Wisniewski, Hayden Carruth, Ted Genoways, Virginia Holman, Mary Gordon, Joe Ashby Porter, Michael Dennis Browne, Rebecca McClanahan, Virginia Holman, Diann Blakely, Daniel Orozco

PAST POETRY EDITORS—H. L. Van Brunt, Naomi Lazard, Lynne Spaulding, Herb Leibowitz, Jon Galassi, Grace Schulman,

14

*Carolyn Forché, Gerald Stern, Stanley Plumly, William Stafford, Philip Levine, David Wojahn, Jorie Graham, Robert Hass, Philip Booth, Jay Meek, Sandra McPherson, Laura Jensen, William Heyen, Elizabeth Spires, Marvin Bell, Carolyn Kizer, Christopher Buckley, Chase Twichell, Richard Jackson, Susan Mitchell, Lynn Emanuel, David St. John, Carol Muske, Dennis Schmitz, William Matthews, Patricia Strachan, Heather McHugh, Molly Bendall, Marilyn Chin, Kimiko Hahn, Michael Dennis Browne, Billy Collins, Joan Murray, Sherod Santos, Judith Kitchen, Pattiann Rogers, Carl Phillips, Martha Collins, Carol Frost, Jane Hirshfield, Dorianne Laux.*

ROVING EDITORS—*Lily Frances Henderson, Genie Chipps*

EUROPEAN EDITORS—*Liz and Kirby Williams*

MANAGING EDITOR—*Hannah Turner*

FICTION EDITORS—*Jack Driscoll, David Means, Joseph Hurka*

GUEST POETRY EDITORS—*David Baker, Linda Gregerson*

EDITOR AND PUBLISHER—*Bill Henderson*

# CONTENTS

THE
PUSHCART PRIZE, XXX

# PRESENTLY IN RUINS

fiction by GREGORY BLAKE SMITH

from STORYQUARTERLY

THE NAMES HAD THE SOUND of the History Channel: Pearl Harbor, Eniwetok Atoll, Guam. His father had been to each during the Second World War and he, the son, had never known about it. Fifty-one years he'd been alive and to find out who his father had been he had to get like this: drunk, lost, estranged from a minimum of two wives, and a murderer in the eyes of his sister, and maybe the state of Indiana.

He was in a hotel room drinking bourbon and typing bits and pieces of his father's life into Google—the name of the ship he'd served on in the South Pacific, the New England factory he'd worked in for thirty-eight years—zooming the JPEGs to 150% and searching for his father's face in the half-empty bleachers at Braves Field or in the back row of the 1948 Clifton Glee Club. In half a dozen photos he could take this or that man's brushy hair, improvise on a nondescript face, and come up with his father, CPO William Pike. Second Tenor Willy Pike. He had been there, if not in the photos then in the real world—rooting for the Boston Braves, singing "Shenandoah" in his one suit. That rocky outcrop just off the Eniwetok beach was where he'd maybe sat shirtless in the equatorial sun, had maybe relieved himself there, fretted, wished he was back home in wintry New England. A small, quiet, dreamy man. The Japanese had torpedoed his ship just off the Philippines.

❀

They had grown up, he and his sister, in a sad manufacturing town in the northwestern corner of Connecticut. It had been what his sociol-

23

ogy textbook would later call a depressed area, a blue-collar world filled with OK Used Cars and out-of-work older brothers. What lingered in his memory was the feeling of having nothing to do. Hanging around on front porches, on front lawns that were nothing but packed dirt, at night sitting in the television room with his mother and sister, watching "F-Troop" while his father worked on his model railroad in the cellar.

It was one of the oddities of his childhood—the presence in the cellar of a 1:87 scale version of the town he was growing up in. Only this was his town circa 1926, a quarter century before he was born, not the Clifton he knew with its closed factories, its empty downtown, its mammoth brass mill turned into a block-square heap of brick like a New England Hiroshima, but the Clifton of his father's boyhood, recreated in plaster and epoxy and scale timber. *There* the American Brass Mill had its sawtooth roof intact; the valleys surrounding the town had orchards on their hillsides, kids fishing in the brooks, Model Ts motoring up the gravel roads. He had known, even as a child, that his father had lived more in that world than in the real world. That in the real world he was a shy misfit, an object of fun in the factory, of taunting by the neighborhood kids. The son, from his earliest memories, had been ashamed of him.

When, forty years later, he and his sister had come east to help sell the house after their mother died, they had had to break up the railroad, take an ax from one of the yard-sale tables and bludgeon the layout into a heap of plaster and wood and then haul it out to a dumpster at the side of the road. There had been no other way. While they did it, their father had stood in his walker on the tarred driveway, his back to the house, watching the clouds sail between the trees.

❖

The *USS Shadwell*, he learned in between bourbons, had been named after the birthplace ("presently in ruins") of Thomas Jefferson. On the website, there were pictures of it, a big, ungainly thing with a crane used to service amphibious equipment and landing craft. There were links to shops where you could purchase caps, coffee mugs, sweatshirts with "USS Shadwell LSD-15" on them, and a link to information about a reunion.

His father had told him—that last night—that the torpedo had been meant for a tanker, but that the convoy had maneuvered and the *Shadwell* had taken the hit instead of the larger ship. That did not make the official history. Neither did the five hundred men standing on deck in their Mae Wests, waiting for the ship to sink. Or CPO Pike in the midst of them, having to take a leak but not daring to go to the head.

Had there been a need, after all, that last night, to communicate something? To say something about mortality while his son took out of his briefcase the bottle of Seconal, the plastic bag, the pantyhose?

*

After the yard sale, after closing on the house, they had loaded up a small U-Haul trailer and driven from Connecticut to his sister's in Indiana, spending a night in a motel along Interstate 80 in Pennsylvania. It had been a painful trip for their father. They had had to help him switch back and forth from sitting in the front seat to lying in the back. He was suffering from Paget's Disease, a condition in which the bones gradually grow soft and misshapen. The prognosis typically includes disintegration of the spine, and compression of the brain as a result of the skull growing malformed. Its chief symptom—the Paget's Disease Support Website had informed the son when he had first logged on three years ago—was pain.

At Harpswell House the residents dined in a common dining room. They had church services, and Bingo, and singing. A hair stylist visited every Tuesday. The aides washed you. They helped you get dressed, pull your socks on, Velcro your running shoes. They would not, however, cut your toenails. Why they wouldn't, when the son pressed them during one of his semi-monthly visits, was unclear. It had something to do with being an operation in which actual parts of the body were removed. Which was different from washing, or dressing, or brushing teeth.

They had furnished the room with things brought from the old house. A table and two chairs. A lamp. A bookcase. They bought a twenty-five inch TV, and from a medical supply store a lounger that had a motorized lift mechanism to assist the infirm in standing up. In the bookcase were all his old New England railroad books, and on top of the bookcase a solitary 2-8-2 freight engine. No. 23, a USRA Light Mikado, weathered with oil spots and grime and a touch of rust.

On the TV the Boston Braves, who had become the Milwaukee Braves and were now the Atlanta Braves, were on TBS nearly every night. The whole country could watch them. Their uniforms still had the same script-written *Braves* underlined with the same tomahawk. But it wasn't like walking down Commonwealth Avenue on a May afternoon, paying your twenty-five cents for a bleacher seat, being one of maybe 4,000 men in coats and ties watching a young Casey Stengel manage, the lefty Eddie Carnett pitch, Babe Dahlgren bat. Not the same as when you were young, alive, with an eye out for the girls. Maybe it was fifty cents.

✿

The website mentioned that the USS *Shadwell's* gunners had "splashed a Zeke," that it had steered by "trick wheel." What did these things mean? Who was left to tell him?

✿

The first time his father tried to kill himself was about a year after he'd moved into the Harpswell House. Jean had called to tell her brother and the two had spoken in low voices, disbelieving, with long silences. What hung on the line between them was the paradox of their timid, funny, pointless, ineffectual father—the man who when he had first gone to school, had been placed in the Opportunity Room—killing himself, taking a bottle of pills, actually doing it. (Also, sadly, bitterly—though this thought might have occurred only to the brother—the aptness that he would fail.)

They spoke of depression, of the death of their mother, of the pain of the Paget's. They asked each other in hushed tones to imagine the prospect of such pain, the certain knowledge that you would end up bedridden, your bones squeezing you from the inside, your body glowing with pain. The sister had said that: glowing with pain.

On the model railroad there had been one figure down in the freight yard, a boy a half-inch tall watching a switch engine making up a milk train. There was a bike propped against his side, a baseball cap on his head. "That's me," the father had said once and smiled into the scale distance. That was him as a boy in 1926.

✿

His first wife had found his father funny. His second wife had not. He had left his first wife. The second had left him.

✿

When they were kids and went shopping as a family, their father would lag behind, dreamily looking at this thing, at that thing, while their mother directed the sister and brother in what they were shopping for, how much they could spend. When they passed something that was stitched—handbags, suitcases, shaving kits—the father would stop and inspect them, looking to see if the stitching had been done with one of the "Puritan" machines that his company manufac-

26

tured. He could tell by the type of stitch. When he found one, he touched it with a surprised smile, as if he had found some part of himself functioning properly in the world.

Now in the hotel room, waiting for the police if the police were going to come, the son typed <puritan sewing Clifton> into Google to see what came up.

Then he typed <'w.w. mertz' 'department store' Clifton>.

Then he typed <'elizabeth skibisky' 'Clifton high school' 'Class of 1969'>.

Why? he wondered. What was he doing?

✻

The second attempt was with black-market Valium the sister had gotten. They had talked it over on the phone. She knew someone in the plant who knew someone who could get it for her: this, the brother marveled, from the girl who had gone to college in the late sixties and had never to this day done drugs, as far as he knew. She wanted him to know that it was just for their father's peace of mind, a kind of insurance policy, something whose presence in the nightstand drawer would calm him when he got scared of the pain to come. It was a sort of escape clause, the brother realized, a psychological feint that allowed her to do what was otherwise emotionally off the charts. He, on the other hand, had wanted to know how strong the pills were, would they do the job. She'd answered that the guy in the plant had said it was the really strong stuff. What did that mean? he had asked a little testily, how many milligrams? And there it was in the silence between them, the old antagonism of their childhood: she a little scattered, myopic, trusting; he, exacting, demanding, wanting to pin things down and know what he was about—the future patent attorney. But he had let it go. If she was willing to do this—he could hear the struggle in her voice, the cost, the fear—then never mind the milligrams.

They turned out, by the hospital lab's evaluation, to have been the smallest commercially available dose—2 mg, twenty of them— enough to put their father out for 48 hours and to make the six days in the hospital an amnesiac gray, but with no lasting effect. They were monitoring him now, his sister told him over the phone. They would start him on physical therapy in a few days. She had been through an ordeal, she said. She had been terrified the police would ask where the pills came from. That was it for her. She couldn't do any more.

27

What really annoyed him was that months earlier, after the first attempt, he had gone online and looked up The Hemlock Society, e-mailed them for their literature. There was a right way of doing it. There was even a step-by-step procedure in the booklet, a sidebar with Dos and Don'ts. He had mailed it to her months ago. When he had talked to her on the phone afterwards she'd said it was too ghastly. It was too gruesome: asphyxiation. The elastic bands, the turkey-sized oven bag: she couldn't do it. But she'd asked around and now she knew of a guy in the plant. . . . The brother should've insisted on the milligrams. Instead he'd let her hide down in the cellar.

(Their mother could have done it, he knew, could have gotten the right stuff, seen to its administration, followed through, closed the deal . . . but she was gone. She was gone and, if it was going to get done, he would have to be the one to do it.)

"Four thousand dollars," his father had chuckled when the son finally called. They were speaking of the hospital bill. "Who would think not dying would cost so much?"

✿

He searched for <'the katzenjammer kids'>, for <'rheingold beer'>, for <chucklehead>.

"The Katzenjammer Kids" because they were part of his earliest memory, sitting in his father's lap and being read to from the Sunday funnies. "Rheingold Beer" he remembered being in the icebox. And "Chucklehead" had been his father's name for him when he was little.

Chucklehead. Why Chucklehead? What was its derivation? Why had it died out?

✿

They should have saved him. They should have saved the boy from 1926, pried his feet from the painted plaster, brought him with them to Indiana, placed him on the bookcase next to the USRA Mikado.

That, and the Boston Braves on TBS, and a model of the USS Shadwell atop the TV. 1:245. A scale world to breathe in. To move in without pain, loss, regret.

About a month after the second attempt the son had made a dogleg from Washington on his way back to San Jose and gone to visit. His father was back in the Harpswell House by then, able again to get to the dining room for meals, to sit in his power recliner and watch TV. He joked with the staff, teased the kitchen help. They called him "Trouble." "Here comes Trouble," they said, as the eighty-five-year-old man

28

made his slow, misshapen way along the corridor. They knew, of course, but they played along. It almost seemed as if he were happy. Teasing, almost flirting. He was blossoming out, Jean said.

But when the son knocked on his father's door the second morning, there had come from inside the room a tremendous groan. A horrible, animal sound. The son knew from Jean that getting out of bed was the worst. A flame of pain that ran from his father's hip to his spine into his head. The son opened the door and stepped inside in time to see the father standing on the other side of the bed, with his face trying to recover. Smiling, for god's sakes.

(What the son's first wife had liked about the father—had found sweet, endearing—was the bashful, little-boy-lost, eyes-averted teasing. She had slipped easily into the game, always had a ready comeback. The father had renamed one of the factories on the railroad after her. Annelise Industries. And he'd urged his son the chucklehead to buy stock in it, a sly compliment to the wife whose pretty face beamed as she teased back, "Don't you sass now!" She was from Georgia. He had left her because she wasn't intellectual enough, didn't read Stephen Jay Gould or Elaine Pagels, didn't know who V.S. Naipaul was.)

"They're sanding me away," his father said that morning after he'd made it around the foot of the bed and into his Assist-a-Lift chair. He held up a piece of pumice stone. "The nurses. They're sanding me away."

✿

The Katzenjammer Kids' names were Hans and Fritz. There was Mama and Der Captain and Der Inspector. They spoke in outrageous accents, Mama spanking them with an "Ach, Himmel!" while Hans and Fritz gleefully eyed the snoring Captain—"Mit such snortling only dynamite could vake him!"—and in the next panel attaching an outboard motor to the Captain's bed, sending him putt-putting out to sea.

Who knew? Maybe that was it, the strip that had been read to him, sitting on his father's lap on a Sunday afternoon, in Eisenhower's America.

✿

He tried to get his sister to talk to him. Did they not have a responsibility to help their father? He was in pain. He could not deliver himself. Was there not a moral obligation on the adult children to ease the parent's hurt? Had he not done that for them when they were lit-

29

tle, picked them up when they had fallen, held them until the pain was gone? They were not a religious family: There was no question of the soul. No trespass on God-given property. Their father's mind was sound. The prospect of unbearable pain was not a prelude to *non compos mentis* but a spur to rational decision. How could they not help him?

She sat in an overstuffed chair, feet pulled up under her, arms crossed as if to lock herself in. She had had breast cancer five years ago and one of her breasts, he knew, was gone.

"I can't," she said.

He went at it again, laid out the ethics of it, the logic. He knew he sounded like a lawyer, but he also believed what he was saying. What if she were dying, in horrible pain, with nothing to look forward to but the pain worsening, her personality reduced to drugged-out nothingness, would she not want someone to help her? Would she not want him, her brother, to help her kill herself?

"Yes," she said.

Then . . .?

She looked out the window at the white birches with their leaves gone. "I can't do it."

Okay, then he needed to know if he went it alone, if he talked to their father and found that they were on the same page, if he did it—not this weekend, but soon, before it was too late—if the police came to talk to her afterwards, could she tell them she didn't know anything about it? Could she do that? Could he rely on her?

❖

(His second wife hadn't liked any of them—father, mother, daughter, and as it turned out, son. She had said the father had Avoidant Personality Disorder, that he displayed a withdrawn pattern with core features of shyness, dysphoria, distorted cognition in relation to self-effacement. The model railroad was a paradigmatic case of magical thinking. Some people had astrology, alien abduction, Atlantis to make them feel empowered. His father found narcissistic omnipotence in a scale model recreation of Clifton circa 1926. She recommended the triazolobenzodiazepine drug Alphrazolam. His father named a casket factory after her.)

❖

"Chucklehead," according to the *Online Webster's Dictionary*, was "a stupid, gauche person; BLOCKHEAD; DOLT"; and derived from the obsolete adjective "chuckle" meaning "clumsy" or "stupid," which in

30

turn derived "[perh. irreg. fr.]" from the now dialect "chuck" meaning "a log or lump" which in turn gave itself to the term for a cut of dressed beef consisting of the neck and part of the shoulder ("chuck steak," "ground chuck"), which in turn described the lumpish, shouldery shape of a lathe or drill press chuck, his father having been a master machinist.

He clicked on the little speaker icon, and let the laptop call him "chucklehead."

✲

The next time he flew in, his father was in a wheelchair. He had to be helped out of bed, helped into the wheelchair, wheeled from his room down to the dining hall. He had to be helped on and off the toilet. The nurse disbursed his pain medication in daily rations, standing over him while he took it to make sure he wasn't squirreling it away. There was a noticeable drop in his abilities, in his concentration, in his memory. He had begun to drift, sometimes to repeat himself.

"I waited too long," he said on the second day of the visit. They were sitting on the little deck the Harpswell House had in the rear of the building, watching the chickadees fly to and from a bird feeder. Though the son had practiced sentences on the airplane, ways of bringing up the matter, he hadn't been able to do it the day before. Now his father was going to do it for him.

"Too long for what?"

The old man made a finger-pistol and raised it to his temple.

The son nodded, like of course he understood. "There's a way," he said, quietly.

"Too late."

"There's a way with a plastic bag."

The father dropped his eyes, stared at his lap. He'd already tried that, he said after a minute. He had made "a dry run" and had found the suffocation too awful. The plastic stuck to your face.

"Yes," the son intoned gently. One of his legs—how strange!—was quivering inside his pant leg. "But there's a way." And he detailed the Hemlock Society's method: Seconal to calm you, plastic bag held on by rubber bands or pantyhose, a painter's mask to keep the plastic from being sucked into the mouth and nostrils, a baseball hat to keep it off your face. He had practiced saying this, ran through it now as if he were back in law school, in moot court where he'd always had his arguments memorized.

31

"A painter's mask," his father was repeating. His face registered the ingenuity of it. "That might work."

*

On eBay there was a purse with W. W. Mertz on the label. He clicked on the enlargement, studied the name of the department store of his childhood. Just the sight of the familiar letters brought back to him the smell of perfume, the salesladies behind their glass cases with the makeup and lipstick. The mezzanine with its balustrade, the elevator operator in his uniform. How many afternoons had he gone there after school to smell the baseball mitts, to browse through the records? Hi-Fidelity albums for $2.99, Stereophonic $3.99. Standing on the narrow wood flooring and reading through the song titles, trying to decide. They were long gone now, those wooden floors. The salesladies with their costume jewelry. The winter afternoons.

The purse was from the late 1950s, the eBay description said, a black leather bucket purse with peach faille lining, in fine to excellent condition. It didn't mention the stitching.

Was everybody like this? he wondered. Did the past, the inconsequential past, seem to everyone so monstrous? He could have understood it if it were the meaningful past that haunted him—his draft number, say, or the time he'd tried to kiss Elizabeth Skibisky and she'd laughed at him. But this, this awe of the ruined everyday—the way the wallpaper of his childhood bedroom had become so full of consequence, of dread—what did it mean?

*

His father had never once phoned him. Never, not when he was away at college or at law school. Or later when he was married, when his children were born or when they had their birthdays. Not once.

"Maybe you can't get free," he said now. "That'd be okay."

"No, I can come."

"Okay. All right."

"If you're sure you want me."

There had been a pause on the line, and then a too-emphatic voice, a voice trying not to be frightened: "What the heck, it's time!"

*

There was no Elizabeth Skibisky. No matter what he typed, or how he tried to manipulate the search engine. There were no Skibiskys in Clifton anymore, in the whole of Connecticut. What had happened to her? Married and remarried, name changed, dead? How could he find her?

32

(All the bourbon from the minibar was gone. It was midnight; the police weren't coming. He'd have to start on scotch.)

❁

He had done his research. It was not illegal in the State of Indiana to be present at a suicide. It was only illegal to assist. Just what might constitute assistance would be up to the local DA.

He carried onto the plane, in his attorney's briefcase, a half bottle of Seconal, a painter's mask, a Glad turkey-roasting bag, a Boston Braves baseball cap, an ice bag, a pair of his current wife's pantyhose, the Hemlock Society pamphlet, and a pair of rubber gloves. He would have to make sure that the Seconal bottle and the rubber gloves were disposed of afterwards.

He got a room at the Indianapolis Hyatt. He had an idea Jean would not want him staying at the house.

In the rental car he tried for the hundredth time to think what they would say when the time came, what symbolic, ritual thing would ease the terrible moment. But there was nothing. There had been no center to their lives together, and there was nothing that they could call on now. He doubted if they would even be able to say they loved one another. And yet it was an act of love, wasn't it? what he was doing?

He reached Jean on the cell phone. She had spent the afternoon with their father, had dropped hints about her brother flying in that evening but the old man wouldn't come clean. And no, he had not said goodbye in any special way. She had tried, but he wouldn't let her.

When he drove up to the Harpswell House his father was sitting crumpled in his wheelchair, facing the front door, waiting. He had a magazine on his lap. When his son came through the door, he held up the front cover.

"Makes me nostalgic," he said.

It was an illustrator's painting of a New England homestead in winter: white clapboard siding and black shutters, split-rail fence, cozy pasture and waiting sleigh. There was smoke curling from the chimney.

"For what?" the son found himself asking. His father turned the magazine back to himself, blinked, screwed up his mouth.

"I don't know," he said and laughed as though the joke was on him. He tossed the magazine onto a nearby chair.

"You're all going to vanish," he told an aide as they went slowly

33

down the corridor. He made a magic-wand arabesque in the air. "Little Willy the Magician!"

"Little Willy the Trouble-maker, you mean!" the aide called with her nursing-home bonhomie. She smiled after them, watched them go.

Under his breath his father muttered, "Yeah, yeah, yeah."

Down in his room he had divided his possessions into two piles, one on either side of the table. There were photographs of the Clifton house, of Jean's wedding, of Annelise. There was a photo of their mother circa 1943 with a come-hither look that the son had never seen before. There was his honorable discharge from the service. A micrometer. Scale model plans for the roundhouse at the New Canaan yard. In front of each pile was a kind of place card. "Jean" one of them said; the other said "William."

"Self-evident," his father said with a wave of his hand.

◊

He remembered—strange! where did such a memory come from?—he couldn't have been but five or six: they were walking, the four of them, along an abandoned railroad right-of-way. It was the sort of thing they did Sunday afternoons: his father with paper and pencil, tape measure in hand, his sister collecting leaves, and he, little William, holding his mother's hand and negotiating the weeds between the railroad ties. His father would go ahead of them, writing things down, "checking for ghosts," he said, finding the occasional foundation of a way house or a shed, and taking measurements. From time to time he would stand up and look around at the blue-green trees, listen to the buzzing meadow, as if he could somehow see, somehow hear, in a world which was presently in ruins, a past that was alive and lit with meaning.

But on that day, on the day he remembered now with such peculiar clarity, his father had gotten too far ahead of them and the son, watching him grow smaller, losing him from time to time behind a bush or a leafy branch, had gotten scared and begun to cry. His mother had picked him up and carried him, told him it was all right, pointed at his father ahead of them—see?—and yet still he had cried, full of childish dread, stretching his arms out to his father who had stopped just where the roadbed curved into the dark trees, his pant legs in bright sun, his head and shoulders in shadow, turned for a moment to look back at them, smiling, waving to them. . . .

◊

They did a dry run. He helped his father out of the wheelchair and into bed, laid out the items from the briefcase. They tried the painting mask first, just to get used to breathing through it. The son helped put the baseball cap on, then after a minute the icebag. That was so he would keep cool, the son explained. It would get hot once the plastic bag was on. Was he all right? Was it comfortable? The son did everything with the plastic gloves on. He didn't want his fingerprints on anything.

They tried the plastic bag. He waited a few minutes and then mock-tied the pantyhose on, showed the father how to slip his fingers between the hose and his neck whenever he wanted to breathe. The Seconal would eventually put him to sleep, but until then he could breathe whenever he wanted. Did he understand? Was he okay?

They took the items off, one by one.

It was then that his father told him about the *Shadwell*, about the torpedo, about standing around on deck waiting to sink, having to relieve himself.

"It's hard to kill little Willy, you know," he said. He went through a funny pantomime his son hadn't seen since childhood: licking a make-believe stamp on the tip of his thumb, then stamping it on his chest like a badge of approval. "Twice now," he said, "three times if you include the Japs." He made his little chuckle; then: "How long's it take those pills to work?"

The son said twenty minutes, maybe half an hour.

He nodded, looked off into space, then over at his nightstand. He twiddled his thumbs, laughed. "Ever show you this?" he asked and lifted off the nightstand a toy that the doctors had given him. It was a battery-powered gizmo—Pull it! Bop it! Twist it!—about the size and shape of a nightstick. The son had seen it before. When you turned it on, it commanded you to pull a lever or bop a button or twist a shaft. If you did it quickly enough the thing whistled with glee, if you didn't, it screamed bloody murder at you. It was supposed to help maintain coordination and reflex.

Now when the old man turned it on and the thing cried "Bop it!" he pulled instead and got screamed at. He let the toy fall to the floor. "Story of my life," he said. He shrugged, whistled a little tune, then: "Well, let's have them."

The son kept himself from saying anything. It was one of the rules he'd set: if it turned out his father had worked up the courage, then he would not get in the way. And yet as he handed the pills two by two to the old man, helped him drink, he knew he had been half-hoping his father would call it off. He was a timid man, wasn't he? The world had been too much for him, hadn't it? But it was the son who found himself having to suppress the stirrings of panic.

"Now what? We wait?"

It was a horrible place to die. He didn't mean the Harpswell House—which was horrible in its own way—but Belmont, Indiana, so far from the New England of their birth, even if the New England of their birth was not the New England of magazine covers but a nineteenth-century mill town gone to twentieth-century ruin. Why didn't his father mind? This exile from everything that he knew—the flat land, the cornfields, the southern-inflected accents of the people. It was, once again, as if the outside world didn't matter, as if what mattered was what he carried within—his model railroad like a gene in the recesses of his personality, carried into the Opportunity Room when he was five years old, into the engine room of the USS *Shadwell*, into the deep sleep of a dozen Seconal.

"I feel funny."

The son looked up in time to see his father's eyes flutter closed, then open. "It's the drug," he said.

The old man looked around, looked at the wheelchair, at the mirror, at the door. It was as if he were checking on the world.

"The bag?"

"When you start to get sleepy."

He nodded. He had his hands folded on his lap.

There had to be something else, the son thought. There had to be more. He had half an impulse to apologize, to say he was sorry for something, maybe sorry for not loving Annelise as he should have. And then he thought he should get up, go get the 2-8-2, give it to his father, let him hold it. But it seemed stupid, corny, a gesture. His hands were hot inside the rubber gloves.

On the other side of the wall someone flushed a toilet. His father's breathing grew regular, deep.

"Dad?" he said when a few more minutes had passed. The old man stirred.

"What?"

The plastic bag lay at the foot of the bed. He did not want to make the decision himself if his father fell asleep.

"Is it time?"

The son couldn't help himself: "You don't have to do it," he said. The old man managed to open his eyes. He blinked, tried to rouse himself. He motioned for the gear.

"Now or never."

"You can just sleep."

Again, the gesture. Tired, over and done with. "C'mon."

He watched his hands do it—the painter's mask, the baseball cap, the plastic bag, the pantyhose. And then he heard himself show his father again how to let air into the bag when he needed it. The old man nodded, seemed to smile behind the painter's mask: he understood. After a minute the plastic bag began to cloud with condensation.

What he remembered then—idly, inconsequentially—was how his father had used to like putting his eye down to track level, watching the trains from the vantage of a scale-model person. They looked real that way, he'd said. What the son had liked was the vista leading into Clifton, the granite bluffs and the Naugatuck River below, the track snaking its way alongside the acrylic water—it had looked real, hadn't it?—the scrubby junipers clinging to the cliffs, a heron wading in a sheltered pool. He had used to sit on the cellar stairs and watch his father work, forbidden to help but sitting there anyway and imagining—

"It's not my fault," his father said suddenly from under the painter's mask. The son's eyes snapped back. He could barely see inside the bag for the condensation.

"What?" he managed to say.

"It's all been forced on me," the father murmured and he lifted his arm in a gesture that somehow included the room around him, the middle-aged figure of his son, and the dull sound of the world outside the window. It was the last thing he said.

*

He had turned the computer off. He had turned the lights off. He stood at the hotel window looking out at the twenty-first century city, at the pyramids of light and the postmodern office towers. He had his cellphone in hand. He had just woken up his wife.

"It's over," was the first thing he said. He could hear her stirring, sitting up in bed.

"William?"

"We did it. It's done."

"Good Lord," she said. "Are you all right?"

He was all right. He wanted to tell her all about it, if she could bear hearing about it. Not now, he said, but when he got home. And he would tell her about all these weird things he'd been looking up on the web. And about this day he kept remembering, this day when he was little and they were all out walking along an abandoned railroad track and he had gotten scared. But even as he said it—even as he listened for sounds of sympathy in her voice, for a sign that things were all right, that she wanted him back home—he felt how impossible it was, how far away he was, and how he would never be able to tell her, never get her to see that summer day . . . the dark greenery that had seemed so threatening to his five-year-old mind, the curving withdrawal of the roadbed, the eerie buzz of a cicada, the invisible life that seemed to palpate in the tall grass, in the eddying trees, the aquamarine, the sunny gold, the way his father had smiled back at them, back at his crying son in his wife's arms, the way he had waved to them—and then turned and stepped into the dark-green shade.

*Nominated by StoryQuarterly, Joyce Carol Oates*

# THE THIRD THING

## by DONALD HALL

from POETRY

Jane Kenyon and I were married for twenty-three years. For two decades we inhabited the double solitude of my family farmhouse in New Hampshire, writing poems, loving the countryside. She was forty-seven when she died. If anyone had asked us, "Which year was the best, of your lives together?" we could have agreed on an answer: "the one we remember least." There were sorrowful years—the death of her father, my cancers, her depressions—and there were also years of adventure: a trip to China and Japan, two trips to India; years when my children married; years when the grandchildren were born; years of triumph as Jane began her public life in poetry: her first book, her first poem in the *New Yorker*. The best moment of our lives was one quiet repeated day of work in our house. Not everyone understood. Visitors, especially from New York, would spend a weekend with us and say as they left: "It's really pretty here" ("in Vermont," many added) "with your house, the pond, the hills, but . . . but . . . but . . . *what do you do*?"

What we did: we got up early in the morning. I brought Jane coffee in bed. She walked the dog as I started writing, then climbed the stairs to work at her own desk on her own poems. We had lunch. We lay down together. We rose and worked at secondary things. I read aloud to Jane; we played scoreless ping-pong; we read the mail; we worked again. We ate supper, talked, read books sitting across from each other in the living room, and went to sleep. If we were lucky the phone didn't ring all day. In January Jane dreamed of flowers, planning expansion and refinement of the garden. From late March into

October she spent hours digging, applying fifty-year-old Holstein manure from under the barn, planting, transplanting, and weeding. Sometimes I went off for two nights to read my poems, essential to the economy, and Jane wrote a poem called "Alone for a Week." Later Jane flew away for readings and I loathed being the one left behind. (I filled out coupons from magazines and ordered useless objects.) We traveled south sometimes in cold weather: to Key West in December, a February week in Barbados, to Florida during baseball's spring training, to Bermuda. Rarely we flew to England or Italy for two weeks. Three hundred and thirty days a year we inhabited this old house and the same day's adventurous routine.

What we did: love. We did not spend our days gazing into each other's eyes. We did that gazing when we made love or when one of us was in trouble, but most of the time our gazes met and entwined as they looked at a third thing. Third things are essential to marriages, objects or practices or habits or arts or institutions or games or human beings that provide a site of joint rapture or contentment. Each member of a couple is separate; the two come together in double attention. Lovemaking is not a third thing but two-in-one. John Keats can be a third thing, or the Boston Symphony Orchestra, or Dutch interiors, or Monopoly. For many couples, children are a third thing. Jane and I had no children of our own; we had our cats and dog to fuss and exclaim over—and later my five grandchildren from an earlier marriage. We had our summer afternoons at the pond, which for ten years made a third thing. After naps we loaded up books and blankets and walked across Route 4 and the old railroad to the steep slippery bank that led down to our private beach on Eagle Pond. Soft moss underfoot sent little red flowers up. Ghost birches leaned over water with wild strawberry plants growing under them. Over our heads white pines reared high, and oaks that warned us of summer's end late in August by dropping green metallic acorns. Sometimes a mink scooted among ferns. After we acquired Gus he joined the pond ecstasy, chewing on stones. Jane dozed in the sun as I sat in the shade reading and occasionally taking a note in a blank book. From time to time we swam and dried in the heat. Then, one summer, leakage from the Danbury landfill turned the pond orange. It stank. The water was not hazardous but it was ruined. A few years later the pond came back but we seldom returned to our afternoons there. Sometimes you lose a third thing.

The South Danbury Christian Church became large in our lives. We were both deacons and Jane was treasurer for a dozen years, utter mis-casting and a source of annual anxiety when the treasurer's report was due. I collected the offering; Jane counted and banked it. Once a month she prepared communion and I distributed it. For the Church Fair we both cooked and I helped with the auction. Besides the Church itself, building and community, there was Christianity, the Gospels, and the work of theologians and mystics. Typically we divided our attentions: I read Meister Eckhart while Jane studied Julian of Norwich. I read the Old Testament aloud to her, and the New. If it wasn't the Bible, I was reading aloud late Henry James or Mark Twain or Edith Wharton or Wordworth's *Prelude*. Reading aloud was a daily connection. When I first pronounced *The Ambassadors*, Jane had never read it, and I peeked at her flabbergasted face as the boat bear-ing Chad and Mme. de Vionnet rounded the bend toward Lambert Strether. Three years later, when I had acquired a New York Edition of Henry James, she asked me to read her *The Ambassadors* again. Late James is the best prose for reading aloud. Saying one of his inter-minable sentences, the voice must drop pitch every time he interrupts his syntax with periphrasis, and drop again when periphrasis interrupts periphrasis, and again, and then step the pitch up, like climbing stairs in the dark, until the original tone concludes the sentence. One's larynx could write a doctoral dissertation on James's syntax.

Literature in general was a constant. Often at the end of the day Jane would speak about what she had been reading, her latest in-tense and obsessive absorption in an author: Keats for two years, Chekhov, Elizabeth Bishop. In reading and in everything else, we made clear boundaries, dividing our literary territories. I did not go back to Keats until she had done with him. By and large Jane read in-tensively while I read extensively. Like a male, I lusted to acquire all the great books of the world and add them to my life list. One day I would realize: I've never read Darwin! Adam Smith! Gibbon! Gib-bon became an obsession with me, then his sources, then all ancient history, then all narrative history. For a few years I concentrated on Henry Adams, even reading six massive volumes of letters.

But there was also ping-pong. When we added a new bedroom, we extended the rootcellar enough to set a ping-pong table into it, and for years we played every afternoon. Jane was assiduous, determined, vi-cious, and her reach was not so wide as mine. When she couldn't reach a shot I called her "Stubbsy," and her next slam would smash me in the groin, rage combined with harmlessness. We rallied half an hour without keeping score. Another trait we shared was hating to lose. Through bouts of ping-pong and Henry James and the church, we kept to one innovation: with rare exceptions, we remained aware of each other's feelings. It took me half my life, more than half, to discover with Jane's guidance that two people could live together and remain kind. When one of us felt grumpy we both shut up until it went away. We did not give in to sarcasm. Once every three years we had a fight—the way some couples fight three times a day—and because fights were few the aftermath of a fight was a dreadful gloom. "We have done harm," said Jane in a poem after a quarrel. What was *that* fight about? I wonder if she remembered, a month after writing the poem.

Of course: the third thing that brought us together, and shone at the center of our lives and our house, was poetry—both our love for the art and the passion and frustration of trying to write it. When we moved to the farm, away from teaching and Jane's family, we threw ourselves into the life of writing poetry as if we jumped from a bridge and swam to survive. I kept the earliest hours of the day for poetry. Jane worked on poems virtually every day; there were dry spells. In the first years of our marriage, I sometimes feared that she would find the project of poetry intimidating, and withdraw or give up or diminish the intensity of her commitment. I remember talking with her one morning early in New Hampshire, maybe in 1976, when the burden felt too heavy. She talked of her singing with the Michigan Chorale, as if music were something she might turn to. She spoke of drawing as another art she could perform, and showed me an old pencil rendering she had made, acorns I think, meticulous and well-made and nothing more. She was saying, "I don't *have* to give myself to poetry"—and I knew enough not to argue.

However, from year to year she gave more of herself to her art. When she studied Keats, she read all his poems, all his letters, the best three or four biographies; then she read and reread the poems and the letters again. No one will find in her poems clear fingerprints of John Keats, but Jane's ear became more luscious with her love for Keats; her lines became more dense, rifts loaded with ore. Coming from a family for whom ambition was dangerous, in which work was best taken lightly, it was not easy for Jane to wager her life on one number. She lived with someone who had made that choice, but also with someone nineteen years older who wrote all day and published frequently. Her first book of poems came out as I published my fifth. I could have been an inhibitor as easily as I was an encourager—if she had not been brave and stubborn. I watched in gratified pleasure as her poems became better and better. From being promising she became accomplished and professional; then—with the later poems of *The Boat of Quiet Hours*, with "Twilight: After Haying," with "Briefly It Enters," with "Things," she turned into the extraordinary and permanent poet of *Otherwise*.

People asked us—people still ask me—about competition between us. We never spoke of it, but it had to be there—and it remained benign. When Jane wrote a poem that dazzled me, I wanted to write a poem that would dazzle her. Boundaries helped. We belonged to different generations. Through Jane I got to be friends with poets of her generation, as she did with my friends born in the 1920s. We avoided situations which would subject us to comparison. During the first years of our marriage, when Jane was just beginning to publish, we were asked several times to read our poems together. The people who asked us knew and respected Jane's poems, but the occasions turned ghastly. Once we were introduced by someone we had just met who was happy to welcome Joan Kenyon. Always someone, generally a male English professor, managed to let us know that it was *sweet*, that Jane wrote poems too. One head of a department asked her if she felt *dwarfed*. When Jane was condescended to she was furious, and it was only on these occasions that we felt anything unpleasant between us. Jane decided that we would no longer read together.

When places later asked us both to read, we agreed to come but stipulated that we read separately, maybe a day apart. As she published more widely we were more frequently approached. Late in the 1980s, after reading on different days at one university, we did a joint question-and-answer session with writing students. Three quarters of the questions addressed Jane, not me, and afterwards she said, "Perkins, I think we can read together now." So, in our last years together, we did many joint readings. When two poets read on the same program, the first reader is the warm-up band, the second the featured act. We read in fifteen-minute segments, ABAB, and switched A and B positions with each reading. In 1993 we read on a Friday in Trivandrum, at the southern tip of India, and three days later in Hanover, New Hampshire. Exhausted as we were, we remembered who had gone first thousands of miles away.

There were days when each of us received word from the same magazine; the same editor had taken a poem by one of us just as he/she rejected the other of us. One of us felt constrained in pleasure.

43

The need for boundaries even extended to style. As Jane's work got better and better—and readers noticed—my language and structure departed from its old habits and veered away from the kind of lyric that Jane was writing, toward irony and an apothegmatic style. My diction became more Latinate and polysyllabic, as well as syntactically complex. I was reading Gibbon, learning to use a vocabulary and sentence structure as engines of discrimination. Unconsciously, I was choosing to be as unlike Jane as I could. Still, her poetry influenced and enhanced my own. Her stubborn and unflagging commitment turned its power upon me and exhorted me. My poems got better in this house. When my *Old and New Poems* came out in 1990, the positive reviews included something like this sentence: "Hall began publishing early . . . but it was not until he left his teaching job and returned to the family farm in New Hampshire with his second wife the poet Jane Kenyon that . . ." I published *Kicking the Leaves* in 1978 when Jane published *From Room to Room*. It was eight years before we published our next books: her *The Boat of Quiet Hours*, my *The Happy Man*. (When I told Jane my title her reaction was true Jane: "Sounds too depressed.") I had also been working on drafts of *The One Day*, maybe my best book. Then Jane wrote *Let Evening Come, Constance*, and the twenty late poems that begin *Otherwise*. Two years after her death, a review of Jane began with a sentence I had been expecting. It was uttered in respect, without a sneer, and said that for years we had known of Jane Kenyon as Donald Hall's wife but from now on we will know of Donald Hall as Jane Kenyon's husband.

We did not show each other early drafts. (It's a bad habit. The comments of another become attached to the words of a poem, steering it or preventing it from following its own way.) But when we had worked over a poem in solitude for a long time, our first reader was the other. I felt anxious about showing Jane new poems, and often invented reasons for delay. Usually, each of us saved up three or four poems before showing them to the other. One day I would say, "I left some stuff on your footstool," or Jane would tell me, "Perkins, there are some things on your desk." Waiting for a response, each of us already knew some of what the other would say. If ever I repeated a word—a habit acquired from Yeats—I knew that Jane would cross it out. Whenever she used verbal auxiliaries she knew I would simplify, and "it was raining" would become "it rained." By and large we ignored the predicted advice, which we had already heard in our heads and dismissed. Jane kept her work clear of dead metaphor, knowing my crankiness on the subject,

44

and she would exult when she found one in my drafts: "Perkins! Here's a dead metaphor!" These encounters were important but not easy. Sometimes we turned polite with each other: "Oh, really! I thought that was the best part . . ." (False laugh.) Jane told others—people questioned us about how we worked together—that I approached her holding a sheaf of her new poems saying, "These are going to be good!" to which she would say, "Going to be, eh?" She told people that she would climb back to her study, carrying the poems covered with my illegible comments, thinking, "Perkins just doesn't get it. And then," she would continue, "I'd do everything he said."

Neither of us did everything the other said. Reading *Otherwise* I find words I wanted her to change, and sometimes I still think I was right. But we helped each other greatly. She saved me a thousand gaffes, cut my wordiness and straightened out my syntax. She seldom told me that anything was *good*. "This is almost done," she'd say, "but you've got to do this in two lines not three." Or, "You've brought this a long way, Perkins"—without telling me if I had brought it to a good place. Sometimes her praise expressed its own limits. "You've taken this as far as the intellect can take it." When she said, "It's finished. Don't change a word," I would ask, "But is it any *good*? Do you *like* it?" I pined for her praise, and seldom got it. I remember one evening in 1992 when we sat in the living room and she read through the manuscript of *The Museum of Clear Ideas*. Earlier she had seen only a few poems at a time, and she had not been enthusiastic. I watched her dark face as she turned the pages. Finally she looked over at me and tears started from her eyes. "Perkins, I don't *like* it!" Tears came to my eyes too, and I said, rapidly, "That's okay. That's okay." (That book was anti-Jane in its manner, or most of it was, dependent on syntax and irony, a little like Augustan poetry, more than on images.) When we looked over each other's work, it was essential that we never lie to each other. Even when Jane was depressed, I never praised a poem unless I meant it; I never withheld blame. If either of us had felt that the other was pulling punches, it would have ruined what was so essential to our house.

We were each other's readers but we could not be each other's only readers. I mostly consulted friends and editors by mail, so many helpers that I will not try to list them, poets from my generation and poets Jane's age and even younger. Jane worked regularly, the last dozen years of her life, with the poet Joyce Peseroff and the novelist Alice Mattison. The three of them worked wonderfully together, each supplying things that the other lacked. They fought, they laughed, they rewrote and cut and rearranged. Jane would return from a workshop exhausted yet unable to keep away from her desk, working with wild excitement to follow suggestions. The three women were not only being literary critics for each other. Each had grown up knowing that it was not permitted for females to be as aggressive as males, and all were ambitious in their art, and encouraged each other in their ambition. I felt close to Alice and Joyce, my friends as well as Jane's, but I did not stick my nose into their deliberations. If I had tried to, I would have lost a nose. Even when they met at our house, I was careful to stay apart. They met often at Joyce's in Massachusetts, because it was half way between Jane and Alice. They met in New Haven at Alice's. When I was recovering from an operation, and Jane and I didn't want to be separated, there were workshops at the Lord Jeffrey Inn in Amherst. We four ate together and made pilgrimages to Emily Dickinson's house and grave, but while they worked together I wrote alone in an adjacent room. This three-part friendship was essential to Jane's poetry.

Meantime we lived in the house of poetry, which was also the house of love and grief; the house of solitude and art; the house of Jane's depression and my cancers and Jane's leukemia. When someone died whom we loved, we went back to the poets of grief and outrage, as far back as *Gilgamesh*; often I read aloud Henry King's "The Exequy," written in the seventeenth century after the death of his young wife. Poetry gives the griever not release from grief but companionship in grief. Poetry embodies the complexities of feeling at their most intense and entangled, and therefore offers (over centuries, or over no time at all) the company of tears. As I sat beside Jane in her pain and weakness I wrote about pain and weakness. Once in a hospital I noticed that the leaves were turning. I realized that I had not noticed that they had come to the trees. It was a year without seasons, a year without punctuation. I began to write "Without" to embody the sensations of lives under dreary, monotonous assault. After I had drafted it many times I read it aloud to Jane. "That's it, Perkins," she said. "You've got it. That's it." Even in this poem written at her mortal bedside there was companionship.

*Nominated by Wesley McNair*

# BRIGHT WORLD

## by CARL PHILLIPS

from FIELD

—AND IT CAME TO PASS, that meaning faltered; came detached
unexpectedly from the place I'd made for it, years ago,
fixing it there, thinking it safe to turn away, therefore,
to forget—hadn't that made sense? And now everything
did, but differently: the wanting literally for nothing
for no good reason; the inability to feel remorse at having
cast (now over some; now others), aegis-like, though it
rescued no one, the body I'd all but grown used to waking
inside of and recognizing, instantly, correctly, as mine,
my body, given forth, withheld, shameless, merciless—
for crying shame. Like miniature versions of a lesser
gospel deemed, over time, apocryphal, or redundant—both,
maybe—until at last let go, the magnolia flowers went on
spilling themselves, each breaking open around, and then
apart from, its stem along a branch of stems and, not of
course in response, but as if so, the starlings lifting, unlifting,
the black flash of them in the light reminding me of what I'd
been told about the glamour of evil, in the light they were
like that, in the shadow they became the other part, about
resisting evil, as if resistance itself all this time had been
but shadow, could be found that easily . . . *What will you do?*
*Is this how you're going to live now?* sang the voice in my
head: singing, then silent—not as in desertion, but as
when the victim suddenly knows his torturer's face from

47

before, somewhere, and in the knowing is for a moment
distracted, has stopped struggling—And the heart gives in.

*Nominated by Field, Richard Burgin, Martha Collins, Rachel Hadas,*
*Rita Dove, Susan Hahn, Sherod Santos, Marilyn Hacker*

# HADRIAN'S WALL

fiction by JIM SHEPARD

from MCSWEENEY'S

W<small>HO HASN'T HEARD BY NOW</small> of that long chain of events, from the invasion by the Emperor Claudius to the revolt of Boudica and the Iceni in the reign of Nero to the seven campaigning seasons of Agricola, which moved our presence ever northward to where it stands today? From the beginning, information has never ceased being gathered from all parts of the province, so it's not hard to see how historians and scribes of the generation before me have extended the subject's horizons.

In my father's day, before my morning lessons began I would recite for my tutor the story of the way the son of all deified emperors, the Emperor Caesar Trajan Hadrian Augustus, after the necessity of keeping the empire within its limits had been laid on him by divine command, and once the Britons had been scattered and the province of Brittania recovered, added a frontier between either shore of Ocean for eighty miles. The army of the province built the wall under the direction of Aulus Platorius Nepos, Propraetorian Legate of Augustus.

I would finish our lesson by reminding the tutor that my father had worked on that wall. He would remind me that I had already reminded him.

The line chosen for the wall lay a little to the north of an existing line of forts along the northernmost road across the province. The wall was composed of three separate defensive features: a ditch to the north, a wide, stone curtain-wall with turrets, milecastles and

49

forts strung along it, and a large earthwork to the south. Its construction took three legions five years.

I have memories of playing in material from the bottom of the ditch, after it had been freshly dug. I found worms.

The ditch is V-shaped, with a scarp and counterscarp and a square-cut ankle-breaker channel at the bottom. Material from the ditch was thrown to the north of it during construction to form a mound to further expose the attacking enemy. As for the wall, the turrets, milecastles, and forts were built with that fortification as their north faces. Double-portal gates front and rear at the milecastles and forts are the only ways through. The country-side where we're stationed is naked and windswept. The grass on the long ridges is thin and sere. Sparse rushes accentuate the hollows and give shelter to small gray birds.

The milecastles are placed at intervals of a mile; the turrets between them, each in sight of its neighbor, to ensure mutual protection and total surveillance. The forts are separated by the distance that can be marched in half a day.

This then is the net strength of the Twentieth Cohort of Tungrians whose commander is Julius Verecundus: 752 men, including 6 centurions, of which 46 have been detached for service as guards with the governor of the province, assigned to Ferox, legionary legate in command of the Ninth Legion. Of which 337 with 2 centurions have been detached for temporary service at Coria. Of which 45 with 1 centurion are in garrison in a milecastle six miles to the west. Of which 31 are unfit for service, comprising 15 sick, 6 wounded, and 10 suffering from inflammation of the eyes. Leaving 293 with 3 centurions present and fit for active service.

I am Felicius Victor, son of the centurion Annius Equester, on active service in the Twentieth Cohort and scribe for special services for the administration of the entire legion. All day, every day, I'm sad. Over the heather the wet wind blows continuously. The rain comes pattering out of the sky. My bowels fail me regularly and others come and go on the continuous bench of our latrine while I huddle there on the cold stone. In the days before his constant visits my father signed each of his letters *Now in whatever way you wish, fulfill what I expect of you.* My messmates torment me with pranks. Most recently they added four great boxes of papyrus and birch leaves for which I'm responsible to two wagonloads of hides bound for Isurium. I would have already gone to collect them except that I do not care to injure the animals while the roads are bad. My only friend is my own counsel, kept in this Account. I enter what I can at days' end, while the others play at Twelve Points, and Robber-Soldiers. I sit on my clerk's stool, scratching and scratching at numbers, while even over the wind the bone-click of dice in the hollow of the dice box clatters and plocks from the barracks. Winners shout their good fortune. Field mice peer in at me before continuing on their way.

Our unit was raised in Gallia Belgica according to the time-honored logic concerning auxiliaries that local loyalties are less dangerous when the unit's not allowed to serve in its native region. Since spring, sickness and nuisance raids have forced the brigading of different cohorts together to keep ourselves at fighting muster.

Scattered tribes from the north appear on the crests of the low hills opposite us and try to puzzle out our dispositions. The wind whips through what little clothing they wear. It looks like they have muddy flags between their legs. We call them *Brittunculi*, or "filthy little Britons."

They don't fully grasp, even with their spies, how many of the turrets and milegates go undermanned. Periodically our detachments stream swiftly through those gates and we misleadingly exhibit strength in numbers.

We've been characterized by the governor of our province as shepherds guarding the flock of empire. During our punitive raids all males capable of bearing arms are butchered. Women and children are caravanned to the rear as slaves. Those elderly who don't attempt to interfere are beaten and robbed. Occasionally their homes are torched.

Everyone in our cohort misses our homeland except me. I would have been a goat in a sheep pen there, and here I contribute so little to our martial spirit that my barracks nickname is Porridge. When I asked why, with some peevishness, I was dangled over a well until I agreed that Porridge was a superior name.

Every man is given a daily ration of barley. When things are going badly and there's nothing else about to eat and no time to bake flatbread, we grind it up to make a porridge.

I was a firebrand as a brat, a world-beater. I was rambunctious. I was always losing a tooth to someone's fist. My father was an auxiliary conscripted in his twenty-first year in Tungria, granted citizenship and the privilege of the tria nomina—forename, family name, and surname—after his twenty-five-year discharge. I was born in the settlement beside the cavalry fort at Cilurnum. My mother worked in a

51

gambling establishment whose inscription above the door was DRINK, HAVE SEX, AND WASH. My father called Cilurnum a roaring, rioting, cock-fighting, wolf-baiting, horse-riding town, and admired the cavalry. My mother became his camp wife, and gave him three children: a sickly girl who died at birth, Chrauttius, and me. Chrauttius was older and stronger and beat me regularly and died of pink-eye before he came of age. Our father was on a punitive raid against the Caledonii when it happened. He returned with a great suppurating wound across his bicep and had a fever for three days. When my mother wasn't at work in the gambling establishment, she attended to him with an affectionate irritation. She dressed and bound his wound with particular vigor. Neighbors held him down and I was instructed to sit on his chest, and while she flushed the cut with alcohol his bellows filled our ears. When he was recovered he brooded about his elder son. "Look at him," he said to my mother, indicating me.

"Look at him yourself," she told him back.

He favored a particular way of being pleasured that required someone to hold his legs down while the woman sat astride him. Usually my mother's sister assisted but during his fever she feared for her own children so I was conscripted. I'd been on the earth for eight summers at that point. I was instructed to sit on his knees. I was frightened and first faced my mother but then she asked me to turn the other way. I held both ankles and pitched and bucked before my father kicked me off onto the floor.

At the start of my eighteenth summer I armed myself with a letter of introduction from him to one of his friends still serving with the Tungrian cohort. My father's command of the language was by no means perfect and since my mother had had the foresight to secure me a tutor for Latin and figures, I helped him with it. *Annius to Priscus, his old messmate, greetings. I recommend to you a worthy man* . . . and so on. I've since read thousands.

I then presented myself for my interview held on the authority of the governor. I had no citizenship but the exception was made for the son of a serving soldier and I was given the domicile *castris* and enrolled in the tribe of *Pollia*. Three different examiners were required to sign off on a provisional acceptance before I received my advance of pay and was posted to my unit. Attention was paid to my height, physical capacity, and mental alertness, and especially my skill in writing and experience with arithmetic. I was told that a number of offices in the legion required men of good education: that the details of duties, parade states, and pay were entered daily in the ledgers, with as much care as revenue records were by the civil authorities.

Thus I was posted to my century, and my name entered on the rolls. I trained for two summers in marching, physical training, swimming, weapons, and field-service so that when I was finished I might sit at my stool and generate mounds of papyrus and birch-bark beside me, like an insanely busy and ceaselessly twitching insect.

I have a cold in my nose.

We're so undermanned that during outbreaks of additional sickness, detachments from the Ninth Legion are dispatched for short periods to reinforce our windblown little tract. "Felicius Victor," I overheard a centurion scoff outside my window after having conducted some business with me. "Any rag-a-bend from any backwater announces he's now to be called Antonius Maximus."

There are other auxiliaries manning the wall on both sides of us. Asturians, Batavians, and Sabines to our east, and Frisiavones, Dalmatians, and Nervii to the west.

My father's agitating to be put back on active duty. He's discovered the considerable difference in practice between the standard of living possible on a soldier's pay and on a veteran's retirement pension. He's tried to grow figs and sweet chestnuts on his little farm, with a spectacular lack of success. He claims he's as healthy as ever and beats his chest with his fist and forearm when he tells me. He's not. The recruiting officers laugh at him to his face. Old friends beg to be left alone. He's asked me to intercede for him, as he interceded for me. He believes I have special influence with the garrison commander. "Oh, let him join up and march around until he falls over," my mother tells me, exasperated.

He rides his little wagon four miles each way every day to stop by my clerk's stool and inquire about his marching orders. The last phrase is his little joke. It's not clear to me when he acquired his sense of humor. When the weather is inclement he presents himself with his same crooked smile nonetheless, soaked and shivering. His arms and chest have been diminished by age. "This is my son," he tells the other clerk each day: another joke. "Who? This man?" the other clerk answers, each time. There's never anyone else in our little chamber.

Sometimes I've gone to the latrine and he waits, silent, while the other clerk labors.

Upon hearing that I still haven't spoken to the garrison commander, he'll stand about while we continue our work, warming himself at our peat fire. Each time he refashions his irritation into patience. "I've brought you sandals," he might say after a while. Or, "Your mother sends regards."

"Your bowels never worked well," he'll commiserate, if I've been gone an especially long time.

On a particularly filthy spring day, dark with rain, he's in no hurry to head home. Streams of mud slurry past our door. The occasional messenger splashes by; otherwise, everyone but the wall sentries is under cover. The peat fire barely warms itself. The other clerk and I continually blow on our hands, and the papyrus cracks from the chill if one presses too hard. I work surreptitiously on a letter to the supplymaster in Isurium, asking for our boxes of letter material back. My father recounts for us bits of his experiences at work on the wall. The other clerk gazes at me in silent supplication.

"We're quite a bit behind here," I finally remind my father.

"You think *this* is work?" he says.

"Oh, god," the other clerk mutters. The rain hisses down in wavering sheets.

"I'm just waiting for it to let up," my father explains. He gazes shyly at some wet thatch. He smells faintly of potash. He re-knots a rope cincture at his waist. He seems to be developing the chilblains. He stands like someone who sees illness and hard use approaching.

"Were you really there from the very beginning?" I ask. The other clerk looks up at me from his work, his mouth open.

My father doesn't reply. He seems to be spying great sadness somewhere out there in the rain.

"Without that wall there'd be Britons on this very spot at this very moment," I point out.

The other clerk gazes around. Water's braiding in at two corners and puddling. Someone's bucket of moldy lentils sits on a shelf. "And they'd be welcome to it," he says.

It was begun in the spring of his second year in the service, my father tells us. Following yet another revolt the season before in which the Britons couldn't be kept under control. He reminds us that it was Domitius Corbulo's adage that the pick and the shovel were the weapons with which to beat the enemy.

"What a wise, wise man was he," the other clerk remarks wearily.

Nepos had come from a governorship of Germania Inferior. Three legions—the Second Augusta, the Sixth Victrix Pia Fidelis, and the Twentieth Valeria Victrix—had been summoned from their bases and organized into work parties. The complement of each had included surveyors, ditch diggers, architects, roof-tile makers, plumbers, stonecutters, lime burners, and woodcutters. My father had been assigned to the lime burners. Five years, with the working season from April to October, since frosts ruled out mortar work.

Three hundred men, my father tells us, working ten hours a day in good weather extended the wall a sixth of a mile. The other clerk sighs and my father looks around for the source of the sound. Everything was harvested locally except iron and lead for clamps and fittings. The lime came from limestone burnt at very high temperatures in kilns on the spot. The proportion of sand to lime in a good mortar mix was three to one for pit-sand and two to one for river sand.

"Now I've written *two to one*," the other clerk moans. He stands from his stool and crushes the square on which he was working.

"Water for the lime and mortar was actually one of the biggest problems," my father continues. "It was brought in continuously in barrels in gigantic oxcarts. Two entire cohorts were assigned just to the transport of water."

The other clerk and I scratch and scratch at our tablets.

As for the timber, if oak was unavailable, then alder, birch, elm, and hazel were acceptable.

While I work, a memory-vision revisits me from after my brother's death: my father standing on my mother's wrist, by way of encouraging her to explain something she'd said.

Locals had been conscripted for the heavy laboring and carting, he tells us. And everyone pitched in when a problem arose. He outlines the difficulties of ditch digging through boulder clay, centurions checking the work with ten-foot rods to insure that no one through laziness had dug less than his share, or gone off line.

The rain finally lets up a bit. Our room brightens. A little bit of freshness blows through the damp. My father rubs his forearms and thanks us for our hospitality. The other clerk and I nod at him, and he nods back. He wishes us good fortune for the day. And you as well, the other clerk answers. He acknowledges the response, flaps out his cloak, cinches it near his neck with a fist, and steps out into the rain. After he's gone a minute or two, it redoubles in force.

On my half-day of rest I make the journey on foot to their little farm-stead. When I arrive I discover that my father's gone to visit me. He never keeps track of my rest days. A cold sun is out and my mother entertains me in their little garden. She sets out garlic paste and radishes, damsons and dill. My father's trained vines to grow on any-thing that will hold them. There's also a small shrine now erected to Viradecthis, set on an altar. It's a crude marble of Minerva that he's altered with a miniature Tungrian headdress.

I ask if he's now participating in the cult. My mother shrugs and says it could be worse. One of her neighbors' sons has come back from his travels a Christian. Worships a fish.

She asks after my health. She recommends goat cheese in por-ridge for my bowels. She asks after gossip. It always saddens her that I have so little. How did her fierce small wonderboy grow into such a pale little herring?

She smiles and lays a hand on my knee. "You have a good posi-tion," she reminds me proudly. And I do.

It would appear from my father's things that a campaign is about to begin. His scabbards are neatly arrayed next to his polishing tin. His kit is spread on a bench to dry in the sun. His marching sandals have been laid out to be reshod with iron studs. A horsefly negotiates one of the studs.

She tells me that he claims at intervals that he'll go back to Gallia Belgica, where the climate is more forgiving for both his figs and his aches. And having returned from service in Britain as a retired cen-turion, he'd be a large fish in that pond. But he knows no one there, and his family's dead, and there's ill feeling bound to be stirred up by the family of a previous wife who died of overwork and exposure.

Besides, there's much that the unit could do with an old hand, she complains he's always telling her. Sentry duty alone: some of the knot-heads taking turns on that wall would miss entire baggage-trains headed their way.

She asks conversationally about my daily duties. A soldier's daily duties include muster, training, parades, inspections, sentry duty, cleaning our centurions' kit, latrine and bathhouse duty, firewood and fodder collection. My skills exempt me from the latter four, I tell her.

She wants to know if my messmates still play their tricks on me. I tell her they don't, and that they haven't in a long while. I regret having told her in the first place.

When I leave she presents me with a wool tunic with woven decorations. I wear it on the walk back.

During training, those recruits who failed to reach an adequate standard with any particular weapon received their rations in barley instead of wheat, the wheat ration not restored until they'd demonstrated proficiency. And while I was quickly adequate with the sword, I was not with the pilum, and could hit nothing no matter how close I brought myself to the target. Even my father tried to take a hand in the training. My instructor called me the most hopeless sparrow he'd ever seen when it came to missile weapons. For three weeks I ate only barley, and had the shits forever afterward. On the one and only raid in which I took part, I threw my pilum immediately, to get it over with. It stuck in a cattle pen.

Night falls on the long trek back to the barracks. I strike out across the countryside, following the river instead of the road, the sparse grasses a light thrashing at my ankles. At a bend I stop to drink like a dog on all fours and hear the rattle-trap of my father's little wagon heading toward the bridge above me. When he crosses it his head bobs against the night sky. He's singing one of his old unit's songs. He's guiding himself by the light of the moon. It takes him a long while to disappear down the road.

By any standards, our army is one of the most economical institutions ever invented. The effective reduction and domination of vast tracts of frontier by what amounts in the end to no more than a few thousand men depends on an efficiency of communication which enables the strategic occupation of key points in networks of roads and forts. Without runners we have only watchfires, and without scribes we have no runners.

In my isolation and sadness I've continued my history of our time here. So that I might have posterity as a companion, as well.

More rain. Our feet have not been warm for two weeks. We are each and every one of us preoccupied with food. We trade bacon lard, hard biscuits, salt, sour wine, and wheat. The wheat is self-milled, made into bread, porridge, or pasta. We trade meat when it's available. Ox, sheep, pig, goat, roe deer, boar, hare, and fowl. We hoard and trade local fruit and vegetables. Barley, bean, dill, coriander, poppy, hazelnut, raspberry, bramble, strawberry, bilberry, celery. Apples, pears, cherries, grapes, elderberries, damsons and pomegranates, sweet chestnuts, walnuts and beechnuts. Cabbages, broad beans, horse beans, radishes, garlic, and lentils. Each group of messmates has their own shared salt, vinegar, honey, and fish sauces. Eight men to a table, with one taking on the cooking for all. On the days I cook, I'm spoken to. On the days I don't, I'm not. The other clerk runs a gambling pool and is therefore more accepted.

The muster reports worsen as the rain goes on. Eleven additional men are down with whipworm and roundworm. One of the granaries turns out to be contaminated with weevils.

For two nights one of the turrets between the milecastles—off on its own on a lonely outcropping here at the world's end, the wall running out into the blackness on each side—contains only one garrisoned sentry. No one else can be spared. He's instructed to light torches and knock about on both floors, to speak every so often as though carrying on a conversation.

It's on this basis that we might be able to answer the puzzling question, how is it that our occupation can be so successful with so few troops? The military presence is by such methods made to seem stronger and more pervasive than it actually is. We remind ourselves that our detachments can appear swiftly and cavalry forts are never far away.

This could also be seen to illuminate the relationship between the core of the empire and its periphery. Rome has conquered the world by turning brother against brother, father against son: understanding that the periphery of the empire could be controlled and organized with troops raised from areas which themselves had just been peripheral. Frontiers absorbed and then flinging themselves outward against other frontiers. They used Spaniards to conquer Gaul, Gauls to conquer Tungrians, Tungrians to conquer Britain. That's been their genius all along: turning brother against brother and father against son. Since what could have been easier than that?

Peace on a frontier, I've come to suspect, is always relative. For the past two years of my service there've been minor troubles, small punitive raids, our units spending much of their time preventing live-stock-rustling and showing the flag. The last few days we've noted our scouts—lightly armed auxiliaries in fast-horsed little detachments—flying in and out of our sally ports at all hours. Rumors fly around the barracks. Having no friends, I hear none of them. When I ask at the evening meal, having cooked dinner, I'm told that the Britons are after our porridge.

My night-watch duty comes around. I watch it creep toward me on my own duty lists, the lists we update each morning to ensure that no one's unjustly burdened or given exemption. The night my turn arrives it's moonless. The three companions listed to serve with me are all laid low with whipworm.

At the appointed hour I return to the barracks to don my mail shirt and scabbard and find my helmet. As I'm heading out with it under my arm one of my messmates calls wearily from across the room, "That's mine." At the duty barracks I'm handed a lantern that barely lights my feet and a small fasces with which to start the warning fire. All of this goes in a sack I sling over my shoulder on a short pole and carry the mile and a half through the dark along the wall to the turret. Before I leave, the duty officer ties a rawhide lead to the back of my scabbard with two old hobnailed sandals on the end of it, so I'll sound like a relieving party and not a lone sentry.

"Talk," he advises as I step out into the night. "Bang a few things together."

The flagstone paving is silver in the starlight. With the extra sandals and my kit sack I sound like a junk dealer clanking along through the darkness. Every so often I stop along the wall and listen. Night sounds reverberate around the hills.

I'm relieving a pair of men. Neither seems happy to see me. They leave me an upper story lit by torches. Two pila with rusted striking-blades stand in a corner. A few old cloaks hang on pegs over some battered oval shields. A mouse skitters from one of the shields to the opposite doorway. In the story below, past the ladder, I can see the glow of the open hearth. There are two windows that look out over the heath but with the glare from the torches I'm better off observing from outside. With the moonlessness I won't have much way of tracking time.

After a few minutes I find I haven't the heart to make noise or clatter about. I untie the rawhide lead with the sandals. I don't bother with the hearth and in a short time the lower story goes dark. The upper story still has its two torches and is nicely dry though a cold breeze comes through the windows. I alternate time on the wall and time inside. It takes minutes to get used to seeing by starlight when I go back out.

Some rocks fall and roll somewhere off in the distance. I keep watch for any movement in that direction for some minutes, without success.

My father liked to refer to himself in his home as stag-hearted. He was speaking principally of his stamina on foot and with women. "Do you miss your brother?" he asked me once, on one of those winter fortnights he was hanging about the place. It was only a few years after my brother's death. I still wasn't big enough to hold the weight of my father's sword at arm's length.

I remember I shook my head. I remember he was unsurprised. I remember that some time later my mother entered the room and asked us what was wrong now.

"We're mournful about his brother," my father finally told her.

He was such a surprising brother, I always think, with his strange temper and his gifts for cruelty and whittling and his fascination with divination. He carved me an entire armored galley with a working anchor. He predicted his own death and told me I'd recognize the signs of mine when it was imminent. I was never greatly angered by his beatings but so enraged by something I can't fully remember now, involving a lie he told our mother, that I prayed for the sickness which later came and killed him.

"I prayed for you to get sick," I told him on his deathbed. We were alone and his eyes were running so that he could barely see. The pallet around his head was yellow with the discharge. He returned my look with amusement, as if to say, Of course.

Halfway through the night a bird's shriek startles me. I chew a hard biscuit to keep myself alert. The rain's a light mist and I can smell something fresh. My mother's wool tunic is heavy and wet under the mail.

When I'm in the upper story taking a drink, a sound I thought was the water ladle continues for a moment when I hold the ladle still in its tin bucket. The sound's from outside. I wait and then ease out the door and stay down behind the embrasure to listen and allow my eyes to adjust. I hold a hand out in the starlight to see if it's steady. The closest milecastle is a point of light over a roll of hills. My heart's pitching around in its little cage.

60

There are barely audible musical clinks of metal on stone down below extending off to my left. No other sounds.

The watchfire bundle is inside to prevent its becoming damp. In the event of danger it's to be dumped into a roofed and perforated iron urn mounted on the outer turret wall and open-faced in the direction of the milecastle. The bundle's soaked in tar to light instantly. The watchfire requires the certainty of an actual raid, and not just a light reconnaissance. You don't get a troop horse up in the middle of the night for a few boys playing about on dares.

There's the faint whiplike sound of a scaling rope off in the darkness away from the turret. When I raise my head incrementally to see over the stone lip of the embrasure, I have the impression that a series of moving objects have just stopped. I squint. I widen my eyes. I'm breathing into the stone. After a moment, pieces of the darkness disattach and move forward.

When I wheel and shove open the turret door there's a face, wide-eyed, smash-toothed, smeared with black and brown and blue. It lunges at me and misses and a boy pitches off the wall and into the darkness below with a shriek.

Behind him in the turret, shadows sweep the cloak pegs between me and my watchfire. A hand snatches up my sword.

I jump, the impact rattling my teeth when I hit. When I get to my feet, something hits me flush in the face.

On the ground I hear two more muffled blows, though I don't seem to feel them. I'm face down. Pain pierces inward from any mouth movement and teeth loll and slip atop my tongue. When my septum contacts the turf a drunkenness of agony flashes from ear to ear.

When it recedes there are harsh quiet sounds. One of my ears fills with liquid. There's commotion for a while, and then it's gone. In the silence that follows I begin to make out the agitated murmur of the detachment left to guard the now-opened gates.

Fluids pour across my eyes. Lifting my head causes spiralling shapes to arrive and depart. I test various aspects of the pain with various movements. The detachment doesn't move any farther away and doesn't come any closer. At some point, silently weeping, I stop registering sensations.

In the morning I discover they'd been pouring over the wall on both sides of me, the knotted ropes trailing down like vines. Everyone is gone. Smoke is already high in the sky from both the milecastle and the fort. When I stand I teeter. When I look about me only one eye is working. The boy from the door is dead not far from me, having landed on rock. His weapon is still beside him, suggesting he was overlooked.

The rain's stopped and the sun's out. My mother's wool tunic is encrusted and stiff. I walk the wall throwing back over those ropes closest to my turret, blearily making my dereliction of duty less grotesque. It requires a few hours to walk across the heather past the milecastle, and to the fort. I can't move my jaw and presume it's broken. Two of the fort's walls have been breached but apparently the attack was repulsed. Legionaries and auxiliaries are already at work on a temporary timber rampart. Minor officers are shouting and cursing. The Brittunculi bodies are being dragged into piles. The Tungrians rolled onto pallets and carried into the fort.

My head is bound. A headache doesn't allow me to raise it. My first two days are spent in the infirmary. My assumption about my jaw turns out to be correct. I ask if my eye will be saved and I'm told that that's a good question. A vinegar-and-mustard poultice is applied. Two messmates come by to visit a third dying from a stomach wound. They regard me with contempt, tinged with pity. Over the course of a day I drink a little water. My father visits once while I'm asleep, I'm informed. I ask after those I know. The clerk who shared my little room died of burns from the barracks fire. He survived the night and died just as I was brought in. Somehow the location of the raid was a complete surprise, despite the rumors.

It takes all of six days for four cohorts of the Ninth Legion, with its contingents of light and heavy horse, supported by two of the tattered cohorts of the Tungrians, to prepare its response. The Romans suffer casualties as if no one else ever has. There are no speeches, no exhortations, among either the legionaries or the auxiliaries. The barracks ground is noisy only with industry. The Romans, hastily camped within our walls, go about their business as if sworn to silence and as if only butchery will allow them to speak.

I live on a little porridge, sipped through a straw. No one comments on the joke. On the fifth day I report my ready status to my muster officer. The muster officer looks me up and down before moving his attention to other business. "All right, then," he says.

On the sixth day of our muster my father appears in the barracks, over my pallet, the first thing I see when I wake. He's wearing his decorations on a harness over his mail and the horsehair crest of his helmet sets some of our kitchenware, hanging from the rafters, to rocking. He's called himself up to active duty and no one's seen fit to argue with him.

It's only barely light. He tells me he's glad for my health and my mother sends her regards and good wishes and that he'll see me outside.

At the third trumpet signal the stragglers rush to take their positions in the ranks. A great quiet falls over the assembled units and the sun peeks across the top of the east parapet. The herald standing to the right of a general we've never seen asks three times in the formal manner whether we are ready for war. Three times we shout, *We are ready.*

We march all day, our advance covered by cavalry. The sun moves from astride our right shoulder to astride our left. By nightfall we've arrived at a large settlement with shallow earthen embankments and rickety palisades. Are these the men, or the families of the men, responsible for the raid? None of us care.

Their men are mustering themselves hurriedly into battle order before the settlement, unwilling to wait for the siege. They wear long trousers and have animals painted on their bare chests: Caledonii. Is this their tribal territory? I have no idea.

We are drawn up on the legion's left. At the crucial time, we know, the cavalry will appear from behind the settlement, sealing the matter. On this day with my father somewhere lost in the melee off to my right, we will all of us together become the avenging right arm of the Empire. We will execute what will be reported back to the provincial capital as a successful punitive raid. I will myself record the chronicle with my one good eye. I will write, *When we broke through the walls and into the settlement we killed every living thing. The women, the children, the dogs, the goats were cut in half and dismembered. While the killing was at its height pillaging was forbidden. When the killing was ended the trumpets sounded the recall. Individuals were selected from each maniple to carry out the pillaging. The rest of the force remained alert to a counter-attack from beyond the settlement. The settlement was put to the torch. The settlement was razed to the ground. The building stones were scattered. The fields were sown with salt.* My comrades-in-arms will think no more of me than before. My father and I will continue to probe and distress our threadbare connections. And what my mother will say about her marriage, weeping with bitterness in a sun-suffused haze a full summer later, will bring back to me my last view of the site after the Twentieth Tungrians and the Ninth Legion had finished with it, pecked over by crows and studded with the occasional shattered pilum: "We honor nothing by being the way we are. We make a desolation and we call it peace."

*Nominated by McSweeney's*

# PROMENADE

## by JOSHUA MEHIGAN

from DOGWOOD

*Bowne Park, Queens. Labor Day morning.*
*A man stumbles across a wedding.*

This is the brief departure from the norm
that celebrates the norm. The wind is warm
and constant through the field set at the heart
of the impervious borough, yet apart.
This day and this place, born from other days
and places as a parenthetic phrase,
and this sky, where a businessman may write
the purposeless, brief beauty of a kite,
are like the possibilities of love.
The kite leaps up, rasps fifty feet above
until it is almost unusual,
and fastens there. The wind's predictable
but private method with it sets it free
to dive toward greater plausibility
and finish its digression in the wide
municipal burlesque of countryside.
What distantly appear to be festoons
of white, white bunting, trefoils of balloons
in white, improve the black affectless trees
where three girls stand like caryatides
patiently holding crepe bells to a bough.
Something exceptional will happen now.

But first the fat, black, wind swept frock will swerve
past the buffet to steal one more hors d'oeuvre.
He floats like an umbrella back to where
his book is, smoothes his robe, and smoothes his hair.
Yellow grass undulates beneath the breeze.
Couples file through the corridor of trees
toward rows of folding seats. Bridesmaids unhook
from groomsmen's arms. Every face turns to look;
and when the bride's tall orange bun's unpinned
by ordinary, inconvenient wind,
all, in the breath it takes a yard of hair
to blaze like lighted aerosol, would swear
there was no greater miracle in Queens.
Wish is the word that sounds like what wind means.

*Nominated by Dogwood*

# JOYAS VOLADORAS

## by BRIAN DOYLE

from THE AMERICAN SCHOLAR

CONSIDER THE HUMMINGBIRD for a long moment. A hummingbird's heart beats ten times a second. A hummingbird's heart is the size of a pencil eraser. A hummingbird's heart is a lot of the hummingbird. *Joyas voladoras*, flying jewels, the first white explorers in the Americas called them, and the white men had never seen such creatures, for hummingbirds came into the world only in the Americas, nowhere else in the universe, more than three hundred species of them whirring and zooming and nectaring in hummer time zones nine times removed from ours, their hearts hammering faster than we could clearly hear if we pressed our elephantine ears to their infinitesimal chests.

Each one visits a thousand flowers a day. They can dive at sixty miles an hour. They can fly backwards. They can fly more than five hundred miles without pausing to rest. But when they rest they come close to death: on frigid nights, or when they are starving, they retreat into torpor, their metabolic rate slowing to a fifteenth of their normal sleep rate, their hearts sludging nearly to a halt, barely beating, and if they are not soon warmed, if they do not soon find that which is sweet, their hearts grow cold, and they cease to be. Consider for a moment those hummingbirds who did not open their eyes again today, this very day, in the Americas: bearded helmet-crests and booted racket-tails, violet-tailed sylphs and violet-capped wood-nymphs, crimson topazes and purple-crowned fairies, red-tailed comets and amethyst woodstars, rainbow-bearded thornbills and glittering-bellied emeralds, velvet-purple coronets and golden-bellied star-frontlets, fiery-tailed awlbills and Andean hillstars, spatuletails and pufflegs, each the most amazing thing you have never seen, each thunderous wild heart the size of an infant's fingernail, each mad heart silent, a brilliant music stilled.

Hummingbirds, like all flying birds but more so, have incredible enormous immense ferocious metabolisms. To drive those metabolisms they have race-car hearts that eat oxygen at an eye-popping rate. Their hearts are built of thinner, leaner fibers than ours. Their arteries are stiffer and more taut. They have more mitochondria in their heart muscles—anything to gulp more oxygen. Their hearts are stripped to the skin for the war against gravity and inertia, the mad search for food, the insane idea of flight. The price of their ambition is a life closer to death; they suffer heart attacks and aneurysms and ruptures more than any other living creature. It's expensive to fly. You burn out. You fry the machine. You melt the engine. Every creature on earth has approximately two billion heartbeats to spend in a lifetime. You can spend them slowly, like a tortoise, and live to be two hundred years old, or you can spend them fast, like a hummingbird, and live to be two years old.

The biggest heart in the world is inside the blue whale. It weighs more than seven tons. It's as big as a room. It *is* a room, with four chambers. A child could walk around in it, head high, bending only to step through the valves. The valves are as big as the swinging doors in a saloon. This house of a heart drives a creature a hundred feet long. When this creature is born it is twenty feet long and weighs four tons. It is waaaaay bigger than your car. It drinks a hundred gallons of milk from its mama every day and gains two hundred pounds a day and when it is seven or eight years old it endures an unimaginable puberty and then it essentially disappears from human ken, for next to nothing is known of the mating habits, travel patterns, diet, social life, language, social structure, diseases, spirituality, wars, stories, despairs, and arts of the blue whale. There are perhaps ten thousand blue whales in the world, living in every ocean on earth, and of the largest mammal who ever lived we know nearly nothing. But we know this: the animals with the largest hearts in the world generally travel in pairs, and their penetrating moaning cries, their piercing yearning tongue, can be heard underwater for miles and miles.

Mammals and birds have hearts with four chambers. Reptiles and turtles have hearts with three chambers. Fish have hearts with two chambers. Insects and mollusks have hearts with one chamber. Worms have hearts with one chamber, although they may have as many as eleven single-chambered hearts. Unicellular bacteria have no hearts at all; but even they have fluid eternally in motion, washing from one side of the cell to the other, swirling and whirling. No living being is without interior liquid motion. We all churn inside.

So much held in a heart in a lifetime. So much held in a heart in a day, an hour, a moment. We are utterly open with no one, in the end—not mother and father, not wife or husband, not lover, not child, not friend. We open windows to each but we live alone in the house of the heart. Perhaps we must. Perhaps we could not bear to be so naked, for fear of a constantly harrowed heart. When young we think there will come one person who will savor and sustain us always; when we are older we know this is the dream of a child, that all hearts finally are bruised and scarred, scored and torn, repaired by time and will, patched by force of character, yet fragile and rickety forevermore, no matter how ferocious the defense and how many bricks you bring to the wall. You can brick up your heart as stout and tight and hard and cold and impregnable as you possibly can and down it comes in an instant, felled by a woman's second glance, a child's apple breath, the shatter of glass in the road, the words *I have something to tell you,* a cat with a broken spine dragging itself into the forest to die, the brush of your mother's papery ancient hand in the thicket of your hair, the memory of your father's voice early in the morning echoing from the kitchen where he is making pancakes for his children.

*Nominated by The American Scholar, Tracy Mayor*

# HER FIRST ELK

fiction by RICK BASS

from THE PARIS REVIEW

$S$HE HAD KILLED AN ELK ONCE. She had been a young woman, just out of college—her beloved father already three years in the grave—and had set out early on opening morning, hiking uphill through a forest of huge Ponderosa pines, with the stars shining like sparks through the pines' boughs, and owls calling all around her, and her breath rising strong in puffs and clouds as she climbed, and a shimmering at the edge of her vision like the electricity in the night sky that sometimes precedes the arrival of the northern lights, or heat lightning.

The hunt had been over astonishingly quick; years later, she would realize that the best hunts stretch out four or five weeks, and sometimes never result in a taking. But this one had ended in the first hour, on the first day.

Even before daylight, she had caught the scent of the herd of elk bedded down just ahead of her, a scent sweeter and ranker than that of any number of stabled horses; and creeping closer, she had been able to hear the herd sounds, their little mewings and grunts.

She had crouched behind one of the giant trees, shivering from both the cold and her excitement—sharply, she had the thought that she wished her father were here with her, that one morning, to see this; to participate—and then she was shivering again, and there was nothing in her mind but elk.

Slowly, the day became light, and she sank lower into the tall grass beneath the big pines, the scent of the grass sweet upon her skin;

and the lighter the day became, the farther she flattened herself down into that yellow grass.

The elk rose to their feet just ahead of her, and at first she thought they had somehow scented her, even though the day's warming currents had not yet begun to ascend the hill—even though the last of the night's heavier, cooling currents were still sliding in rolling waves down the mountain, the faint breeze in her face carrying the ripe scent of the herd downhill, straight to her.

But they were only feeding, wandering around now, still mewing and clucking and barking and coughing, and feeding on the same sweet-scented grass that she was hiding in. She could hear their teeth grinding as they chewed, could hear the clicking of their hoofs as they brushed against rocks.

These creatures seemed a long way from the dinners that her father had fixed out on the barbecue grill, bringing in the sizzling red meat and carving it quickly before putting it on her child's plate and saying, "Elk"; but it was the same animal, they were all the same animal, nearly a dozen years later, and now the herd was drifting like water, or slow flickering flames, out of the giant pines and into a stand of aspen, the gold leaves underfoot the color of their hides, and the stark white trunks of the aspen grove making it look as if the herd was trapped behind bars; though still, they kept drifting, flowing in and out of and between those bars: and when Jyl saw the biggest one, the giant among them, she picked him, not knowing any better—unaware that the meat would be tougher than that of a younger animal—and raising up on one knee, the shot was no more difficult for her than sinking a pool ball in a corner pocker, tracking with the end of her rifle and the crosshairs of the scope the cleft formed just behind his right shoulder as he quartered away from her—she did not allow herself to be distracted by the magnificent crown of antlers atop his head—and when he stopped, in his last moment, and swung his huge head to face her, having sensed her presence, she squeezed the trigger as she had been taught to do back when she'd been a girl, and the giant elk leapt hump-shouldered like a bull in a rodeo, then took a few running steps before stumbling, as if the bullet had not shredded his heart and half his lungs but had instead merely confused him.

He crashed heavily to the ground, as if attached to an invisible tether; got up, ran again, and fell yet again.

71

The cows and calves in his herd, as well as the younger bulls, stared at him, trying to discern his meaning, and disoriented too by the sudden, explosive sound. They stared at the source of the sound—Jyl had risen to her feet and was watching the great bull's thrashings, wondering whether to shoot again—and still the rest of the herd stared at her with what she could recognize only as disbelief.

The bull got up and ran again. This time he did not fall—having figured out, in his grounded thrashings, how to accommodate his strange new dysfunction in such a way as to not impede his desire, which was to escape—and with one front leg tucked high against his chest, like a man carrying a satchel, and his hind legs spread wider for stability, he galloped off, running now like a horse in hobbles, and with his immense mahogany-colored rack tipped back for balance: what was once his pride and power now a liability.

The rest of the herd turned and followed him into the timber, disappearing into the forest's embrace almost reluctantly, and still possessing somehow that air of disbelief; though once they went into the timber, they vanished completely, and for a long while she could hear the crashing of limbs and branches—as if she had unleashed an earthquake, or some other world force—and the sounds grew fainter and farther, and then there was only silence.

Not knowing any better, back then, she set out after the herd, rather than waiting to let the bull lie down and bleed to death. She didn't know that if pushed, a bull could run for miles with his heart in tatters, running as if on magic or spirit, rather than the conventional pump-house mechanics of ventricles and aortas; that if pushed, a bull could run for months with his lungs exploded or full of blood. As if in his dying the bull were able to metamorphose into some entirely other creature, taking its air, its oxygen, straight into its blood through its gaping, flopping mouth, like a fish; and as if it were able still to disseminate and retrieve its blood, pressing and pulsing it to the farthest reaches of its body and back again, without the use of a heart, but relying instead on some kind of mysterious current and desire—the will to cohere—far larger than its own; the blood sloshing back and forth, back and forth, willing the elk forward, willing the elk to keep being an elk.

Jyl had had it in her mind to go to the spot where the elk had first fallen—even from where she was, fifty or sixty yards distant, she could see the patch of torn-up earth—and to find the trail of blood from that point, and to follow it.

She was already thinking ahead, and looking beyond that first spot—having not yet reached it—when she walked into the barbed-wire fence that separated the national forest from the adjoining private property, posted against hunting.

The fence was strung so tight that she bounced backward, falling much as the elk had fallen, that first time; and in her inexperience, she had been holding the trigger on her rifle, with a shell chambered in case she should see the big bull again; and as she fell, she gripped the trigger, discharging the rifle a second time, with a sound even more cavernous, in its unexpectedness, than the first shot.

A branch high above her intercepted the bullet, and the limb came floating slowly down, drifting like a kite. From her back, she watched it land quietly; and she continued to lie there, bleeding a little, and shaking, before finally rising and climbing over the fence with its *Posted* signs, and continuing on after the elk.

She was surprised by how hard it was to follow his blood trail: only a damp splatter here and there, sometimes red though other times drying brown already, against the yellow aspen leaves that looked like spilled coins—as if some thief had been wounded while ferrying away a strongbox, and had spilled his blood upon that treasure.

She tried to focus on the task at hand but was aware also of feeling strangely and exceedingly lonely—remembering, seemingly from nowhere, that her father had been red-green colorblind, and realizing how difficult it must have been for him to see those drops of blood. Wishing again that he were here with her, though, to help her with the tracking of this animal.

A drop here, a drop there. She couldn't stop marveling at how few clues there were. It was easier to follow the tracks in the soft earth, and the swath of broken branches, than it was the blood trail—though whether she was following the herd's path, or the bull's separate path, she couldn't be sure.

She came to the edge of the timber and looked out across a small plowed field, the earth dark from having just been turned over to autumn stubble. Her elk was collapsed dead out in the middle of it—the rest of the herd was long gone, nowhere to be seen—and there was a truck parked next to the elk already, and standing next to the elk were two older men in cowboy hats. Jyl was surprised, then, at

73

how tall the antlers were—taller than either man, even with the elk lying stretched out on the bare ground; taller even than the cab of the truck.

The men did not appear happy to see her coming. It seemed to take her a long time to reach them. It was hard walking over the furrows and clods of stubble, and from the looks on the men's faces, she was afraid that the elk might have been one of their pets: that they might even have given it a name.

It wasn't that bad, as it turned out, but it still wasn't good. Their features softened a little as she closed the final distance, and they saw how young she was, and how frightened—she could have been either man's daughter—and as she approached there seemed to be some force of energy about her that disposed them to think the best of her; and they found it hard to believe, too, that, had she killed the elk illegally, she would be marching right up to claim it.

There were no handshakes, no introductions. There was still frost on the windshield of the men's truck, and Jyl realized they must have jumped in their truck and cold-started it, racing straight up to where they knew the herd hung out.

Plumes of fog breath leapt from the first man's mouth as he spoke, even though they were all three standing in the sunlight.

"You shot it over on the other side of the fence, right, over on the national forest, and it leapt the fence and came over here to die?" he asked, and he was not being sarcastic: as if, now that he could see Jyl's features, and her fear and youth, he could not bear to think of her being a poacher.

The other man, who appeared to be a few years the elder—they looked like brothers, with the older one somewhere in his sixties, and fiercer looking—interrupted before she could answer and said, "Those elk knew never to cross that fence during hunting season. That bull wouldn't let them. I've been watching him for six years, and any time a cow or calf even looks at that fence, he tips—tipped—his antlers at them and herded them away from it."

Jyl saw that such an outburst was as close to a declaration of love for the animal as the old man would be capable of uttering, and the three of them looked down at the massive animal, whose body heat they could still feel radiating from it—the twin antlers larger than any swords of myth, and the elk's eyes closed, and still only what seemed like a little blood dribbling down the left shoulder, from the

74

exit wound—the post-rut musk odor of the bull was intense—and all Jyl could say was, "I'm sorry."

The younger brother seemed almost alarmed by this admission.

"You didn't shoot him on our side, did you?" he asked again.

Jyl looked down at her feet, and then again at the bull. She might as well have shot an elephant, she thought. She felt trembly, nauseated. She glanced at her rifle to be sure the chamber was open.

"Yes," she said quietly.

"Oh, Christ," the younger man said—the older one just glared at her, hawkish, but also slightly surprised, now—and again the younger one said, "Are you sure? Maybe you didn't see it leap the fence?"

Jyl showed him the scratch marks on her arms, and on her face. "I didn't know the fence was there," she said. "The sun was coming up and I didn't see it. After I shot, I walked into the fence."

Both men stared at her as if she were suddenly some kind of foreigner, or as if she were making some fabulous claim, and challenging them to believe it.

"What was the second shot?" the older man asked, looking back toward the woods. "Why did it come so much later?"

"The gun went off by accident, when I walked into the fence," she said, and both men frowned in a way that told her gun carelessness was even worse in their book than elk poaching.

"Is it unloaded now?" the younger brother asked, almost gently.

"No," she said, "I don't guess it is."

"Why don't you unload it now?" he asked, and she complied, bolting and unbolting the magazine three times, with a gold cartridge cartwheeling to the black dirt each time, and then a fourth time, different sounding, less full sounding, snicking the magazine empty; and she felt a bit of tension release from both men.

The older brother crouched down and picked up the three cartridges and handed them to her. "Well goddamn," he said, after she had put them in her pocket and stood waiting for him to speak— would she go to jail? would she be arrested, or fined?—"that's a big animal. I don't suppose you have much experience cleaning them, do you?"

She shook her head.

The brothers looked back down the hill—in the direction of their farmhouse, Jyl supposed. The fire unstoked, the breakfast unmade. Autumn chores still undone, with snow coming any day, and a whole year's worth of battening down, or so it seemed, to do in that narrow wedge of time.

"Well let's do it right," the elder said. "Come with us back down to the house and we'll get some warm water and towels, a saw and ax and come along." He squinted at her, more curious than unkind. "What did you intend to do, after shooting this animal?" he asked.

Jyl patted her hip. "I've got a pocketknife," she said. Both brothers looked at each other and then broke into incredulous laughter, with tears coming to the eyes of the younger one.

"Might I see it?" the younger one asked, when he could catch his breath—but the querulous civility of his question set his brother off to laughing again—they both broke into guffaws—and when Jyl showed them her little folding pocketknife, it was too much for them, and they nearly dissolved. The younger brother had to lean against the truck and daub at his rheumy eyes with a bandana, and the morning was still so cold that some of the tears were freezing in his eyelashes, which had the effect, in that morning sunlight, of making him look delicate.

Both men wore gloves, and they each took their right glove off to shake hands with her, and to introduce themselves: Bruce, the younger, Ralph, the elder.

"Well, congratulations," Ralph said, grudgingly. "He is a big damn animal."

"Your first, I reckon," said Bruce, as he shook her hand—she was surprised by the softness, almost a tenderness, of his hand—Ralph's had been more like a hardened flipper, arthritic and knotted with muscle—and he smiled. "You won't ever shoot a bigger one than this one," he said.

They rode down to their cabin in the truck, Jyl sitting between them—it seemed odd to her to just go off and leave the animal lying there in the field—and on the way there, they inquired tactfully, she could tell, about her life: whether she had a brother who hunted, or a father, or even a boyfriend. They asked if her mother was a hunter, and it was her turn to laugh.

"My father used to hunt," she said, and they softened a bit further.

They made a big breakfast for her, bacon cut from hogs they had raised and slaughtered, and fried eggs from chickens they likewise kept, and cathead biscuits, and a plate of pork chops (both men were as lean as match sticks, and Jyl marveled at the amount of work the two old boys must have performed daily to pour through such fuel and yet have none of it cling to them); and after a couple of cups of black coffee, they gathered the equipment required for disassembling the elk, and drove back up on the hill.

The frost was burning off the grass and the day was warming so that they were able to work without their jackets. Jyl was struck by how different the brothers seemed, once they settled into their work: not quite aggressive, but forceful with their efficiency. And even though they were working more slowly than usual, in order to explain to her the why and what of their movements, things still seemed to unfold quickly.

In a way, it seemed to her that the elk was coming back to life and expanding, even in its diminishment and unloosening: the two men leaning into it like longshoremen, with Jyl helping them, laboring to roll the beast over on its back, and inverting the great head with the long daggered antlers, which now, upended, sank into the freshly furrowed earth like some mythic harrow fashioned by gods, and one which only certain and select mortals were capable of using, or allowed to use.

And once they had the elk overturned, Ralph emasculated it with his skinning knife, cutting off the ponderous genitals quickly and tossing them farther into the field, with no self-consciousness, it was merely the work that needed doing—and with that same large knife (the handle of which was made of elk antler), he ran the blade up beneath the taut skin from crotch to breastbone, while Bruce worked to keep the four legs splayed wide, to give Ralph room to work.

They peeled the hide back to the ribs, as if opening the elk for an operation, or a resuscitation—how can I ever eat all of this animal? Jyl wondered—and again, like a surgeon, Bruce placed twin spreader bars between the elk's hocks, bracing wide the front legs as well as the back. Ralph slit open the thick gray-skin drum of fascia that held beneath it the stomach and intestines, heart and lungs and spleen and liver, kidneys and bladder: and then looking like nothing so much as a grizzly bear grubbing beneath boulders on a hillside, or burrowing, Ralph reached up into the enormous cavity and wrapped both arms around the stomach mass—partially disappearing into the carcass, as if somehow being consumed by it, rather than the other way around—and with great effort, he was able finally to tug the stomach and all the other internal parts free.

As they pulled loose they made a tearing, ripping, sucking sound; and once it was all out, Ralph and Bruce rolled and cut out with that same sharp knife the oversized heart, as big as a football, and the liver, and laid them out on clean bright butcher paper on the tailgate of their truck.

Then Ralph rolled the rest of the guts, twice as large as any medicine ball, away from the carcass, pushing on it as if shoving some boulder away from a cave's entrance. Jyl was surprised by the sudden focusing of color in her mind, and in the scene. Surely all the colors had been present all along, but for her it was suddenly as if some gears had clicked or aligned, allowing her to notice them now—some subtle rearrangement or recombination blossoming now into her mind's palette—the gold of the wheat stubble and the elk's hide, the dark chocolate of the antlers, the dripping crimson blood midway up both of Ralph's arms, the blue sky, the yellow aspen leaves, the black earth of the field, the purple liver, the maroon heart, Bruce's black and red plaid work shirt, Ralph's faded old denim—and the richness of those colors, and their bounty, was illuminated so starkly in that October sunlight, that it seemed to stir chemicals of deep pleasure in Jyl's own blood, elevating her to a happiness and a fullness she had not known earlier in the day, if quite ever; and she smiled at Bruce and Ralph, and understood in that moment that she, too, was a hunter.

She was astounded by how much blood there was: the upended ark of the carcass awash in it, blood sloshing around several inches deep. Bruce fashioned a come-along around the base of the elk's antlers and hitched the other end to the iron pipe frame on the back of their truck—the frame constructed like a miniature corral, so that they could haul a cow or two to town in the back when they needed to, without having to hook up the more cumbersome trailer—and he began to ratchet the elk into a vertical position, an ascension. To Jyl it looked like nothing less than a deification: and again, as a hunter, she found this fitting, and watched with interest.

Blood roared out from the elk's open carcass, gushing out from between its huge legs, a brilliant fountain in that soft light. The blood splashed and splattered as it hit the newturned earth—Ralph and Bruce stood watching the elk drain as if nothing phenomenal at all were happening; as if they had seen it thousands of times before—and the porous black earth drank thirstily this outpouring, this torrent. Bruce looked over at Jyl and said, "Basically, it's easy, you just carve away everything you don't want to eat."

Jyl couldn't take her eyes off how fast the soil was drinking in the

78

blood. Against the dark earth, the stain of it was barely even notice-able.

When the blood had finally stopped draining, Ralph filled a plastic washbasin with warm soapy water and scrubbed his hands carefully, leisurely, precisely, pausing even to clean the soap from beneath his fingernails with a smaller pocket knife—and when he was done, Bruce poured a gallon jug of plain water over Ralph's hands and wrists to rinse the soap away, and then Ralph dried his hands and arms with a clean towel and emptied out the old bloody wash water, then filled it anew, and it was time for Bruce to do the same; and Jyl marveled at, and was troubled by, this privileged glimpse at a life, or two lives, beyond her own—a life, two lives, of cautious competence, fitted to the world: and she was grateful to the elk, and its gone-away life, beyond the sheer bounty of the meat it was providing her; grate-ful to it for having led her into this place, the small and obscure if not hidden window of these two men's lives.

She was surprised by how mythic the act, and the animal, seemed. She understood intellectually that there were only two acts more an-cient—sex and flight—but here was this third one, hunting, suddenly before her. She watched as each man worked with his own knife to peel back the hide, working on each side of the elk in the way that a river unbraids to the left and the right of a boulder placed mid-stream. Then, with the hide eventually off, they handed it to Jyl, and told her it would make a wonderful shirt or robe. She was astonished at the weight of it.

Next they began sawing the forelegs and stout shins of the hind legs; and only now, with those removed, did the creature begin to look reduced or compromised.

Still it rose to an improbable height, the antlers seven feet beyond the eight-foot crossbar of the truck's pole rack—fifteen feet of animal stretched vertical, climbing into the heavens, and the humans work-ing below, so tiny—but as they continued to carve away at it, it came to seem slowly less mythic, and more steerlike; and the two old men working steadily upon it began to seem closer to its equal.

They swung the huge shoulders aside, like the wings of an im-mense flying dinosaur, and then pulled them free, each man wrap-ping both arms around the slab of shoulder to hold it above the ground. They stacked the shoulders in the truck, next to the rolled-up fur of the hide.

Next the hindquarters, one at a time, and severed with a bone saw,

79

both men working together to heft that weight into the truck, and the remaining length of bone and antler and gleaming socket and ribcage looking reptilian, like some reverse evolutionary process, some metamorphic errancy or setback; though the pile of beautiful red meat in the back of the truck, as it continued to mount, seemed like an embarrassment of riches; and again, it seemed to Jyl that perhaps she had taken too much.

She thought how she would have liked to watch her father render an elk. All gone into the past now, however, like blood drawing back into the soil. How much else had she missed?

•

The noonday sun was mild, almost warm now. The scavenger birds—magpies, ravens, Steller's jays and gray jays—danced and hopped nearby, swarming and fluttering, and from time to time as Ralph or Bruce took a rest, one of the men would toss a scrap of gristle or fascia into the field for the birds to fight over, and the sound of their angry squabbles filled the lonely silence of the otherwise quiet and empty hills, beneath the thin blue of the Indian summer sky.

They let Jyl work with the skinning knife—showed her how to separate the muscles lengthwise with her fingers before cutting them free of the skeleton, and the quartered ham and shoulder—the backstrap unscrolling beneath the urging of her knife—the meat dense as stone, it seemed, yet as fluid as a river, and so beautiful in that sunlight, maroon to nearly purple, nearly iridescent in its richness, and in the absence of any intramuscular fat—and now the skeleton, with its whitened bones beginning to show, seemed less an elk, less an animal, than ever; and the two brothers set to work on the neck, tenderloins, butt steaks and neck loins. And while they separated and then trimmed and butchered those, Jyl worked with her own knife at carving strips of meat from between each slat of ribcage.

From time to time their lower backs would cramp, from working so intently, at such strangely unaccustomed work, work which presented itself now even in the best of years but two or three times annually—a deer, an elk, and sometimes an antelope—and they would have to lie down on the ground, all three of them, looking up at the sky and spreading their arms out wide as if on a crucifix; and they would listen to, and feel with pleasure, the subtle popping and realigning of their vertebrae, and would stare up at that blue sky and listen to the cries of the feeding birds, and feel intensely their richness at possessing now so much meat, clean meat, and at simply being alive, with the blood from their labor drying quickly to a light crust on their hands and arms. They were like children, in those moments, and they might have napped.

They finished late that afternoon, and sawed the antlers off for Jyl to take home with her. Being old school, they dragged what was left of the carcass back into the woods, returning it to the forest—returning the skeleton to the very place where the elk had been bedded down, when Jyl had first crept up on it—as if she had only borrowed it from the forest for a while—and then they drove back down to their ranch house and hung the ham and shoulder quarters on meat hooks to age in the barn, and draped the backstraps likewise from hooks, where they would leave them for at least a week.

They ran the loose scraps, nearly a hundred pounds' worth, through a hand-cranked grinder, mixed in with a little beef fat to make hamburger, and while Ralph and Jyl processed and wrapped that in two-pound packages, Ralph cooked some of the butt steak in an iron skillet, seasoned with garlic and onions and butter and salt and pepper, mixed with a few of the previous spring's dried false morels, reconstituted—and he brought them small plates of that meal, thinly sliced, to eat as they continued working, the three of them grinding and wrapping, and the mountain of meat growing on the table beside them.

They each had a tumbler of whiskey to sip as they worked, and when they finally finished, it was nearly midnight.

The brothers offered their couch to Jyl, and she accepted; they let her shower first, and they built a fire for her in the woodstove next to the couch; and after Bruce and then Ralph had showered, they sat up visiting, each with another small glass of whiskey, Ralph and Bruce telling her their ancient histories, until none of them could stay awake—their eyes kept closing, and their heads kept drooping—and with the fire burning down, Ralph and Bruce roused from their chairs and made their way each to his bedroom, and Jyl pulled the old elk hides over her for warmth and fell deeply and immediately asleep, falling as if through some layering of time. That elk would not be coming back, and her father would not be coming back. She was the only one remaining.

•

She killed more elk, and deer too, in years after that, learning more about them in the killing, year by year, than she could ever learn otherwise. Ralph died of a heart attack several years later, and was buried in the yard outside the ranch house, and Bruce died of pneumonia the next year, overwhelmed by the rigors of twice the amount of work, and he, too, was buried in the yard, next to Ralph, next to an aspen grove, through which passed on some nights wandering herds of deer and elk, the elk direct descendants of the big bull Jyl had shot. The elk sometimes paused to gnaw at the bark of those aspen whose roots reached now for the chests of the buried old men.

Remembering these things, a grown woman now woven of losses and gains, Jyl sometimes looks down at her body and considers the mix of things: the elk becoming her, as she ate it, and becoming Ralph and Bruce, as they ate it (did this make them somehow, distantly like brothers and sister, or uncles and niece, if not fathers and daughter?)—and the two old men becoming the soil then, in their burial, as had her father—becoming as still and silent as stone, and her own tenuous memories of them. And her own gone-away father, worm food, elk food, now: but how he had loved it.

Mountains in her heart now, and antlers, and mountain lions and sunrises and huge forests of pine and spruce and tamarack, and elk, all uncontrollable. She likes to think now that each day she moves farther away from him, she is also moving closer to him.

As if within her, beneath the span of her own days, there are other hunts going on continuously: giant elk in flight from the pursuit of hunters other than herself, and the birth of other mountains being plotted and planned—other mountains rising, then, and still more mountains vanishing into distant seas—and that even more improbable than her encountering that one giant elk, on her first hunt, was the path, the wandering line, that brought her to her father in the first place: that delivered her to him, and made him hers, and she, his—the improbability and yet the certainty that would place the two of them in each other's lives, tiny against the backdrop of the world, and tinier still against the mountains of time.

*Nominated by Joyce Carol Oates, Yiyun Li*

# SECRET NAMES

## by DAVID MAMET

from THREEPENNY REVIEW

W̲ᴇ ᴀᴍᴇʀɪᴄᴀɴs love nicknames and acronyms.
I think this is rather charming.

My other people, the Jews, do too. Maimonides, the medieval scholar, was, in Hebrew, Rabbi Moishe Ben Maimon, or the Ram-Bam. Israel Bal Shem Tov is known as the BESHT.

We Jews treasure the secret names of things, those things we hug to ourselves. As we Americans do. We award those we love with the secret name. The Yankee Clipper, the Sultan of Swat, Ray Boom-Boom Mancini, Elvis The King.

We also know the habit of awe.

All new parents automatically and universally refer to "The Young One," "The Little One," "You-Know-Who." This is an attempt to distract or subvert the evil eye, a force so powerful it need not be named.

Similarly, we, for the last decades, have referred to our Presidents by their trilateral initials. This is at once an expression of awe and an attempt to co-opt the terrible through familiarity. We were told (it seems it was a fabricated story, but it was a good one) that the Republicans, on taking the White House, found that all the computers had had their "w's" removed. Mythologically, this is priceless: the losers attempt to weaken the victor through removal of his most distinctive trait.

Awards ceremonies now each have to possess a self-awarded diminutive. The Oscars, the Emmys, et cetera. This phenomenon, we are told, began historically when Bette Davis looked at the statue of the Motion Picture Academy and thought its derriere looked like that of a friend of hers named Oscar.

The ceremony swelled in importance, and *other* awards groups, craving that power, came up with their own diminutives, their own "w's," as it were. These were not naturally occurring, but an attempt to arrogate to themselves a prerogative.

The grand hailing sign of urban decay is the blandishment of street nicknames on street signs.

State Street "That Great Street," Fifty-Second Street as "Swing Street"—these are all well and good. They are spontaneous expressions of affection. Their display, however, is an attempt to sustain a power which is waning, or has disappeared.

Just so with pet names and baby talk.

We all know the phenomenon of the true marital fight, which begins with the resurrection of long-dead endearments and pet names: to wit, "I called you this once, and look what you have become." Mary McCarthy writes of "the baby name, the surest sign of a partner incapable of that final marital swoon." Lenny Bruce spoke of the power of the intimate pet name. A widower, after a time of mourning, avails himself of female companionship. His wife has been gone some years; he is in bed with a woman, and calls her by his wife's old pet name. His wife, though dead, pops up from behind the headboard. "What," she says, "you called her *blahblah?*" "Hey, honey," the man says, "I knew you were there . . . I was joking . . . what do you think? I WAS *JOKING* . . ."

The Bible tells us the most secret name of God, the Shem Ha Meforesh, could be uttered only by the high priest in the afternoon of Yom Kippur. He would alone enter the Holy of Holies, and there would say the name. He would have a rope tied around his ankle, so that, should he die while in the Holy of Holies, he could be gotten out. No one else, of course, being permitted to enter there.

Why could they not enter? The Spirit of God dwelt therein, and anyone else entering would be slain by that power. Why were they afraid the high priest would die? He might die if he were insufficiently cleansed, if he uttered the name with insufficient sanctity. He would be consumed.

My rabbi told this story in the synagogue, and added: you may find this story simplistic, or picayune. But, say I had a booth up here, and you in the congregation knew the Sacred Name. How many of you would want to put to the test both your sanctity and the operation of the ban, with its penalty? That's right. No takers.

Just like Lenny Bruce and his dead wife.

Just as with the dread name cancer. Which we will not utter. We understand the phenomenon of the secret name. We treat this name in a spirit best expressed by the Talmudist who said, "We do not believe in superstition. On the other hand, it is good to be careful."

We understand how the secret name works, and that it must and will be treated with respect. Who would not be careful in the face of the Ineffable? Who would invert Pascal's wager, and walk into the Holy of Holies, and utter The Name? Someone, perhaps, but not you or I.

Note: we see this strongly in the movie business.

A business notably subject to the whims of fate. No one who has made a film would think to say, on the set, "Well, it looks like a nice day," or "Gosh, things are going well . . ." That person is looked upon, not as a fool, but absolutely as a blasphemer, and outcast as such.

So we do, it seems, remember the commandment. There are certain names of The Lord which we might take in vain, but the secret, the operative names, the *true* secret names, we will not.

Seneca cautions us to treat Fortune as if she were actually going to do to us everything it is in her power to do. I am working on a film with the most practical of men. He is a technical advisor on a political thriller. He was, for many years, an operator of Delta Force, in rather continuous combat for thirty years. He spoke of a fellow on his first mission who said, "We're going to kick their ass and take names" as he got onto the helicopter. The other soldiers looked at him with incomprehension and dread, and, at the end of the day, the man had indeed been shot up, and his military career ended.

And which of us has not had the experience of the old friend to whom we say, or who says to us: This is one friendship which will *never* end. And we feel that cold wind, whose premonition is, of course, fulfilled. Not only are there no atheists in foxholes, there are, I believe, no atheists *anywhere*. We just call our gods by different names. Indeed, psychotherapy may be nothing more than the attempt to find those names, and so challenge their power.

I recommend to you the story of Rumpelstiltskin. In which myth we see the very force, or opponent, *explaining* the method of his own defeat to his victim. The poor girl is forced to spin flax into gold; her savior, Rumpelstiltskin, becomes her oppressor, and demands, as payment for rescuing her from the Evil King, her first-born child. She will be exempted if she can tell him his real name.

Rumpelstiltskin is an example of the compulsion to repeat. The poor girl marries a king who is evil. Boo hoo. Her new friend *also* proves to be false, exacting an even worse tax. *If she finds out his secret name,* she will be freed (the promise, again, of psychiatry).

He proclaims his secret name as soon as she decides to "follow him around." This "following" is, in effect, watching his operations. That is, she has either become sufficiently brazen or "hit bottom" (perhaps the two are the same) and now will/must confront the actual operations of her world.

The instant she does, she is freed. The neurosis proclaims itself, it says its secret name, and it is now powerless. Now, his name is nonsense. Who, then, *is* he? Who has no name? He is the King, the Evil King she married in the first place. And lo, she has married him *again*. The compulsion to repeat, now revealed, is conquered.

The old Russian proverb has it, "Laughing bride, weeping wife. Weeping bride, laughing wife." Those of us of a certain age saw two or so decades of marriages go awry, and may have thought back to the self-confected vows to "try" to "respect each other's space," to "grow and to allow to grow," and we may have sighed and understood, too late, in those cases or perhaps our own, the power of ritual, and the price of its absence.

Another perversion of the power of names is, of course, advertising. The highest achievement of advertising, public relations, is to get the manufactured, manipulative idea "off the page," as it were, and accepted as part of speech. E.g., "Let's have a Coke" or "I'll FedEx it." And I remember a television commercial of fifty years ago—many of you do too—of the tobacco auctioneer bawling out his lightning-quick, incomprehensible, wonderful litany, concluding with "Sold American." Or that velvet voice at the conclusion of the Chesterfield cigarette ad, reminding us "And they are *mild . . .*" Tag-phrases of the day. Minted to sell a product, they transcended conscious resistance to manipulation and became part of the language. As advertising is, or has become, the attempt to subvert, weaken, or bypass conscious resistance to an idea—to implant in the victim an idea while obscuring its origin, and so influence behavior.

All parents in the audience understand this process all too well. And we appreciate its difficulties, and revel in its unfortunately all-too-occasional triumphs. My friend, the comedian John Katz, had a joke about the inept hijacker. This is years ago; the joke is no longer performable, but I will share it with you in this protected setting. "Take this plane to Tucson." The pilot says, "But it's going to Tucson." Guy says, "Act like it's my idea, nobody gets hurt . . ."

Back to the theme:

The assignment of nicknames, the application of jargon, is an understood tool for the manipulation of behavior. We know the quote "charismatic" boss who is making up "cute" and idiosyncratic names for his or her employees. "I alone know and I alone will assign you your name." This is a powerful (and impolite) tool. It is an arrogation of power and a useful diagnostic. For those who grin and tilt their heads to have their ears rubbed at the new name have surrendered their personality to the oppressor; they have given up their soul.

And for them to, should they wish it, gain it back, they will have to go through the upheaval and shamed self-examination of Rumpelstiltskin's victim.

For the complicity, though impolite, though exacted by one who does not wish us well—by, in effect, an enemy—the complicity is *shaming*. And it is this feeling of shame which ensures continued compliance. For we are structured such that we would rather suffer, in most cases, the delusion than take arms against that sea of troubles. Like the rape victim who might wonder, "*Was* my skirt too short?" rather than accept the reality that she is again being oppressed, this time by the legal system. And so, as Freud informed us, the resistance *is* the neurosis. And the very mechanism of awe of the secret name is employed in the service of oppression.

This may occur, as we see, in neurosis, through advertising, or, in a mixture, in political discourse. If we say that "the government" has "lowered the threat level," we must mean that the government is in charge of the threat. Semantically, what else is the meaning of this "color code"? One cannot act differently on a day coded red than on one coded orange, and indeed no one even suggests that one can. We are urged to "be more vigilant," but the phrase cannot be acted upon. He who defends everything defends nothing, as Napoleon said.

So semantically—that is, as judged by the way in which words influence thought and so action—the proclamation of the threat level is an admission *that there is no threat*. Or that if a threat exists, the government is powerless to deal with it. And that those who accept the reiteration of the threat level have submitted, like the employee who accepts docilely her new pet name, and are thenceforward complicit in their own manipulation, daily trading submission first for an abatement of anxiety and, as time goes by, for painful and shameful self-examination.

A public relations genius insisted that the Warner Brothers cable network be referred to as The WB. For as we do it, we are theirs.

The construction itself has no special meaning, it is simply an obeisance, and as such is in fact *more* powerful for the absence of content. As this obeisance passes, like "Sold American," from the conscious into the automatic, we no longer recognize its provenance; it becomes a habit.

I instance the phrase "weapons of mass destruction." This formulation is overlong, clunky, and obviously confected. This is not to say that this or that dictator, or indeed well-meaning soul, may or does not possess such tools. But the formulation *itself* is unwieldy and, to the American ear, unfortunate. It is the cadence of "I'm not going to tell you again." Rhythmically, it is a scold. And its constant enforced repetition by the newscasters (you will note that the people in the street do not use it often, and then with little ease), its very awkwardness, ensures that the phrase, and thus its reference, pass beyond the borders of consideration. Like The WB.

For our mind tends toward the creation of habit. And the choice, faced with the unacceptable phrase, is this: constant, vigilant, unpopular opposition, or habitual acceptance. We submit in order to avoid the burden of hypocrisy.

I will recommend to the interested Bruno Bettelheim's writings on the Nazi salute.

Similarly, *homeland security* is a concept close to all of our hearts. We live in a wonderful country, which has for years enjoyed a blessed freedom from attack. The phrase "Homeland Security," however, is confected and rings false, for America has many nicknames. The Vietnam servicemen referred to it as The World; we might call it, lovingly, the U. S. of A. Many of us have thrilled to the immigration officer who stamps our passports and says, "Welcome home," a true act of graciousness. But none of us has *ever* referred to our country as The Homeland. It is a European construction, as Die Heimat, or The Motherland, or Das Vaterland. There is nothing wrong with the phrase; I merely state that it is confected, it is not a naturally occurring American phrase, and it rings false. And *as* it rings false, we, correctly or not, will question the motives of those who created it for our benefit. As we do the "coalition of the willing."

Names are powerful.

No one involved in a "relationship" ever had a good time. One may be courting, seducing, experimenting sexually, dating, married, keeping company, and so on. But anything called "a relationship" must eventually result in sorrow, as the participants are unwilling to examine and name its nature.

The nexus of the conscious and the unconscious is of short duration. The unconscious mind can slough off the useless, or, indeed, the unlovely. When its reiteration is coupled with compulsion, we may be due for grief.

*Nominated by Threepenny Review*

# WALKER EVANS IS A SPY ON THE LEXINGTON AVENUE LOCAL

fiction by VALERIE SAYERS

from ZOETROPE: ALL STORY

AGNES O'LEARY FEELS A PECULIAR THRILL riding the subway, now
that the question is not if the Germans will bomb New York but
when. The Huns know no bounds, as her father says, as all the men
at Farrell's say. This month it's Greece and Yugoslavia. If they can
send panzers across the breadth of Europe, why not fighter planes
across the Atlantic? And what if you're riding the train when it happens? Agnes pictures the dim car blackening: she fumbles for her
glasses, stumbles through the smoky tunnel, calls out for Joe and
Bernie. She knows it is wrong, deeply selfishly wrong, to be more excited by this possibility than scared, but the truth is: she's excited.
They've been waiting forever.

And the man across the aisle, halfway down the car, has been staring at her forever, or so she guesses—she cannot say for sure because
she's not wearing those glasses she would have to fumble for in the
event of an air strike. Glasses are always unseemly, but they are unthinkable under a hat or a new hairdo, and Agnes has both: pin curls
courtesy of her sister Loretta (who is not capable of much else, poor
girl) and a green tam meant to bring out the blue in her eyes that
people sometimes mistake for grey. She senses the mystery man
sneering at her vanity.

"I've seen that fellow before. I think he's taking pictures of people."

Joe-and-Bernie, a pair of boys she's so desperately in love with she thinks of them as one, snap to attention on either side of her. Bernie spots him right away: a pale middle-aged man, jumpy as a schoolboy, fiddling in the pocket of his spring coat. "What's he got up his sleeve, a line to the shutter? By jove."

By jove. Bernie slays her: he's always putting on an accent, playing the fool for her amusement. In the contest over Agnes (she doesn't mean to be vain about that too) Bernie believes he's already lost. Because he's short, because unlike her he does wear his glasses; because Joe is a tall graceful track star with a flap of ash-blond hair over his forehead that Agnes can't take her near-sighted eyes off of. So she stares at Joe more than she stares at Bernie. She is flabbergasted all over again by how dim boys—men—are. Bernie is brilliant, for God's sake, he speaks German and Latin and French and this spring he's been admitted to Harvard and Columbia, not to mention Fordham and Notre Dame, but he has decided already that it will be City College for him: a sacrifice he'll make for his widowed ma, who cannot afford to clothe him suitably for the Ivy League, much less cough up the tuition. Not that any of their families could. No wonder Joe-and-Bernie spotted her at the Dominican-Xavier dance: she might just as well have worn a sign, SCHOLARSHIP GIRL.

Today, as they do every week, Joe-and-Bernie waited for her at the side-door exit for employees of B. Altman, where she sells stockings afternoons and Saturdays. Every Saturday she slips her hands into their crooked arms, one on either side, and allows them to escort her downtown. Every Saturday the three of them pretend they are the kind of swells who might actually enroll at Princeton, who might actually wear the shoes they wear at Sarah Lawrence (and what shoes might those be? Crocodile high heels with the toes showing cleavage?). They bound out of the train at Bleecker Street and march off to one ornate coffee house or another, where they sit at little marble tabletops to ogle dark paintings, to suck soup, to suck coffee, to suck talk, talk, talk for their Saturday night supper. Sometimes at the end Joe orders a monte bianco they all share: she has never tasted chestnuts before, and when she licks the cream off her spoon she thinks indecent thoughts involving nipples.

Joe-and-Bernie go into a reverent trance, watching her eat her dessert, and then they are running late. They must trot to deliver her

91

on time to her Saturday night job at De Robertis, where she boxes cannolis for the hoi polloi of First Avenue (good old cannolis, stuffed with perfectly decent solidified cream). Agnes O'Leary is the only O'Anything who's ever worked the counter: Joe, who lives around the corner and knows the family, got her the job. Sometimes she wishes he hadn't. By nine o'clock her feet are so swollen that she slips out of her pumps (they are not made of crocodile) and, leaning on the glass counter she has just polished, strokes one stockinged ankle with the other. Joe and Bernie come in at 10 P.M. acting like customers, and at eleven they walk her out to the car waiting at the opposite curb: her father's friend Matt McClary, who miraculously and coinciden- tally gets off his Consolidated Edison shift at ten forty-five and who can deliver her straight to her doorway in Brooklyn. Agnes suspects that Mr. McClary gets off at 9 P.M., or 8 P.M., or maybe doesn't even work a Saturday shift at all, but drives the streets of Manhattan until it is time for her to go home so that he can say, as they pull away from Bernie and Joe, waving curbside:

"Now that's devotion, those two lugs. What name did you say— Damn Romeo?"

Agnes will giggle as she is expected to. "D'Ambrosio. Joe D'Am- brosio."

"What's this, DiMaggio fever? Falling for the boys with the vowels at the ends of their names!"

She has recently noticed how attentively Mr. McClary watches her when he tells a joke, how suddenly the whole world wants to tell her the punchline. She is, she realizes, one of the world's designated lis- teners. And a good thing, too. Her lack of glasses—her view of the world as pleasantly out of focus—has led to some merry money mis- takes behind her sales counters, but meanwhile she has been listen- ing so closely, smiling so appreciatively, as Bernie says in a British accent, that she has never once been called on the carpet for her blind change-counting.

Joe inclines his head, trying to be ever so suave. "Who's taking pic- tures? That one, with the dented fedora? Who's he think he is, a pri- vate eye?"

"Don't look now. He's got his private eye on us."

Agnes breathes: "Once he had a lady friend with him, A decoy, I guess."

"Are you saying he's a spy?"

It has never occurred to her that the man who spies on his fellow subway passengers actually *is* a spy, but now that Joe's spoken the word it is too delicious. A Nazi spy. "Who would he be spying on, on the Lex?"

"Jews." Bernie says it sharply, without a funny accent, and Joe leans over Agnes to study the look on his face. They do this all the time—lean over her, around her, stare at each other's face to read the intention there—and Agnes is sharp enough to know that, as much as she is in love with the pair of them, they are in love with each other too. Oh, not that way. Not like the skinny mustachioed fellows you see prancing with each other on Waverly Place. But in love nonetheless. This entire year they have been carrying on a debate— sometimes heated, sometimes so cool it is wordless—about the war. Bernie will be first in the enlistment line: it's a wonder Bernie's not in uniform already.

Joe won't enlist, he says, he'll resist. But he'll find a way over there nonetheless, to fight the fascists by smuggling people out, and if it's too late to get to Europe—which of course it is, by years—why then after graduation he'll go down to the Mexican border and he'll escort refugees (the lucky few who have talked their way into some Latin American port) back to New York with him. He talks about saving for a bus ticket, about bribing border guards, and Bernie rolls his eyes at the foolishness. *Look, if you're too pure to fight you're not going anywhere but a jail cell, once this starts.*

Joe sneaks another look at the spy. "Oh . . . my . . . God." He leans forward, inventing a radio script. Worse than she is, with his imagination. "Look at him. Aryan perfection. Of course he's a kraut."

"I beg your pardon," says Bernhard Kelly, in a German accent. His mother is German and she has fed him the language with her mother's milk.

"Really, Joe. What do you think he's doing, sending snapshots of Jews back to Germany?"

"Did you know in Berlin women in *evening* gowns stood around on the sidewalk, pointing out Jews for the brownshirts to pummel?"

No, of course she didn't know and neither do the other girls at the Dominican Academy or anybody else who pays a nickel for the subway. Everything she knows about Germany, about Austria, about Poland or France or the Sudetenland, she knows from Bernie-and-Joe, who apparently read seventeen newspapers a day. When they have a second to spare on their Saturday night pilgrimage, Bernie even dashes over to Christopher Street to pick up a couple of foreign newspapers for good measure. He's showing off, of course, but she's impressed just the same. The nuns do not discuss international politics—though they were the first to moan about the priestly blood running in the streets of Barcelona—and the O'Leary apartment is generally innocent of newsprint, unless her grandmother Babe is reading Jimmy Cannon in the *Post*. Since Joe-and-Bernie, Agnes has been hungry, ravenous to hear the news, but Babe commandeers the Philco for baseball and her father wants it for the opera.

Bernie says: "Maybe he's working for America First or the Christian Front, right here in the subway."

"Did I ever tell you about my Grandmother and the Christian Front?"

It has taken Agnes years—and Joe-and-Bernie—to sort out her grandmother Babe's contradictions. The Christian Front, according to Babe, is a pack of cretins, but anybody who follows Father Coughlin needs something to hang onto. She does not herself attend Mass but the girls must, under pain of the back of Babe's spoon. And speaking of silver spoons: FDR is an arrogant bastard leading us into war so his pals can get richer than they already are; but anybody who votes Republican is a traitor to working people. Those other Republicans, the Spanish ones, were fools and Communists and priest killers, not that there aren't a few priests she'd like to murder herself. Babe has raised her four granddaughters to mistrust priests—even as they're kneeling at the altar rail and thrusting out their plump pink tongues for Communion—to mistrust all men while they're at it. *Men are weak*: they die too soon, the way Babe's husband did, or turn to mush on a barstool the way Agnes's father has done. The only men worthy of respect are ballplayers, but that does not mean you can trust them either. Agnes's grandmother follows DiMaggio's numbers the way brokers used to follow the market—adoringly—but she complains too that Joe's a big Italian goofball, *with those teeth*.

"Bernie, Joe, Joe, Bernie"—Agnes is in the habit of mixing up the order, so they won't guess which one she's soft on—"he's not a spy. He thinks he's another Weegee." She's pleased to move the conversation from politics to pictures, though Weegee is the only photographer she's ever heard of, so she won't be able to keep this up for long. She doesn't have to.

"Couple of months ago they rounded up—"

"You told me."

94

"Ten thousand in Vienna. *Times* didn't even put it on the front page—why do you think they buried it?"

"I don't know. Too much war news?"

"Took all their jewelry and shipped them east. What do you suppose they'll do with them there?"

She hates these quizzes, which she never answers correctly. "Make them work for the Nazi cause? I know it's terrible, but Bernie, I don't know what we can do about it, riding the local."

"Don't be naive, Agnes." Lately, this is why she's leaning toward Bernie, because he is so firm with her, because if he's guilty about his German mother, he's slithered out of guilt's clutches too, by knowing exactly what he has to do. And he may be short but he has a dark beard, a beard that begins to emerge, bristle by black bristle, late on a Saturday afternoon, emphasizing his authority.

"Let's none of us be naive, shall we?" Joe understands that Bernie's won a momentary advantage and retaliates in his best imitation of a Jesuit. "If he's just some innocent photographer, he'll say so."

"Oh, Joe. You're not going to ask him."

"Think of it, Agnes. He could be spying, and you'd let him get away because you're *embarrassed*?"

One thing to have a firm hand in the small of your back, guiding you in the right direction, and quite another to have two boys bossing you around. She's a little tired of all the sanctimony. They're eighteen years old, for heaven's sake, and she's seventeen, and while their classmates are out dancing at the Roosevelt and throwing back manhattans they're working two jobs apiece so they can be the first on their blocks to get to college. All right, so Joe won't make it next year, war or peace—college is so frivolous a concept to the D'Ambrosios that he will have to save up not just for his tuition but for his lost wages too. Anyway, sooner than they know the two of them will be shipping out for France or Belgium, even Joe, who thinks he knows what he believes but is so impetuous—Mexico, spies—he'll change his mind in a crunch. Agnes can't imagine a boy she knows, a boy who goes to Xavier or Regis, not doing his duty. Meanwhile, can't they ever just have a laugh? There's nothing they can do about the poor Jews shipped out of Vienna, not a thing in the world, and before every boy she knows gets drafted they might as well . . . She hears her father's sweet tenor voice gathering in her own throat—*break your heart, poor bastards*—and remembers why she lets these two toy soldiers trail her around. At least they do not lie flat in the steam-roller's path, the way her father does.

She giggles and then, confused by the false sound of her own laughter, finds herself gazing past Joe to study the out-of-focus photographer. He has finally settled down, engrossed in the women opposite him. She knows, more or less, how he works: he's hidden the camera in his coat, the lens between two buttons but buried well enough that she only glimpsed it once, that time he came with his lady friend and let his guard down. Sometimes he stands and pretends he's studying the map or ogling the lush girl in the Chesterfield ad, which means he's about to shoot the length of the car; but mostly he sits and fools with his pocket. It just kills her how many women stare right back at him: well, he is attractive in a skittish nightclubby sort of way, a rich layabout amusing himself by spying on the subway class. His clothes are expensive but wrinkled, because he throws them on a chair at night. She can't say for sure, but from here his profile suggests a ski-slope nose. She herself has a Roman nose—a little large, maybe not Roman exactly—and with her dark hair she could be taken for Jewish by a spy snapping pictures.

Their spy grins suddenly, as if he knows he's just snapped a good mug shot, and her windpipe tightens. How can they move ten thousand people overnight? She calculates how many people could squeeze onto this subway car at rush hour: a hundred and fifty? One seventy-five? How could you feed thousands of people, along the way?

"Joe," she says, "on the way to Mexico, what will you eat?"

"What?"

"When you go down to Mexico on the Greyhound. Have you figured out how many meals that will be?"

"Agnes, don't. Just when he's given up on it."

"I haven't given up on it." It's hard to know anymore if Joe is just being stubborn in the face of Bernie's disdain. "You'll wrap me enough cannolis for my journey." Joe laughs that manly low-register laugh he and Bernie have been trying out: Bernie's is a little bitter (Gary Cooper) but Joe's is delighted with itself (Clark Gable). "You'll keep me nourished, Agnes. For the refugees' sake." She lets his knee press up against hers. Other lovers whisper sweet nothings, but this pair of Romeos is trying to drag her to the altar by her conscience.

Their spy leans back, looking for new prey. Photographers are always spying, even when you know they're taking the picture: a photographer's always trying to steal something you want to hide. When she was a kid, she could recognize everyone in the family pictures but herself. She is the happiest of the four O'Leary sisters, merry and blithe, and yet the line of family portraits in their dim entryway shows a very unmerry Agnes, a grim, lips-set, murderous Agnes, an Agnes who threw a tantrum every year when it was time for the O'Leary girls to queue for a new photo down at the parish hall. How she resisted: her uniform blouse tugged on over her arched back, her lank hair brushed and watered and brushed some more (Loretta hadn't perfected pin curls yet), the long walk from the South Slope to SFX to stand in line with other families who all knew perfectly well that Babe didn't go to confession and said rude things about the Dodgers. Agnes hissed at Loretta not to smile for the camera. Where was her grandmother getting the money for this—or was it another humiliating handout from smug Sister Sebastian? She was beside herself with dark fury, and there is the evidence on the grimy apartment wall: year after year, the merry child revealed! She was really a miserable child after all, her jaw set so tight that her face looked plain as a turnip, her nose looming, her far-set eyes watery and . . . grey.

Well who wouldn't be a little gloomy, without a mother? Still, Agnes has always thought Babe an excellent substitute, fat and capacious, able to hold two or three of them on her lap at once. Why should she miss a mother who, as Babe never fails to remind them, *would put you through such a thing?* Not that Agnes can remember such-a-thing. She was four, Babe tells her: Mame was eight, Rose Marie six, Loretta two. It was only last year that it came to her whole that if she and her sisters were two-four-six-eight then it was time for another baby. Her mother must have been pregnant. Agnes has been well enough trained by the Josephites (Brooklyn) and the Dominicans (Manhattan) to understand the dread that might be attached to *that*. Their mother sent them down to the corner for a loaf of semolina: Babe says they all went everywhere together, the two younger tied to the two older at the wrist, with a length of clothesline. And when they returned, the note was on the door again: GET YOUR FATHER, DON'T COME IN. I LOVE YOU ALWAYS.

Well. It was the fourth time she'd taped the note to the door, and three times before Mame had dutifully dragged the chain gang of them all over the Slope to locate their father, who was unemployed but not unoccupied in those Prohibition years (Agnes's father has never been much of a drinker, but he has always found his company in the confraternity of drunks). Of course Mame could have simply led them all downstairs to rouse their grandfather Vito from his corpses and his marble slabs: they lived, then, above the Cozzi Funeral Parlor. But the little girls couldn't say what scared them more—their grandfather or the stiffs—and Mame evidently thought it would save some trouble this time to rescue their mother herself. Maybe she didn't fully understand that their mother had tried the oven twice before and once a bottle of phenobarbital: those are the details Babe bandies about, but Mame and Rose Marie never, ever talk about it. They are surly, demanding girls who will probably never marry because they are so ill-tempered, and Agnes knows she is supposed to put up with them because of what they saw. But, after all, she saw it too—and maybe she can't remember it, but Babe has told the story so many times that she can feel herself pushing in the front door behind Mame and Ro, tugging Loretta along. She can feel the clothesline cutting into her wrist. If she could fill in the picture, if she could say for sure what she witnessed . . . Babe's story always stops at the front door, but sometimes Agnes takes a few more steps.

Their spy turns, suddenly, and she is pretty sure that he is staring directly at her: or no, that he is reaching in his pocket and pressing the line to the shutter. Criminy, she has not even told Bernie and Joe that her mother was a suicide. The first one she tells will be the one she marries. Beside her, Joe draws in his breath.

"C'mon Agnes, he knows we're onto him."

"I don't know, Joe . . . I'm a little scared of him." She raises a gloved hand to Joe's sleeve to restrain him, or maybe just to touch him. Photographers think nothing of intruding on strangers, of entering their darkest, most private thoughts. Her father said as much when he showed her a picture of refugees on the SS *St. Louis*, a picture that shocked him enough to actually bring the paper home: *Look at this; it would break your heart. The photographer caught just how hopeless those little Jewish girls feel.* Two little girls leaning on their elbows at the open window, two little girls dressed in raincoats, as if they expected to be walking the wet streets of New York by breakfast. But by the time Agnes stared at their picture, their faces said they would not be leaving the boat in the port of New York, not for breakfast or lunch or dinner, and they would not be leaving in Havana or Buenos Aires either. One of them—the blond child, a prisoner on an oceanliner—looked like Loretta, and Agnes imagined a kinship. Her father said: *Poor bastards*.

"Whatever happened to those refugees from the *St. Louis*?" Though she knows exactly what happened. The boat sailed back to Germany.

"Some of them got to France." Bernie doesn't hide his frustration. "But if they're rounding them up in Vienna . . ."

She hangs her head, ashamed as she often is when she actually says something, instead of just giggling, and ends up garbling the words and forgetting the thought. They are pulling into Astor Place. The photographer rises langorously and dances with the pole on his way out the doors. Joe is on his feet, and now so is Bernie, and Agnes has no choice but to follow them, though this is a stop too early and will throw off the entire Saturday ritual. This will send her rushing to work even hungrier than usual.

The photographer-spy has paused on the platform, as if to let them catch up. He pats his pockets, but what he retrieves is not his secret shutter-closing device but a box of Chesterfields. He lights one with a wry Fred Astaire face, amused at himself, amused at them. The three of them tumble toward him.

"Look here," Joe says, and the spy nods as if he's been expecting this interrogation.

"You blew my cover."

Though Agnes should not be surprised by how easily he laughs at them—this is a man at home in the world—her windpipe tightens further still. She longs for the boys to move closer, so she can get a good look, and wonder of wonders, the three of them do crowd in. She was right: the man's coat is crumpled and expensive, his hat pushed back at the angle men adopt when they've had a martini or two, the fringe of hair that shows strangely tousled, boyish. He takes a careful drag on his cigarette and tilts his head slightly to blow the smoke out of their range. He must be the same age as her father and she sees now—finally—that he wears glasses: they are rimless, and that is why she could not make them out from half a car-length away. She takes his glasses as permission to remove her own from her pocket, but her ears burn scarlet as she hooks on the humiliating horn rims.

"We just need to know," Joe begins anew, smooth as a radio announcer, smooth as Father Coughlin, "whether you were taking pictures of Jewish passengers."

The spy jerks his head with a sense of wonder that strikes Agnes as fake and real all at once, as if the only way he knows how to show his shock is to repeat a gesture he's rehearsed a thousand times before. "Jewish passengers!"

Now Joe's confused. "Because at a time like this—"

"That's what you thought I was doing!" He smiles, the spy, but does not laugh at them. He takes his time unbuttoning his coat, motions them in, co-conspirators, and reveals a dull black camera: "My Contax," he says. With her glasses in place Agnes can see that the shiny parts have been painted dark for camouflage. He pulls from his pocket a slender cord to which is attached . . .

". . . a shutter release," Bernie says.

"Precisely."

"We thought maybe you were spying," Joe says, not embarrassed in the least, though he's the one who's really garbled things.

"Well I suppose I *am* spying, in a way, but good grief, not on Jews."

"That's a relief," Joe says. "We were just checking."

The spy shakes his head in wonder—Agnes decides this time that the gesture is completely authentic—and leans in to consider his words. "I'm collecting . . ." He reads the mistrust on Bernie's face and changes tracks. "Look, let me send you a copy of my new book. So you'll know I'm legit. To restore your faith in humanity." He pats his pocket, this time for a pen, and withdraws a scrap of paper so that they can write an address.

Bernie shakes his head no and retreats a step. "No need."

"No need," Joe repeats. "Sorry to trouble you. Can't be too careful."

". . . In this day and age?" The spy looks directly at Agnes for the first time: he's as old as her father, and she falls in love with him too while she's at it, with the glint off his glasses and the way he smiles without his teeth. "It was you, wasn't it? *You* were onto me."

She thinks to say: "I'd like a copy of the book. If it's not too much trouble."

She's never done such a thing and knows that behind her Bernie-and-Joe are shocked at her forwardness. Probably they're shocked at the glasses too: and underneath a tam, of all the comical hats. She is tempted to turn the spy's paper over: it's a bank deposit slip. Meanwhile it's hard to get her address down—the pen keeps slipping between the fingers of her glove, especially when she gets to "Brooklyn," and naturally it's a good pen, sleek and silver. When she hands the slip back she meets the photographer's eyes through two layers of glasses and sees that his are as smudged as her own. And as she moves down the platform after Bernie to wait for the next train, she hears, from a distance: "Good *somebody's* paying attention." She turns to acknowledge him, but he's disappeared, vaporized.

"He's never going to mail you a book," Bernie mutters. "He thought we were little kids playing spy games." But Agnes, in love with three men now, knows that Bernie's just jealous and that the photographer will keep his word.

And she looks for the package, for a week or two, when she comes home at night, shaky with hunger after the school day and the stockings and the long train ride home. After a while she begins to forget about the book, the way worldly men forget schoolgirls in glasses. She has been distracted, anyway, by the news. She splurges on the *Times* almost every day now, so she can keep up with Joe-and-Bernie on Saturday nights. She pretends that the paper's a gift for Babe, who has started a photo collection of DiMaggio, of the Dago twisting his long body into one graceful, audacious swing. Babe doesn't think much of the so-called sports reporting in the *Times*, but a picture's a picture.

Dinner's on when Agnes walks in the door: the sweet smell of carrots and turnips night after night, Babe's fidelity to root vegetables meant to balance her father's infidelity to his jobs. At least he's working at the moment, as an insurance investigator (Babe found him the job, the way she finds the girls scholarships and hand-me-downs). Just now he sits at the kitchen table stunned by the effort of his day. They all look a little stunned, the six of them squeezed around a wobbly card table. In the corner Loretta wears a face suggesting, as it often does, that she might burst into tears any minute.

"So, Aggie, let's have the news," Babe says. Mame and Rose Marie promptly examine their fingernails for chips. They are file clerks downtown and they are not interested in Agnes's news, a recent feature of the dinner hour, one she suspects is designed to keep providing Babe with newspaper photos.

"Ma, I thought you were going up to the Stadium today."

"Ladies Day." They all know what Babe thinks of Ladies who need a Day to lure them to the ballpark. "I thought better of it."

Agnes says: "They rounded up five thousand Jews in Paris, and it wasn't even on the front page. I didn't notice till tonight."

"Can't you get in free on Ladies Day?"

"I could get all the way up there and McCarthy pulls Rizzuto? I like the little mutt. Give him time."

"Five thousand," her father says, and shakes his head. "Poor bastards."

"Agnes! I forgot. Package for you today. Something from the college, I suppose."

"May I be excused?"

"Leave it for later," Babe says. Agnes's hoity-toity Manhattan academy has already caused enough bitterness.

Agnes rises. "No, for the bathroom." They all know she will grab the package from the hallway and take it with her to the bathroom, the only room in the apartment where the door fits properly into its frame, the only room where four sisters who live in one jail cell can retreat when they want to hoard a secret.

She sits precariously on the curved side of the clawfoot tub and unwraps the brown paper as quietly as she can. It's the book, finally. Looking for a note, an inscription, she shakes out the packaging, but there's only the book itself, with a little portfolio of pictures at the beginning: *Photographs by Walker Evans*. He's famous. She knew it. She's shaking with anticipation but already feels cheated: if he went to all the trouble of having the book sent, he could have signed it for her. TO THE CHARMING BLUE-EYED GIRL WHO SPIED ME FIRST. YOUR ACCOMPLICE IN CRIME, WALKER EVANS. Men like that always have last names for first.

She flips through the picture pages in front and sees that the spy Walker Evans has not sent her pictures of subway riders at all. What's this? Okies? Page after page of poor country people: she feels again the weight that Joe-and-Bernie have been suggesting she should carry. Is she supposed to do something about these people too? She is poor but she cannot imagine this kind of poverty, posing for a rich man with your own face grubby and your clothes streaked and torn. The Depression is over but this Mr. Walker Evans is still groveling in it the way the wealthy sometimes do. Only the rich don't stay awake at night: she's the one who will lie sleepless, in bed with Loretta, who twitches with all her sorrows.

This bathroom, she feels certain, is very like the one they fled when her mother killed herself. That was a limestone and this is a tenement, but the shape of the rooms is surely the same and there is the high window, the promise of light if not the delivery. Probably she will always have a long narrow bathroom in her life: a coffin. At

102

her college scholarship interview, she said she might study psychology and was surprised to hear the word come out of her mouth. The committee thought that was grand: women have a gift for counseling, and there'd be plenty of need during wartime. Or was she perhaps interested in the moral development of children?

The apartment is very quiet, as if they are waiting in the kitchen for her to betray herself by turning the pages of her book. In the silence she sees Joe D'Ambrosio entering a jail cell, Bernie Kelly shipping out. In the paper tomorrow (but not on the front page) she will read how the Vichys arranged the food when they rounded up the Jews; they held the men and sent the women home for provisions, as if they were being sent to pack for a picnic.

She flips to the front of the book again, but now she feels a dark fury rising. It's not just that the photographer wants her to imagine what he's witnessed—he wants her to imagine what it's like to live that life, when she cannot even imagine what it was like to be her own childhood self. Isn't it enough that tonight she will lie listening to Loretta's weeping?

She shifts and the brown paper makes a racket, only now she doesn't hear it. Now she is riding a train in the dead of night. She sits in the terrible silence as if she might imagine moving past this helplessness, as if one day she will decide the way Bernie and Joe have decided what it is she is supposed to do. She is riding a train. When Joe gets released from federal prison, when Bernie comes home from the war beyond the reach of language, she will sit with them in a silence darker and deeper than this one, and she will wonder if she will ever be able to shed her sense of shame.

She is riding a train in the dead of night but she does not know what she can do about it. *Poor bastards*. She slaps the book shut— she's not ready for any of this yet—and lifts herself up from the side of the tub just as the doorknob rattles. Mame's fuming: "Aggie, it's your night for the dishes and you know it."

In a few minutes, Babe will commandeer the radio again, and then Marty Glickman's voice will rumble through the apartment with the replays of Ladies Day on "Today in Baseball." Maybe DiMaggio has roused himself from his slump, and then the mood in the O'Learys' will lift. Meanwhile, she'll plunge her hands in the dishwater and dream about climbing on a Greyhound bus with Joe, to go rescue refugees in Mexico. She'll dream about marrying Bernie and buying him spare pairs of glasses for the war.

103

In the hallway, she stops in front of the portraits of the poor motherless O'Leary girls, row after row in the dim bare-bulb light. She looks her eight-year-old self in the eye, her glasses in her pocket even then: a mysterious scowling girl who wants to raise holy hell but grows up giggling instead.

"Da," she hears herself bellow, though no one but Babe is allowed to bellow in this household. "Dad," and even before she hears the scrape of his chair the sentence has formed: *I'm going to lose my mind if you say* "poor bastards" *one more time*. Even before she sees his confused face appear in the hallway she understands that it is not just her father she is admonishing, that it is not just Joe-and-Bernie she is choosing between.

*Nominated by Zoetrope: All Story*

# SONGS FROM THE BLACK CHAIR

## by CHARLES BARBER

from BELLEVUE LITERARY REVIEW and UNIVERSITY OF NEBRASKA PRESS

A THOUSAND MEN EACH YEAR sit in the black chair next to my desk. I am a mental health worker at the Bellevue Men's Shelter. These men are between 18 and 80 years old, usually black or Hispanic, usually with a psychiatric problem and a substance abuse history (crack, heroin, and alcohol), often with a forensic history (usually released from prison that day), and quite often with a major medical illness.

At some point during the interview with these men, I get around to the questions: "Are you hearing voices?" "Have you ever seen things that other people didn't see?" "Have you ever tried to hurt yourself?" A few times a month I hear responses like, "I thought about jumping in front of the subway," or "I can't tell you whether I'm going to hurt myself or not." Or I am shown wrists that have recently been cut, or bellies and limbs and necks with long scars. At that point, I calmly tell my client in the black chair that I think they need to go to the hospital in order to be safe. Almost always they agree without complaint.

I call 911 and write a note addressed to the Attending Psychiatrist, Bellevue Hospital Emergency Room, detailing my observations and my assessment of their mental status. Fortunately, the hospital is only one block away. Within ten minutes, the police and EMT's arrive. "Good luck," I always say to the men as they are taken away. To my amazement, they almost always say, "thank you."

The staff and I are instructed to classify the men we see into one or more of the following official categories of disability or distress, as promulgated by the New York City Department of Mental Health:

SPMI [seriously and persistently mentally ill]
MICA [mentally ill chemical abuser]
Axis II [personality disordered]
Medical
Forensic [released from jail or prison]
Over 60 Years Old
Mentally Retarded/Developmentally Disabled
Immigration
Physically Disabled
Vocational
Domestic

It's a nice list of nice bureaucratic categories, but it means nothing, really. I've created my own list. These, I've learned in my two years of sitting next to the black chair, are the far more descriptive and pertinent categories:

*The Travelers and the Wanderers*
*Guided by Voices*
*Vietnam Vets*
*Waylaid tourists, usually recently robbed*
*Criminals*
*"No English" and no papers*
*Various persons destroyed by alcohol, crack, heroin or some other substance*
*Alzheimer's patients and other victims of senility*
*Manic in America*
*People who choose to live underground and in darkness*
*The truly weird, from whom we can find no category that fits*

But all this I keep to myself. I sit at the computer and duly check off the city's official list.

In truth, they are *all* travelers and wanderers. They come from Jamaica, Georgia, Colombia, Kuwait, Poughkeepsie, Italy, Oregon, Taiwan, Wyoming, Poland, Detroit, and Bosnia. And it is Manhattan—not Brooklyn, Queens, or the Bronx—that they want to come to.

Countless times I've found myself in the following exchange:

"*Brooklyn*! That's all the beds you got tonight! *Just Brooklyn*! Shit!"

"Yes, that's the only place that there are beds tonight."

"Shit. I ain't going to no *fucking Brooklyn*! You sure that's it? Nothing in Midtown, or maybe the Wall Street area?"

"No. That's it. All we have is the shelter in Bedford Stuyvesant."

"Fuck, if that's all you got, I'm leaving. I gotta be in Manhattan, man. Maybe I'll come back tomorrow night."

And they get up and leave, back to the streets or park or wherever.

I've learned that homeless people prefer to be in Manhattan, just like everybody else. At first I was indignant—these people are *choosy* about where they're going to stay? But I thought about it, and realized the sources of their livelihood, such as they are, are far more lucrative in Manhattan. Panhandling goes much better in Times Square than in Far Rockaway. The men tell me that if you do it respectfully, and look decrepit enough—but not so decrepit as to scare people—you can make between twenty and eighty dollars an hour panhandling in a prime location in Midtown. They may be mentally ill, but they're not crazy: it is Manhattan that the voices tell them to go to, and not, for example, Staten Island.

"So, why did you come to New York . . . that is, Manhattan?" I almost always ask the people in the black chair.

Some of the answers I've heard over the years:

"Because Jesus told me to."

"Because someone was trying to kill me in Las Vegas."

"Because where I was staying they only let you stay in chairs, and I want a bed."

"Because when I got out of prison in Baltimore, I read that Giuliani had brought the crime rate down so I decided to return to New York."

"Because this is where the bus brought me."

"Because I can get better health insurance here than in Puerto Rico."

"Because I can't find my way home. I left my house on Walters Street in the Bronx ten years ago and I can't find my way back."

"Because I'm John the Baptist—a truth serum given to me at Trenton State Hospital in 1969 proves it—and can you get me a bed

107

near the St. John the Divine Cathedral because I have to go there and tell them I've arrived."

"Who said I was in New York?"

"Because when I was working on the chicken farm in Georgia last week, a voice told me to come here."

"Because I always wanted to see the Empire State Building."

"Because the people here are less crappy here than they are in Florida."

"To compete in a Karate championship."

"Because I want to open a blacksmith shop in Queens."

"Because my so-called best friend stole everything I had."

"Because I always wanted to go where no one would find me."

But even among the travelers, there are the prodigious and cease-less ones, the ones who are committed to motion as a way of life. Traveling around America—which in this case means visiting one shelter and soup kitchen and church basement and subway station and bus depot and abandoned building after another—is their pro-fession. In the warmer weather, and even in the colder weather, a lot of them camp out, whether it is in Central Park, the woods of upstate New York, or the beaches of California. It doesn't seem to matter re-ally where they are, as long as they can move away from it quickly. A lot of them are actually offered permanent or semi-permanent lodg-ing—half-way houses, community residences, and the like—and they invariably turn them down, to move on to the next city. Their desti-nations are much like those featured in travel advertisements: New Orleans, Las Vegas, L.A., Hawaii, and New York.

There is a specific look to the professional travelers, instantly iden-tifiable; there is almost invariably a certain healthy and woodsy glow about them, no matter how high or drunk or crazy they are. They tend to have long straggly beards and wild eyes and dusty backpacks and sleeping bags. In the summer, they wear as little as possible, and sport dark tans, and hair bleached blond from the sun; in the winter, they wear layers of sweaters and their cheeks are rosy pink. They are usually lean. A few of them, self-consciously or not, adopt the romantic trappings of the old hoboes; one night, a man plaintively played a harmonica in the waiting room, entertaining his fellow way-farers. Once I walked past Central Park and saw a group of hoboes sitting around and roasting marshmallows at a campfire, like some-thing out of *The Treasure of the Sierra Madre*. The parallel universe of Central Park West and its fabulously expensive French restaurants, celebrity apartment houses, and endless medical—and typically psychiatrists'—offices, was just thirty feet away.

The shelter staff came to me one night, exasperated, saying there was a white guy somewhere in the building who had been eluding them for hours. The shelter workers had been trying to take his photograph and his fingerprints—submission of which is required to enter the shelter—but this person, whoever he was, had been stealthily moving from chair to chair and room to room all night long. In other words, he was a traveler even within the confines of the shelter.

"Where is he now?" I asked the security officer.

"In the bathroom—we think," he said, and led me there.

The bathroom was a predictably dingy, rank affair, distinguished only by the curious fact that the dividers between the stalls were made of marble, with beautiful gray swirling patterns. On the marble was written, in magic marker: "Bums never have a nice day," and "Suck my homeless dick." The man sitting on the toilet had tousled reddish blond hair—lots of it—and a thick beard. He was rocking back and forth on the toilet, with his pants on. He looked, I thought, like a psychotic Viking.

"Excuse me," I said to the psychotic Viking on the toilet. "Would you mind going to have your photograph taken in the screening room? And when you're done, would you mind coming to my office down the hall?"

"Oh yeah, sure, sure, sure," he replied.

And I left there as quickly as possible, thinking that I had done my job for the night and that I would never see him again. But when I turned around a moment later, back in the office, the Viking was sitting quietly in the black chair next to me.

"What's your name?" I said.

"Leif," he said. It sounded Nordic or Danish or something, confirming my Viking theory. He probably would have been a great Viking, I thought; a few thousand years ago his wildness would have served him well. As I was contemplating this, he began doing a kind of dance in the chair—arms and legs and hands and neck bouncing away, all of them flowing to different beats—and embarked upon this rushed monologue:

"In case you wanted to know, I'm Norwegian, Ukrainian, Swedish, Danish, Irish," he began. "I've lived in Florida, Hawaii, Alaska, Okla-

109

homa, all over Canada, and Cheyenne, Wyoming, but mainly I grew up in South Jersey.

"The malls there suck, you know? I slept under a car last night. I was in jail for a rape I didn't commit of my half-sister. What else do you need to know?"

"Have you been in the shelter system before?" I asked.

He looked directly at me. "I need help. I need help! No one's helping me after I got out of detox," he said, and as he said it I noticed for the first time that his breath stank of liquor. "I didn't have nowhere to go. That's why I'm here. But not for long. Thinking of going back to Cheyenne. That was my favorite place. Happy there. That's where I got convicted of the rape I didn't commit of my half-sister"—I noticed he used the exact same phrasing to describe the alleged crime—"and I want to clear my record. Clear my name!"

"Have you been in the hospital recently?" I said.

"I have very bad nerves," he said, not exactly to me, but, it seemed, to something beyond me—a general statement to or about the world. *Very bad nerves,*" he added for emphasis. "You know who helped me? The nuns helped me. The nuns were fucking *awesome!*" he shouted to the ceiling, and then smiled broadly.

"Do you take any medications?" I asked.

"I brought it all on myself," he said. "Nobody's fault but mine." He stood up and produced from his pockets a series of smudged and torn-up hospital papers. The papers said that he had been in a hospital in Maine, and before that a detox in Providence, and before that a psychiatric hospital in Kansas, and before that a rehab in Oregon, and that he had severe diabetes, a seizure disorder, and bipolar disorder. The medical diagnoses surprised me: he had that healthy look of the travelers, that unworried and rural look that made it seem that, at a moment's notice, he could set off on a fifty mile hike in the woods.

Suddenly he lurched forward in the chair and thirty syringes fell to the floor. They seemed to have fallen out of his red sweatshirt, but from where exactly, I couldn't tell. He picked up the syringes, one after the other, and stuffed them into his pockets and what seemed like a pouch in his sweatshirt. As he picked up the needles, he kept on talking, not stopping for a second, about nuns, disputed rapes, Cheyenne, and bad malls in Jersey. At one point he took out a thick wad of bills, again from some mysterious place on his person. "See this!" he said, waving the money close to my face. "It's chump change, and it means nothing," he said, and immediately went back to picking up syringes. Finally he was done, and I got him to sit down again.

"When was the last time you took your meds?" I said.

"The physical shit is nothing. It's a test, a test! I wish I woulda died after the seizure, I wish I woulda never woken up. Then I wouldn't have to deal with the *hassle*. The physical shit is nothing. It's a test by Jesus Christ, a test by God to see how much you can take. The only thing, man, is I gotta keep moving. Death is being static, dude."

I was about to ask him more about tests by Jesus Christ and hassles and nuns, because I liked him and was interested, when he jumped again—as if electrically shocked by something in the chair—and ran out of the room. By the time I got out into the hallway, he was gone. A few syringes had fallen out of his pocket and were bouncing on the hard shiny floor of the shelter. Fortuitously, the security officer hadn't been at his post, and Leif, the psychotic Viking, the adventurer, was able to leave undetected, free to re-enter his world.

Last January I was asked by the security staff to go to the entrance of the shelter to assess a problem case, some guy in a wheelchair. Security would not let him into the building because he didn't have papers to prove that he was medically cleared to enter the shelter system. When I saw the guy in the strangely ornate entry foyer (it has marble floors and a hand-painted ceiling), I knew why. He was in a wheelchair, had no arms and no legs, and wore a loose cotton hospital gown that was open to the waist, revealing a still oozing stomach wound. He was distressingly thin, had black curly hair, and looked Italian. A teddy bear was in his lap. A sparkly heart-shaped balloon, with the words "I love you" printed on it in expansive letters, was attached by a string to the back of his wheelchair. "I'm Richie Vecchio," he said, smiling at me. He appeared to be in no distress.

I wheeled him down the dark hall to the waiting room. The security guards looked at us dubiously—all they knew was that he wasn't authorized to come in. I looked closely at his hospital papers. It indicated that he had been an inpatient at Bellevue for the last four months.

111

"Which unit?" I said.

"16-North," Richie said. "I was in an accident," he added, happily.

I told him that they wouldn't let him into the shelter unless he got a form from a doctor stating that he was medically stable.

"You better go back to the hospital. Then you can come back here," I said.

"Oh, I'm not going back there," he said. "I've been there for four months."

As a legal matter, I said, they weren't going to let him in.

"Oh that's okay," he said, reassuring me. "I'm just happy to be out of the hospital."

"Did you sign yourself out?" I asked.

"Yup," he said with satisfaction.

"But where will you go?"

"Oh, I'll figure something out," he said.

I started in on the legalese I'd been trained with: "It is, of course, your right to leave the hospital, but I strongly urge you . . ." when he interrupted me.

"It's all right, man, I'm just happy to be free," Richie said. "But I was wondering, do you think you could let me stay in the building long enough so I could recharge my wheelchair? The batteries don't last long in the cold."

He had spotted the electrical outlet in the corner. He pushed his chin down into his chest, and engaged a button on a metal plate that lay on his collarbone. The wheelchair whirred forward.

"See the cord in the back? Could you plug it in?" he said. "It takes about forty-five minutes to charge up," he said happily. I plugged in the cord.

"Is your wound okay?"

"Yeah," he said, looking down at it as if for the first time. "Jeez," he observed. "I guess it is oozing a little."

"What happened to you anyway?" I said.

"Lost my limbs in a motorcycle accident. My fault," he said. "I'm an addict. Heroin, coke, everything. Now I'm just on methadone, and a ton of medications." It was as if he were talking about varieties of ice cream.

He directed me to a pouch on the back of his wheelchair. In it was a hospital paper stating he had hepatitis and HIV, along with fifteen bottles of medications.

"Are you *sure* you don't want to go back to the hospital?"

"No way!" he said almost violently. "Four months is enough. They won't take me back anyway."

"Let me see if I can find anything for you," I said.

There are, in New York City, strange entities called "drop-in centers." They are intended to work as adjuncts to the city shelter system. They are meant to assist those who aren't medically cleared or not deemed "appropriate" for the regular system. That is, they serve those poor souls who have been rejected even by the New York City shelter system. The drop-in centers are usually a couple of basement rooms in a church somewhere. Contractually they are not allowed to provide beds. The clients of the drop-in centers sit on chairs all night long.

I called the four drop-in centers in Manhattan. I made my usual mistake, which is to ask if they have beds.

"You mean *chairs*," said an annoyed voice at the first drop-in center.

"Yes, chairs," I said.

"No chairs," the voice replied, and hung up the phone.

I called the next drop-in center. "Do you have any . . . er . . . slots?"

"You mean chairs," said the voice. "No, didn't you notice? It's cold outside. No chairs." Click.

No chairs were to be had at the other drop-in centers either.

When I returned to the waiting room there were three more clients waiting. Normally the guys in the waiting room never talk to one another, sitting silently with their heads down, avoiding eye contact at all costs. But these three were all talking to Richie. One was sharing his sandwich with him, and another was reading him a story from the newspaper.

"I'm sorry, I couldn't find anything for you. Do you have any money?" I said.

"One hundred and thirty dollars," said Richie, precisely.

The last resort for shelter were the Bowery flophouses. They charged $10 a night for a "room" with walls made of chicken wire. I called The Palace, The Rio, The Sunshine; none of them had beds. "It's cold outside," the voices on the other end of the line said.

My last call was to the YMCA, ten blocks away.

"We have a bed, but you gotta get here quick," said the attendant.

"How much?"

"Sixty-five dollars a night." In New York, even the Y's are expensive.

"Oh that's fine," Richie said, after I told him about the Y. "I'll go there."

"But you only have enough for two nights."

"It's okay. Don't worry, man. I'll figure something out." He depressed his chin, engaged the button and rolled out of the waiting room. "See you guys later. Thanks a lot," he said, nodding to his instant friends.

I left the shelter with Richie. Smoke or steam or whatever it is that emanates from the city's innards was billowing up through an open manhole to the surface of First Avenue. The wind had picked up and it must have been twenty degrees. Richie told me he had a jacket in his pouch. I pulled out the flimsy windbreaker and settled it over his shoulders. All he had on underneath was the cotton hospital gown.

I pointed him in the direction of the McBurney YMCA. "Do you think the wheelchair will make it?"

"We'll see," he said, laughing. "It looks like it's downhill." He headed out onto the street.

Then he stopped and shouted back to me. "See ya later! Thanks a lot, Charlie, I mean it. I really appreciate everything you've done for me. You're a great social worker or doctor, or whatever you are."

Richie crossed First Avenue, nearly colliding with the M15 bus. He whirred unsteadily down one side of the avenue, in the precarious slip of pavement between the parked cars and the oncoming traffic. The last I saw of Richie was the back of his wheelchair, the heart-shaped balloon bouncing in the wind, as he cut through the cloud of steam escaping from the city's netherworld.

Homelessness doesn't stop on holidays, but it does slow down. I've worked most holidays at Bellevue: Independence Day, Thanksgiving, Christmas, Labor Day. I think even the clients know it's a little tough to be in a homeless shelter on Christmas, and they stay away.

I watched the millennium come in at the shelter, saw the digital clock turn to 12:00:01 am, 2000. Here at the shelter, nothing changed. No one celebrated. Homelessness in the new millennium seemed to be just about the same as it was in the last one.

But the holiday I'll always remember was last July 4th. The shelter, about fifty yards from the East River, is a great spot to watch the fireworks. The explosives are set off by Macy's in barges in the middle of the river. The city closes down the F.D.R. Drive for the night and the crowds arrive two or three hours before the display to get a good view. At Bellevue, we have a front-row view all to ourselves.

That night I watched the fireworks from the shelter waiting room. There was nobody there but me, and I looked down upon the vast, noisy crowds, nearly fifty yards thick, packed in behind police barricades on the streets. After watching the psychedelic explosions for half an hour, I returned to my office.

Out my window I could see the massive residential wing of the building. A hundred turn-of-the-century casement windows faced me across the garbage-strewn courtyard. As the fireworks continued, I noticed a few faces quietly, tentatively peering out of a few windows. At first everything was murky, but as the side of the building lit up for a few seconds in the startling pink or green or purple aftermath of the explosions, I could see that there were dozens and dozens of faces—almost all of them black—peeking out of the windows. It was like a delayed strobe: every twenty seconds or so, I could see those heads, each time lit with a different color. As I stared long enough, and my eyes adjusted to the strobe, I could read the expressions on the faces. They all wore the same expression, an odd look, one that I'd never seen before at the shelter, where most people try to be as numb as possible: it was an expression of shy longing, a wish to be a part of something that was unavailable to them. America, it seemed, was a party that they could observe, but not attend.

All of them, I thought, every single one of the residents of the black chair, wanted to embrace the pink and green and purple light, to merge into those streaming lights over Manhattan. All of them possessed songs, songs sung in the midst of despair—songs about mythical places like Cheyenne, or about bobbing red balloons, songs proclaiming there is something much greater out there somewhere, songs hopeful that perhaps somehow, some way, someday . . . In a moment, I realized how strangely and cruelly exhilarating, how terribly and punishingly great it is to spend my nights listening to songs from the black chair.

*Nominated by Jewel Mogan and Bellevue Literary Review*

# THE NIGHT RICHARD PRYOR MET MUDBONE

## by A. VAN JORDAN

from RIVENDELL

> *"It is spiritless to think you cannot attain to that which you have seen and heard the masters attain. The masters are men. You are also a man."*
>
> *Hagakure: The Book of the Samurai*
> Yamamoto Tsunetomo

The moon hung orange as any sun
Just before it faces evening,
Like a flaming breast in the sky
Calling my name, and I walked out

Under it and rubbed the moonlight
All over my face and hands the way
The old folks used to do with the sunlight
On Wednesdays, because back in those times—

The hard times, harder than any of this shit
We're faced with today—they said, *The only
Time the sun came out was on Wednesday—
If you were lucky—and a boy had to get*

*His ass up early just to catch that.* Well,
It was a day like that that I'm about to tell you

116

About, a day when all I could see were
The mismatched symbol on the slot machine

Of my life. Surprisingly, this isn't a story
About a woman. All my relationships with women
Were one long-legged story in high heels.
But I'm not even trying

To get to sex here, for once.
What I'm trying to say is when your foot
Brushes a woman's toes under the sheets,
When you feel her breath on the back of your neck,

Turning your spine into a tall building,
When your eyes meet hers while making love,
You know you're looking at the truth.
The truth is what I found whenever I thought life

Could prove better than the craps game I was born into,
Although it's always just a roll of dice;
Like that time in Vegas when I walked out
On stage—half high, half drunk—

In 1968, and there sat Dean Martin in the front row,
Drink in one hand and a half-burned out cigarette
In his other cuff-linked hand, and I looked at his
Seal-hide hair and his wax-figure of a face,

And the rest of the audience went out of focus,
All the voices were put on mute; all I could hear was
Dino stirring the ice in his drink and I asked myself
What the fuck am I doing here, my skinny, black

Ass from Peoria, Illinois? I walked out on stage and a switch
Flipped off inside my head. The room went white.
My agent told me—like in the movies, man,
Told me on the phone real chill like—that I'd never work

In this life again. But then I realized
It wasn't neon marques, gangsters

Or headline acts I was afraid of—it was me.
I spent years imitating Bill Cosby, telling jokes

That fit me like a suit two sizes too big;
I struck a sad figure on stage, even when I was good.
Don Rickles came up to me once and said,
*What a great show! It's amazing how much you sound*

*Like Cosby*. And then I wondered if everyone else could
Tell I had climbed inside his skin and zipped him up;
I wondered who else would unzip my monologue
And find me there trembling.

After Vegas I headed to New York and got to open
For Miles Davis at the Village Gate, and Miles
Looked through me just like Rickles had, but he did
Something that was as beautiful as his music:

Miles knew I was looking for a way
To fall off the planet's edge, gettin' high and wanting more,
So one night as I sat drinking in my dressing room,
The emcee comes in right before curtain and tells me

Miles changed the line up. I thought I was fired, man.
But Miles decided that he was going to open for *me*.
Do you know what a bad muthafucka you gotta be
To have Miles Davis open for you? That's like God, Jack.

So I go out on stage, and as I'm about to go into my best
Bill Cosby impression, I see this old man with coal-
Colored skin sitting on the edge of the stage.
He's lookin' at me like, *Well, boy, let's see what*

*You've got. And I don't want to hear none of that Bill Cosby shit,*
*Either*. And he said tell them about badass Oilwell; about the Wino;
Or about Miss Rudolph, the Hoodoo lady, *How she had one titty*
*That had an eye tattooed on it and 'nother that had*

*A mouth, and how when that one titty blew a kiss*
*And the other winked, you knew, for the first time,*

*You had smoked enough of that shit.*
I asked the old man his name and he said

*They call me Mudbone; I was born in Tupelo, Mississippi.*
I looked at him sideways, and he said, *That's a city, boy.*
*I was born there a long time ago. So long ago it ain't worth*
*Rememberin' when exactly, because after a certain while,*

*It's just a long time ago.*
Like me, I could tell he died
Many times and had some stories to tell;
*You don't live this long being a fool.*

*There's a whole lot of wise, young men*
*Deader than a muthafucka,* he said.
Yes, I thought, my meditations on Death keep me alive,
Too; Death would show up, from time to time,

Like a distant relative
Who thought I had been away too long.
The funny thing is, I spent years searching—
Laughing on the tip of a needle,

Crying between a woman's legs, imitating
Other people's work—just to come
Back to a man who had been there all along saying,
*Hey, look over here at me,* but I had ignored him

Thinking he didn't have anything to say.
So I stood there with a cigarette throbbing in one hand
And a microphone rocking in the other
And I told them about the fallen angels of my life.

And I grabbed a handful of the glow from the spotlights,
Rubbed it all over my body, right on stage, naked,
In front of everybody, and I smiled, and they smiled back,
As the light, growing brighter now from the rafters,

Turned to sunshine.

*Nominated by Rita Dove, Reginald Gibbons, Stuart Dischell, Rivendell*

# MY UNOPENED LIFE

## by TESS GALLAGHER

from NEW ORLEANS REVIEW

lay to the right of my plate
like a spoon squiring a knife, waiting
patiently for soup or the short destiny
of dessert at the eternal picnic—unsheltered
picnic at the mouth of the sea
that dares everything forgotten to huddle
at the periphery of a checked cloth spread
under the shadowy, gnarled penumbra
of the madrona.

Hadn't I done well enough with the life
I'd seized, sure as a cat with
its mouthful of bird, bird with its
belly full of worm, worm like an acrobat of darkness
keeping its moist nose to the earth, soaring
perpetually into darkness without so much as
the obvious question: why all this darkness?
And even in the belly of the bird: *why
only darkness?*

The bowl of the spoon
collects entire rooms just lying there next
to the knife. It makes brief forays into
the mouth delivering cargoes of ceilings

and convex portraits of teeth
posing as stalactites of
a serially extinguished cave

from whence we do nothing but stare out
at the sea, collecting little cave-ins of
perception sketched on the moment
to make more tender the house of the suicide
in which everything was so exactly
where it had been left by someone missing.
Nothing, not even the spoon he abandoned
near the tea cup, could be moved without
seemingly altering the delicious
universe of his intention.

So are we each lit briefly by engulfments
of space like the worm in the beak of
the bird, yielding to sudden corridors
of light-into-light, never asking: *why,*
*tell me why*
        *all this light?*

*Nominated by New Orleans Review*

# BOYFRIENDS

fiction by CYNTHIA WEINER

from PLOUGHSHARES

Give or take a day or two, I've had a boyfriend for the past twenty-five years, starting with Nicky Braun when I was ten and up to Eddie now, and when I say *boyfriend*, I really do mean the *boy* part: I'm not a big fan of men, if you want to know the truth. There have been a couple of what I guess you could call manfriends (bow ties, pension plans, some Winston Churchill biography on the nightstand), but it's really boys I like best. I like the way they hang tacky souvenirs off the rearview mirror in their cars, the way they shave their heads when they're going bald, the way they stare at your mouth when they want to kiss you, the way they buy you silly presents like kazoos and Flintstones vitamins. Boys like to hold hands, and they like to watch porn, and they like to fix things around the house. Men'll say, "Your breasts are lovely in the moonlight" or "candlelight" (they've always got moonlight or candles around; what's that about?), whereas a boy will say, "You have great tits," and maybe it's me, but I can't think of a more honest phrase in the English language. Show me the hunger in "Your breasts are lovely." Show me the passion, the conviction, the need. That's the thing about boys: they need you in a way that a man never will.

Nineteen boyfriends in twenty-five years, and I had to break up with each and every one of them. You can probably guess what happened: they became men. Tony got a promotion at work and suddenly wanted to be called Anthony. I admit, I wasn't as enthusiastic as I might have been. I said, "Anthony's not even your real name." (He kept a framed copy of his birth announcement on the coffee

122

table, Tony Brian Miller, next to—what else?—a picture of his mother. Boys worship their mothers.) He said, "They're giving Anthony an office with two ficus trees." I put my arms around his neck, rubbed myself against his jacket. I said, "How come you never call me kitten anymore?" His eyes were shining. "One ficus tree is de rigueur," he said, "but two is a genuine coup." Where had he learned to talk like that? He wouldn't even take off his tie until I examined his upgraded stock options.

With Jerry, it started when his best friend's wife got pregnant. One night I woke up to a thermometer wedged under my tongue—he'd begun secretly charting my ovulation cycle. The next morning at brunch he gazed moonily at a set of twins at the table beside ours, though they were both bawling so loud their own parents finally gave in and started bawling, too. Within a month, he was claiming *Toy Story* as his favorite movie (and believe me, he didn't mean the X-rated version that we'd once gotten such a kick out of, with its vibrating gadgets and blow-up dolls).

I'm not sure what exactly got into Ritchie, but one day he began referring to me as a woman, as in "What a challenging woman you are." I cringed every time I heard it. *Woman* makes me think of chapped lips and public television. Women are earnest in that self-congratulatory, beige-pantyhose way, and they always have a lot of plants in their apartments. Women make *me* nervous, and I (at least in chromosome, if not spirit) *am* one.

Next came Bob, who on his thirtieth birthday stopped shaving his head, and then went out and bought a pair of crepe-soled shoes like his grandfather's.

Danny picked me up a box of tampons on the way to my apartment, without a word of protest.

Rudy gave up meat and started watching tennis on TV. Soon he was asking permission to kiss me.

See what I mean? Even Nicky Braun, my first true love, my wild, skateboarding delinquent, joined the math club in junior high, spending every afternoon in heated debate over fractions vs. decimals. Fractions and tennis and *woman* and tampons: maybe these all seem like little things, but put enough little things together, and what do you get? You get "Not tonight, honey—my ulcer's acting up." You get "Isn't that skirt a little on the short side?" You get "What do you mean, you don't know what OPEC stands for?" You get a pear-shaped diamond and a stack of monogrammed towels with your husband's initial in the center, no matter what you told everyone about not changing your name. You get a kitchen with too many appliances and a couple of kids who truly believe you're the biggest moron they've ever met. You get an oncologist who thinks you've got a fifty-fifty chance, sixty-forty with radiation. Am I the only one who understands this?

My friend Karen asked me to spend a few hours at her daughter's kindergarten for what was being billed as Grandparents and Special Friends Day. Grandparents are evidently a rare quantity these days, what with most of these kids' parents in their forties and fifties—someone must have figured the "special friends" would fill out the house a little. But when I got there, it was just a bunch of kids fooling around with tissue paper and pipe cleaners, and about a half-dozen elderly people nearly toppling off those tiny school chairs. The two teachers were huddled by the gerbil cage, arguing about whose turn it was to clean it. "Last time I looked," one of them whispered, "*somebody* did nothing but dump a pound of shavings over the old poop"; the other one made a face and said, "*Somebody* better watch their tone of voice unless they want the kids to find out what really happened to Twinkle's brother." I could've listened all day, the two of them in their plaid kilts and Peter-Pan-collared blouses, but they spotted me and put on big, sunny smiles. "You must be Allie's special friend," one of them chirped. "She was petrified you wouldn't show up!"

Actually I was only about fifteen minutes late, but I've noticed that people who spend all their time with children get a little snotty when it comes to adults. Maybe they've gotten used to bossing everyone around, or maybe they just started out like that, but either way it's one of the reasons I'm a little wary about having kids of my own. When you've got kids, you're at the mercy of all their teachers, and their principals and pediatricians, not to mention the various toy store managers, shoe store salesmen, and zookeepers you encounter throughout the day. It's bad enough when you're by yourself in the world—everyone I know seems to feel perfectly free to make pronouncements on my job (or lack thereof), my wardrobe (or lack thereof), my maturity (do I need to say "or lack thereof" again?), but once you've got children, forget it: you're *really* public property. It's apparently everyone's duty to remark on how you're raising them, and the worst part is that a lot of the time you have to listen, or at least look like you're listening. If your son bites another kid's ankle, you can't tell the principal to mind her own business when she asks what's going on at home. You can't voice much opposition when the guy manning the Ape House suggests you read Dr. Spock, not if your daughter's just pulled up her dress to try to entice a chimpanzee.

I told the teachers I'd been at an important conference and was lucky to have gotten away at all (I thought "conference" had an impressive ring to it, with its vaguely medical implications), and then I went over to Allie, who didn't look especially petrified, just a little befuddled as she tried to bend a pipe cleaner into the shape of a flower stem. She's a smart kid, not the most dexterous, maybe, but good at card games and knock-knock jokes, which is why we get along so well. Next to her was a boy with black hair and that milky white skin that's nearly translucent. He was looking down at the table, his head cocked to the side like he was contemplating the properties of linoleum. He glanced up when Allie called my name, and I saw that his eyes were blue, steel blue verging on gray, with a look of absolute gravity as he regarded me.

He said, "Hello, Fiona."

Something came over me. I still can't explain it. That hot-cold feeling like when you're in the grip of the flu, or when you've just gotten caught in a whopper of a lie. He had a vertical crease over the bridge of his nose, faint circles under his eyes that spoke of restless nights, of raising the window to stare out at the constellations. I thought about my boyfriend Eddie—his sailboat pajamas with the buoys on the sleeves, Lucky Charms for breakfast. Suddenly they seemed to have lost some of their luster. Over the course of a lifetime, how many of those yellow marshmallows are you really meant to ingest?

"James doesn't like making flowers," Allie informed me. "But he does like to sing songs, though."

She smiled at him. Was she flirting? I was having trouble catching my breath. I thought: when he's my age, I'll be sixty-five. A mouthful of bridgework, but half-price at the movies—not such a bad deal, right? If you look at it that way? "Flowers can be very attractive," I said, inanely, "but music is, you know, the food of love and everything."

Had I really said that? He appeared to consider my words. "That's true," he said finally. His voice was husky, judicious. No one had ever taken anything I'd said so seriously.

There was a message from Karen on my answering machine when I got home, saying she hoped no one at Allie's school had tried to hit me up for a donation, and also that she'd spotted Eddie on the subway that morning reading the newspaper and was I aware that *Family Circus* made him laugh so hard his eyes teared? She hung up abruptly: she's got another kid besides Allie, a two-year-old son who starts chewing paper clips when he thinks she's been on the telephone too long. For a moment I considered calling back and telling her about James, the jigsaw puzzle we'd worked on close to an hour, and how as the picture gradually came clear—a zebra's eye here, then a flank, then a hoof; the mane of a lion, its ear and then its tail— we named each animal together, like some twenty-first-century Adam and Eve. But I wasn't sure what she might do with that anecdote (for instance, ban me from her apartment, considering she's got Charlie running around day and night in nothing but a diaper), and if I tried to explain that it was James I found so compelling, James specifically, the James who'd shaken my hand when it was time for me to leave and said, "I hope you'll visit us again," I wouldn't even put it past her to get a little competitive, like, what—Charlie can't shake your hand and exchange a few pleasantries? Charlie's not *specific* enough for you?

It seems to me that parenthood's a real trade-off, in terms of what happens to your brain. The minute your kid's born, all this space gets cleared out for the new knowledge you're going to need (how to clean an umbilical stump, or gauge the tenor of a burp for forthcoming spit-up), but all that space was once filled with something other than stumps and burps, right? So something gets lost in the shuffle, and my vote goes to common sense, at least based on my admittedly sketchy observation. Did you know that if you cut a baby's fingernails on a Friday, there's a good chance they'll forever grow back crooked, and the same for his hair, on a Sunday? That a crib facing south can lead to colic and/or jaundice and/or pinkeye? What I mean is that parents aren't always the most rational of people, and so I decided not to tell Karen about James, even though I thought it was obvious that our connection had been a cerebral one. "Incorporeal" was the word that kept running through my head, but you try explaining that to someone who freaks if her kid swallows a watermelon seed.

126

And for a different reason, I didn't tell Eddie, either. Although once in a while we explore the possibility of having a baby—"Want to maybe do it without a condom?" he asks; I say, "I don't know, do you?" and he says, "Maybe in a couple of weeks?"—I think it's fair to say that we're both somewhat ambivalent. But I think it's also fair to say that of the two of us he's the less ambivalent (I *am* aware that *Family Circus* makes him laugh so hard his eyes tear). I didn't want him getting the idea that my affinity with a child might mean I was ready for one of my own. I'm not so sure I'm cut out to be a mother. I get along really well with kids unless I happen to be related to them, and then I'm struck with self-consciousness, the kind that gives you clammy hands and a stutter, the kind that usually overcomes you in the middle of a job interview when you recognize how flagrantly unqualified you are for the position. I get so flustered around my nieces and nephews that I mispronounce their names; I babble nostalgically about movies they've never seen, and ask them age-inappropriate questions like *Can you believe how much a tank of gas costs these days?* or *Does my butt look bigger since the last time you saw me?* Maybe I'm just one of those people whose DNA gets uneasy when it senses itself nearby, in which case procreation may be a bit of a gamble.

So I didn't tell anyone about James, but it was days before I stopped shivering whenever I thought about him—when I thought about the way he'd held the door for me as I left the classroom; when I thought about his solemn eyes on mine, in the moment before it swung shut.

That Sunday I woke up with only half an hour to get ready for the baby shower I had to go to at noon. I'd stayed awake way too late the night before watching a movie on one of those obscure cable channels, a science-fictiony thing where some microbe got into the water and reversed the aging process. Everyone was born old and got younger and younger, so that people who started off at eighty turned seventy-nine twelve months later, and then seventy-eight, and by the time they were thirty they had enough old-age wisdom to truly appreciate their stamina and their youthful good looks. It wasn't the kind of movie you could switch off in the middle, plus I had Eddie asleep next to me making his familiar, but still somehow always alarming, grunts and mumbles, plus I wasn't exactly overjoyed about going to a baby shower, anyway, my tenth this year. Look: I understand what it is about babies that gets people worked up—the tiny fingers and toes, the hope for a new generation, etc.—but at most showers the baby isn't due for at least a couple of months, so why are the women already so—I don't know—so *giddy*? Today, for instance, there were pink and blue streamers hanging from every doorway in such profusion it felt like walking through a car wash, and the hostess had filled several of those infant bathtubs with fruit punch, which she was encouraging guests to drink out of baby bottles *with* the nipples still attached. She'd also fallen prey to the newest trend of serving only the foods that the mother-to-be has been craving the past few months, though is anyone really meant to eat anchovies sprinkled with cinnamon, or peanut butter and turkey sandwiches?

Still, all that was bearable for an hour—I was able to scrape clean a couple of bites of turkey, and I even managed to smile politely through the usual chitchat about episiotomies and rectal lacerations and placental discharge—but the minute the plates were cleared, a woman in a Gymboree T-shirt announced that it was game time. Someone always wants to play games at a baby shower, and that *someone* invariably turns out to be a mother, especially when the majority of guests don't have children. Then the other mothers started cheering and rushing to move the chairs into a circle; it makes you wonder if the games aren't a way to even things up a little with the non-mothers, a kind of subconscious retaliation for every tactless remark and impatient shake of the head. It's not that I'm unsympathetic. Honestly, if I had to endure one too many hints about the wonders of Ritalin, or if I got reproachful looks in restaurants no matter how discreetly I unhooked the clasp on my nursing bra and lifted my child to my breast, it might be me proposing a diaper-sniffing contest, urging the non-mothers in particular to don blindfolds and guess if the smear in the crotch is mustard or soy sauce. I might be the one coaxing them to sing "You're Having My Baby," and I might even get so caught up in the excitement that I'd not only award a pacifier to the one who sang most off-key, but exhort her to suck on it while I took her picture. ("Smile, Fiona," said the hostess, adding kindly, if not especially helpfully: "Pretend it's a rubber thumb.") I suppose I might even get a kick out of the game where everyone has thirty seconds to safety-pin a cloth diaper on a balloon, or a doll, or the person sitting beside her. And although I do hope I'd draw the line at passing out ice cubes with little plastic babies frozen inside, insisting that the first guest whose ice cube melts shout,

128

"My water broke!"—well, if I had to hear "It must be so relaxing, being out of the rat race" even once, I can't swear that isn't a line I wouldn't cross.

I slipped out as this last game was getting underway. I was still carrying the paper cup with the ice cube inside, but it seemed somehow churlish, I guess, or at least a little improvident, to just drop it in one of the garbage cans along the sidewalk. The air had that electric feeling to it, the type of day that swivels back and forth between sunshine and rain. *Antsy*, my mother used to call it, the sky blue streaked with gray, and then a minute later gray with patches of blue, but I decided to walk home through the park, anyway. I passed the entrance to one of those spooky old tunnels my friends and I used to hang out in after school, the kind that's damp and echoey inside with a million cigarette butts on the ground that no one ever seems to clean up, and it occurred to me that that's where I'd want my own baby shower to take place, if the day ever came to pass. Seriously: no chocolate-covered sardines, and no molding babies out of clay or soap or chewing gum, just a lot of dopey trash-talk about boys, and maybe a sénce for old time's sake as the sun went down, and then we could all go back to one of our parents' apartments and raid the liquor cabinet and search the phone book for people with the same names as celebrities so we could crank-call them.

The air got even mistier as I walked past the baseball diamonds, and by the time I got to the playground a few yards away from the park's exit, it had started drizzling. Parents were packing up shovels and juice boxes while the kids took a last ride down the slide. I was thinking about the scene in the science-fiction movie that I'd liked best: a middle-aged woman planting roses in her garden for the first time, her eyes lighting up as she pats the soil into place with once-arthritic fingers. In the playground there was one boy left on the jungle gym, hanging from a set of bars a few feet above the ground. It was his watch I recognized first, a clunky block of steel on a leather band that he'd told me was a gift from his uncle, and I recognized his wrist, too, pale and slender with a small scar alongside the vein. (A dying dog'll bite if you pet her, he'd explained when we were putting together the jigsaw puzzle. That's the only way she knows how to say goodbye.) I leaned against the entrance gate to watch him—there were a few adults still collecting toys and zipping jackets, but I didn't hear anyone call his name, and it seemed entirely possible that he was here in the park by himself.

He saw me and dropped to the ground, then took a couple of steps in my direction. "Your cup has flowers on it," he said. "Did you go to a party?"

"A baby shower," I said. I tilted the cup so he couldn't see the plastic baby inside. It seemed suddenly kind of obscene, especially since the ice cube had melted off everything but its backside.

He was looking at me in that pensive way I remembered, his eyes bluish-gray like the sky, but steady. "Babies aren't supposed to take showers. They can drown."

"Tell me about it," I said, glancing again into the cup.

"I think it's because babies aren't very good at holding themselves up, so the water would hit their heads too hard and knock them over," he said. I was studying his face, his black hair falling into his eyes, and it took me a moment to get that he hadn't recognized my "Tell me about it" as rhetorical. "Plants and radios don't go in the shower, either," he added, "but that's for completely different reasons."

He emphasized "completely" in a way that reminded me of a friend I once had, a very tall girl who'd fallen for a guy who barely reached her shoulder. "I'd completely marry him," she liked to say, "if we could sit down at the altar." As I watched James push his hair out of his eyes, I was thinking about this friend, who wound up marrying not the guy who reached her shoulder but an even shorter one who hardly reached her bicep, and I was also thinking about the rose-planting lady in the movie and how her knuckles had gone from swollen to smooth in a picturesque, time-lapsey way, and then I thought that I ought to start coming to the park every Sunday afternoon. Why not? It was just a short walk from my apartment, and there were certainly a number of things I knew that James could benefit from knowing, too, such as about baby showers and rhetorical statements, for starters, and also other things like how to wrap a comic book in Mylar so the pages don't yellow, and how to help a girl out of a taxi so that her legs won't get tangled in her skirt. I could come every Sunday for, say, a year or two, and if that year or two went smoothly then for another year or two, and after another year or two and then another—well, sooner or later he'd be old enough for us to spend time together in a venue other than a playground, right?

The rain was starting to fall a little harder. He pointed to a girl sitting on a bench who was holding an umbrella over her head and talking on a cellphone, and said she was his babysitter and that her favorite color was purple. The wind began to pick up, enough so that the swings were twisting and swaying on their own, but we stood there a while longer, not saying much, just watching the rain and listening to the creak of the swings. Toward the end of that science-fiction movie, the rose-planting lady, now a little girl in a velvet dress with lace at the hem, approaches an old man on the deck of an ocean liner. There's some talk about canasta, how she used to play it with his grandmother; then he says, "So, how old are you these days?" and she laughs and says, "The funny thing is, I've lost track." That's the closest I can get to what it felt like, standing with James in the rain.

Just in case you ever find yourself in a situation similar to mine, let me spare you countless hours of research, not to mention a slew of bewildered questions from a talent agent and some less-than-pretty insinuations from a board of ed. official: it's impossible to rent a child for an afternoon. It doesn't matter what your needs are—decoy purposes, for instance, so that your unaccompanied presence in a playground week after week doesn't arouse suspicion—nothing doing. Even if you've got more selfless motives, like a mansion in the country with a swimming pool and a trampoline and a bunch of cute puppies just aching to be romped around with on your vast, verdant lawn, you still can't get a child for a day. Believe me; I asked.

One ought to be able to borrow a child now and then. That's all I'm saying.

Eddie's parents were driving down from Hartford on Saturday, and much of the next week was devoted to helping him choose a restaurant for dinner. I was generally fond of them, though they could be a bit exhausting, what with their dogged pursuit of fun. (Or at least their idea of what constituted fun, their tastes being of the high-school-kids-on-spring-break variety: comedy clubs, theme restaurants, margaritas with extra salt and little umbrellas. The last time they visited, as we gallivanted from video arcade to bowling alley to Times Square to trawl for defunct peepshow houses, I thought I overheard Eddie's father tell Eddie that he wasn't sure I was "plucky" enough for him, though Eddie later insisted he'd said "plucking"—something to do with the width of my eyebrows.) In the midst of our investigations, Eddie suggested I move in with him. I suggested we discuss it after the weekend. He suggested we discuss it during the weekend, since after all it was his father's name on the apartment lease and it might not be a bad idea to consult him. I suggested we see how dinner went before bringing it up, considering my lack of either pluckiness or tidy eyebrows. All these suggestions gave a kind of portentous undertone to our debates about the WWF Café vs. Sir Gawain's Bar and Grill, though I tried to lighten the mood by renting his favorite X-rated videos three nights in a row. They restored a measure of harmony between us, enough so that we were able to settle on a haunted house cum Mexican restaurant for Saturday night, but by the time we got there, Eddie's mood had plummeted again, since really porn can only go so far when cohabitation issues are at stake.

"All this," he said sourly, frowning at a display of what looked like bloody fingers on a shelf above the bar, "for the price of a burrito."

"You're a burrito," I said, nonsensically but supportively, and I put my arm around his shoulder and kissed his cheek as we were led to our table because I genuinely wanted to cheer him up, and also because I was inadvertently slipping into this fantasy state that sometimes comes over me when I'm out with a boyfriend in public, which goes something like: my real and final boyfriend is in the room, the one I haven't met yet but who's going to, I don't know, redeem me, and I have only a few minutes to impress upon him my kind and affectionate nature. I'm not sure what brings it on, but tonight it must have been the sight of all the kids in the restaurant, one big blur of boy in the faint light cast by the chandeliers.

Though shouldn't there be some ordinance against kids dining at tables that are carved into the shape of coffins, especially when they're topped with glass so that the heaps of dirt-sprinkled bones inside are fully visible?

It was another half hour before Eddie's parents arrived, their faces flushed and their hair windblown, as if maybe they'd veered off I-84 for a quick stroll by the Housatonic. His father was wearing a wide tie the color of toast with a scatter of yellow, melted-butter-looking squiggles, and his mother had on a yellow, squiggle-matching dress. Her name was Priscilla, which was what she'd told me to call her, though she referred to herself as "Silly," as in "My friends say, Silly, you're insane to keep a ferret as a pet." They complimented Eddie on his choice of restaurant. His mother called it "moody." His father said, "We could be in Vincent Price's living room." They peered around, chuckling over a display case in which a werewolf knelt beside the prone body of a bride, blood and gore at her throat and down the front of her wedding dress. Eddie grinned, vastly enlivened by the presence of his parents, and pointed out a shark by the waiters' station, one sandaled foot with pink-painted toenails sticking out of its mouth. From a couple of speakers embedded in the ceiling came the creepy-cello notes of Verdi's *Requiem*. I was starting to feel a little jittery, like when you get an overseas call and for the first few seconds all you hear is that windy, moaning sound over the line; I was starting to feel the kind of thirst I'd felt the day after my favorite aunt died, when her name was printed in the newspaper not as Bess Kagan but as Boss Keegan. I drank a glass of water in one gulp. Body parts were swinging from the rafters on long stretches of rope. A waiter came to our table holding a pad in one hand and a scythe in the other, and Eddie's father ordered refried beans for all of us. He said he thought we should drive out to Coney Island after dinner. Eddie's mother said that the week before she'd forgotten the word for carousel. Eddie's father said the week before that, she'd forgotten the word for stethoscope.

They all roared with laughter. I thought about how Eddie'd said Boss sounded cooler than Bess, like a mafiosa. I thought about how he'd told me that the day after he was born, his father reserved a burial plot for himself, Eddie, and Eddie's mother in a Las Vegas cemetery. I downed another glass of water. How do I describe what I was feeling? There was static in my ears. There was a pain in both my ankles, as if I had my shoes on the wrong feet. There was sweat collecting at the back of my neck, behind my knees, in my palms. The bones in our coffin were glowing like they'd been coated in radioactive waste. Eddie's mother unfolded her napkin and placed it on her husband's lap. She said, "My friends say, Silly, you're losing your marbles." Eddie grabbed my hand and told his parents he had something to discuss. A kidney swung so close to my head I thought it might smack me in the face. His father said, "Something to disgust?" and his mother said, "The story about Nixon and the garter belt?"

They all shook with laughter again.

I said, "Eddie, I'm sorry, but this isn't going to work."

It wasn't what I'd meant to say. I'd meant to say something about refried beans—how I'd heard that an oddly high number of death-row inmates requested them for their final meal; how if no one minded, I thought I'd get an order of nachos—but now the words were out, and I can't say I wasn't relieved. Eddie was staring at me, looking confused and then hurt and then confused again, and I figured the least I could do was help him make up his mind. If I told him the truth, he'd from now on get to brand me as the wayward one in our relationship, the one who'd flipped and broken his heart instead of the other way around, thus ensuring future girlfriends' sympathy. So I started at the beginning, Grandparents and Special Friends Day, the pipe-cleaner flowers and the scar on James's wrist. The static in my ears faded. The bride with the gore got to her feet, and the werewolf brushed some dust off her dress. Eddie's mother said, "I didn't know that's why dying dogs bite." His father said, "Son, I'm not saying I'm pleased with what I'm hearing, but you have to admit there's some pluck involved." I told them about the jigsaw puzzle and the baby in the paper cup. I mentioned the word "incorporeal," though I was kind of winding down by that point, plus the waiter had set the beans on the table but was nevertheless lingering. Eddie's father asked for three Coronas, and a Shirley Temple for me. His mother said, "Oh, are we allowed to joke?" His father spooned beans onto his plate. "Fiona's kidding," he said. He smiled at me with more warmth than I'd ever felt from him. He  said, "You're kidding, right?"

I shook my head and glanced at Eddie. He was fiddling with the rubber spider he'd found under his napkin, but his shoulders sagged, and his face had that gloomy last-game-of-the-season look that made my heart break a little.

"Kidding," he said, pronouncing it like two separate words. "Sort of the way I'd go sledding or canoeing."

"Sort of," I agreed, not exactly sure what I was agreeing with but happy to let him have the last word. Though I did add that I guessed I ought to be going, and all of them, including the waiter, said that would probably be best.

A friend of mine, the one who married the guy who hardly reached her bicep, once calculated how many days of her life the average woman has her period. Five days a month for thirty-seven years—that's 2,220 days and somewhere in the neighborhood of eleven thousand tampons; that's over fifty thousand hours' worth of cramps and crankiness and a greater-than-usual awareness of the reproductive mechanism lodged inside your body, the same body that you feed Devil Dogs and cram into too-tight jeans and settle on various, and often suspiciously sticky, bar stools. This is what I was thinking about when I left my apartment Sunday afternoon, premenstrual spasms like darts below my rib cage. I was also thinking that considering the night I'd had the night before, I'd looked surprisingly the same in the mirror this morning. I'd thought I might look something like when I quit smoking last year—lonely and fearful, but also virtuous and wise—but there was nothing of that in my face, just a general fatigue I imagine had to do with a nonstop bout of dreams involving Tom Jones and a tombstone. And as I got closer to the park, I was also thinking about James, and what I was going to say when I saw him. The sky was one of those mild blues that makes it seem like nothing bad can possibly happen, but I was still nervous, and my usual tension-easing conversation starters—*Did you know that forty percent of Americans have never been to a dentist?* or *Did you hear the one about the nun and the vacuum cleaner?*—were obviously unsuitable.

It was the first really sunny day in weeks, and the playground was overrun with kids in shorts and T-shirts. I sat down at the end of a bench beneath a cluster of trees, occupied by a row of sleepy-looking women with tiny babies strapped to their chests. I had on a billowy shirt so I could pass for pregnant-and-therefore-here-to-observe-and-anticipate in case anyone questioned me, and I was carrying a roll of Tums and a box of Raisinets in my handbag as my mother had through three pregnancies, but the women hardly glanced my way after a couple of quick, weary smiles. It occurred to me that James might be here with one or both of his parents, a potential encounter it seemed a good idea to avoid, although after a minute I spotted his babysitter on a bench by the sandbox. Her eyes were closed, and her head was tipped back to face the sun. James was sitting a few feet away on the edge of the sandbox with a book on his lap, observing an argument a group of kids were having over who'd brought which shovel to the park today. My nervousness subsided a little as I watched him watch them. All the boys I've ever liked have been fidgety, the gum-chomping leg-shaking knuckle-cracking type, whereas James was so still he seemed almost like an element of the park instead of the crowd that would leave at the end of the day, like the water in the water fountain or a branch on the tree behind the seesaws. I think I could have sat there all afternoon watching him, but then he turned his head and saw me. He said something to his babysitter, and she smiled vaguely in my direction before pushing her sleeves above her elbows and leaning her head back again.

I guess I must have looked to her like just another tired mother on a bench, though I certainly didn't *feel* like a tired mother, the violent jump in my heart as James walked toward me. There was a cut on his knee I hadn't noticed from a distance, a smudge of dirt and a tiny speck of blood. He carried the book in one hand, his finger inside, I guess, to mark the page he'd read up to. The pedagogic chatter I'd rehearsed (rhetorical statements, comic books, etc.) deserted me: he sat down and the only thing I could think to say was, "Fancy meeting you here," a phrase I not only detest but that was barely audible, anyway, my throat was so dry.

He squinted at me, holding his hand over his eyes to shield them from the sun.

"Fancy?"

"It's a way of saying hello," I stammered. "Kind of like, Oh, we're both in the park—what a coincidence." I cleared my throat and added, "I'm usually more of a hi kind of person, but I guess today felt like a fancy day." He looked a bit bewildered. How much longer was I going to stay with this topic? A little longer, apparently; I said, "If I were you, I'd just stick with hello. Or hey. Or hi." I knew that millions of conversations like this were going on around the world at that very moment, girls on a mountain range in Nepal or in a Lithuanian forest trying to impress the boys they liked, and yet it was hard to imagine a clumsier performance in any language.

"Okay," he said. "Hi."

"Right back at you," I replied. I wasn't sure where to go from there, but I figured I'd better stop talking for a few minutes. I rummaged through my handbag until I found a Band-Aid, and he thanked me as I set it over his cut. Then we sat quietly, watching a couple of toddlers chase after a squirrel, listening to the chirps and murmurs of the babies and mothers beside us. After a while he held his book out to me. I flipped through a couple of pages—it wasn't a work I was familiar with; something to do with blueberries—but I'd often seen couples reading together in the park, lounging on a rock or a patch of grass with a picnic basket at their feet, and I liked the idea of being part of such a romantic tableau.

I said, encouragingly, "It looks like a very soulful story."

He nodded. "Yes, I think the little bear is about to get lost on the mountain trail." As he turned to look at me, a piece of hair fell in his eyes. He said, "Do you have this book in your house?"

*Outsmarting the Female Fat Cell, Meditation for Dummies*—that's the type of book that was in my house, but I didn't think this was the

136

appropriate time to divulge my shoddy taste in literature. "Please don't take this the wrong way," I said, "but a little bear on a mountain trail—well, that's sort of for children, isn't it?"

His hair was still in his eyes, and I brushed it away, my heart jumping again when I saw that his gaze was one of those searching ones, the kind a boy gives a girl when he wants to ask her something personal, or tell her something he's never told anyone, something that she senses will change everything between them. The kind of look a boy gives a girl when he's about to kiss her for the very first time.

His gaze fell to the Band-Aid on his knee, then he glanced back up at me and said, "But aren't you somebody's mother?"

It's funny how certain moments you remember only pieces of. You try to fix the full force of your memory on the whole, but different parts keep slipping just out of grasp. You can see the silver span of the first plane you ever flew on, but you can't hear the roar of its takeoff; you can feel the slide of your grandmother's iced tea down your throat, but the taste is permanently gone. Except that this wasn't one of those moments. James placed his hand on the book, and even now I can picture it next to mine, less than half the size and his nails smooth and small as a doll's. I could describe the chalky remains of the Tums I was sucking on, though I'll spare you that, and I'll also spare you the ache in my side as my period began, and the scent of azaleas in the air. I'll just tell you that there was something grave but also kind in his eyes as he moved a little closer, that he pressed his shoulder to mine and said, "Could you read to me for a little while?" And with the most perfect clarity I can still recall the wail that went up from our bench, because I swear I'm not making it up when I tell you that every last baby chose that moment to start crying, first one and then a second and then all eight or nine, like some miniature Greek chorus.

*Nominated by Stacey Richter*

# CHILD, DEAD, IN THE ROSE GARDEN

fiction by E. L. DOCTOROW

from THE VIRGINIA QUARTERLY REVIEW

SPECIAL AGENT B. W. MOLLOY, now retired, tells the following story: One morning the body of a child was found in the Rose Garden. The sun had just risen. A concert had been given the night before in celebration of the National Arts and Humanities Awards, an event held every year in May. The body was discovered by Frank Calabrese, sixty, the groundskeeper, who had arrived in advance of his workers to oversee the striking of the performance tent. Dew was on the grass and the air was fresh. The light inside the tent was soft and filled with shadows. What Calabrese saw under two folding chairs in a middle row at the east end of the tent was a small Nike running shoe protruding from a shroud-like wrapping. Not knowing what else to do, he phoned the Marine guard post.

In a matter of moments the on-duty Secret Service were at the site. They secured it and radioed the FBI. At the same time the President was awakened, the measures for emergency evacuation of the White House were put in motion, and in short order he, separately, and his family, their overnight guests, and the resident staff were away from the area.

The shroud was scanned and then unwrapped by the FBI bomb squad. The body was that of a boy, white, perhaps five or six years old. It bore no explosives. It was photographed, covered again, put in a plastic bag, and taken away in the trunk of an unmarked Agency sedan.

After the public rooms of the White House and the grounds had been gone over, the President's party was allowed to return. The workers who had been held with their truck outside the gates were waved in and a few hours later all trappings of the ceremony of the night before had been removed and the White House grounds and gardens stood immaculate under the mid-morning sun.

At seven-thirty that same morning Agent Molloy, a twenty-four-year veteran of the Bureau, who worked in the Criminal Investigation Division, met with the chief of the Washington field office. You're the SAC on this one, his chief said. Whatever you need. I don't have to tell you—they are livid up there.

And so, just a few months from retirement, Molloy found himself the agent in charge of a top-priority case. It didn't matter that the event was without apparent consequences. There was no place in the world with tighter security than the White House complex, and someone had breached it—someone who seemingly could carry a dead child wrapped in a sheet past all manner of human and electronic surveillance.

He had delicate issues to deal with. He wanted first of all to have all military and Secret Service personnel on duty the night before account for their actions. He wanted everything diagrammed. The agents he assigned this task looked at each other and then at him. I know, I know, Molloy said. They have their routines, we have ours. Go.

From the White House social secretary Molloy procured the list of the previous night's guests. Three hundred and fifty people had been invited to the evening's concert—awardees, their families, their publishers, dealers and producers, cultural figures, Washington A-list culls, members of Congress. Then there were the orchestra players, various suppliers, and press. Maybe as many as five hundred names and SS numbers to check. He called his chief and got the manpower. Dossiers, if any, were to be pulled. He hoped research would reduce the need for interrogations to a fraction of the attendees.

With everything up and running, Molloy had the groundskeeper brought to his office. Calabrese was a simple man and somewhat stunned by the high-powered reaction to his discovery. He had been in government service all his working life and had years of White House clearances. He was a widower who lived alone. He had a married daughter, a lawyer, who worked in the Treasury Department.

139

I just seen this sneaker, he said. I didn't touch a thing. Not the chairs. Nothing.

Were the chairs moved?

Moved?

Out of line.

No, no—they was straight. And this sneaker sticking out. It was a kid, wasn't it? A dead kid.

Who told you?

Nobody had to tell me. Imagine. And all wrapped around in white, like a cocoon. That's what it reminded me. A cocoon.

Calabrese had nothing more to offer. Molloy told him he was not to speak of the matter to anyone, and had already sent him out to await a lift back to the White House when a call came from one Peter Herrick, a White House deputy assistant secretary in the Office of Domestic Policy, saying the groundskeeper was to be detained incommunicado under provisions of the counterterrorist statutes until such time as all investigative questions had been answered to the President's satisfaction. A formal authorization would be coming shortly from the Attorney General's office.

The gall rose in Molloy's throat. In my judgment that is a mistake, he said.

We've got to put a lid on this, Herrick said. Nobody other than the President knows the reason for this morning's alert. If this is in the nature of a terrorist act of some kind, it should not be given air.

Without a doubt, Molloy said. But when Calabrese is reported missing, we'll end up answering more questions than we want to. His daughter's a lawyer in Treasury.

I'll get back to you, Herrick said.

Molloy says that only when the line went dead did it occur to him to wonder why the White House liaison re this matter was the Office of Domestic Policy.

At noon he heard from Forensics. The boy had been dead from forty-eight to sixty hours. There were no signs of abuse, no grievous injuries—death was from natural causes.

Molloy went to the lab to see for himself: The body was supine, its hands clenched at its side. Attached to a lanyard around its neck was a bronchodilator. The mouth was open. The face was florid. The eyelids did not completely cover the bulging eyes. The little chest was expanded, as if the kid was pretending to be Charles Atlas. He had black hair a bit longer than it should have been. Molloy had the impression he might be Hispanic.

No foul play here, the pathologist said. You're looking at respiratory failure. The airways spasmed and closed up.

From what?

Kid had asthma. The worst kind—status asthmaticus. Comes a time when no inflammatories or dilators can control it. To keep him breathing, because he can't get rid of the carbon dioxide, he would have to be put on a respirator. I guess where he was, there was none available.

The boy's clothing had been sealed in plastic bags: T shirt, jeans, briefs. Gap items. No nametags. Together with the shroud, and the Nikes, the clothing was still being analyzed. He hoped for something, he didn't know what. Maybe a lot identification that would indicate origin of shipment.

At eight the next morning, Molloy went back to the Rose Garden and stood looking at the White House from where the orchestra platform had been. Fifty feet away and somewhat to the side was a staked ribbon to show the body's position. He wondered when a wrapped body could have been brought into the tent so that it would not be noticed by any one of hundreds of people until the groundskeeper came to work the following morning. Conceivably, it could have been brought in after the concert was concluded and everyone had left and the lights were turned off—but that was a scenario he didn't want to think about. It meant he would need to direct his investigation to persons who would not have been required to leave the premises once the evening was over.

Over the next several days considerable manpower was used in an attempt to identify the child. Once they knew who he was, the question of who had brought him onto White House grounds would begin to answer itself. In the meantime, the agents called him P.K., for Posthumous Kid. With photos in hand, they checked missing-children files, visited hospital pediatric wards, and interviewed pulmonologists in D.C., Virginia, and Maryland. No leads were forthcoming. The Bureau's national data bank showed no reported kidnappings to match his description. As the paper piled up on Mol-

141

loy's desk, he remembers he wondered at what point these inquiries, which were bound to create gossip, would come to the attention of someone whose profession it was to ask questions.

In order to comply with directives calling for interagency cooperation, Molloy held a briefing for a deputy of the Secret Service, an electronic-security expert assigned to the NSA, and a psychologist consultant to the CIA whose specialty was terrorist modalities.

Molloy didn't know any of them. I don't have much time, he said, and quickly filled them in.

Secret Service sat tall in his chair, a man in his late thirties, early forties who obviously used the gym, his suit as if tailored to his musculature. Well, he said with an icy smile, are we clean?

So far, Molloy said.

The electronics man with the NSA said he could run a system check, but the system was self-monitoring. It sends out an EKG that would have shown something, he said. So we'd already know.

Molloy's own techs had told him the same thing.

The psychologist held his chin in his hand and frowned. Would you say this was a symbolic action, Agent Molloy?

I'd say.

I remind you that 9/11 was strongly symbolic, in case you think what we have here is necessarily over and done. You might be tempted to invoke the sixties as historical precedent, when you had those anti-nuke activists trespassing on government property and pouring blood on missile housing and so on. Where they were more interested in propagandizing than doing real damage. But you would be wrong. Those hippie types were American. They put their bodies on the line. They took jail terms. They didn't sneak in, leave their calling card, and sneak out. So this is something else entirely. Something more ominous.

Like what, Molloy said.

Like a warning. As in, We've done this so you see we can.

So a dead boy doesn't mean anything in particular? Molloy said. He's just a calling card?

Well, they brought him from somewhere, the consultant said. This feels to me like an Arab thing.

Secret Service said, Still no I.D.?

No.

Nothing ethnic?

No. A white kid. He could be anything.

Then he could be from where they hate us, the psychologist said. He could be a Muslim kid.

In the second week of the investigation, a break came when a district commander of the D.C. police, John Felsheimer, called Molloy and invited him for an after-hours beer. The two men had worked together on occasion over the years, and while they were not exactly friends, they had a high regard for each other's professionalism. That they were of the same generation, family men with grandchildren, was another bond between them.

Once they'd exchanged amenities, Felsheimer withdrew a letter from his breast pocket. He said he was sorry he had not learned of the FBI investigation of a missing person until he happened to pick up some scuttlebutt that very day. He said the letter had been left at his district station a week before. Unsigned, undated, it was a single page, with just one computer-typed sentence. "You should know that a child was found, dead, in the Rose Garden."

Felsheimer explained that Molloy was holding a Xerox copy—the original had been kept by the White House. He had put the original in a glassine envelope and taken it to the office that liaised with the D.C. police. Rather hastily, he'd been shunted over to the Office of Domestic Policy, which he thought odd. A deputy assistant, a Peter Herrick, had heard him out and expressed surprise that he, Felsheimer, would attach any importance to a crank letter. But then Herrick had said he would hold on to it.

Felsheimer, on his second beer, recalled the conversation:

So you're saying there was nothing in the Rose Garden?

No, I didn't say that, Commander Felsheimer. What it was, was an animal.

An animal?

Yes. A raccoon. FBI did the tests. It died of rabies. It just came in there to die.

We don't see much rabies in Federal City.

Well, you live and learn. Just to be safe, we had the First Dog tested, checked the kids of staff, and so on. Negativo problems. It just wandered in and died. End of story.

So, Brian, Felsheimer said to Agent Molloy after a pause. Am I wrong to put two and two together? Is that why the FBI is into missing-persons work now? You're looking to make an I.D. on a dead kid?

Molloy thought awhile. Then he nodded yes.

And the kid was found where the letter said?

Molloy said: John, for both our sakes, I have to ask for your word. This is a classified matter.

Felsheimer drew another letter from his pocket. Of course you have my word, Brian. But you may be glad you leveled with me. Here's a letter that came this morning addressed to the district commander, meaning me. When I heard you were running the show, I knew better than to go back to the White House.

This letter text was exactly the same as the first. Computer-printed, Times Roman, fourteen-point. And unsigned. But unlike the first letter, it had come through the mail. And the envelope had a Houston postmark.

Molloy did not blame himself for assuming, from the lab report of time of death—forty-eight to sixty hours before the body was examined—that the child had lived and been treated in D.C. or Virginia or Maryland. He put in a call to the chief of the FBI field office in Houston, whom he had known since their days as agent trainees, and asked for the complete paid obituary notices in all the Texas papers for the month of May. And throw in Louisiana, Molloy said.

Naturally, knowing you, the chief said, I'm to put this at the top of my things-to-do list.

You got that right, Molloy said.

He called his secretary into his office and told her to run the National Arts and Humanities Awards guest roster through the computer to tag all names with Texas addresses. The names as of today? she said. It's down to under a hundred. The original list, Molloy told her.

He sat back in his chair and considered the mind of the person or persons he was dealing with. They had wanted it made public. Why then had the press not been tipped off? Why wasn't it now a rumor flying all over the Internet? Only a note delivered to a district station and, upon a lack of response, a note mailed, this time almost as a reminder to the district commander? How peculiar to rely on authority when authority is what had been subverted. But there was something else, something else . . . a presumption that a line could be drawn between those powers who might be trustworthy, like local police, and those who were thought not to be, like himself. It did not square with the boldness of this bizarre act that the person who committed it had a hopeful regard for the law. Molloy had from the beginning theorized that he was dealing with eco-terrorists. But he had now the scintillating sense of a presiding amateurism in the affair.

It was time for a meeting with the White House liaison, Peter Herrick. Molloy found a balding blond young man who wore Turnbull & Asser shirts with French cuffs. Herrick had been a hotshot regional director in the last campaign, a President's man. Molloy had seen his like over the years. They came and went but, as if it were a genetic thing, always managed a degree of condescension for federal employees putting in their time.

You heard from John Felsheimer, Molloy said.

Who?

D.C. police. You took a piece of evidence from him.

I suppose so.

I'll have it now, Molloy said.

Just sit down, Agent Molloy. There are things you don't know.

Withholding evidence is a chargeable offense, even for White House personnel.

Perhaps I was overprotective. I'll dig it up for you. But you appreciate why we can't have any leaks. It would be like the other party to jump on this for political advantage. There's so little else they have going. And this is the kind of weird shit that sticks in the public's mind.

What things don't I know?

What?

You said there were things I don't know.

No, I was speaking generally about the political situation. I wonder why we haven't heard your working hypothesis. I assume you have one? Wouldn't you think it figures, from this crowd, something disgusting like this? The desecration of a beloved piece of ground? Not that I ever expect the artists, the writers, to show gratitude to the country they live in. They're all knee-jerk anti-Americans.

You let a hypothesis limit an investigation and you can get off on the wrong track, Molloy said.

I'm thinking of the cases musical instruments come in. That kid could have fit into a cello case, a tuba.

The program was Stephen Foster and George Gershwin, Molloy said. There are no tubas in Stephen Foster or George Gershwin.

I used that as an example.

145

The cases are left back at the hotel. The instruments are examined on the bus.

Writers were on hand whose books are adversarial to the Republic. Painters of pictures you wouldn't want your children to see. Our reward for these socialist giveaway programs.

Molloy rose. I do admire your thinking, Deputy Assistant Secretary of Domestic Policy Herrick. You have any more helpful ideas, pass them on to my office. Meanwhile, I'll expect that letter.

Molloy knew that as a piece of evidence, the letter was useless. It would be dimestore stationery, just like the one in his possession, and overhandled at that. But he had to make a point. This group trusted only themselves. Molloy was certainly no liberal, but he detested politically driven interference in a case.

He was put in a better mood that same afternoon when one of his agents brought him a missing-persons bulletin taken from the interstate police net: Frank Calabrese, widower, age sixty. The report had been filed by Ann Calabrese-Cole, his daughter. Molloy smiled and told his secretary that when a call came from the Office of Domestic Policy, she was to say he was out.

He now had dossiers—some thirty of the guests had files. He set to work. A while later he looked up and noticed that the windows of his office had grown dark. He turned on his desk light and kept reading, but with a growing sense of dissatisfaction: There were book publishers and art dealers who'd marched against the Vietnam War. A playwright who'd met with a visiting Soviet writer's delegation in 1980. University teachers who'd refused to sign loyalty oaths. Contributors to the Southern Christian Leadership Conference. A lawyer who'd defended priests in the Sanctuary movement. A professor of Near Eastern studies at George Mason. A folksinger who'd gotten an arts award several years before . . . He knew only halfway through the pile that it was useless, as if he could hear the voice that had written You should know that a child was found dead in the Rose Garden. It was not the voice of any of these files. These were the files of people who, no matter for what cause, were by nature self-assertive. What he heard here was a circumspect voice going quietly about an unpleasant duty. It sounded to him like a woman.

Molloy was handed a FedExed 250 MB Zip disk from Houston when he arrived at work the next morning. He gave it to a young agent nerd whom he suspected somewhere down the line of having considered a career in criminal hacking. Would have done quite well, too: In an hour the nerd produced published notices for every child twelve and under who had died in every city and county in Texas and Louisiana in the month of May, then a refined list by city and county of male child deaths in south Texas and southwest Louisiana, and, under that, a target list of all young male deaths in south Texas and southwest Louisiana that had occurred within seventy-two hours of the ceremonial in the Rose Garden.

Molloy sighed and started in on the target list. He first looked for the age and struck out names of kids over seven. Then he eliminated names that to his mind connoted black children. With the names remaining, he read in detail the simply worded expressions of heartbreak: beloved son of . . . alive in our hearts . . . classmate of . . . taken from us . . . in the bosom of Jesus . . . It was not with any sense of satisfaction, but with something like a disappointment in himself, that he came upon what he knew he had been looking for. In the Beauregard, Texas, *Daily Record* a boy named Roberto Guzman, age six, had been remembered in three paid obits—by his parents, by his cub scout troop, and, crucially, by someone unidentified, who had written, "Rest in Peace, Roberto Guzman, it was not God who did this to you."

Molloy told his secretary to make out the appropriate travel forms and book a next-day flight to Houston with a car rental at the airport. He had a pile of paperwork to go through—the agent interviews were still coming in—but he thought he'd have another look at the cadaver. He seemed to remember there was a small brown mole on the kid's cheek. The on-site flash photos weren't any good. He requisitioned a Sony Cyber-shot and went off to the morgue.

The kid was not there.

Molloy, stunned, questioned the attendant, who knew nothing about it. Wasn't on my shift, the attendant said.

Well, someone took it. You people keep a book, don't you? Bodies just don't fly in and out of here.

Be my guest.

Molloy found nothing written to indicate a child's body had been received or taken away.

Immediately, he called his bureau chief. He was told to come right over.

Now, what I'm about to tell you, Brian, his chief said—you have to understand a policy decision has been made that was explained to the director, and however reluctantly, he has chosen to go along.

What policy decision?

The investigation is concluded.

Right. Where's the kid? I'm pretty sure I've made an I.D.

But you're not listening. There is no kid. There was no body in the Rose Garden. It never happened.

So where'd they bury him?

Where? Where they would not be questioned, where nobody would see them at two in the morning.

The two men looked at each other.

They panicked, the chief said.

Did they, now?

They shouldn't have detained that groundskeeper who found the body.

You're so right.

Someone tipped his daughter over in Treasury. So they swore him to secrecy, sprung him, and allowed as they'd been holding him as a material witness on some classified matter. But they also told her that they'd perceived signs of dementia. So if he does say something—

That's really low.

It wasn't just that. The *Post* is nosing around. Someone sent them a letter.

From Texas.

Well, yes. How did you know?

I can tell you what it said, Molloy said.

When Agent Molloy got back to his office, he was seething. He sat down at his desk and, with his forearm, swept the stack of paperwork to the floor. There'd been a pattern of obstruction from the start. He'd felt an operative intelligence in the shadows all through this business. On the one hand they wanted answers, as why wouldn't they, given an intolerable breach of security? On the other hand they didn't. They may have made their own investigation—or they may have known from the beginning. Known what? And it was so sensitive it had to be covered up?

Whenever Molloy needed to cool off, he went for a walk. He remembers how, when he first came to Washington as a young trainee, he'd been moved almost to tears by the majesty of the nation's capital. Quickly enough it became mere background to his life, accepted, hardly noticed. But in his eyes now it was the strangest urban landscape he had ever seen. Classical, white, and monumentalized, it looked like no other American city. It was someone's fantasy of august government. On most any day of the week, out-of-town innocents abounded on the Mall. The believers. The governed. He kept to the federal business streets, where the ranks of dark windows between the columns of the long pedimented buildings suggested a nation's business that was beyond the comprehension of ordinary citizens.

Back in his office, Molloy scrambled around on the floor looking for the awards-ceremony guest list. When he found it, it was as he'd thought—no Texas residents. At this point it occurred to him that if the President had had personal friends staying over that night, they might not have been on this list. Personal friends were big-time party supporters, early investors in the presidential career, and prestigious moneyed members of his social set. They were put up on the second floor, in the Lincoln Bedroom or across the hall in the suite for visiting royalty, these friends.

Molloy left a message with the White House social secretary. By the end of the day his call had not been returned. This told him he might not be crazy. Like everyone else in Washington, he knew the names of the in crowd. A couple of them had cabinet appointments, others had been given ambassadorships, so they were not possibles. But one or two of perhaps the most important held portfolios as presidential cronies.

On a hunch, he called the controllers' tower at Dulles. He would have to show himself with his FBI credentials to get the information, but he thought he'd give them a head start: Molloy wanted to know of any charter or private aircraft logged out of Dulles with a flight plan for anywhere in Texas the morning after the awards event.

In heavy rush hour traffic he drove to the airport. He was tired and irritable. His wife would be sitting home waiting for him to appear for dinner, too inured to the life after all these years even to feel reproachful. But his spirits lifted when an amiable controller in a white shirt and rep tie handed him a very short list. Just one plane matched his inquiry: a DC-8 owned by the Utilicon Corporation, the Southwest power company, with home offices in Beauregard, Texas.

He had some leave time coming and put in for it and flew to Houston on his own money. Looking down at the clouds, he wondered why. Over the years he'd been involved in more than his share of headline cases. But in the past year or two he'd felt his official self beginning to wear away—the identity conferred by his badge, his commendations, the respect of his peers, the excitement of being in on things, and, he had to admit, that peculiar sense of superiority as a tested member of an elite, courteous, neatly dressed, and sometimes murderous police agency. In his early days he would bristle when the FBI was criticized in the press; he was more judicious now, less defensive. He thought all of this was his instinctive preparation for retirement.

How would he feel when it was over? Had he wasted his life attaching himself to an institution? Was he one of those men who could not have functioned unattached? He had suspected of some of his colleagues that they had taken on the federal agent's life as much for their own protection as anyone else's. Whatever his motives, it was a fact that he'd spent his life contending with deviant behavior, and only occasionally wondering if some of it was not justifiable.

He picked up a car at the airport. Beauregard was about an hour's drive to the east. He could see it miles away by the ochre cast of sky.

At the outskirts, he turned off the interstate and continued on a four-lane past petrochemical plants, oil storage tanks, and hardscrabble lots that were once rice paddies.

The Beauregard downtown looked as if it had succeeded in separating itself from the surrounding countryside: a core of glass-curtain office buildings, a couple of preserved old brick hotels with the state flag flying, chain department stores, and, dominating everything else, the skyscraping Utilicon building, a triangular tower faced in mirrors.

Molloy did not stop there but went on through the residential neighborhoods where imported trees shaded the lawns, until, after crossing the railroad tracks, he was bumping along on broken-down roads past bodegas and laundromats and packed-dirt playgrounds and cottages with chain-link fences bordering the yards.

He pulled over at the Iglesia de la Bendida la Virgen. It was a clapboard church, unusual for Catholics. The priest, Father Mendoza, a younger man than Molloy, slender, with a salt-and-pepper beard, explained that it had been built by German immigrants in the 19th century. Their descendants live in gated communities now, he said with a wry smile.

They sat in the shade on the rectory porch.

You realize I can say nothing.

I understand, Molloy said.

But yes, Juan and Rita Guzman are my congregants. They are righteous people, a virtuous family. Hardworking, strong.

I need to talk to them.

That may be difficult. They are being detained. Perhaps you can tell me what exactly is the motivation of the INS.

I have no idea. That is not my bailiwick.

I will tell you the child had last rites. A mass. Everything from that point to burial a scrupulous celebration of the Mystery.

Molloy waited.

Unfortunately, in the shock of bereavement, in the sorrow of their loss, people are at their weakest, the father told him. Sometimes the consolations of the Church and the assurance of Christ do not quite reach to the depths of the heart of even the most fervent believer. Are you a Catholic, Mr. Molloy?

Not as much as I used to be.

This is a poor congregation, the priest said. Working people who just get by, if that. They love their Blessed Virgin. But they are learning to be Americans.

The Guzman bungalow was like any other on the street, except for the little front yard—it was not burnt-out, it was green. It had hedges for a fence and a carefully tended border of the kind of wildflowers that Mrs. Johnson, the former First Lady, had once designated for the medians of Texas highways.

The inside of the house was dark, the shades drawn. A stout old woman in black and a girl of about twelve watched Molloy as he looked around.

In the sitting room, a boy's grade-school photo was the centerpiece of a makeshift shrine on a corner table: Roberto Guzman in life, with a big smile and a little brown mole on his cheek. The picture was propped against a bowl of flowers placed between two candles. On the wall behind it was a carved wooden crucifix.

Molloy glanced at the girl: his older sister, with the same

151

large dark eyes but without Roberto's deep shadows underneath.

Special Agent Molloy with the image of the dead boy in his mind felt the shame of someone who had seen something he shouldn't have. He mumbled his condolences.

The old woman said something in Spanish.

The girl said: My grandmamma says, Where is her Juan? Where is her son?

I don't know, Molloy said.

The old woman spoke again and shook her fist. The girl remonstrated with her.

What does she say?

She is stupid, I hate her when she is like this.

The girl began to cry: She says the Devil came to us as a señorita and took my mama and papa to hell.

The two of them, the old woman and the girl, were both crying now.

Molloy went through the little kitchen and opened the back door. There in the hazy sun was a formal garden with brick-edged flowerbeds, shrubs, small sculpted trees, grass as perfect as a putting green, and a small rock pool. It was very beautiful, a composition.

The girl had followed him.

Molloy said, Is Señor Guzman a gardener?

Yes, for Mr. Stevens.

Stevens, the chairman of the power company?

What is the power company?

Utilicon.

Sí, of course the Utilicon, the girl said, tears running down her cheeks.

Before he left, he took down a phone number from a pad beside the wall phone: in faded ink, el médico.

He found the Beauregard City Library and read Glenn Stevens's C.V., in *Who's Who*. It was a long entry. Utilicon's nuclear and coal plants provided power for five states. Molloy was more interested in the personal data: Stevens, sixty-three, was a widower. He had sired one child, a daughter. Christina.

Molloy got into his car and drove to the Stevens estate and was admitted by a gatekeeper. Several hundred yards down a winding driveway were the front steps.

———

I thought this was all settled, Glenn Stevens said as he strode into the room. Molloy stood. The man was well over six feet. He had graying blond hair combed in pompadour style, a ruddy complexion, and a deep voice. He wore white ducks and a pale yellow cashmere sweater and loafers with no socks.

Just tidying up some loose ends, Molloy said. He had waited twenty minutes to be received. The Stevens library was paneled in walnut. Settings of big leather chairs, polished refectory tables with the major papers and magazines laid out in neat rows. The french windows opened onto a deep stone terrace with potted trees and balusters wound with white flattened flowers.

But the books in the scantily stocked shelves—Durant's *Story of Philosophy*, the collected works of Winston Churchill, Richard Nixon memoirs, Henry Kissinger memoirs, and ancient best-sellers in Book-of-the-Month-Club editions—were not up to scratch.

I didn't know the Bureau was involved, Stevens said. Nobody told me that. Molloy was about to reply when a young man in pinstripes and carrying a briefcase came into the room. As fast as I could, he said, mopping his brow.

I thought I'd better have counsel present, Glenn Stevens said, and sat down in a leather armchair.

Our concern is we were told the Bureau had been called off.

That's true, Molloy said. The incident is not only closed, it never happened.

You have to understand that Mr. Stevens would never embarrass the President, whom he admires as no other man. Or do anything to bring disrepute to the great office he holds.

I do understand.

Mr. Stevens was one of the President's earliest supporters. But more than that, the two men are old friends. The President regards Mr. Stevens almost as a brother.

I can understand that too, Molloy said.

And he has shown the tact and grace and compassion so typical of him in assuring Mr. Stevens that nothing of consequence has happened and that their relationship is unchanged.

Molloy nodded.

So why are you here? the lawyer said.

This is a family matter, Stevens chimed in. And while it may be ex-

153

tremely painful for me personally, it is only that, and if the President understands, why can't the damn FBI?

Mr. Stevens, Molloy said, we do understand that this is a family matter. It has been judged as such and sealed. Nobody is building a case here. But you must understand a serious breach of security occurred that calls into question not only the Bureau's methods but the Secret Service's as well. We have to see that such a thing never occurs again, because next time it may not be a family matter. We would not be fulfilling our mission were we to be as casual about the President's safety as the President.

So what do you want?

I would like to interview Miss Christina Stevens.

Absolutely not, Mr. Stevens! the lawyer said.

Sir, we're not interested in her motives, the whys or wherefores. Molloy flashed an ingratiating smile and continued: But she pulled something off that I, as a professional, have to admire. I just want to know how she did it, how this young woman all by herself managed to leave egg on the faces of the best in the business. I know it's been difficult for you, but considering it purely as a feat, it was quite something, wouldn't you say?

She betrayed my trust, Stevens said hoarsely.

Mr. Stevens means his daughter is not well, the lawyer said.

Look, sir, sure she did. But there will be an internal investigation of our procedures. And I'm sure you appreciate how it is with company men—we have to cover our ass.

Out on the gravel driveway at the bottom of the steps the lawyer gave Molloy his card. Anything else, from now on, you deal with me direct. No more unscheduled visits, Agent Molloy, agreed?

Where is this place?

Do you know Houston?

Not very well.

When you get there, give them a call and they'll lead you in. It's no mystery, you know.

What is?

How she did it. One look at Chrissie Stevens and you'll understand.

The lawyer was smiling as he drove off.

Molloy stayed that night at the Houston Marriott, eating room service and watching CNN. He liked the bureau chief here but didn't want to have to answer for himself. What he did was put in a call to Washington—a lady friend from his bachelor days, a style writer for the *Post*, who had since moved up in marital increments to her present life as a Georgetown power hostess.

The gal has quite a history, Molloy. Isn't this a little late for your midlife crisis?

You'll be discreet, I know, Molloy said.

Chrissie Stevens is a flake. She was riding pillion with a Hell's Angel at the age of fourteen. Then she found religion, Zen wouldn't you know, and spent a couple of years in Katmandu in some filthy ashram. Oh, and she lived in Milan for a year with some Italian polo player till she dumped him, or he dumped her. You want more?

Please.

Not just once has she been in for detox at Betty Ford. That's the talk, anyway. You know my theory?

Tell me.

Lives to pay Daddy back for the life he's provided her. I mean, that may be her true passion—they are really a very intense couple, Glenn and his daughter Chrissie. But you know what's most remarkable?

No.

You sit across from her at the dinner table and she is spectacular. A vestal virgin, not a sign of wear and tear. Brian, she has the most beautiful skin you can imagine, coloring I would die for. Goes to show.

The phone number Molloy had found in the Guzman kitchen was for the office of a Dr. Leighton, a pulmonologist, one of three associates in a clinic a few blocks from the Texas General medical complex. The waiting room was packed, aluminum walkers and strollers abounding: women with children on their laps, the elderly, both black and white, clutching their inhalators. Three TV sets hung from the walls. Eyes were cast upward—a chorus of labored breathing and bawling children blocked out the sound. It was a world of eyes sunk in hollow sockets.

A nurse, turning pale at the sight of Molloy's credentials, had him wait in an examining room. Molloy sat in a side chair next to a white metal cabinet on which sat racks of vials, boxes of plastic gloves. On the facing wall, a four-color laminated diagram of the human lungs and bronchia. In a corner, on the other side of the examining table, a

155

boxy looking machine hung with a flexible tube and mask. Nothing out of place, everything immaculate.

Dr. Leighton came in, equally immaculate in his white coat over a blue shirt and tie. He was a bit stiff, but quite composed and professional-looking behind wire-framed glasses. He leaned back against a windowsill and with his arms folded looked as fresh as if he had not been tending all morning to an office full of people who had trouble catching their breath. Molloy remarked on the crowd.

Yes, well, the smog has been worse than usual. You put enough nitrogen oxide into a summer day and the phones light up.

I wanted to ask you about the Guzman boy who died last week, Molloy said. I understand he was your patient.

Am I obligated to talk with you?

No, sir. Do you know a Christina or Chrissie Stevens?

The doctor thought a moment. A sigh. What would you like me to say—what is it you want to hear? The boy suffered terribly. On days like this, he was not allowed to go to school. He tried so hard to be brave, to control his terror, as if it was unmanly. He was a great kid. The more scared he was, the more he tried to smile. In this last attack, they rushed him up here—Chrissie and the priest and the boy's father—and I put him on intubation. I couldn't reverse it. He died on me. Roberto didn't need a respirator, he needed another planet.

Chrissie Stevens had been checked in to the Helmut Eisley Institute, a sanitarium for the very wealthy.

Molloy found her in the large, sunny lounge to the right of the entrance hall. She was seated on a sofa, her legs tucked under her, her sandals on the carpet. He had not expected someone this petite. She was the size of a preteen, a boyishly slim young woman with straight blond hair parted in the middle. Her elbow propped on the sofa arm, her chin resting on her hand, she was posed as if thinking about Molloy as she stared at him.

But don't you people travel in twos? she said with a languid smile.

Not all the time, Molloy said.

Behind her, standing in attendance, was a very young Marine in olive drab too warm for the climate. He had the flat-top haircut, the ramrod posture, the rows of ribbons, of a recruitment poster.

This is my friend Corporal Tom Furman.

When the corporal put his hand on her shoulder, she reached back and covered his hand.

Tom is visiting. He just flew in today.

Where are you stationed, son?

When he didn't answer, Chrissie Stevens said, You can tell him. Go ahead—nothing's going to happen. It's been decided.

Sir, I'm posted at the White House.

Well, Molloy said, that's a plum assignment. Does it come with the luck of the draw or is it saved for the very exceptional?

Sir, yes. We're chosen I suppose, sir.

Ah me, ah me, Chrissie Stevens said. Can we all sit down, please? Pull up a chair for Agent Molloy and you sit beside me here, she said to the Marine as she patted the sofa cushion.

And so the two men sat as directed. Molloy hadn't anticipated Chrissie Stevens as a Southern belle. But she was very much that. His own daughters, straightforward field-hockey types, would have taken an instant dislike to her.

She was strikingly attractive, very pale, with high cheekbones and gray eyes. But what was mesmeric was her voice. That was where the vestal-virgin effect came from. She had a child's soft Southern lilt, and when she lowered her eyes, her long blond lashes falling like a veil over them, it was as if she had to examine in her mind the things she was saying to make sure they were correct, and the effect of an ethereal modesty was complete.

I'm not here of my own volition, Agent Molloy. Apparently I've done something for which the only possible explanation is that I've gone off the deep end. But if that is true, what other questions are left to ask?

I have just a few.

Though it's not at all bad here, she said, turning to the corporal. They fatten you up and give you a pill that makes you not care about anything much. They stand there until they see you swallow it. I'm out to pasture right now. Are my words slurred? I mean, why not, why not, you can dream your life away, she said with her sad smile. That's not so bad, is it?

Molloy said: Did you know that the boy's parents are faced with deportation?

Clearly, she didn't.

But I think that can be stopped, he said. I think there's a way to see that it doesn't happen.

She was silent. Then she mumbled something that he couldn't hear.

I beg your pardon?

Deport me, Agent Molloy. Send me anywhere. Send me to Devil's Island. I'm ready. I want nothing more to do with this place. I mean, why here rather than anywhere else? It's all the same, it's all horribly awful.

Molloy waited.

Oh Lord, she said, they always win, don't they. They are very skillful. It didn't come out quite as we planned—we are such amateurs—but even if it had, I suppose they would have known how to handle it. I just thought maybe this could restore them, put them back among us. It would be a kind of shock treatment if they felt the connection, for even just a moment, that this had something to do with them, the gentlemen who run things? That's all I wanted. What redemption for little Chrissie if she could put a tincture of shame into their hearts. Of course I know they didn't give our gardener's son the asthma he was born with. And after all they didn't force his family to live where the air smells like burning tires. And I know Daddy and his exalted friends are not in their personal nature violent and would never lift a hand against a child. But, you see, they are configured gentlemen. Am I wrong to want to include you, Agent Molloy? Are you not one of the configured gentlemen?

Configured in what way?

Configured to win. And fuck all else.

Her Marine reached over and held her hand.

What do you think? Chrissie Stevens said. Am I making sense? Or am I the family disgrace my father says I am?

The both of them were looking at Molloy now. They made a handsome couple.

Would you like some refreshment, Agent Molloy? There's a bell over there—they bring tea.

Back at his desk in Washington, Molloy caught up on the cases that he'd left when the call came in about the dead child in the Rose Garden. One of the cases, a possible racketeering indictment, was really hot, but as he sat there he found his mind wandering. His office was a glass-partitioned cubicle. It looked out on the central office of lined-up desks where the secretaries and less senior agents worked away. There was a nice hum of energy coming through to him as phones rang and people went briskly about their business, but Molloy couldn't avoid feeling that he was looking at a roomful of children. Certainly everyone out there was at least twenty years younger. Younger, leaner, less tired.

This is what he did: He put in a call to Peter Herrick at the Office of Domestic Policy and quietly told him, though not in so many words, that if the parents of the dead child were not released by the INS and allowed to return home, he, Molloy, would see to it that the entire incident became known to every American who watched television or read a newspaper.

Molloy then sat at his computer and composed a letter of resignation.

The last thing he did before he turned out the lights and went home to his wife was to write, by hand, a letter to Roberto Guzman's parents. He said in the letter that Roberto's grave might be unmarked but that he rested in peace at the Arlington National Cemetery among others who had died for their country.

*Nominated by The Virginia Quarterly Review*

# BEST AND ONLY

## by ANDREW FELD

from MICHIGAN QUARTERLY REVIEW

*I: THE SHIP OF STATE*

The way a carp's speckled brown and white head
flashes just below the surface of the Potomac
night waters, Richard Nixon's penis almost enters

the national consciousness, as a thin gold thread
of urine stitches him to an August night in 1973,
on the stern of the *Sequoia*. Standing beside him

is the Cuban financier Bebe Rebozo, who is also
pissing into the river. The image is a small shame
in the middle of many greater ones: the damp dots

on his pants as he shakes off with an awkward
drunk step back and zips up: the president pissing
on the Republic, over which he stands. Exposed

briefly before being pulled back below decks,
the two men are easy targets for anyone's
anger or condescension. Jowly, soft with

the executive spread of men in the area before
exercise was invented, their bodies bulge oddly,
pumpkin-like growths swelling the crotches

and stomachs of their pin-stripped suits, as if
their own flesh had risen up against them. But for
the marksman stationed near, their appearance

at his post is an allegation he'd die to deny. Eyes
trained to see elsewhere, he holds his cool
weapon and a bead drops from the little jungle

of his armpit as twin diesel engines push the boat
past the riverbank where the hippie who jumps up
to grab a Day-Glo Frisbee out of the air hears

their voices and mistakes the drunken laughter
of two old men in a boat for the drunken laughter
of two old men in a boat, unaware that History

is passing so close he's breathing its exhaust,
its strain of scorched fuels distinct for a few
seconds and then folded back into the ordinary

summer night smells of mass transportation
and river water. We now know on this particular
August night they're shifting funds, arranging pay-offs

for the plumbers and harassing Henry the Jew,
denying they've *even heard* of Cambodia, as they sail
several martinis outside anyone's jurisdiction.

For these and other crimes, may they be lodged
in the sulphurous cavern of Satan's anus forever.
But what of the genuine warmth all the biographers

agree burnt between these two men, the actual,
human love they felt for each other: is it only
the gaseous fire of butane tentacles wrapping around

a bushel of asbestos logs in the below-deck bar's
mahogany dark, or is it the quicksilver spirits
in the funneled glasses they lift to each other,

a whisper of vermouth tasting like amnesia
in the gin's frostbitten false fire, the warmth
in each sip drawing them closer together?


II: *From the Apocrypha of Bebe Rebozo*

3.
Protesters under the cherry trees: notice
how each fallen petal rots from the inside
with a small brown dot on its delicate center-seam,
like a piece of used toilet paper:
so corruption is essential in us. It's in our guts.

7.
The young no longer dance.
Instead they *twitch*, as if
their electric guitars were electrodes
taped to their genitals. If only.

But their children will rediscover
the steps they abandon
and follow them back to us.

12.
Richard, I dreamed we walked the fine silver sands
shoring the Bay of Pigs, and there, beside your wing-
tip's tip, we found a gull poking its bill into the gills
of a still-living fish. Out in the surf, girls' voices called

for your attention as Tricia and Julie came riding shoreward
on the crests of waves; and this length of scaled muscle
was eaten alive at our feet, drowning in our oxygen.


III: *19—: An Elegy*

Apollo. Bebe Rebozo. Beatniks.
The Car. Counting backwards.
Cold Warriors. The century

I was born in. Disney. The Great
Depression and Anti-Depressants.
Everest. The Evil Empire. Electric
light and atomic energy. Frost
at Kennedy's Inaugural. Fucking.
Free love. Gridlock. Harley-Davidson
and Hell's Angels. *Ho Ho Ho Chi Minh*.
The Ivory-billed woodpecker. The Iron
Curtain. Joke: how many right-wing
neo-conservative, conspiracy theory,
survivalist, NRA, MIA, VFW,
free-market, anti-establishment
radio talk show host-loving loners
does it take to screw in a light bulb?
The Killing fields. Love-Beads.
Love-Ins. Love Canal. The Mall
of America. Medical waste. Richard
Nixon. No one's home. The century
when oral sex came into its own.
The overdose. *People*. Peaceniks.
Plutonium. Post-. Pop-. Plastic-wrapped
bundles of cocaine washing up
on Florida beaches. Queer theory.
Race. A small car like a stereo
on wheels, the Soul-Singer's voice
tearing through paper speaker cones
the way the spirit is formed and deformed
by the flesh. The century of the Teenager.
Televangelists. Uncut. Unadulterated.
Vietnam. Watergate. World Wars. The X-ray.
Yeah Yeah Yeah. Zen Koan. Grown Zero.

*Nominated by Martha Collins*

# END OF THE LINE

fiction by AIMEE BENDER

from TIN HOUSE

THE MAN WENT TO THE PET STORE to buy himself a little man to keep him company. The pet store was full of dogs with splotches and shy cats coy, and the friendly people got dogs and the independent people got cats and this man looked around until in the back he found a cage, inside of which was a miniature sofa and tiny TV and one small, attractive brown-haired man, wearing a tweed suit. He looked at the price tag. The little man was expensive, but the big man had a reliable job, and thought this a worthy purchase.

He brought the cage up to the front, paid with his credit card, and got some free airline points.

In the car, the little man's cage bounced lightly on the passenger seat, held by the seat belt.

The big man set up the little man in his bedroom, on the nightstand, and lifted the latch of the cage open. That's the first time the little man looked away from the small TV. He blinked, which was hard to see, and then asked for some dinner in a high, shrill voice. The big man brought the little man a drop of whiskey inside the indented crosshatch of a screw, and a thread of chicken with the skin still on. He had no utensils, so he told the little man to feel free to eat with his hands, which made the little man irritable. The little man explained that before he'd been caught he'd been a very successful and refined accountant who'd been to Paris and Milan multiple times, and that he liked to eat with utensils, thank you very much. The big man laughed and laughed, he thought this little man he'd bought was so funny. The little man told him in a clear, crisp voice that dollhouse

164

stores were open on weekends and he needed a bed, please, with an actual pillow, please, and a lamp and some books with actual pages if at all possible. Please. The big man chuckled some more and nodded.

The little man sat on his sofa. He stayed up late that first night, laughing his high, shrill laugh at the late night shows, which annoyed the big man to no end. He tried to sleep and could not, a wink. At 4 a.m., exhausted, the big man dripped some antihistamine in the little man's water drip tube, so the little man finally got drowsy. The big man accidentally put too much in, because getting the right proportions was no easy feat of mathematical skill, which was not the big man's strong suit anyway, and the little man stayed groggy for three days, slugging around his cage, leaving tiny drool marks on the couch. The big man went to work and thought of the little man with longing all day, and at five o'clock he dashed home, so excited he was to see his little man, but he kept finding the fellow in a state of murk, drooling all over the cage. When the antihistamine finally wore off, the little man awoke with crystal-clear sinuses and by then had a fully furnished room around him, complete with chandelier and several very short books, including *Cinderella* in Spanish, and his very own pet ant in a cage.

The two men got along for about two weeks. The little man was very good with numbers and helped the big man with his bank statements. But between bills, the little man also liked to talk about his life back home and how he'd been captured on his way to work, in a bakery of all places, by the little-men bounty hunters, and how much he, the little man, missed his wife and children. The big man had no wife and no children, and he didn't like hearing that part. "You're mine now," he told the little man. "I paid good money for you."

"But I have responsibilities," said the little man to his owner, eyes dewy in the light.

"You said you'd take me back," said the little man.

"I said no such thing," said the big man, but he couldn't remember if he really had or not. He had never been very good with names or recall.

After about the third week, after learning the personalities of the little man's children and grandparents and aunts and uncles, after hearing about the tenth meal in Paris and how le waiter said the little man had such good pronunciation, after a description of singing tenor arias with a mandolin on the train to Tuscany, the big man took to torturing the little man. When the little man's back was turned, the big man snuck a needle-thin droplet of household cleanser into his water and watched the little man hallucinate all night long, tossing and turning, retching small pink piles into the corners of the cage. His little body was so small it was hard to imagine it hurt that much. How much pain could really be felt in a space that tiny? The big man slept heavily, assured that his pet was just exaggerating for show.

The big man started taking sick days at work.

He enjoyed throwing the little man in the air and catching him. The little man protested in many ways. First he said he didn't like that in a firm, fatherly voice, then he screamed and cried. The man didn't respond, so the little man used reason, which worked briefly, saying: "Look, I'm a man too, I'm just a little man. This is very painful for me," and also, "Even if you don't like me, it still hurts." The big man listened for a second, but he had come to love flicking his little man, who wasn't talking as much anymore about the art of the baguette, and the little man, starting to bruise and scar on his body, finally shut his mouth completely. His head ached and he no longer trusted the water.

He considered his escape. But how? The doorknob was the Empire State Building. The backyard was an African veldt.

The big man watched TV with the little man. During the show with the sexy women, he slipped the little man down his pants and just left him there. The little man poked at the big man's penis which grew next to him like Jack's beanstalk in person, smelling so musty and earthy it made the little man embarrassed of his own small penis tucked away in his accountant pants. He knocked his fist into the beanstalk, and it grew taller and, disturbed, the big man reached down his pants and flung the little man across the room. The little man hit a table leg. Woke up in his cage, head throbbing. He hadn't even minded much being in the underwear of the big man, because for the first time since he'd been caught, he'd felt the smallest glimmer of power.

"Don't you try that again," warned the big man, head taking up the north wall of the cage entirely.

"Please," said the little man, whose eyes were no longer dewy, but flat. "Sir. Have some pity."

The big man wrapped the little man in masking tape, all over his body, so his feet couldn't kick and there were only little holes for his mouth and his eyes. Then he put him in the refrigerator for an hour.

When he came back, the little man had fainted and the big man put him in the toaster oven, at very, very low, for another ten minutes. Preheated. The little man revived after a day or two.

"Please," he said to the big man, word broken.

The big man didn't like the word "please." He didn't like politesse and he didn't like people. Work had been dull, and no one had noticed his new coat. He bought himself a ticket to Paris with all the miles he'd accumulated on his credit card, but soon realized he could not speak a word of the language and was too afraid of accidentally eating veal brains to go. He did not want to ask the little man to translate for him, as he did not want to hear the little man's voice with an accent. The thought of it made him so angry. The ticket expired, unreturned. On the plane, a young woman stretched out on her seat and slept since no one showed up in the seat next to hers. At work, he asked out an attractive woman he had liked for years, and she ran away from him to tell her coworkers immediately. She never even said no; it was so obvious to her, she didn't even have to say it.

"Take off your clothes," he told the little man that afternoon.

The little man winced, and the big man held up a bottle of shower cleanser as a threat. The little man stripped slowly, folded his clothing, and stood before the big man, his skin pale, his chest a matted grass of hair, his penis hiding, his lips trembling so slightly only the most careful eye would notice.

"Do something," said the big man.

The little man sat on the sofa. "What?" he said.

"Get hard," said the big man. "Show me what you look like."

The little man's head was still sore from hitting the table; his brain had felt fuzzy and indistinct ever since he'd spent the hour in the refrigerator and then time in the toaster oven. He put his hand on his penis and there was a heavy sad flicker of pleasure, and behind the absolute dullness of his mind, his body rose up to the order.

The big man laughed and laughed, at the erection of his little man, which was fine and true but so little! How funny to see this man as a man. He pointed and laughed. The little man stayed on the sofa and thought of his wife, who would go into the world and collect the bottle caps strewn on the ground by the big people and make them into trays; she'd spend hours upon hours filing down the sharp edges and then use metallic paint on the interior, and they were the envy of all the little people around, so beautiful they were and so hearty. No one else had the patience to wear down those sharp corners. Sometimes

167

she sold one and made a good wad of cash. The little man thought of those trays, trays upon trays, red, blue, and yellow, until he came in a small spurt, the orgasm pleasureless, but thick with longing.

The big man stopped laughing.

"What were you thinking about?" he said.

The little man said nothing.

"What's your wife like?" he said.

Nothing.

"Take me to see her," the big man said.

The little man sat, naked, on the floor of his cage. He had changed by now. Cut off. He would have to come back, a long journey back. He'd left.

"See who?" he asked.

The big man snickered.

"Your wife," he said.

The little man shook his head. He looked wearily at the big man. "I'm the end of this line for you," he said.

It was the longest sentence he'd said in weeks. The big man pushed the cage over, and the little man hit the side of the sofa.

"Yes!" howled the big man. "I want to see your children too. How I love children!"

He opened the cage and took the little floral-print couch into his hand. The little man's face was still and cold.

"No," he said, eyes closed.

"I will torture you!" cried out the big man.

The little man folded his hands under his head in a pillow. Pain was no longer a mystery to him, and a man familiar with pain has entered a new kind of freedom.

"No," he whispered into his knuckles.

With his breath clouding warmly over his hands, the little man waited, half-dizzy, to be killed. He felt his death was terribly insignificant, a blip, but he still did not look forward to being killed, and he sent waves of love to his wife and his children, to the people who made him significant, to the ones who felt the blip.

The big man played with the legs of the little armchair. He took off the pillow and found a few coins inside the crevices, coins so small he couldn't even pick them up.

He put his face close to the cage of his little man.

"Okay," he said.

———

Four days later, he set the little man free. He treated him well for the four days, gave him good food, and even a bath and some aspirin and a new pillow. He wanted to leave him with some positive memories and an overall good impression. After the four days, he took the cage under his arm, opened the front door, and set it out on the sidewalk. Unlocked the cage door. The little man had been sleeping nonstop for days, with only a few lucid moments staring into the giant eye of the big man, but the sunlight soaked into him instantly, and he awoke. He exited the cage door. He waited for a bird to fly down and eat him. Not the worst death, he thought. Usually the little people used an oil rub that was repellent-smelling to birds and other animals, but all of that, over time, had been washed clean off him. He could see the hulking form of the big man to his right, squatting on his heels. The big man felt sad, but not too sad. The little man had become boring. Now that he was less of a person, he was easier to get along with and less fun to play with. The little man tottered down the sidewalk, arms lifting oddly from his sides, as if he had wet hands or was covered in paint. He did not seem to recognize his own body.

At the curb, he sat down. A small, blue bus drove up, so small the big man wouldn't have noticed it if he hadn't been looking at foot level already. The little man got on. He had no money, but the bus revved for a moment and then moved forward with the little man on it. He took a seat in the back and looked out the window at the street. All the little people around him could smell what had happened. They lived in fear of it every day. The newspapers were full of updates and new incidents. One older man with a trim, white beard moved across the bus to sit next to the little man, and gently put an arm on his shoulder. Together, they watched the gray curbs passing by.

On the lawn, the big man thought the bus was hilarious and walked next to it for a block. Even the tires rolled perfectly. He thought how if he wanted to, he could step on that bus and smush it. He did not know that the bus was equipped with spikes so sharp they would drive straight through a rubber sole, into the flesh of the foot. For a few blocks, he held his foot over it, watching bus stops come up, signs as small as toothpicks, but then he felt tired, and went to the corner, and let the bus turn, and sat down on the big, blue plastic bus bench on his corner made for the big people.

When the big man's bus came, he took it. It was Saturday. He took it to the very end of the line. Here, the streets were littered with trash, and purple mountains anchored the distance. Everything felt like it was closing in, and even the store signs seemed too bright and overwhelming. He instantly didn't like it, this somewhere he had never been before, with a different smell, that of a sweeter flower and a more rustic bread. The next bus didn't come for an hour, so he began the steady walk home, eyes glued to the sidewalk.

He just wanted to see where they lived. He just wanted to see their little houses and their pets and their schools. He wanted to see if they each had cars or if buses were the main form of transport. He hoped to spot a tiny airplane.

"I don't want to harm you!" he said out loud. "I just want to be a part of your society."

His eyes moved across grasses and squares of sidewalk. He'd always had excellent vision.

"In exchange for seeing your village," he said out loud, "I will protect you from us. I will guard your front gates like a watchdog!" He yelled it into the thorny shadows of hedges, down the gutter, into the wet heads of sprinklers.

All he found was a tiny, yellow hat with a ribbon, perched perfectly on the yellow petal of a rose. He held it for a good ten minutes, admiring the fine detail of the handiwork. There was embroidery all along the border. The rim of the hat was the size of the pad of his thumb. Everything about him felt disgusting and huge. Where are the tall people, the fatter people? he thought. Where are the aliens the size of God?

Finally, he sat down on the sidewalk.

"I've found a hat!" he yelled. "Please! Come out! I promise I will return it to its rightful owner."

Nestled inside a rock formation, a group of eight little people held hands. They were on their way to a birthday party. Tremendous warmth spread from one body to the other. They could stand there forever if they had to. They were used to it. Birthdays came and went. Yellow hats could be resewn. It was not up to them to take care of all the world, whispered the mother to the daughter, whose yellow dress was unmatched, whose hand was thrummed with sweat, who watched as the giant outside put her hat on his enormous head and could not understand the size of the pity that kept unbuckling in her heart.

*Nominated by Tin House*

# PORTRAIT OF THE ARTIST AS AN OLD MAN

by EDWARD HIRSCH

from TIN HOUSE

## 1. MEETING

IT STARTLES ME TO REALIZE that William Maxwell was already an old man when I fell in love with him. I looked into his slightly sunken, radiant face, which seemed transparent to me, and suddenly felt overwhelmed by his actual presence, his odd vulnerability. I had been reading him for years, and yet I wasn't really prepared for the person opening up in front of me. Whatever he felt seemed instantly visible in his lined, paper-thin face, some of which had been carved away by surgery. He was like an X-ray held up and exposed to the light. You could see through him.

We came together over a shared admiration for the poet William Meredith. William had suffered a stroke some years before, and a number of his friends and admirers got together in a little theater to read his work aloud. It was a poignant occasion. Mr. Maxwell was one of the last to recite. He was in his late seventies, and when he stood at the podium I was startled by how fragile he looked, how disconcertingly thin. He had an intimate, slightly quavering voice, which also had something steely in it. He was someone who could not be deterred. He swayed a bit as he talked and the years—the decades—fell away from him. He was a rapturist. He said, "Listening to William Meredith's poems being read aloud, I felt as if I could die with happiness."

At the dinner after the reading, I glued myself to his side. I was not the only one distracted by his wife Emmy's natural beauty. It must have been that way her entire life. Other people entered the conversation; people came and went. He said things that startled me. He said that when he first read Yeats's early poetry he felt as if fairy dust had been sprinkled on him. He said that in college he had written poetry that was of no consequence. He said that he couldn't enjoy the work of any novelist (Trollope, for example) who didn't have some degree of the poet in him.

Poets had figured into his life. He remembered that when he first met Robert Fitzgerald he had driven him up the wall by praising the plays of J. M. Barrie. Fitzgerald was still an undergraduate at Harvard—Maxwell was a graduate student—but he had been introduced to modernism by Dudley Fitts and took a more advanced position. Fitzgerald got him to give up Galsworthy, introduced him to *The Waste Land*, and taught him that literature is "serious business." Maxwell also spoke of Louise Bogan. Both had a profound effect on him, and he couldn't bear it that they had passed away. He was not reconciled. "People die and they're gone," he said. "I'll never get used to it."

I had never met anyone, let alone an old man, who seemed so emotionally present. It went against the grain of my experience to find someone who had not been stunted or closed up, who had not been overwhelmed or defeated by old age. One knew that he had been an editor at the *New Yorker* for forty years, where he had worked with O'Connor, Welty, Salinger, Nabokov, Cheever, Gallant, Updike, Woiwode, Brodkey, and innumerable others, a distinction that he wore lightly, like his pale green seersucker suit. He was modest and incisive. He had an unassuming urbanity mixed with a strange forthrightness. What surprised me was that one could see directly through to the child in him, the rail-thin kid from Lincoln, Illinois, the heartbroken boy who had lost his mother and never got over it—he stubbornly refused to—but also the novelist of childhood, of a vanished Midwestern world.

After dinner, the Maxwells and I rode across town in a cab together. It was understood we would become friends. The gift of his attention seemed inexplicable, but real. I can still remember the sound of the cab door slamming in front of his apartment building on the Upper East Side, over by the river. He bounded out with alarming speed, like someone half his age. "Good night," he shouted through the open window, and disappeared.

Good night? I was so magnetized by the quality of his affections that I could scarcely sleep at all. It took me a few more hours to re-member something apropos that he had written about Sylvia Townsend Warner's initial visit to the *New Yorker* in 1939. He said, "Her conversation was so enchanting that it made my head swim. I did not want to let her out of my sight. Ever."

## 2. Story of Friendship

I must have written him an excited letter, because he wrote back and said that it allowed us "to dispense with the five or ten years it takes people to become friends when they leave it to circumstance." He also spoke of Meredith's heart-stopping recital of his own poems ("I felt I was pushing a wheelbarrow over Niagara blindfolded, until he got the last word out") and of the poet who had unexpectedly leaned over to him in the auditorium and said, "I can't tell you how many times in my life I have been Lymie Peters," whereupon he pulled out a copy of *The Folded Leaf* for an autograph. Maxwell was astonished. "I was only Lymie Peters once," he confessed, "and I don't dare think what it could have been to repeat and repeat the experience."

Our friendship feels as if it happened all at once, as if it arrived full-blown, but of course it didn't. There were stages. The chronol-ogy confuses me a little, or maybe it doesn't seem that important. I remember the letter in which he enclosed his phone number and the first time he called to praise something I had written. I remember a high-spirited dinner party with the Wilkinsons and the Colliers. Bill said that he wished it were like an egg timer so that he could turn it upside down and begin all over again, at any time he liked. It was the way life ought to be.

My initial visit to the Maxwells in their apartment on Eighty-sixth and East End set the pattern. I came on time and stayed too long. I had trouble tearing myself away. We sat in the living room, which was long and spacious. We drank tea from china cups and nibbled cookies. Emmy visited for a while and drifted off. I pulled things down from the white bookcases. We stood at the large windows in the far corner of the room and gazed at the street, eight floors below. We sat next to each other on the couch and talked about books and childhood, our irrepressible first subject.

It's hard to describe the exact character—the quality—of Max-well's attention. It was undivided. It was disarmingly frank. He asked you all about your childhood, which he marveled at, and gave freely of his own. He talked about growing up in a small town, about the way the houses set back calmly from the wide streets and the elms cast a pattern of light and shade on the pavement. People didn't lock their doors at night and their faces were filled with kindness. He believed that only a few things had happened to him in his life, but some of them he had felt deeply.

It didn't take long to discover that when he talked about the past, it was vividly, even painfully, present to him. It was as if at any moment he could close his eyes and slip through a thin membrane in time. He didn't need a *petite madeleine* to send him there. I once asked him if he missed the past. He looked at me with some surprise and replied that he didn't miss the past because he was never separated from it. He said, "I have a huge set of memories, which I carry around like a packed suitcase."

Maxwell's past was so immediate to him because there was such a clear Before and After in his life, which was sundered in two by the death of his mother. Everything was fastened at a specific moment in time when his childhood was lost forever. That's when he discovered what he called, in a resonant phrase, "the fragility of human happiness." I have the harrowing image of him as a ten-year-old boy pacing up and down the floor of an empty house at night with his father, both of them in bewildered mourning, in numb grief, unable to comfort each other. His fate was sealed on those nights. There's a telling moment near the end of *So Long, See You Tomorrow* when the narrator is talking to his psychiatrist about his mother's death. He means to say, "I couldn't bear it," but what comes out of his mouth is "I can't bear it," and then he rushes into the city in tears. He says, "New York City is a place where one can weep on the sidewalk in perfect privacy." There is something Maxwellian about inconsolable grief. The loss of his mother was so traumatic and intolerable for him that his memory, supplemented by imagination, set out to defy it.

I first felt the inconsolable nature of Maxwell's work when I read his second novel, *They Came Like Swallows*, a book that has left me in tears more than once. One of the early reviews called it "heartwarming," a common opinion about his work, which grates on me because it misses the mark. On the contrary, I find his work intensely sad and quietly heartbroken. It is very American. The surface is calm, the sentences poised and deceptively offhanded, but what drives them is a desperate need to hold on to a world irrevocably gone. At

174

one point I asked him—I suspect it was because I liked the form—where he had written the three sections of the novel. He copied out his answer in my edition of the book: "The first section was written over a year at a farmhouse in Wisconsin. Part 2 in a summer at the MacDowell Colony where Robert Fitzgerald was translating, I think, *The Alcestis* of Euripides. Part 3 was written in two weeks in an old house in Urbana, Illinois, walking the floor and in tears."

Grief had a deep hold on him, and yet I have seldom known anyone who took such deep interest in the inner lives of his friends. His sympathy seemed boundless for both books and friends. "To be up to the eyebrows in a great work of literature is such happiness," he wrote to me once. "I remember crying in Greek over the death of Socrates."

It's hard to write about your friends, as Bill once told me when he was trying to write an obituary piece about Francis Steegmuller, whom he had known for fifty years. "If you write too fondly it comes out mush, and if you aren't careful they become a character in a story, which is inappropriate."

Maxwell wasn't a wisdom machine, or a figure in a story. Yet it strikes me as a triumph of character that someone who suffered such early sorrow later developed such a capacity for friendship, for shared happiness. Sometimes, when you asked him a question, he closed his eyes for a long time and drifted off—where was he going?—but when he came back he gave an irresistibly truthful answer. It was as if he had let you into his daydreaming process. He seems never to have resisted a generous impulse. We were giddy in each other's presence. We suffered from all we had to say to each other.

Time had a way of stopping when you were in his presence. Eventually, it was necessary to leave. I always felt dazed after one of our marathon visits. I had been seduced all over again. I am surely not the only one who came away from his apartment feeling that I was loved in excess of my actual worth. Every visit felt like a last one, which was part of its mystique. We had ten years of friendship, yet our mutual happiness in each other's presence was tinged with the inevitable sadness of parting.

3. INTERVIEW IN YORKTOWN HEIGHTS

I never worked with Maxwell as an editor, but I did get a taste of how he worked when I was commissioned to write a piece about him for

*DoubleTake* magazine. I was daunted by the thought of writing about each one of his books in turn, so I procrastinated endlessly about the piece. Finally, I confessed my dilemma to him. He wrote back: "My life seems to me a subject too thoroughly (if anything) dealt with in one place or another. The books I don't have any ideas about. I just did them. But it occurs to me that we might have a conversation about old age and what it is like to be aware that your days are numbered. That may interest you. I don't know what I think about these two things and would be interested to find out." He went on to suggest that I could hang the piece on an occasion, like his birthday party. It was a perfect (and practical) solution. Thus Maxwell not only became the subject of my piece; he also taught me how to conceptualize and write it.

One August morning in the summer of 1996, I caught an early morning train from Manhattan to Croton-Harmon. Emmy met me. At seventy-five, she was still a radiant presence, utterly charmed and charming, preternaturally gracious, though there was also something coltish in her, something wild just under the surface. Her dark brown eyes always seemed unusually wide open, wide apart. They were filled with light. She was a Westerner with a spiritual side. Her favorite song was "Don't Fence Me In." It was hard not to want to linger in her presence. We took our time. We drove through a couple of picturesque villages, meandered off to admire a local waterfall, and traveled down various country lanes before turning into the gravel driveway of the house on Baptist Church Road, where Bill came rushing out of the house.

I liked coming out to their country place, a tiny prefab house that arrived in Westchester on a flatbed truck sometime in the early 1920s. Bill had bought it for about five thousand dollars in the early 1940s, before he was married. Over the years, the Maxwells enclosed the front porch and converted it into Bill's study, built a freestanding screened-in gazebo, and built a studio for Emmy, who was a painter. Bill was mad for flowers, and as we drove up to the house I could see the grounds covered with large patches of color. I carried my suitcase into the house, settled into the guest room, and then went looking for Bill again, who had disappeared. "Oh, he's already in the study," Emmy said. "He's ready to work."

Sure enough, Bill was stationed at his desk—a simple sturdy piece of pearwood—in his small study crammed with papers, books, photographs, paintings, records—the accumulation of years. "I am slowly being crowded out by the objects," he told me, "but even more by the associations around the objects."

I noticed photographs of his two daughters, Brookie and Kate; a couple of Emmy's paintings depicting places where they had lived; a postcard of a young man with one hand on his forehead, bent over a piece of paper, lost in thought. Bill called it "a picture of the inner life."

There was an oversize photograph of Colette, a photograph of the Wisconsin novelist Zona Gale—the first writer he ever met and a sort of literary fairy godmother to him ("She had one foot in the mystic camp," he once told me)—and another of Robert Fitzgerald. "I knew he was something I needed, and that he didn't suffer fools gladly," Bill had explained about their first meeting. "I loved him on first sight. He was so difficult, so intransigent, so obviously a true poet."

Over the years Bill had developed his own eccentric way of conducting an interview. I had heard about the ritual many times before, and I was amused to be participating in it. It went like this. I'd lob a question aloud. Bill would take a moment, swivel around on his chair, grab a sheet of blank paper, and then start typing on his old Smith Corona 1200. He had a sort of pecking, rapid-fire method of typing. "All the thoughts are in the typewriter," he told me. I liked watching him work. He'd pause, type, stop, read what he had written, scowl, then start typing again, faster now, following the heartbeat of a thought, the development of an idea. When he was done he peeled off the page and handed it to me, searching my face while I read the answer. If I had a follow-up question he'd take the paper and insert it back into the type-writer. If I had a new question, he'd reel in a new sheet and start firing away. I found it strangely effective—a way of mixing the intimacy of conversation with the precision of writing.

While Bill answered the questions, I snooped around the bookshelves. I found a full set of Chekhov's stories—an obvious model—two shelves of works by Sylvia Townsend Warner, a couple of shelves of his own books in no particular order, a collection of Welty's photographs (preface by William Maxwell). There were no biographies, a genre he distrusted, but lots of collections of letters. I found full editions of the letters of Horace Walpole, William James, and Robert Louis Stevenson. There was also *The Happiness of Getting It Down Right*, his own recent epistolary exchanges with Frank O'Connor.

While our interview was proceeding, the preparations for the party were also going into full swing. A friend of Emmy's arrived to help set things up. The gardener stopped by; someone dropped off wine. The phone rang constantly. Some well-wishers wouldn't be put off, and so Bill was called off to the kitchen. He'd come right back and sit down at his desk. All morning there were the questions of whether or not it would rain (it wouldn't rain on Bill's birthday!) and where the luncheon should take place. It was finally decided to have the lunch in Emmy's airconditioned studio rather than on the outdoor porch (a good thing, too, since it ended up pouring rain). There was also the question of Harriet Sheehy's fish. Harriet had sent a salmon from Ireland and it still hadn't arrived. A flurry of international calls turned up that it had been delayed in customs at Kennedy Airport. Listening to the party taking shape all over the house, asking Bill questions and then watching his long hands floating fluidly over the typewriter, I started to feel as if I were participating in a Chekhov story.

### 4. SOME THINGS HE SAID

I once said to Joe Mitchell that the only part about dying that I minded was that when you are dead you can't read Tolstoy.

I am no longer surprised at being as old as I am because I went through two or three preliminary shocks that prepared me for it. They all occurred in front of the bathroom mirror while I was shaving. The first was "What am I doing attached to that old man?" The second, a few days later, was "But I don't want to leave the party."

It isn't so much that time seems mysterious to me as that I wonder if it is necessary.

There was a time when I was able to feel (even though I knew it was irrational) that they would all be waiting for me when I died— my mother, my uncle Doc, my aunts Edith and Annette. What that amounts to is that the child expected it, and the man humored him in this idea.

There was a woman, one of several surrogate mothers, who lived on a farm in Wisconsin, where I went to work when I was eighteen, and which afterward became a second home to me. She was a very vital woman. She lived to be ninety-five or ninety-six, and told her daughter at the end of her life that she was tired, that she had lived long enough. This has been a great comfort to me.

I did things I shouldn't have but have been on the whole so fortunate that it would seem ungrateful to regret anything. But you haven't asked about my mind. It is beginning to fray . . . There is slippage in the upper story.

I used to think that when I got to be an old man I would sit in a wheelchair and drink Scotch all day. Now that I am an old man I find I don't like Scotch and one glass of red wine at dinner is all I can manage comfortably.

The energy that it requires to imagine a novel and then carry this idea through to the final page is simply not there anymore. When people ask me, "What are you writing?" even though I know they have asked the question only out of politeness, I want to pick up something and throw it at them. Which must mean some resentment on my part at the diminishment of certain powers that old age inevitably means.

About kindness. I have taken so much of my emotional "attitudes," if that is the right word, from my mother. When I was a very small child I was out riding with my father and mother one evening after supper and as they were going through town, my father suddenly pulled on the reins and stopped the carriage. A little boy had darted into the street and been run over just ahead of us. He was about my age, and the son of a doctor, and he was carried into his father's office. My father and mother got the carriage and, taking me with them, went into the waiting room. My mother disappeared behind a glass wall and I could tell she was holding the boy and talking to him, saying, "Now, now, now, now . . ." Using just the tone of voice she used when I was upset. But it sunk in that anyone in trouble had a claim on her feelings.

On another occasion we were at dinner and the phone rang, and when my mother came back from the telephone she said, "There has been a cyclone in Matoon, and they want people to send food down in a freight car to the station." Whereupon she took all the food off

179

the table, when we had barely started to eat, wrapped it in a cloth and gave it to my father who took it downtown, and I went to bed hungry.

"Bravely frank!" How can you say such a thing! I am truthful only once in a month of Sundays. And only when I am fairly sure the person can stand it. Mostly people can't, as Eliot said, bear very much reality. If I were to die and go to heaven, if there were a heaven, I would go around telling the truth all day long, never mind the angels and their harping.

When I was a child and would tell my mother, "My feelings are hurt," I felt that they existed, my feelings, with the solidity of material objects. Because my older brother teased me and nobody could make him stop, I cried at least once a day until he went away to college, after which I didn't cry any more than people normally do. But I listened, in a manner of speaking, to my feelings, and when it was sensible always tried to act on them.

When I am writing a novel or even a story it is as if I had entered a room and closed the door behind me. The concentration it takes to shape a story, to watch characters emerge and become in the round, to move sentences around a dozen times until they are locked into place usually involves a withdrawal from one's present and exterior life.

Don't you and the poet live side by side and lie awake with insomnia in the same bed at night?

I have come to put more faith in what actually happened. I have come to feel that life is the Scheherazade.

[My sense of my mother's death changed from book to book.] In *They Came Like Swallows* it was pretty much raw grief. In *The Folded Leaf* she is a shadowy figure in the background of Lymie Peters. I don't remember if it is in the novel or not, but when, in actual life, I did cut my throat with the intention to die, it was also with the expectation that I would join my mother.
The woman in *Time Will Darken It* is not drawn from her, though she lived in my mother's house.
In *So Long, See You Tomorrow* I wasn't so much writing about her

(although I did briefly) as her absence. But perhaps emotionally speaking there is no difference.

In *Ancestors* the chapters about the happiness of our family life were a kind of testifying. It was also like painting. As if years and habits and feelings could also be made visual. But it is done, I think, from a distance and with acceptance.

By the time I came to write the two stories about the black people, Billie Dyer and his sister who was my mother's housekeeper, I tried to abandon the child's viewpoint and see my mother as an adult would have. Allowing her to be less than perfect, but at the same time, with no withdrawal of love. More as if I had become Isherwood's camera and were photographing her in this or that moment.

But also, I wrote less about how she was, what she meant to me, and more about what she was and meant to other people.

When I was in analysis I wrote a full-length play which I told to Theodore Reik, lying on the couch. My mother arrived at a mysterious airport, having managed a return to life in this world. Only to find that my father had remarried and didn't need her. That I was on the point of marrying, and if she stayed I would be torn between my love for her and my love for the young woman I was about to marry. Feeling that there was no longer any place for her, that life had closed over and she was shut out, she returned to the airport. The curtain line was the "I" character saying to his fiancée, "Hold me!"

Whether you want to or meant to or not, in old age you find yourself thinking whatever is simply is and must be accepted. I suppose the child goes on grieving. The man—

What life resembles sometimes, though fortunately not too often, is a jack-in-the-box.

My own part I would be more satisfied with if I had said that Emmy has kept my body and soul together for more than fifty years, that I never tire of looking at her face, that if I hadn't married her I wouldn't have married anybody and so wouldn't have been able to write about a life that was in any way whole.

## 5. DYING

*Old age is what you make of it, and what old age makes of you.*

What he made of his circumstance, and what it made of him,

turned him into the most lovable person I've ever known. I once asked him how he managed it. He said that in his thirties he was terribly alone and that he decided that he wanted to be loved more than anything else. The way to do that was to love other people unreservedly. He said, "I saw people all around me, saw what they were like, understood what they were going through, and without waiting for them to love me, loved them."

It worked beyond measure. It never failed to surprise him, even at the very end of his life, that so many people loved him so completely. During the last few weeks of their lives, when Emmy was dying of cancer and Bill was declining rapidly from old age, I would sometimes stop over just to be near them. I was one of the circle, all of us inconsolable. The week before he died I confessed that I didn't think I could stand it without him, and he said to me, "I've lived with death my whole life, and I know that the people we love we carry with us always. They're part of us."

His curiosity—his interest in other people—never lagged. For example, he wanted me to see the Chardin show at the Met, which he and Emmy had gotten out of their deathbeds to visit. I was teaching a course on reading poetry for high school teachers, and it was hard to get away during the week. One night I came back to a telephone message from his nurse waiting for me at my hotel. The red light blinked on and off in the dark. "Mr. Maxwell wants to know if you have seen the Chardin show yet."

The day before Emmy died, I was standing behind Bill's wheelchair while he gazed at her face. A group of us were gathered around her bed. She was wearing a Chinese brocade jacket. It was hard to take your eyes off her. Her hair was cropped short, her face thin but luminous. Her eyes were deep brown pools lit from within. "I think of all the men she could have made happy," he tossed up at me. "All of them poets." She had saved him, as he had said many times, and he never got over his great good fortune at having found her.

Emmy wanted to dispel the sadness. She wanted each of us to take a glass of champagne. The cork popped. We toasted and sang "Don't Fence Me In." Bill held her hand. He whispered and hummed along. Emmy closed her eyes and was ready to slip away. She wanted to hear "Death and the Maiden." One felt that she was going somewhere, that she believed in something on the other side. Each of us said good night, goodbye. "This is the hardest thing I've ever had to do," she whispered to me as I leaned over to kiss her cheek. Her voice was so low that I couldn't tell if I was hearing her right. "Rilke says that each of us must die his own death. Now I have to die mine." And then she was asleep.

In the end, he was waiting for her to die first. It was a final act of love, a last courtesy. The night after Emmy died, I had an irresistible urge to be near him, and so I showed up unannounced at his apartment around 10 P.M. He heard my voice in the hallway and called me into his bedroom. He looked incredibly fragile lying on the bed. "Her hand was warm," he said. He remembered that after his mother died her hand was ice cold, the touch of a corpse that had stayed with him for eighty years. But he was comforted by the fact that Emmy's hand had retained its warmth for several hours. I kissed him good night.

When I was going out the door, he whispered, "Have you seen the Chardin show yet?" I hadn't. I was stunned that he could think of it. I went the next morning—the paintings have a kind of deathly beauty that has haunted me ever since—and then flew right over to his apartment to please him. I told him the only thing missing from the show was that he wasn't there to see it with me. He said, "I *was* there with you."

In the days before Maxwell died, he talked about the lightness of being. He was so thin and bony that one felt as if he could simply float away. He ate a little. He resolved that he would live as long as he could for the sake of his daughters. He said that he had been so lucky in his life that to wish for anything more would be greedy. Unlike his wife, he did not believe in the other side. His religion had been literature. He closed his eyes and said that he liked to think of dying as taking a permanent nap.

I can't reconcile myself to the fact that he is gone. The night before he passed away I stood on the sidewalk outside his apartment building and burst into tears. I was grieving in advance. I couldn't bear to be without him. I still can't. William Maxwell knew something about inconsolable grief. People hurried by on either side of me, but no one even glanced my way. It started to rain. The night opened its arms. New York City is a place where one can weep on the sidewalk in perfect privacy.

*Nominated by Daniel Henry, Grace Schulman, Charles Harper Webb,*
*Susan Hahn, Joan Murray, Tin House*

# AFTER HERODOTUS

## by TOM SLEIGH

from AGNI

"Seven furlongs of papyrus
and flax cables
lie shredded and entangled,
floating sodden

on the Hellespont's
storming waters,
the remains
of Xerxes bridge,

Xerxes the Invader:
but you, Great King Xerxes,
chosen son of Cyrus,
you gave the waves

three hundred lashes,
you hurled chains
into those traitor waves,
you branded

their rebellious,
restless sides
with hissing irons.
Then you rounded up

the engineers,
chopped off
their heads:
then new engineers

took over, lashing
together triremes
and galleys,
360 vessels

moored head-on
to the current
to lessen the strain
on cables groaning;

then timbers
were laid down,
brushwood on timbers,
and finally earth

tamped over all,
basketful on basketful
trampled hard
by the cavalry's hooves;

and now, Great King Xerxes,
you sit on
your marble throne
high on the highest hill

above the plain of Abydon:
your troops swarm
the beaches and fill
every inch of ground,

your armada's sails
blot out the waves,
your centipeding oars
scuttle across

those subject waters:
for seven days and nights
day and night
the army crosses . . .

but look: the Great King weeps:
for he feels his fate
in all the arms and legs
milling beneath his eyes:

*O what use to be a King,*
*what use to rule*
*East and West*
*from Susa*

*to Sparta's plains,*
*for in a hundred years' time,*
*not one of all my soldiers*
*will be left alive . . ."*

*Nominated by Agni, David Wojahn*

# WILD PLUMS IN BLOSSOM

## by TED KOOSER

from NATIONAL POETRY REVIEW

In a light, cold rain, at the edge of the woods,
a line of brides is waiting, hand in hand.
Their perfume carries far across the fields.
They have been brought here from the east
to marry farmers, and were left on the platform.
The dark old depot of the woods is locked
and no one has come for them but me.

*Nominated by National Poetry Review*

# ACKERMAN IN EDEN

fiction by DONALD HAYS

from THE SOUTHERN REVIEW

Tomorrow, he knows, they will come back with their Thorazine and their rules, but now Ackerman, alone of all his kind, stares into a pool of water and thinks of spearing fish in a twilit eddy of the far Euphrates. For tomorrow, when they return, they will not find him. He will be in the marshlands south and west of Babylon and Babel. The war, he's sure, will begin tonight. Shock and awe. But he and the dark princess, whom he has lavished with love and poetry, have planned their escape for days. In but hours, the watchman will come to her, accept his bribe, and in exchange give her Ackerman's confiscated cards of identity and access and a duplicate key to the doomed city's western gate. Already a car awaits them. They will flee the horror, cross the God-plagued desert until they reach a place of safety, an oasis where, after dining on fish and rice and fruit, they will lie naked together outside a hut of woven reeds, share a pipe of Afghan opium, and make love beneath the flaming skies of Eden.

"You still puddling around here, Doc?" It is the first watch of the night, and so it is Rasheed, the keeper of the early evening. "You ain't careful, bub, you gon' miss supper. We might even have a poetry reading after." His head jerks down, up, the emphatic affirmative. "You never know. What you think, Wally? See if we can't stop the war that way?" Sometimes he calls Ackerman Wally, sometimes Doc, and sometimes Dr. Hip. That's because on Ackerman's first night here, Rasheed had asked him what he was a doctor of. Poetry. Ackerman had said. I teach it and I write it. What's it like, your poetry? Rasheed had asked. Wallace Stevens, said Ackerman, except hip. And then, for many minutes, he had declaimed poems and bits of poems from his most recent collection, *Parallel Loves.*

Rasheed walks over to the sink. "What a man's got to do here is just pull the plug and watch it all go down the drain." Ackerman stares at him. Rasheed is a mystery. He pulls the plug. "See," he says.

They watch the water swirl and disappear. Ackerman looks away and sees. He is in a white room. There is a bed, a window, blinds. Slits of dusk light seep through. He looks again at the sink. White and empty. Vanished waters. There is a mirror above the sink. A black man and a white one. Ackerman stares into first the black face and then the white. "How can we sing the Lord's song," he asks, "in a strange land?"

"You just got to keep right on at it, Dr. Hip," Rasheed says. "A man like you, ain't no other way." He takes Ackerman by the elbow and turns him away from the sink.

"I write letters home," says Ackerman earnestly. "I read paragraphs on the sublime."

They step into a hallway. It is empty now, but it leads toward the western gate and, beyond that, the world.

"But you gon' eat your supper now, Wally. Right up here. We having fish tonight."

Tonight the television is on. Inside it, bombs burst on Babylon.

"Baghdad," the dark princess says. "You got to quit calling it Babylon. All that's gone."

"Ah," says Ackerman. "Another world."

She reaches across the table and touches the back of his hand. "Let it go," she says. "None of it's going to be any good if you don't let this go."

A third person at the table, an old man, says, "You want your fish?"

Ackerman stares deep into the princess's dark eyes. "I am a poet," he tells her. "I am in love with loss."

"You a special kind of fool," she says.

With his fork, the old man spears her fish.

Deep in the night he comes to her, the young woman, dark and lost. She is sleeping. He stands above her and watches her breathe. Comely, he thinks, as the tents of Kedar, as the curtains of Solomon. Her face is dark against the white cloth. Ackerman leans down and kisses her lips, her neck. Her smell, he thinks, is like the smell of

Lebanon. He wants to undress and lie beside her—the first man and the first woman. But time is short. A terrible army crosses the desert, racing toward them. Already the fires of war have smudged the night. The air itself hums with threat. So they must go. They must hide together in the marshes at the edge of Eden. When the terror passes, they'll flee to Ur and join the great caravan to Ophir, where songs still map the world.

He straightens and stares down at her again. She opens her eyes and there's a moment of wonder. He wants to speak of that wonder. He wants to ask her how she can sleep on such a night. But all he can say is, "The key?"

She shakes her head. "It's not done yet. Too early. You go on back and bide your time. It'll be all right."

But he stands and looks.

"Go on," she says. "Don't leave your room. You gon' mess it all up."

So he leaves, returns to his room. He does not see the watchman. He lies in his bed, curled like a frightened child. He waits. He listens. Again and again, he tells himself not to mess it all up. What must be done must be done. A sacrifice for freedom.

Twice he rises and paces his room, then returns to his bed and curls into himself again. He listens. Nothing. The institutional hum. He fears that the other world is lost, that there is only dread and madness.

Then the footsteps. Ackerman sits up. He wants to stop the man. Instead, he merely sits there, wide-eyed, staring into the imprisoned night. He begins to rock back and forth. He wants to pray. He has always wanted to pray.

When at last she comes to him, he does not see her. His eyes are closed. He is still rocking. He is reciting, in a whisper, "Esthétique du Mal."

She touches his forehead. He opens his eyes. "Is it . . ." She touches his lips with her index finger. "Night men are easy," she says.

Ackerman wants to say something, fresh words from the heart. He opens his mouth to speak but finds nothing now save silence and sorrow.

She is dressed in jeans, sweater, sneakers. "All right," she says. "It's running time, rhyming man."

As he had promised he would be, the keeper of the night is now watching war in the sun room. They slip past the door and turn down the other hallway. It is white and empty. They slip down it, passing other rooms. Some of the doors are closed, some half open. All of the rooms are dark. Inside them, patients sleep. Behind the reinforced glass lining the upper half of the nurses' station, the light is bright and harsh. The head nurse, head bent with concentration, is writing something in a patient's chart. A life there, Ackerman thinks, symptoms, diagnosis, prescription. He would like to steal his chart, his file. Steal it and take it with him. Deprive them of all they know. But it would be a fool's risk. And what does it matter? It is a kind of truth, that chart, but it is only their truth, a formula, cribbed and condensed. There is Eden, too.

The girl pauses, looks back at Ackerman, and makes a downward motion with her right hand. On hands and knees, pressed against the white wall beneath the brightened station glass, they crawl past the nurse. Once they are well beyond her and her light, they stand and, carefully, quickly, walk toward the door at the end of the hall. The princess slips the duplicate key into the lock and turns it. Ackerman follows her into the silent hall, the opening world, beyond.

At the edge of Nasiriyah, atop the ziggurat of Ur, Ackerman looks east across the broad Euphrates and the flatlands and marshlands beyond. Cornfields, pastureland, cattle and sheep. Carp-filled ponds, mud-walled gardens, landholders' houses. He turns his face northward and searches the edges of the shadowed world. Beyond all light, in the darkness that covers the curve of the world, are the thirteen city-states where man invented meaning. Extinction, he thinks, the great, gone kingdoms and caliphates. And yet except for us the total past felt nothing when destroyed.

The girl touches his forearm. "You're talking to yourself again," she says.

"Borrowed words."

"Sometimes that's all there is," she says.

"And silence. Borrowed words and silence."

"You're going all grim again," she says. "There's a road leading west. We keep driving, we be all right."

"We have enemies everywhere," he tells her. "Arrogant armies, moonward fedayeen."

She pulls at his arm, turns him to face her. "Look at me," she tells him. "This is Fort Smith, not Nasiriyah or An Najaf. That's the Arkansas, not the Euphrates. You're William Ackerman. People say you're a pretty good poet. But you went nuts. I'm Tamika Jones, a runaway nigger girl that's never known nothing but crackhead projects and hard-dick foster homes."

191

Ackerman nods, then turns his face again toward the water. She turns it back to her. "We got your money. We got your car. We refilled the prescriptions you had before you went in the hospital. You got a chance now and I want you to have it. Ain't nobody ever been as good to me as you. But you keep this up, I'll leave your ass. So you got to get this in your head. Neither of us has ever seen Babylon. Not much chance we ever will. You keep pouring pixie dust over everything, we'll end up someplace worse than what we left."

"You were getting gas," Ackerman says. "I walked up on the bridge. That's all."

"You looked like you were fixing to jump. Up here talking to yourself, moving off into that other world again."

He turns and looks across the river again. He nods. "It's just Oklahoma," he says.

"Get back in the car," she tells him. And he does.

"Amarillo is not Ophir," she insists. "Tucumcari ain't Tikrit. Those are gullies, or maybe arroyos—they ain't wadis. And that's just one more mirage, not Habbaniyah Lake. Nobody out here ever heard of Harun al-Rashid or Jafar the Barmecide or Pale Ramon or any of that other crazy shit you always talking about. I don't want to hear no more about nobody descending nowhere on extended wings." She nods toward the windshield and points toward the road ahead. "You keep your mind fixed on what's right here in front of you. You got to give up all this Shadrach, Meshach, and Abednego shit."

They cross the width of Oklahoma, the Panhandle of Texas, enter New Mexico. She never allows Ackerman to drive the car. He is trying hard to hold on to the world.

They take a room in Tucumcari. Ackerman pays with cash they have gotten from an ATM in Amarillo. They will eat, sleep, and move on, the princess tells him. Then she looks at him and says it again, "We will eat, sleep, and move on."

Ackerman stares at her. She touches the back of his hand. "You gonna take your pills," she tells him. "And you gonna sleep."

He nods slowly. "The night has no bedroom," he says.

"Yeah, well, we renting it one now."

In the night, she eats and then sleeps. Ackerman does neither. He sits in the chair beside his bed and watches the war on the bolted-down TV. The sound is off. He does not want to wake the princess. The English have taken Basra. There are marines in An Najaf, where

Ali, the Prophet's son-in-law and cousin, is buried. A rectangular wall surrounds the sanctuary, two storeys with a golden dome, that holds the tomb. Ali, a gentle man who became caliph after the murders of Omar and Othman and ruled until he was murdered at the door of the mosque in Kufa. He was succeeded by his enemy, first of the Ommayad caliphs, who for the next century ruled from Damascus.

The Shiah and the Sunni. Believers and their wars. Infidels are not allowed entry into the sanctuary of Ali's tomb, and Ackerman is everywhere an infidel—in Bethlehem and Jerusalem as much as An Najaf. But beyond the cemetery and the thin stretch of palm-lined fields along the far Euphrates, there is but desert, black and endless. Desert.

As he watches the television, tears come to his eyes. He must let the girl go.

When she wakes he stares into her soft eyes, watches as they become wary. A new day. What must be done must be done. "Tamika Jones," he says. He closes his eyes. Tamika Jones. He opens his eyes and sees her again. Tamika Jones. "Let be be finale of seem," he says.

She stares at him. "You didn't take your pills, did you?"

He shakes his head. "I've gone too far."

"Ain't that the truth?" she says, shaking her head. "You listen to me. I'm gon' get up now. I'm gon' shower. I'm gon' put my clothes back on. Then we gon' go out and get us some breakfast. We get back, we gon' get in your car and drive to Phoenix."

"Yes," says Ackerman. "Phoenix."

Phoenix is what happens when there is no poetry, Ackerman thinks. Then he says it aloud to Tamika Jones. "Well, we fix that," she says. "You be there tonight."

Casually and splendidly naked, she rises from the bed and goes into the shower. The body itself, thinks Ackerman, should be wonder enough.

While she showers, he watches the silent TV. Retired colonels and ignorant anchormen. An ad for a purple pill. Phoenix, thinks Ackerman. He has been there. There is nothing real in Phoenix. The rainbow lawns, the blue pools, the desert denied. Can no one hear the sucking sound of greed?

Tamika Jones walks out of the bathroom still drying herself with a white towel. My dark princess, he thinks. But, yes, he must leave her. His desire has become the twin of his despair. Ackerman watches her dress. She doesn't need the sweater now. Just the jeans, the T-shirt, the shoes. There is much he wants to say to her. She looks at him, her face a question.

"I can't eat," he says.

"Well, you wait right here. I'm going down the street, get me some eggs and shit. I'll be right back."

She leaves. Ackerman waits. Then he has to force himself to wait some more. Then he has to force himself to rise. There is a small writing desk against the wall opposite the door. Ackerman walks to the desk and takes his wallet out of his back pocket. He takes the bills out of the wallet. Most of them are hundreds. He decides to count them. Twenty, thirty. Then he decides to stop. He sets them on the desk, places an ashtray on top of them. He takes out his ATM card and three of his four credit cards. He places the credit cards next to the money. He puts his wallet in his pocket. He lays the bank card on a sheet of motel stationery and, with a cheap motel pen, writes, "The PIN number is 1955." It is the year Wallace Stevens died. But he does not tell her that.

He stands over the desk, staring down at the cards, the money, the sentence he has written. He looks up at the mirror and sees an old man, unshaven, mad eyed, and broken. He closes his eyes and sees her, naked again and drying herself with the white towel. He opens his eyes and sees her again. It will only get worse. He turns and leaves.

After she is gone, Ackerman spends three days in the darkness of another motel room. He hangs the DO NOT DISTURB sign on the out-side doorknob and leaves it there. He keeps the blinds closed. He never turns on the television, never watches the war. He lies on his back, eyes open, and stares at the ceiling. For the first day, his mind races, circles, keens. Then it slows, pauses over old griefs. He re-members his hard, thin-lipped father, all bitterness, resentment, and fear, and his mother, the shrewdness and persistence with which she worked to save him from the hardscrabble family farm in the pine barrens outside Nacogdoches, the sadness and pride with which she saw him off at the station the morning he, her scholarship boy, caught the bus for Houston and Rice, the morning she gave him up to a world beyond her knowing. After that, it was Iowa and the writ-ing program and jobs in Michigan, North Carolina, Kansas, and, fi-nally, Arkansas. The professional pilgrimages of the professor-poet. Until his mother died, Ackerman loved her without qualification. And her love for him was obvious—pure and permanent. After his father's death, Ackerman had moved his mother into the house with him in Lafayette. She lived six more years, and during that time he married and divorced three women. After the second divorce, he had spent a month in Harbor Vista. When he was released, his mother was waiting for him. The house was fine, the world in order. Somehow, from her wheelchair, she had managed. He wrote a poem about it, about her month and his. One of his few purely narrative poems. It was in *Poetry*. It was in *Best American*. It made his mother proud. When she died, two years ago, the book that held that poem was beside her bed in her room in his house. He was proud of that. He had done right by his mother. How many men could honestly say that?

Remembering that is almost enough to cause him to rise and re-enter the world. He does, in fact, rise and shower. But under the shock of water he sees that he is a weak, selfish man who has been loved, truly loved, by no one, by no woman, other than his own mother. He is a joke of a man who thinks he is a poet. No more. He leaves the shower without either turning the water off or drying himself. He returns to his bed, wet and whimpering, and gives himself again to wretchedness and night. Early the next morning, paralyzed by self-pity, he pisses himself.

On the morning of the fourth day, the motel manager knocks on the door and says that he just wants to make sure everything's all right. Ackerman says nothing. The manager knocks again. Then he opens the door and steps into the room. Ackerman can see only the shadow of a man in a shaft of light. He waits. The shadow turns its head and speaks. "You got thirty minutes. You're not gone then, I'm calling the police."

When the man is gone, Ackerman gets out of bed. He looks down at himself. Naked. Then he sees the clothes that have been lying on the floor for he doesn't know how many days. Where to now? Karbala, he thinks. The mosque, the tomb of the great Imam Hussein, grandson of the Prophet. But he knows he is still in Tucumcari.

He pulls on his clothes, and outside the door, piss-stained in hard desert heat, Ackerman stands for long moments in the glare of a desperate sun, willing his eyes to see. Everything is cruel and white. He crosses the potholed parking lot and stops at the edge of the ruins of the empty motel pool. There, alone and far from Eden, he prays for Tamika Jones.

*Nominated by The Southern Review, Michael Heffernan*

# CHRISTMAS 1910

fiction by ROBERT OLEN BUTLER

from STORYQUARTERLY

$M$Y THIRD CHRISTMAS in the west river country came hard upon the summer drought of 1910, and Papa and my brothers had gone pretty grim, especially my brother Luther, who was a decade older than me and had his own adjacent homestead, to the east, that much closer to the Badlands. Luther had lost his youngest, my sweet little nephew Caleb, to a snakebite in August. We all knew the rattlers would come into your house. We women would hardly take a step without a hoe at hand for protection. But one of the snakes had got into the bedclothes and no one knew and Caleb took the bite and hardly cried at all before it was done. And then there was the problem with everybody's crops. Some worse than others. A few had done hardly ten bushels of corn for forty acres put out. We weren't quite that bad off, but it was bad nonetheless. Bad enough that I felt like a selfish girl to slip out of the presence of my kin whenever I had the chance and take up with Sam my saddle horse, go up on his back and ride off a ways from the things my Mama and Papa and brothers were working so hard to build, and I just let my Sam take me, let him follow his eyes and ears to whatever little thing interested him.

And out on my own I couldn't keep on being grim about the things that I should have. There was a whole other thing or two. Selfish things. Like how you can be a good daughter in a Sodbuster family with flesh-and-blood of your own living right there all around you, making a life together—think of the poor orphans of the world and the widows and all the lost people in the cities—how you can be a good daughter in such a cozy pile of kin and still feel so lonely. Mary,

Joseph and Jesus happy in a horse stall, forgive me. Of course, in that sweet little picture of the Holy Family, Mary had Joseph to be with her, not her brothers and parents with their faces set hard and snakes crawling in your door and hiding in your shoe.

So when the winter had first come in, there hadn't been any snow since the beginning of November and it was starting to feel like a drought all over again, though we were happy not to have to hunker down yet and wait out the dark season under all the snow. There was still plenty of wind, of course. Everybody in our part of South Dakota shouted at each other all the time because of the wind that galloped in across the flat land to the west and to the north with nothing to stop it but the buffalo grass and little bluestem and prairie sandreed, which is to say nothing at all. But the winter of 1910 commenced with the world dead dry and that's when he came, two days before Christmas, the young man on horseback.

We were all to Luther's place and after dinner we returned home and found the young man sitting at our oak table in what we called our parlor, the big main room of our soddy. He'd lit a candle. The table was one of the few pieces of house furniture we'd brought with us from Nebraska when Papa got our homestead. Right away my vanity was kicking up. I was glad this young man, who had a long, lank, handsome face, a little like Sam actually, had settled himself at our nicest household possession, which was this table. And I hoped he understood the meaning of the blue tar paper on our walls. Most of the homesteaders used the thinner red tar paper at three dollars a roll. Papa took the thick blue at six dollars, to make us something better. People in the west river country knew the meaning of that, but this young man had the air of coming from far off. We all left our houses unlocked for each other and for just such a wayfarer, so no one felt it odd in those days if you came home and found a stranger making himself comfortable.

He rose and held his hat down around his belt buckle and slowly rotated it in both hands and he apologized for lighting the candle but he didn't want to startle us coming in, and then he told us his name, which was John Marsh, and where he was from, which was Bardstown, Kentucky, county of Nelson, not far down the way from Nazareth, Kentucky, he said, smiling all around, and he wished us a Merry Christmas and hoped we wouldn't mind if he slept in the barn for the night and he'd be moving on in the morning. "I'm bound for Montana," he said, "to work a cattle ranch of a man I know there and

197

to make my own fortune someday." With this last announcement he stopped turning his hat, so as to indicate how serious he was about that. Sam's a dapple gray with a soft puff of dark hair between his ears, and the young man sort of had that too, a lock of which fell down on his forehead as he nodded once, sharply, to signify his determination.

My mama would hear nothing of this, the moving on in the morning part. "You're welcome to stay but it should be for more than a night," she said. "No man should be alone on Christmas if there's someone to spend it with." And with this, Mama shot Papa a look, and he knew to take it up.

"We can use a hand with some winter chores while we've got the chance," Papa said. "I can pay you in provisions for your trip."

John Marsh studied each of our faces, Mama and Papa and my other older brother, Frank, just a year over me, standing by Papa's side as he always did, and my younger brother, Ben, still a boy, really, though he was as tall as me already. And John Marsh looked me in the eye and I looked back at him and we neither of us turned away, and I thought to breathe into his nostrils, like you do to meet a new horse and show him you understand his ways, and it was this thought that made me lower my eyes from his at last.

"I might could stay a bit longer than the night," he said.

"Queer time to be making this trip anyway," my papa said, and I heard a little bit of suspicion, I think, creeping in, as he thought all this over a bit more.

"He can take me in now," John Marsh said. "And there was nothing for me anymore in Kentucky."

Which was more explanation than my father was owed, it seemed to me. Papa eased up, saying, "Sometimes it just comes the moment to leave."

"Yessir." And John Marsh started turning his hat again.

Mama touched my arm and said, low, "Abigail, you curry the horses tonight before we retire."

This was instead of the early morning, when I was usually up before anyone, and she called me by my whole name and not "Abba," so it was to be the barn for John Marsh.

Papa took off at a conversational trot, complaining about the drought and the soil and the wind and the hot and the cold and the varmints and all, pretty much life in South Dakota in general, though that's the life he'd brought us all to without anyone forcing us to leave Nebraska, a thing he didn't point out. He was, however, making sure to say that he held 320 acres now and his eldest son 160 more and that's pretty good for a man what never went to school, his daughter being plenty educated for all of them and she even going around teaching homesteader kids who couldn't or wouldn't go to the one-room school down at Scenic. John Marsh wasn't looking at me anymore, though I fancied it was something he was struggling to control, which he proved by not even glancing at me when Papa talked of my schooling, in spite of it being natural for him to turn his face to me for that. Instead, when the subject of me came up, his Adam's apple started bobbing, like he was swallowing hard, over and over.

I slipped out of the house at that point, while Papa continued on. I walked across the hard ground toward the little barn we kept for the saddle horses, Sam and Papa's Scout and Dixie. When Papa's voice finally faded away behind me, I stopped and just stood for a moment and looked up at the stars. It's true that along with the wind and the snakes and the lightning storms and all, South Dakota had the most stars in the sky of anywhere, and the brightest, and I had a tune take up in my head. *I wonder as I wander out under the sky* . . . Christmas was nearly upon us and I shivered standing there, not from the cold, though the wind was whipping at me pretty good, but because I realized that nothing special was going on inside me over Christmas, a time which had always all my life thrilled me. Luther had even put up a wild plum tree off his land in a bucket of dirt and we'd lit candles on it, just this very night. And all I could do was sit aside a ways and nod and smile when anyone's attention turned to me but all the while I was feeling nothing much but how I was as distant from this scene as one of those stars outside. And even now the only quick thing in me was the thought of some young man who'd just up and walked in our door, some stranger who maybe was a varmint himself or a scuffler or a drunkard or a fool. I didn't know anything about him, but I was out under this terrible big sky and wishing he was beside me, his hat still in his hands, and saying how he'd been inside thinking about only me for all this time. *How Jesus the Savior did come for to die, For poor ornery people like you and like I.* Ornery was right.

I went on into the barn and lit a kerosene lamp and Sam was lying there, stirred from his sleep by my coming to him at an odd time. His head rose up and he looked over his shoulder at me and he nickered

199

soft and I came and knelt by him and put my arm around his neck. He turned his head a little and offered me his ear and waited for my sweet talk. "Hello, my Sammy," I said to him, low. "I'm sorry to disturb your sleep. Were you dreaming? I bet you were dreaming of you and me riding out along the coulee like today. Did we find some wonderful thing, like buffalo grass flowering in December?"

He puffed a bit and I leaned into him. "I dream of you, too," I said. "You're my affinity, Sammy." Like John Marsh not looking my way when Papa spoke of me, I was making a gesture that was the opposite of what I was feeling. My mind was still on this young man in the house. I suddenly felt ashamed, playing my Sam off of this stranger. In fact, I was hoping that this John Marsh might be my affinity, the boy I'd fit alongside of. I put my other arm around Sam, held him tight. After a moment he gently pulled away and laid his head down. So I got the currycomb and began to brush out the day's sweat and the wind-spew and stall-floor muck and I sang a little to him while I did. *"When Mary birthed Jesus 'twas in a cow's stall, With wise men and farmers and horses and all,"* me putting the horses in for Sammy's sake, though I'm sure there were horses around the baby Jesus, even if the stories didn't say so. The stories always made it mules, but the horses were there. The wise men came on horses. There was quite a crowd around the baby, if you think about it. But when he grew up, even though he gathered the twelve around him, and some others, too, like his mama and the Mary who'd been a wicked girl, he was still lonely. You can tell. He was as distant from them as the stars in the sky.

So I finished with Sam and then with Scout, and Dixie had stood up for me to comb her and I was just working on her hindquarters when I heard voices outside in the wind and then Papa and John Marsh came into the barn, stamping around. I didn't say anything but moved behind Dixie, to listen.

And then Papa said, "I'm sorry there's no place in the house for a young man to stay."

"This is fine," John Marsh said. "I like to keep to myself."

There was a silence for a moment, like Papa was thinking about this, and I thought about it as well. Not thought about it, exactly, but sort of felt a little wind-gust of something for this John Marsh and I wasn't quite sure what. I wanted to keep to myself, too, but only so I could moon around about not keeping to myself. John Marsh seemed overly content. I leaned into Dixie.

"I was your age once," my papa said.

"I'll manage out here fine."

"Night then," Papa said, and I expected him to call for me to go on in the house with him, but he didn't say anything and I realized he'd gone out of the barn not even thinking about me being there. Which is why I'd sort of hid behind Dixie, but he'd even ignored my lamp and so I was surprised to find myself alone in the barn with John Marsh. I held my breath and didn't move.

"Hey there, Gray," John Marsh said, and I knew he was talking to Sam. "You don't mind some company, do you? That's a fella."

I heard Sam blow a bit, giving John Marsh his breath to read. It was not going to be simple about this boy. Him talking to my sweet, gray man all familiar, even touching him now, I realized—I could sense him stroking Sam—all this made me go a little weak-kneed, like it was me he was talking to and putting his hand on. It was like I was up on Sam right now and he was being part of me and I was being part of him. But then I stiffened all of a sudden, got a little heated up about this stranger talking to my Sam like the two of them already had a bond that I never knew about. I was jealous. And I was on the mash. Both at once. In short, I was a country fool, and Dixie knew it because she rustled her rump and made me pull back from her. She also drew John Marsh's attention and he said, "Hello?"

"Hello," I said, seeing as there was no other way out. I took to brushing Dixie pretty heavy with the currycomb and John Marsh appeared, his hat still on his head this time and looking like a right cowboy.

"I didn't know you was there," he said.

"Papa was continuing to bend your ear, is why," I said.

John Marsh smiled at this, but tried to make his face go straight again real quick.

I said, "You can find that true and amusing if you want. He's not here to take offense."

John Marsh angled his head at me, trying to figure what to say or do next. He wasn't used to sass in a girl, I guess. Wasn't used to girls at all, maybe. I should have just blowed in his nose and nickered at him.

"He does go on some," John Marsh said, speaking low.

I concentrated on my currying, though it was merely for show since I was combing out the same bit of flank I'd been working on for a while. Dixie looked over her shoulder at me, pretty much in contempt.

I shot her a just-stand-there-and-mind-your-own-business glance and she huffed at me and turned away. I went back to combing and didn't look John Marsh in the eye for a little while, not wanting to frighten him off by being too forward but getting impatient pretty quick with the silence. The eligible males I'd known since I was old enough for them to be pertinent to me had all been either silly prattlers or totally tongue-tied. This John Marsh was seeming to be among the latter and I brushed and brushed at Dixie's chestnut hair trying to send some brain waves over to this outsized boy, trying to whisper him something to say to me. Which horse is yours? Or, You go around teaching, do you? Or, Is there a Christmas Eve social at the school house tomorrow that I could escort you to? But he just stood there.

Finally I looked over to him. He was staring hard at me and he ripped off his hat the second we made eye contact.

"I'll be out of your way shortly," I said.

"That's okay," he said. "Take your time. She deserves it." And with this he patted Dixie on the rump.

"You hear that, Dixie?" I said. "You've got a gentleman admirer." Dixie didn't bother to respond.

"Where's your horse put up?" I said.

"Oh he likes the outdoors. Horses do. It ain't too fierce tonight for him."

"My Sam—he's the gray down there—it took a long time for him to adjust to a barn. But I like him cozy even if it's not his natural way."

"I'd set him out on a night like this," John Marsh said.

"He's better off," I said.

"I'm sure you love him," John Marsh said.

We both stopped talking and I wasn't sure what had just happened, though I felt that something had come up between us and been done with.

John Marsh nodded to me and moved away.

I stopped brushing Dixie and I just stood there for a moment and then I put down the currycomb and moved off from Dixie and found John Marsh unrolling his sleeping bag outside Sam's stall.

I moved past him to the door. "Night then," I said.

John Marsh nodded and I stepped out under the stars.

❀

Then it was the morning before Christmas and I'd done my currying the night before and I'd had a dream of empty prairie and stars and I couldn't see anyway to go no matter how I turned and so I slept on and on and woke late. As I dressed, there were sounds outside that didn't really register, their being common sounds, a horse, voices trying to speak over the wind, and then Papa came in and said, "Well, he's gone on."

Mama said, "The boy?"

"Yep," Papa said. "He wants to make time to Montana. He's got grit, the boy. The sky west looks bad."

I crossed the parlor, past the oak table and Papa, something furious going on in my chest.

"I was his age once," Papa said.

Then I took up my coat and I was out the door. It was first light. Papa was correct. To the west, the sky was thickening up pretty bad. A sky like this in Kentucky might not say the same thing to a man. Even thinking this way, I knew there was more than bad weather to my stepping away from our house and looking to where John Marsh had gone, maybe only ten minutes before, and me churning around inside so fierce I could hardly hold still. Then I couldn't hold still.

I dashed into the barn and Sam was standing waiting and I gave him the bridle and bit and that was all. There was no time. I threw my skirt up and mounted Sam bareback and we pulled out of the stall and the barn and we were away.

There was a good horse trail through the rest of our land and on out toward the Black Hills that rippled at the horizon when you could see it. But there was only dark and cloud out there now, which John Marsh could recognize very well, and Sam felt my urgency, straight from my thighs. I hadn't ridden him bareback in several years and we both were het up now together like this, with John Marsh not far ahead, surely, and we galloped hard, taking the little dips easy and Sam's ears were pitched forward listening for this man up ahead, and mostly it was flat and winter bare all around and we concentrated on making time, me not thinking at all what it was I was doing. I was just with Sam and we were trying to catch up with some other possibility.

But John Marsh must have been riding fast, too. He wasn't showing up. It was just the naked prairie fanning out ahead as far as the eye would carry, to the blur of a restless horizon. What was he running so fast for? Had I frightened him off somehow? Was it so bad to think he might put his arms around me?

I lay forward, pressing my chest against Sam, keeping low before the rush of the air, and I heard Sam's breathing, heavy and steady, galloping strong with me, him not feeling jealous at all that I was using him to chase this man. I closed my eyes. Sam was rocking me. I clung to him, and this was my Sam, who wasn't a gray man at all, not a man at all, he was something else altogether, he was of this wind and of this land, my Sam, he was of the stars that were up there above me even now, just hiding in the light of day, and we rode like this for a while, rocking together like the waves on the sea, and when I looked up again, there was still no rider in sight but instead an unraveling of the horizon. Sam knew at once what my body was saying. He read the faint tensing and pulling back of my thighs and he slowed and his ears came up and I didn't even have to say for him to stop.

We scuffled into stillness and stood quiet, and together Sam and I saw the storm. All across the horizon ahead were the vast billowing frays of a blizzard. I had a thought for John Marsh. He'd ridden smack into that. Or maybe not. Maybe he'd cut off for somewhere else. Then Sam waggled his head and snorted his unease about what we were looking at, and he was right, of course. He and I had our own life to live and so we turned around and galloped back.

The storm came in right behind us that day before Christmas in 1910, and there was no social at the school house that year. We all burrowed in and kept the fires going and sang some carols. *Stars were gleaming, shepherds dreaming, And the night was dark and chill.*

After midnight I arose and I took a lantern and a shovel and I made a way to the barn, the new snow biting at me all the while, but at last I came in to Sam and hung the lantern, and he muttered in that way he sometimes did, like he knew a thing before it would happen, he knew I'd be there, and I lay down by my horse and I put my arms around him. "Aren't you glad you're in your stable," I whispered to him. "I brought you here away from the storm." And I held him tight.

*Nominated by Joyce Carol Oates, StoryQuarterly*

# THE DEATH OF MAYAKOVSKY

by PHILIP LEVINE

from THE KENYON REVIEW

Philadelphia, the historic downtown,
April 14, 1930.
My father sits down at the little desk
in his hotel room overlooking an airshaft
to begin a letter home: "Dear Essie,"
he pens, but the phone rings before he can
unburden his heart. The driver from Precision Inc.
has arrived. Alone in the back seat, hatless,
coatless on this perfect spring day,
my father goes off to inspect aircraft bearings
that vanished from an army proving ground
in Maryland, bearings he will bargain for
and purchase in ignorance, or so he will tell Essie,
my mother, this after he takes a plea
in the federal courthouse in downtown Detroit.
I knew all this before it happened. Earlier that
morning storm clouds scuttled in across Ontario
to release their darkness into our gray river.
Hundreds of miles east my father rolls down
the car window; the air scented with leaves
just budding out along Route 76
caresses his face and tangles his dark hair.
He lets the world come to him, even this world

of small machine shops, car barns, warehouses
beside the Schuylkill. The child I would become
saw it all, yet years passed before the scene slipped,
frozen, into the book of origins to become
who I am. I'd been distracted
in the breathless dawn by a single shot—
the Russian poet's suicidal gesture—
that would crown our narratives, yours and mine.

*Nominated by Richard Jackson, Charles Harper Webb, Dick Allen,*
*Christopher Buckley, Len Roberts, Chard de Niord*

# PROVERBS

## by ANGIE ESTES

from CHAUTAUQUA LITERARY JOURNAL

      Mortise and tenon, tongue and
groove, tongue-in-cheek, the tenor
      holds the note until it dovetails
in air like the white kerchief of
      the Holy Spirit tied around the neck
of God in Masaccio's *Trinity*, the dove
      more banner than bird, which from
the beginning was the word for
      *verb*—part sky, part earth, part
of speech expressing action, occurrence,
      existence. *It is wonderful,*
Stein said, *the number of mistakes*
      *a verb can make. Pardon, scusi*, word
for word, tell me whether the theory
      holds and, if so, how we will
hold up, hold out, hold
      on, and then I will hold you
to your promise the way the arms of God
      hold up the cross, which holds up
Christ. *To have and to hold*: hold
      that thought. *Besides being able to be*
*mistaken and to make mistakes*
      *verbs can change to look like*
*themselves or to look*
      *like something else.* The inscription above

the skeleton below Christ's feet, for example,
     says the same holds
for you: *I was that which you are,*
     *and what I am you will be.* So much
for *vers libre. Do you think he looks*
     *like himself?* they asked, glancing toward
his casket. *In the hold,* in Masaccio's fresco,
     the grave is a wall with a barrel vault
pierced through, deep chamber below
     a coffered ceiling where God holds forth
in rose and black. *Behold,*
     *I show you a mystery*: a ruse
is a ruse is a ruse. In Latin,
     to have verve is to have
words. It could be a version,
     aversion, a verse: please
advise. Not much we can know save
     the redbud, which wears its heart
on its leaves.

*Nominated by Chautauqua Literary Journal, Martha Collins,*
*Erin McGraw, Linda Bierds, Andrew Hudgins*

# NOTES ON URANIUM WEAPONS AND KITSCH

by GEORGE GESSERT

from NORTHWEST REVIEW

## 1.

KITSCH IS A PHENOMENON of empires and industrialized societies. Hunter-gatherers do not have it. It is not found in wilderness, but cats have been bred to resemble teddy bears, and every year more flowers look like roses.

Other examples of kitsch: socialist realist paintings, Disneyland, Hallmark bereavement cards, Frank Sinatra's songs, high-sugar breakfast cereals like Count Chocula, the Princess Diana cult, Hummers, and *Chicago*, the musical. Kitsch can be sentimental or cynical, stylish or hopelessly unfashionable. It can be as naughty as soft-core pornography or as nice as *Bedtime for Bonzo*. It belongs to no particular nation, class, or political faction.

According to Milan Kundera, kitsch is whatever pleases the greatest number of people at any cost. Whether cartoon-like or grandiose, venomous or trite, kitsch is an aesthetic mode that affirms what most serious art and discourse avoid: the pleasures of conformity, pretension, and oversimplification. Kitsch joins isolated individuals to crowds. In Nazi Germany and Stalin's USSR kitsch inoculated against empathy and prepared the way for atrocities.

Kundera is European, and his understanding of kitsch came out of life under Hitler, communism, and consumer culture. Very few Americans directly experienced Nazism or communism, or share

Kundera's belief that kitsch is a sign of social malignancy. More than forty years have passed since Dwight MacDonald warned against kitsch, which he associated with mass culture and control from above. He considered high culture the only viable alternative. There have been no such authoritative warnings since. In the United States high culture came in for radical reappraisal during the 1960s. Susan Sontag defended camp sensibility for its celebration of artifice, exaggerated emotions, and pure style. She noted that much (but not all) camp was kitsch. Pop artists mirrored kitsch, and brought rock-and-roll into galleries.

Kitsch contributed to totalitarianism and the Holocaust in Europe, but perhaps in America what is called kitsch is actually something more innocent, more exuberant, more natural, and above all more democratic. Perhaps here the alchemy of democratic culture turns kitsch into harmless fun.

The marketplace makes no aesthetic judgements. In America the word kitsch has gradually become almost an anachronism. One of the few places that I still occasionally encounter it is in the pages of *Art Forum*. Now and then a critic uses it in passing, a ghost-trace of another world. This is not to say that the phenomenon of kitsch has disappeared—on the contrary, it is more pervasive than ever. Kitsch dominates the media and political spectacle, especially now, in time of war.

2.

General Wesley Clark wrote of the ideal contemporary war as "a high-tech battlefield, viewed through an array of sensors, with battles fought and won by precision strikes and a slimmer ground component."[1] This is not kitsch, but kitsch proliferates around it, transforming war into entertainment. The magic begins like this: if technology can replace much of the work of the soldier, and precision strikes can reduce civilian casualties, then war's toll of suffering and death can be eliminated, or at least dramatically reduced.

By implication world domination and the benefits of empire will not involve much loss of lives or moral capital.

Until 1990 Americans overwhelmingly associated war with Vietnam-style carnage, but following Iraq's invasion of Kuwait, and leading up to the Persian Gulf War, the media widely reported that the US military possessed "smart bombs" and "precision weapons," devices that could deliver "surgical strikes." These weapons promised war that would resemble a medical procedure. Cancerous political entities such as Saddam Hussein could be swiftly excised and American casualties kept low. Even civilians would be spared.

News reports at the time occasionally mentioned something called depleted uranium, but the component of the new weapons that gained the most attention was computer chips. Today computers have little more aura than dishwashers, but in 1990 chips were still magical, trailing promises of limitless economic expansion, revitalized democracy, and even, some said, eventual escape from the body into electronic immortality. If even a fraction of these promises were true, was not war with little or no suffering also possible? The public did not have to actually believe, just suspend disbelief. Politics resembles art, especially on television.

3.

Uranium is 1.7 times as dense as lead, has exceptional tensile strength, and is pyrophoric, that is, it ignites spontaneously on impact. Once lit, it burns with such intensity that it can cut through earth, steel, or solid rock.

Uranium weapons include bunker-buster bombs, precision missiles, uranium-tipped bullets, and tanks with uranium shielding—essential tools of high-tech war.

4.

Kitsch distracts, which is why it is so useful in the entertainment industry and politics.

Some kitsch is ineptly crafted "bad" art, but today the rule is impressive technical skill. Hundred-thousand-dollar fashion ads are like Andrew Wyeth paintings: their high craftsmanship and aesthetic finish project vast authority.

The term "depleted uranium" is politically useful because it implies that uranium can be denatured, made safe. However, uranium is uranium. In the earth, it consists of a mixture of three isotopes, U-234, U-235, and U-238. Of these, only U-235 is fissionable. Through a process called enrichment this isotope can be separated from others, after which it can be converted into nuclear fuel rods or used in atomic bombs.

211

The by-product of enrichment is called depleted uranium, or DU. It consists largely of U-238. Pure U-238 can be handled safely because it emits only alpha particles, which do not penetrate skin, but DU contains residues of U-234 and U-235, which give off beta particles and gamma rays. These have been linked to kidney problems, neurological disorders, leukemia and other cancers, as well as birth defects. DU sometimes also contains other highly radioactive elements, including plutonium, which can be lethal even in minute quantities.

When depleted uranium weapons explode, they produce uranium dust that drifts with wind. Particles fine enough to pass through gas mask filters can be breathed in, buried in wounds, or ingested in food or drink. The danger of radioactivity comes not only from U-234, U-235, and plutonium, but possibly from U-238 as well, because the interior of the body, unlike skin, is vulnerable to alpha radiation. However, systematic, peer-reviewed studies of the effects of exposure to DU have not been done.

6.

Will our time be remembered for kitsch? Who knows? But we can be certain that the residues of uranium weapons will last longer than memory. U-234's half-life is 248 thousand years, and U-235's is 710 million. The half-life of U-238 is 4.5 billion years, which exceeds the fossil record. Nothing that is human fades so slowly. Shakespeare, Sophocles, and the *Lotus Sutra* can't compete, but Roy Lichtenstein's *Drowning Girl* may do a bit better. One version is enamel on steel, and with any luck will endure for over a quarter of a million years.

The half-life of plutonium is a mere 24,000 years, a span of time very roughly equivalent to the known history of the visual arts.

7.

The Israelis probably employed a few uranium weapons in the 1973 Arab-Israeli War, however their first significant use was in the Persian Gulf War in 1991, when almost 320 metric tons of depleted uranium were strewn around Iraq and Kuwait.[2]

The Gulf War lasted seven weeks, during which 148 Americans

were killed in action, and another 121 died in accidents. True, Saddam Hussein remained in power, and Iraqi casualties were in the neighborhood of 100,000, at least according to Defense Department reports at the time,[3] but the war was swift and few Americans were killed, so the promise of war without suffering appeared to be mostly realized.

During the active phase of the Gulf War, the White House and the Pentagon paid scrupulous attention to production values and public relations, and with the cooperation of the major media presented the war as a form of team sports and infotainment. Little carnage aired, but visual effects were stunning. Especially spellbinding were night shots of the bombing of Baghdad. In the green light of night vision, precision missiles drifted earthward, as slow as fireflies. The public was sold.

However, after the ceasefire, when the media lost interest in the Persian Gulf, war reaped its customary harvest. By 2002 the number of civilian dead in Iraq may have been a million, or even more.[4] This bears comparison with Vietnam, where somewhere between 500,000 and 2,000,000 civilians died.

As disasters piled up in Iraq, Gulf War veterans from the United States, Australia, Canada, and Britain reported a range of disturbing symptoms. Among them were nausea, loss of body hair, short-term memory problems, rashes, debilitating fatigue, eye problems, and joint and muscle pain. Cancers and leukemia began to appear, and deaths followed. Children were born with birth defects. This complex of problems came to be known as Gulf War Syndrome.

In most cases the exact cause of Gulf War Syndrome has never been determined. Chemical weapons, vaccines, DU, oil fires, pesticides, and/or infectious disease may all be responsible. The exact role of uranium in Gulf War Syndrome remains unclear. Studies by the Uranium Medical Research Centre indicate that many veterans of the first Gulf War have high levels of uranium in their urine, and that certain problems associated with Gulf War Syndrome may be a result of ingested uranium.[5]

Of the 697,000 American troups who served in the Gulf War, by 2003 28% had sought treatment for illnesses resulting from their military service. 186,000 had sought treatment for Gulf War Syndrome.[6] Many are permanently disabled. About 10,000 have died. Considering the magnitude of suffering among Gulf War veterans and their families, Gulf War Syndrome has been grossly under-reported. As a result, the myth of high-tech war as swift and nearly victimless if only for Americans, remains intact.

8.

High kitsch typically involves virtuoso techniques, glossy surfaces, jewels, and gimmicks. Fabergé's eggs are the epitome, precious in every detail. A taste for shock came later. Dali designed ruby lips parted to reveal pearl teeth. His masterpiece of jewelry, *The Royal Heart*, is made of 60 rubies and contains a mechanism to make it beat.

What was most visionary about Dali's work after the 1930s was that transgression could answer consumer culture's need for innovation. Today kitsch provides everyone with instant transgression.

9.

728,000 tons of DU have accumulated in Department of Energy stockpiles around the U.S.[7] Weapons manufacturers can acquire the metal at almost no cost. Tungsten is an alternative to DU, and could be used to make comparably precise and hardened weapons that are not radioactive. However, tungsten would have to be imported.

10.

In Nazi Germany and the USSR many kinds of expression were suppressed and replaced by kitsch. In the United States the situation is quite different. The public has access to diverse products and sources of information, as well as to a rich variety of art and entertainment. Under these circumstances kitsch is not simply imposed, in spite of the enormous powers of government, mass media and large corporations, but is a collaborative project. The public chooses kitsch.

11.

Writing these notes, I was overcome with a sense of fatality.

The beauty of modern
Man is not in the persons but in the

214

Disastrous rhythm, the heavy and mobile masses, the dance of
the Dream-led masses down the dark mountain.

Jeffers wrote these lines in "Rearmament," which is about the approach of World War II. Like the Japanese and the Greeks, he organized experience aesthetically. His God was inhuman beauty, but he
recognized the great difficulty of assigning aesthetic qualities to contemporary experience without creating obscenities.

He built a tower by the Pacific, and his memory is associated with
that tower. I live in a beautiful part of the Oregon countryside, with
forest in every direction, but for me there is no tower. I feel very little
distance, aesthetic or otherwise, from uranium weapons. Uranium arrives invisibly, through water, air, or food, or through the bodies of organisms. I believe that I am quite safe for now, but that does not settle
the matter. Whether or not the masses are dream-led, my fate is not
separate from theirs. (If I had a choice, it would be.) What is happening today has its own terrible beauty, no doubt, but it is no dance. It
moves in evolutionary time. A slow-motion avalanche comes to mind.

Under such circumstances, what is the artist's role? I considered
tearing up this manuscript. I often reach that point when I write, and
many manuscripts have ended up in the trash. But this time, willingness to let go freed me to recognize the obvious: like nuclear
weapons, uranium weapons numb us with despair. That is part of
their power. Until we break the spell, we can't begin to do much
about the rest.

12.

The single most important reason that the American electorate has
favored the right since 1968 is not money, but narratives. The right
offers the electorate the stories that it most wants to hear. Reagan
was the master of the mode. Whether or not he actually coined for-
mulations like "morning in America," he struck a chord with people
still torn by Vietnam and distressed by the loss of traditional certain-
ties (imaginary or real). By Kundera's definition, Reagan's performance was kitsch: he was an actor who gave as many as possible what
they wanted at any price. The price was partial dismantlement of the
New Deal, massive arms buildup, atrocities in Central America, and
enormous debts. All of this took place quite openly. The public knew
what it was getting.

Warhol made silkscreens of Elvis dressed up as a cowboy, but since the late 1970s artists have not only mirrored kitsch, but produced it. Jeff Koons said, "Aesthetics on its own: I see that as a great discriminator among people, that it makes people feel unworthy to experience art."[8] He is our Fabergé, setting the jewels of mass society. Museums are no longer refuges—not that they ever entirely were. Andrew Wyeth is in the Metropolitan, and Bougeureau seems to be everywhere. At the de Young in San Francisco I encountered a Maxfield Parrish on the same wall as a Ryder seascape, which no doubt reflected some intriguing curatorial theory, but the effect was like juxtaposing Chief Joseph and a My Little Pony.

14.

There's Bambi, and there's Freddy Kruger. Kitsch can be light or dark.

15.

Since the Gulf War, the US has used uranium weapons in the Balkans, Afghanistan, and Iraq, and tested them in five states, Puerto Rico, and Okinawa. During the 1999 NATO operation in Kosovo, ten metric tons of DU were used.[9] Incidences of cancer and other illnesses among soldiers who had served as peace-keepers in the Balkans led the European Parliament to pass a resolution that called for a ban on the manufacture, testing, use, and sale of DU weapons until research on health effects had been carried out. Earlier the United Nations Human Rights Commission had passed resolutions to ban DU weapons.

In May and September 2002 Uranium Medical Research Centre teams in Afghanistan found that all randomly selected civilians near bomb sites in Jalalabad, Kabul, Tora Bora, and Mazar-e-Sharif tested positive for internal uranium contamination. The average person had uranium urine levels more than 30 times above normal, with some levels more than a hundred times normal. Many people suffered from illnesses similar to Gulf War veterans.[10]

## 16.

Most media accounts of uranium weapons focus on depleted uranium, however, nondepleted uranium can also be used to make weapons. The Pentagon claims to have used DU in Afghanistan, but independent researchers have not verified this. DU has an easily identifiable radiological signature. What researchers found instead was evidence of nondepleted uranium, which has far more serious long-term effects.[11]

## 17.

Countries that are manufacturing DU munitions or importing them from the US: Britain, France, Greece, Russia, Turkey, Bahrain, Egypt, Israel, Saudi Arabia, Kuwait, Pakistan, Thailand, North Korea, South Korea, Taiwan.

## 18.

Kitsch evolves. Today it often functions most effectively when audiences scorn it. Television viewers heap contempt on programs that they regularly watch. Both Reagan and G. W. Bush built constituencies by projecting mediocracy and encouraging the perception that they were inferior to the people that they represented.

Fear may underlie the perversity of these relationships. Most Americans know from watching television and reading newspapers that however difficult their lives, there are people in Africa, Asia, and Latin America who have it far worse, at least economically. Given the frightening economic and political possibilities that haunt the world today, the corporate system works well for most people. Even our poor are prosperous by world standards (although not by the standards of industrialized nations). To reject kitsch and the kinds of leaders who project it may be the first step out onto the slippery slope that is the world, maybe even out into post-consumer culture.

Confusion and despair are also at work. The extreme contradictions between ideals inherited from the Republic and the realities of life in a world empire favor aesthetic novocaine.

Television, computers, movies, glossy magazines, radio—arguably ours is the most art-saturated culture that has ever existed.

217

## 19.

Uranium weapons blur the sharp line that traditionally has been drawn between conventional and nuclear weapons, and prepare the public to accept low-yield nuclear weapons.

## 20.

Everything has a price, but kitsch promises that someone else will pay—losers, nature, the future, whatever. In the latest war the Iraqis were supposed to pay with oil. Friends of the president and his family would profit most, but that was nothing new: what was important was that fuel prices might come down.

## 21.

Barbie is a standard for ideal female form. The eleven installments of the "Left Behind" series, which describe the rapture and the tribulation, when the AntiChrist appears and begins his rule through the United Nations, have sold 55 million copies. Kitsch substitutes for lost universals.

## 22.

Antidotes to kitsch: high fiber cereal, peer-reviewed research on the effects of inhaled DU, and body bags. Of course, there's also high art such as *Drowning Girl*. And always there's the starry sky.

## 23.

Toystores are treasure troves. It is not that children need kitsch, or that it restores childhood, but that it embalms innocence. Today kitsch is all that keeps American innocence looking clean and fresh.

## REFERENCES AND NOTES

[1] General Wesley K. Clark, "Iraq: What Went Wrong" in *The New York Review of Books*, Vol. L, No. 16, Oct. 23, 2003. p. 54.
[2] Berrigan, Frieda, "Weapons of Mass Deception" in *In These Times*, June 20, 2003.
[3] In May, 1991, the US Defense Intelligence Agency estimated that 100,000 Iraqis had been killed in action. Over the years that number has been challenged, most dramatically by John Heidenreich (*Jane's Defense Weekly*, March 13, 1993, Vol. 19, No. 11, p. 5), who calculated that only 1,500 soldiers had been killed, and fewer than 100 civilians. Other estimates vary widely.
[4] Probably this estimate is conservative. Saddam Hussein suppressed the revolt of the Shiites and Kurds, which resulted in any-

where from 50,000 to 200,000 deaths. UNICEF estimated that between 1991 and 1998 there had been 500,000 excess deaths among children under the age of 5. (see UNICEF, *Results of the 1999 Iraq Child and Maternal Mortality Surveys*). Most of these deaths were so clearly due to sanctions that in 1998 Denis Halliday, head of UN humanitarian operations in Iraq, quit in protest. I can find no estimates on deaths of older children and adults. No comprehensive survey of the humanitarian situation in Iraq was conducted after 1999, but sanctions were not lifted until after the 2003 war.

[5] Uranium Medical Research Centre, umrc.net/umrcResearch.asp

[6] Berrigan, Frieda. Ibid.

[7] Berrigan, Frieda. Ibid.

[8] Koons, Jeff, "Jeff Koons Interviewed by David Sylvester" in Jeff Koons: *Easyfun-Etherial*. (Berlin, Deutsche Guggenheim, 2000) p. 36.

[9] Berrigan, Frieda, ibid.

[10] Kirby, Alex, "Afghans' Uranium Levels Spark Alert", BBC News, world edition, May 22, 2003.

[11] Kirby, Alex. Ibid.

*Nominated by Northwest Review*

# HUNTERS

fiction by JOHN FULTON

from THE SOUTHERN REVIEW

$K$ATE ANSWERED HIS PERSONAL AD in late summer soon after she'd been told for the second time that she was dying. She had always thought of herself as shy, not the type even to peruse such ads. But the news had been jolting, if not altogether unexpected, and had allowed her to act outside her old ideas of herself.

The first time her doctor told her she would die had been two years before. The cancer had started in her left breast and moved to her brain. She'd had a mastectomy and undergone a full course of chemotherapy to no effect. A divorcée, she was close to only a few people: her sixteen-year-old daughter, Melissa, her widowed mother, who was now dead, and one good woman friend, all of whom she'd told. She'd worried about what to do with Melissa, then fourteen, whose father had been out of touch since he'd left them years before. And then, after worrying, weeping, raging, and undergoing the storm of insanity that, by all reports, was supposed to end in acceptance, she learned that her cancer had mysteriously retreated and that she would live. Her doctors hesitated to use the word "cured." Cancers such as hers were rarely, if ever, cured. And yet they could find no signs of carcinoma cells in her system. She returned to work, got her hair done, went on shopping sprees, and thought about the possibility of reconstructive surgery for her left breast. Even something like a nipple, her plastic surgeon had informed her, could be convincingly improvised. In trying to explain her restored health to her daughter, her coworkers, and her friends, she could find no other word than "cured." And now, once again, the doctors were telling her she had

220

tumors about the size of a pea in her liver and spine. She would die in a matter of months.

The news silenced Kate. This time, she told no one.

She selected his ad because of its unthreatening tone. Other ads had intimidated her with their loud enthusiasm and confidence: "young vital fifty-something looking for lady with love for life." Still others sounded sleazy—"Master in need of pet"—or psychotic, even murderous: "Quiet, mysterious Lone Ranger looking for that special horse to ride into the night." By contrast, his sounded distinctly meek: "Like books and munching popcorn in front of TV." He tended towards "shyness with a goofy edge." He sought "sex, but more, too. Tenderness without attachments." That caught her eye. She wanted sex. She wanted tenderness "without attachments." In the years since her diagnosis, she'd wanted to keep her maimed body to herself. Now a feeling of bodily coldness and desolation had come over her, and she wanted to be brought back to life. She wanted to be touched—maybe for one night, one week, one month.

Kate's daughter heard his message on the answering machine first. "There's a guy on the machine for you," she said when Kate got home from work. Melissa stood next to her in the kitchen while she played it. "Kate," a heavy male voice said, "Charles here. I look forward to meeting you. Gotta say I'm just a bit nervous. I don't know about you, but I've never done this before. Not to say that I don't want to. I do. I'm going on, aren't I? Sorry. You've got other messages to hear, I'm sure." He paused and Melissa laughed. Kate wasn't sure what she thought of this first impression of him, though she liked the fact that he was obviously afraid; his voice was nearly trembling. "I guess I should tell you what I look like. I'm tall and have a moustache. See you on Saturday."

"A moustache?" Melissa smiled suggestively. "I didn't know you were looking for someone."

"I'm not," Kate said. Her daughter had the wrong idea. She'd assumed that Kate was searching for a companion, was healing and moving on with what would be a long life. It wasn't fair to leave her with false impressions, but Kate couldn't go through all the tears again. She wanted her privacy for now. "Don't, please, get any ideas."

"No ideas," Melissa said, laughing. "I think it's great. I think it's what you should be doing."

Kate hardly expected to be afraid. She took every precaution. She'd chosen a popular coffee shop, often crowded on Saturday afternoons, which seemed like the safest time to meet a stranger. Ann Arbor was hardly a dangerous town. It was clean and wealthy and civic minded, she reminded herself. It was an especially hot September day, over ninety degrees, but the air conditioning in the café was crisp and bracing. Kate selected a table in a sunny corner, beside two elderly women wearing pastel sweat suits and gleaming white orthopedic tennis shoes; they made Kate feel still safer. One of the silver-haired women was baby-sitting an infant and kept her hand on the baby carriage, now and then looking down into it with a clownish face. Students sat at other tables and read books. A toddler ran past Kate, its father in pursuit.

She heard him before she saw him. "Are you Kate?"

She stood up, and he presented her so quickly with a red carnation that it startled her—the redness of it, the sudden, bright presence of it in her hand—and she giggled.

"I'm Charles," he said. He wore nice slacks, a button-up shirt, and a blazer; and he was suffering—his forehead glistened—from the extremely hot day. His face was thin, his bony nose and cheekbones complex and not immediately attractive. But it was his hair that surprised her most. Thick, gray, nicely combed: it was the hair of a pleasant, not unattractive older man, a man in his fifties, as his ad had said. Kate hadn't dated for more than six years; her divorce and then her illness had made sure of that. And now, at the age of forty-five, she was shocked to think that this middle-aged man might be her romantic prospect.

When they sat down, Kate noticed the rapid thudding of her heart. She picked up her coffee and watched it tremble in her hand before she took a sip. For some reason, the table was shuddering beneath her. "I'm sorry," Charles said, putting a hand on his knee to stop it from jiggling. "I'm terrible at handling my nerves. I'm no good at meeting people. It's not one of my skills." He took a folded white handkerchief from his back pocket and neatly wiped the sweat from his forehead.

His obvious fear assured Kate that he was harmless and maybe even kind. "I meant to say thank you for the flower." She looked down at the wilted carnation.

"It's not very original of me."

When she picked her coffee up now, her hand was steady. Clearly one of them needed to be calmer. "I liked what you said in your ad about tenderness," Kate said. "That's why I called."

222

"I'm not usually this adventurous." He looked over his shoulder and then at her again. "I'm still getting over a divorce. I guess that's why I'm so jittery about all this."

Things weren't going well, Kate knew. And for some reason, she wanted them to go well with this nervous man, and so she continued to be brave, to say what she was thinking. "'Tenderness without attachments.' That sounded nice. None of the other ads talked about that. I thought that was original."

He wiped his forehead with his handkerchief again. "I just don't want anything serious. But I don't want it to feel, you know, like just an exchange of . . . of . . ."

"Bodies?" Kate said. He sat back in his chair, as if struck, and she felt her face deepen in color. The thought that they were here, in large part, for the prospect of sex was out on the table now. It was a bold and raw motive, for which neither of them, middle-aged and awkward, seemed well suited. But the awkwardness and shame were refreshing, too; Kate hadn't blushed in years.

"I guess," he said. He patted his moustache gently, as if drawing composure from it. "Not that we have to ever get there. We might just become friends. We might just enjoy each other's company."

"Sure," she said, though in fact she felt an unexpected pang of rejection. Was this nervous man already running from her bed?

She changed the subject then, telling him about her job at the bank as a loan officer, a serious job that had always suited her rather too serious character; her love for fresh food and cooking; her sixteen-year-old daughter, who right now was a little too absorbed in her boyfriend. "I wish my kid would fall in love," Charles said, smiling. "He's angry. His mother gave him up when she gave me up. I understand the anger. I'm angry, too. But there's something mean in him that I'd never seen before this." Ryan, Charles's son, had a mohawk that changed colors—purple, yellow, blue—at least once a month and a lizard tattoo on his forearm. Charles owned an office furniture and supply store. "It sounds boring, I know. But I actually sort of enjoy it."

It did sound boring to Kate, who was much more interested to learn that Charles enjoyed hunting. It hardly seemed like something this concerned father and furniture salesman would do. "You kill things?" Kate asked. "You enjoy it?"

He confessed that he did, though he didn't hunt large game.

223

"Deer and elk are beautiful animals and too much of a mess. Field dressing a deer can take the better part of a morning."

"Field dressing?" she asked.

"Gutting them, removing the entrails. You need to do that soon after a kill, before you cure and slaughter it. It's a real mess. I used to hunt large game as a boy with my dad. It's not for me anymore." He shook his head in a way that allowed Kate to picture this mess: the blood, the entrails, the carcass. "I just hunt upland birds now; pheasant, woodcocks, grouse. It's not so much the killing as it is the stalk, the chase. Being out in the open air, seeing the land."

"But you do kill them?"

He nodded. "I suppose you're against that sort of thing."

Kate thought about it for a moment. "Not really. Though I'd say I'm not for it either. I find it odd."

Two hours later, when they walked out of the café, a hot wind was blowing down Washington Street and the concrete beneath her felt as if it were baking through her thin-soled shoes. She felt light headed, buzzed from three cups of coffee, and nervous about what would happen next, how they'd say good-bye. Would they kiss? She couldn't imagine it and was relieved when he reached out with his sweaty hand and shook hers softly. "I enjoyed meeting you," he said. A train of running children shot between them and they both took a step back. She half thought he'd turn away then and walk off, and she'd have to wonder why he put her through two hours of conversation about his divorce, his son, about field dressing and slaughtering deer. But then he asked her if he could call again and she couldn't— as hard as she tried—suppress a smile and the obvious eagerness in her voice when she said, "I'd like that."

Kate didn't feel sick yet. She'd felt healthy now for months, light of body, energetic, strong. She tried not to think of the fatigue and pain to come. But the week the heat wave lifted and the first cooler days of fall arrived, Kate succumbed to fear. She'd been approving a loan for a pregnant couple when it happened. The woman wore a purple maternity dress that said "Mommy" at the place where her belly showed most. She carried her weight with an intimidating, ungraceful physicality, and her face glowed with acne and oil and a smile that was almost aggressive. The woman's scent of flowers and sweat filled Kate's small office, the air suddenly feeling close and tropical. She kept saying "we" in a way that left Kate feeling bereft and excluded. "*We're* looking forward to our first home. This is just what *we* need right now." The woman looked down at the roundness where she had just placed her hands. "Four more months," she said. The questions came to Kate spontaneously. Would she be bedridden by then? Would she be gone? Could she already feel the beginning of fatigue? Would the symptoms she'd experienced last time—the headaches, the facial paralysis, the double vision—begin that very day?

Claiming illness, she left work early that afternoon only to discover Melissa and Mark in her bathroom. The shower had been on, which was no doubt why they hadn't heard Kate climbing the stairs. When she walked into her room, Kate saw steam curling out the open bathroom door before she saw her sixteen-year-old daughter, naked save for the pink strip of her Calvin Klein panties, balancing on her knees and giving pleasure with too much skill, too much expertise, to her standing boyfriend. She took it in for a moment: the bodies moving together in practiced motion, the flayed brown and white of tan lines, her daughter's breasts, mouth, and hands, the curve of her back. "Melissa," Kate said.

Melissa stopped and Mark grabbed his crotch and turned his shuddering backside to Kate. "Mom!" Melissa's naked body lunged at the door and slammed it in Kate's face. "I can't believe you, Mom!"

"Put your clothes on now!" Kate shouted at the door.

"We can't," Melissa said. "Our clothes are all out there."

Kate turned then and noticed the storm-strewn boxer shorts, Levis, soiled white socks; Melissa's blouse and bra, even her pink Keds. Why were Melissa's shoes on Kate's bed? She picked them up, tossed them to the floor, and then started crying. She hardly knew why, though it had something to do with the pregnant woman and the surprise of her daughter, her body so frighteningly womanly, full in the hips and breasts, more beautiful than Kate had ever been, engaged, absorbed in what Kate could only think of now as an adult activity. Her loss of control left her feeling even angrier at Melissa. "I want to talk to you both downstairs in five minutes!" she shouted.

After doing her best to cover up all signs of tears, Kate sat across from Melissa and Mark in the living room. They had a messy, postsex look about them, their hair tousled and their clothes, if secure and in place, somehow looser on their bodies. "I don't know what to say," Kate began.

"We're being careful," Melissa said. "I'm on the pill, Mom. I've had my first pelvic exam. We've both been tested. I'm doing everything I should be doing."

"You were in *my* bathroom," Kate said. These words made Mark look down at the floor.

"You have the large shower," Melissa said. "We were going to clean things up. You weren't supposed to be home yet."

"Your clothes were all over *my* bed. Your shoes were on *my* bed."

Melissa smirked and flashed her blue eyes at Kate. This was her most charming and practiced gesture, and though it usually made Kate fall instantly in love with her daughter, she resisted it now. "Well," Melissa said, "we were in a hurry."

Kate felt her face go red. "You should have been studying."

"We still have time to study," Melissa said.

"You need all the time you can get. You have to apply for college and prepare for the college boards."

"That's next year," Melissa said.

Kate took a deep breath. She was about to do something she had been afraid to do for months. "I don't think what you did was wrong. I'm more concerned about the irresponsibility of neglecting the rest of life so that you could do . . ." Kate couldn't name what they'd done, nor could she keep pretending to herself that it didn't bother her. How could her sixteen-year-old already take on this responsibility? How could she lie on her back in a doctor's office with her legs in stirrups so that she could, as safely as possible, give herself to a boy? A boy who made her lose so much presence of mind that she would throw her dirty shoes on her mother's bed, use her shower, and maybe even afterwards use her bed. Kate had terrifying visions of what would become of these two after she was gone. They'd end up in ten months with a baby and stuck in subsidized housing somewhere. It was possible. But what frightened Kate most was the fact that she herself was responsible for pushing these kids—and they certainly were no more than kids—into each other's arms with her own desperation, her own intensity.

Two years before, when Kate thought she was dying for the first time, she'd panicked. She couldn't sleep. She couldn't stand the aloneness of it, the waiting, the nights of insomnia. Kate clung to Melissa and made her go everywhere with her—the doctor's office, the grocery store, the post office, the accountant's. It didn't take long for Melissa to disappear. She joined the swim team, the debate club, and the school newspaper. In the meantime, Kate kept dying. She suffered from headaches, double vision, loss of balance so extreme that she'd have to lean against the nearest wall to stay upright. Kate saw Melissa only in the late evenings when she'd sit at the kitchen table, her hair stringy from chlorine, wolfing down cereal, toast, and cookies. And so when Kate woke at night and the hours alone in the dark became intolerable, she walked down the hallway to her daughter's room, gently moved aside the large stuffed bear her then fourteen-year-old child slept with, and got into her bed. She tried not to cry, but failed. Melissa said nothing. She stiffened and moved to the edge of her narrow bed. At first light, Kate quietly got up and returned to her room.

Kate slept with her daughter as often as three times a week. She slept with her until one night she opened the door and saw in the dimness a boy next to Melissa. She had met Mark only once before then and knew that he was on the swim team and played tenor saxophone for Central High's jazz ensemble. His thick curly hair was on the pillow, his muscular back was turned to her, and his bare arm was wrapped around Melissa, protecting her from her sick mother.

After that, Kate stayed away from her daughter's room. She might have put an end to Mark's sleepovers if she hadn't been sick and, later, if Melissa and Mark hadn't cooled off soon after the cancer had disappeared. Mark no longer slept over, as far as Kate knew. But her cancer was back, and she could only expect the worst when her daughter found out. So she was finally going to put her foot down, never mind the fact that what bothered her most was not so much their having sex—she had assumed before this afternoon that they'd been having sex—as her having seen it, and having seen Melissa's dirty tennis shoes—that image returned to her and made her wince—on her clean bed. Thrown, tossed with no concern whatever for her mother. "You two need to see less of each other," she said. "It would be better for both of you. You can go out on Friday and Saturday nights. But weekday afternoons and nights are off limits. Got it?"

Melissa looked at Kate with childish fury. "No," she said.

"Don't say no to me." Kate hardly recognized herself. She'd always been tolerant and open with her daughter. She'd always laid out options, pros and cons, and let her daughter make her own decisions.

Melissa shook her head. "No. I'm saying no. We're not going to do it." She stood, took Mark forcefully by the hand, and led him up to her bedroom, where she slammed the door. Kate should have done

227

something. She should have stood at the foot of the stairs and yelled. She should have gone up there and shouted through the door. But she was too tired to go on playing the role of parent. In any case, she wouldn't be a parent much longer.

Her second meeting with Charles took place at 7 A.M. at a small restaurant across from the university hospital's cancer center, where, among other procedures, she'd had her mammogram done more than six times in one sitting. Kate had wanted to suggest another breakfast place, but she kept quiet. She didn't want to have to explain herself. Not yet. A line of scarlet sunrise had just begun to wipe out the last few morning stars when they stepped out of the cold. All the same, waiting to be seated, Kate felt the presence of the black glass façade across the street and couldn't help remembering the pink walls of the waiting booth where she'd spent almost eight hours with plastic pads stuck to her breasts. Only a floor above the mammogram clinic, she would lie on her back some weeks later while a physician's assistant slid a needle deep between two upper lumbar to draw out the spinal fluid in which, it turned out, carcinoma cells were actively dividing. She was told to expect double vision, speech impairment, dizziness, partial paralysis, and any number of random inexplicable sensations due to the tumor that was growing in her brain. And then there was the chemotherapy, the woman named Meg who'd died in the waiting room while reading *Vogue*. It was hardly an appropriate magazine for a cancer ward, Kate had been thinking, when Meg slumped over in her chair and stopped breathing. Kate was amazed at her calm as she broke Meg's fall, sat her upright, and held her in her chair until someone arrived and took her away.

Once she and Charles sat across from each other in a booth, she was able to forget the hospital. A sheet of Levolor-sliced sun fell over their table, and billows of steam rose from their coffee cups in the brightness. He was jittery, tapping his fingers against his cup then running them through his hair. She was already getting used to the rather extreme angularity of his face and finding it vaguely attractive. His blue eyes she noticed for the first time—faint, shallow—after the waitress set their menus down. "Aren't you nervous?" he asked.

She wasn't and she told him so.

"I am," he said, and she could hear it in his voice. "Doesn't it bother you to see a grown man afraid?"

"Apparently not." She laughed, reached across the table and took his hand for the first time. But when he didn't loosen to her touch, she let him go.

The next week, she dropped into his office furniture store just before closing time. Charles seemed to have a great deal more courage, walking briskly through the endless rows of desks, filing cabinets, and computer tables to meet her. "Welcome," he said, smiling, at ease in his suit and tie. He led her around and made her sit in multiple styles of waiting room chairs and ergonomically designed stools for typists and receptionists. The repetition and sameness of objects—chair after chair after chair—spooked her a little. "You think it's terrible," he said. "What I do."

She denied it at first. Then said, "It does seem a little . . . lonely. All these human objects without the humans."

"You want to see lonely?" he said. He walked her into the back: a gray, dimly lit storage facility, in the middle of which stood a forklift surrounded by towers of boxes. The place was remarkably vacant of warmth and life, and a soft roar of wind and emptiness seemed to hum at its center.

She admired his comfort here, his sense of dominion. "I don't mind it. It's quiet. It's like going to the park. It's an escape."

Later that week, they went to the arboretum, where the trees had begun to turn and where they stood beside a glassy, shallow stretch of the Huron river, the pink, unmarked evening sky laid out over its mirror. Two hippie kids in loose clothing sat on a log, holding each other, kissing, giggling. A muddy-colored dog with a red handkerchief knotted around its neck leapt into the river and began drinking. When Kate took Charles's hand and pulled herself close to him, he was trembling. And somehow, just after Kate kissed his cheek lightly, she caught it, too; a rush of fear shook her. She was breathing shallowly when Charles bent down and kissed her on the lips. "I hope that was all right," he said.

When she nodded, he seemed immensely relieved, his step lighter now as they walked hand in hand, swinging their linked arms, up a dirt path until they came to a clearing in the trees. Startled, a deer sprinted through the high grass, dove into the trees, and was gone. In the orange evening light, Charles looked larger, less meek, and Kate couldn't help wondering what this gentle man would be like with a gun. "What's it like to kill something?" she asked.

"You might not like me as much if I told you the truth."

Kate laughed and squeezed his hand. "I promise I'll still like you."

"Ok," Charles said. "It's thrilling. It's why you go out there. It's the fun part."

"It's fun to kill?" If she didn't like him less, it still wasn't the most pleasant answer, nor one she understood.

"Perhaps 'fun' isn't exactly the right word."

On their walk back, the temperature dropped sharply and Kate was shivering so violently that she had to wonder if her vulnerability to the cold had to do with her illness. Was she weaker than she'd suspected? When they parked in front of Kate's house, she kissed him once, but pulled away when he wanted to continue. "I should tell you something," she said, still shivering. The dark inside the car, the fact that she could see only the outline of his face, made it easier to lie to him. "I'm recovering from cancer. Breast," she said, stopping so that odd word stood alone. "Recovered, I mean. I wouldn't mention it, but I need to tell you that I have a scar."

"A scar?" he said.

"I had a mastectomy. My left breast." She hated the feeling of shame that accompanied what she had just said. It was merely a fact and she should have had the presence of mind to treat it as such.

There was a pause before he said, "I'm sorry."

Kate couldn't see the expression on his face, but she sensed that something was different between them. An ease, an excitement was gone. "Does that change things?" she asked.

Again, he took time in answering. "I don't think so."

"You don't think so?" The anger in her voice half surprised her. She didn't know him well enough to be angry with him.

"It's just that . . ." He stopped himself and reformulated his thought. "This was supposed to be a light thing. No commitment. Nothing serious."

"What does this have to do with commitment?"

"I don't know," he said. Then he bumbled out, "It seems serious. It seems . . ."

"All right," she said. She got out of his car, and before she'd closed the door of her house behind her, she heard him say, "I'll call you."

Inside, she found Melissa and Mark on the couch watching a movie in the dark. It was a school night, and they were openly defying the rule she'd set down. She turned the lights on and they looked at her, squinting in the brightness. "Mark has to leave now." Her anger was too pronounced, too obviously out of proportion. And their response to it was to stay frozen in each other's arms. Kate

230

wanted to throw something at them—a shoe, a book, even her purse would have worked. "I said now," Kate said. Mark finally sat up and rushed to put his shoes on.

"Did something happen on your date?" Melissa asked.

"I didn't have a date."

She expected a fight from Melissa. But instead her daughter merely sat up slowly and kept her eyes cautiously on Kate.

Charles called all week and left messages on the answering machine that Kate tried her best to ignore. He was blunt. He stuttered and repeated himself. He admitted that he'd been thinking of her. He regretted the words he'd spoken that night. "I'm calling from the back of the store," he said in one message. "From the warehouse phone. You were right. It is lonely back here." In another message, he became almost desperate. "I guess I just miss you. I hope I'm not saying too much. I realize that this is just an answering machine. I realize that I'm begging." He sounded as hurt and alone as she had felt in the car that night. Nonetheless, she was done with him, until he made what was obviously his final call. "I'm sorry things didn't work out," he said. She picked up the phone and tried her best to stop him from repeatedly apologizing. "OK, Charles," she said. "Apology accepted."

He wanted to see her as soon as possible. That afternoon he and his son, Ryan, had planned to shoot skeet at the gun club. And so Kate ended up on the edge of town shouldering a rifle for the first time in her life and wearing wax earplugs as she blasted away at a "clay pigeon," a little black disk, and tried to follow the instructions Charles shouted out to her to lead the pigeon by at least a foot. The gun club was in the center of a huge abandoned field, which looked dead, yellow, and already ravaged by winter. It was a gray day, the air like white smoke, and Kate was surprised by the pleasing and substantial weight of the weapon in her hands, the delicious, earthy odors of cordite and gunpowder after each blast, the sense—there was no mistaking it—of power and control the weapon gave her when she finally obliterated her target. She did so twice, then three times, awed as the disk disintegrated in the air. Behind her, a small boy of about ten, who wore a camouflage baseball cap and chewed a huge wad of pink bubble gum, pressed a button that released the pigeon every time she shouted out the word "Pull!" She handed the rifle, its barrel as hot as a stove top, to Charles and stood behind him—"Always stand behind the shooter," he'd told her earlier in a grave voice—and watched now as he meticulously hit pigeon after pigeon. She hadn't anticipated her excitement at seeing Charles's skill with a rifle, the quickness with which he trained the barrel on the target and destroyed it. His arms seemed thicker, more powerful, his shoulders broader. There was no sign of weakness, of hesistancy or doubt, and she was awed to see this unexpected competence in a man who, as she was seeing that afternoon, could barely keep his own son in check.

Ryan was a tall kid with deep-set eyes that seemed on the edge of rage every time he looked at Kate. His mohawk, high and stiff and dyed salmon pink, and his multiply pierced ears, lined with studs and hoops, made him seem menacing, especially when he took the shotgun in hand. On the way out to the club, when Charles had stopped for gas and left Kate and Ryan in the car alone, the boy had resisted her every attempt at conversation, and then, after she had given up, he smiled at her and said, "Are you fucking my dad yet?"

"I'm not going to answer that question."

"None of my business, right?" he said. "You've probably already seen that he's a wimp. He lets people do whatever they want to him. He just takes it."

"I'm not that kind of person," Kate said.

Ryan nodded. "Sure you're not."

Whenever Ryan missed his target that afternoon, he cringed and swore, sometimes under his breath, though more often out loud. "Fuck me," he half shouted once, to which Charles merely responded with a warning glance. Kate would have sent him to the car at the very least. Ryan had certainly been right about his father. He did seem willing to take just about anything.

Kate was relieved when they dropped Ryan off at home later that night and went out to a pleasant dinner. They ordered a bottle of wine. When late in the meal Charles sighed and said, "I'm too easy on Ryan. I let him get away with everything," Kate lied.

"I'm not so sure that's wrong," Kate said. "Every kid needs a different approach."

He shook his head. "My motives aren't that noble. I just want him to like me again."

Somehow they'd joined hands across the table. Kate felt terrible for this worried father, this man who just wanted to be liked, and her pity quickly transformed into attraction. She knew already that she wanted to sleep with him that night. She was blushing when she stuttered out an invitation. "You can say no," she added.

But he didn't say no. Kate hardly knew how she'd imagined herself behaving then, though she'd hoped that passion and desire would take over, that she'd know what to do. Instead, she and Charles waited for the bill in utter silence, which persisted as they drove toward Kate's place, the black trees and proper Victorian homes rising on either side of them in the dark. "Let's talk," Kate said.

"OK," Charles said. But they didn't say another word until they stood facing each other on either side of Kate's bed. For a change, Kate was relieved that Melissa had once again defied her and was out that night. "We don't have to do this," Kate said.

"I want to," he said, though he didn't sound as if he did.

When she came out of the bathroom wearing a man's white T-shirt that fell to her thighs, she didn't feel at all attractive. Charles sat on the edge of the bed in his tank top and boxer shorts, his legs skinnier, paler, more covered in thick, dark hair than she'd imagined. His arms were crossed, as if protecting himself from her. "I don't care about your scar," he said.

Kate knew he'd meant to say something that would sound nicer, more romantic. "I want to keep this on," she said, pointing to her shirt.

In the dark, everything became a little easier. He began to kiss her—her face, her neck, her arms—all the while carefully avoiding the place of her absent breast. His moustache tickled a little. She found his erection without meaning to. It was just suddenly there in her hand, and she couldn't help but think of the shotgun she'd been handling earlier that day. Guns and penises. She let out a silly, adolescent laugh. "Is something wrong?" he asked.

"I haven't done this in so long." And now that she held him, she knew she needed to do something. She tried the very act she'd seen her daughter perform only weeks before, but she was indelicate and Charles let out a short cry of pain and then began to laugh himself.

"Is this all right?" he asked when he finally mounted her.

Her left thigh began cramping, but she nodded as the pain gathered into a solid, dense ball. "It's all right," she said. His caution, his concern moved her. If not passionate, it was deeply tender, just as he had promised, and she lifted herself a little to kiss his shoulders, his neck and cheeks. It took him a while—Kate could have hoped for a briefer first time—but as soon as he was finished, he rolled over and said, "You didn't, did you?"

"I will next time."

"I'm sorry."

"Don't be. It was . . ." She paused, looking for a word, and when she finally said it, the fullness and enthusiasm in her voice embarrassed her: "Lovely." She felt a deep and heavy laziness of body. Their legs were tangled. Off in the darkness beside her, the fingers of her hand caressed Charles's neck. She had forgotten for a moment what was happening to her. She was dying, she remembered now. Again. For the second time. And for some reason, it was easy to know. She wasn't afraid, even as she was certain that the fear would return soon. For now she lay next to a man who must have been as spent and physically oblivious as she since he let out an enormous, accidental belch. "I'm sorry," he said.

Half asleep, Kate giggled lazily. "I'm happy," she said.

The next morning, she was dizzy and experiencing double vision. In her bathroom mirror, she saw that her left eye had fallen towards the lower outside corner of her socket. She looked monstrous, and she wanted Charles, who lay slumbering in her bed, out of the house. When she prodded him awake, he rolled over and smiled at her, seeming to expect the kisses and friendliness of a lover. His breath was less than pleasant and his hair was lopsided. She kept a hand over her eye, and when he asked her about it, she said something about an eye infection and eye drops that he didn't question. "I've got to get to work," she said, after which she stood by him while he dressed.

"Is something wrong?" he asked, standing out on the porch in a warmish rainy morning. One of his shoes was still untied and his shirt was partially untucked. He waited in the light drizzle until Kate gave him a peck on the cheek. "Something's wrong," he said. "Tell me what's wrong."

"I'll call you," she said, and then closed the door.

Kate stayed home from work for the next few days. And with the house empty, she thought of Charles more than she wanted to: his ease with a rifle, his pale, awkward nakedness, his postcoital belch, his laughter and patience in her bed. He left four messages on the machine, though she didn't call him until two days later. It was three in the morning, and she'd woken with a dull throbbing pressure in her head that verged on pain. She was hot and opened her windows, but the breeze moving in the curtain sent shadows rushing through the dark of her room—walls of blackness falling on top of her. "Kate," he said sleepily.

"Would you consider coming over here . . . now?"

He was in her bed in fewer than twenty minutes. She could only cuddle that night, and he seemed more than happy to oblige her. "This isn't going to be serious, right?" she asked.

He kissed her ear. "OK."

"It will be pleasant. It will go until one of us says enough," she said.

He moved in closer, sealing their bodies together. "Sure. I mean, unless we decide otherwise."

"I'm pretty sure that I won't decide otherwise."

"That's fine," Charles said.

In subsequent nights, they returned to their lovemaking, vigorous, athletic, more skilled and certain. They did everything they could think of with the eagerness of discovery and the fumbling skill of those who'd done it before. Charles took her from behind with an enthusiastic brutishness—his arm hooked around her neck and his pelvis pounding into her—that left her feeling pleasantly ravished. Kate remembered how to come, straddling Charles and using her thigh muscles to focus on the pleasure. Charles became, at times, almost too fearless, letting out loud howls so that Kate put a hand over his mouth and whispered, "My daughter will hear." In moments of physical exuberance, Charles tried to lift her shirt, but she grabbed his arm forcefully and pushed it back down.

After a week or so of adventurous nights together, Kate was exhausted. Her body felt leaden, fatigued, not exactly sick, but not well either. She wanted closeness, not pleasure, which Charles sensed easily. He spooned her, the weight of his arm folded over her—a good, blanketing weight—and fell asleep more often than not hours before Kate, who lay awake watching the lunar sweep of headlights pass through the room. Charles spoke out of his dreams, which were sometimes pleasant, as when he asked repeatedly for more gravy, please. "Delicious," he would say. And sometimes terrifying. "Stay away!" he shouted one night. "Away! Away!" When she woke him, he looked at her; and she saw the terror pass from his face as soon as he recognized her. "Love," he said sleepily, and then held on to her for a desperate and needy moment before he fell back asleep.

Towards the end of October, Kate arrived home from work one afternoon to find her daughter in tears at the kitchen table. Sitting across from her, Mark looked pale and unwell, and Kate assumed that he had finally broken her daughter's heart. Kate had had a good day and was hardly prepared to deal with this sadness. She'd felt strong, invigorated all through this sunny, slightly chilly afternoon. It was days before Halloween, and at lunch she had seen a group of young schoolchildren dressed as witches and vampires grasping a rope as their teachers herded them safely across Huron Street. Walking home, she took note of the fat pumpkins with bare-toothed grins sitting on porch steps and thought of this holiday that contemplated darkness and fear and death. She'd felt both aware of and pleasantly removed from what was about to happen to her. And now, facing her weeping daughter, she was about to rush upstairs and leave the kids to themselves when Melissa lifted an open letter from the table. "You didn't tell me. You didn't say anything."

"Is that my mail?" Kate asked, setting her briefcase down. From the torn envelope on the table, Kate knew it must be a letter from the hospice where she had already decided she would die, in part to give Melissa her own safe space at home.

"You lied."

"I think Mark should go home," Kate said calmly. "I think you and I need to talk."

"He's not going." Kate's daughter reached over and grasped Mark's hand.

Mark looked shaken, uncertain. He wore a Mountain Dew T-shirt, a new pair of bright blue Nike running shoes, and the same sort of blue sweat pants that Melissa was wearing. They had just returned from swimteam practice and had that sallow, washed-out look of kids who've been in water for hours. A box of Raisin Bran was out on the table and they'd no doubt eaten two or three bowls before Melissa had opened the letter. This time of the afternoon, with the kids gorging on toast and cereal, then sitting in front of the TV or working on homework, could be Kate's favorite part of the day. She enjoyed the house most when they were there, when she felt their presence, which was another reason she never should have put her foot down weeks before. "Should I go, Mrs. Harrison?" Mark asked.

"He's staying," Melissa said again.

"He might want to go," Kate said.

Mark looked timidly over at Melissa. "Maybe I should go." Melissa shook her head and pulled him so forcefully towards her that Mark had to scoot his chair over. "I think I should go."

"Please just . . . ," Melissa growled, unable to finish her sentence.

Kate sat down at the table. "I didn't tell you because I needed some privacy for a while. I needed to get used to it again."

"How long?" Melissa asked.

"Maybe three months. Maybe six. The doctors can't be certain."

"You don't look so sick," Melissa said suspiciously.

"I don't feel very sick. Yet."

"Maybe it won't happen. It didn't happen last time."

"Maybe."

Sitting beside Melissa, Mark seemed to squirm in his chair. He hardly had freedom to move with Melissa clinging to him, and Kate saw how intensely he wanted to escape. She sensed that this second occasion of her dying might be too much for him. She hardly knew if it was a selfish and calculating impulse or true desperation, the better motive by far, that made her say, "You can spend as much time with Mark as you like, Melissa. He can even sleep over now and then. I just ask that you not disappear this time."

Melissa's gaze was cool and unchanged. "You lied to me."

And because Kate couldn't fight, especially over this, she got up and left the room.

Kate was not at all surprised when her daughter disappeared after that. She came home from school late and left first thing in the morning, hopping into Mark's car. She had stopped talking to Kate, or only talked to her to say the most prosaic things. "Got to go. Be home later." Kate could do nothing but watch as her daughter grew distant, watch and hope that Melissa's fury would subside.

It was around this time that Kate began testing Charles, though she hardly knew what she was testing him for. One morning when they woke up together, Kate kissed him and then asked him to shave his moustache. "I'd like to see you without it. It tickles a little."

He touched it contemplatively before he went into her bathroom. After a moment, she heard his electric razor. When he came back out, his face was leaner than she'd expected, though she knew she'd get used to it. What surprised her even more was how willingly, how quickly he'd done as she asked.

She made other requests, too. She asked him to part his hair on the left side rather than in the middle, and he did it. She asked him to wear red—the color that suited him best—more often and discouraged him from ever wearing gray shirts, which washed him out. She woke him at two, three, four in the morning and made him go home without explaining herself. She called him at the same hours and asked him if he would come over and get into bed with her. He came and he left when she asked. And though she wasn't always sure why she made her requests, she was sure that Ryan had been right about her. She was taking advantage of Charles. She was pushing him around.

In the last weekend of October, Charles took Kate hunting. He'd proposed that she hike with him through the woods while he hunted, and been surprised when she insisted on participating. She wrote a note to Melissa, whom she hadn't talked to in days. "Gone hunting. Will return on Sunday." Kate couldn't help feeling startled by the note even as she wrote it: how odd, how unlike herself it sounded. Would Melissa laugh when she read it? Would she worry?

Charles picked her up at five on Saturday morning in what he called his "rig": a huge pickup truck with a camper on the back. It was as dark as night out and freezing, and Kate felt frail and groggy as she locked the front door and pushed herself through the cold air. The truck was warm and smelled of boot leather and wet wool and another odor that Kate could identify now as guns—oil and cordite. A mist clung to the roads and made the dark houses on Washington Street appear caught in spools of web. Kate struggled to stay awake and talk to Charles, but she felt unwell, and the pull of sleep and the pleasure of succumbing to it were too much.

She woke in a little town called Mio, where Charles bought her a hunting license from a large man who wore a hunter's orange hat with earflaps and smiled at Kate. "Wish I could get my wife to hunt. But she won't have it."

"I thought I'd try it this once," Kate said. She felt a little awkward and improper, going out into the woods to kill things.

Outside of Mio, they entered a tract of forest that Charles knew well enough to navigate without a map. By ten that morning, Kate had donned a hunting vest, its pockets weighted down by twenty-gauge shells, and was cradling a shotgun and trampling over a forest floor carpeted with bark and dead leaves. Charles was twenty yards to her right. Their quarry was grouse, and Kate was tense, conscious of wanting to shoot something, though she didn't necessarily want to kill it. The day was sunless and cold enough that Kate could see her breath. When the first bird rose in front of her, the muscular beating of its wings startled her. She shot and missed, after which Charles took the bird down in a cloud of feathers. Terribly enough, the grouse, dark gray and nearly the size of a chicken, was still alive, driving its head into the ground as it flapped one wing. Charles ran to it, took its head in a hand, and snapped its neck with the flick of his wrist, then stuffed it in his game pouch. "You want to do that right away," he said. "There's no reason to let it suffer." How simple, how quick it was. It sickened Kate even as it excited her, even as it made her want to shoot more surely the next time.

The second bird that got up, she missed, as did Charles, who shot after her, and she was half relieved to see the bird soar above the tree line and escape. But early that afternoon, a grouse burst out of a tree no more than five feet in front of her. She was quick to train the barrel on it. The bird went down and immediately began its broken dance, hopping on a leg, leaping into the air and falling again. She ran to it, then stood back when she saw the ripped open wing, a mess of bleeding flesh to which bits of feather stuck. Charles reached her and offered to finish the panicky creature off. "I can do it," Kate said. She grabbed it by the neck, struck by its weight, its absolute terror as its one good wing insisted on struggle. She tried to flick her wrist, as she had seen Charles do, but the bird was stubbornly heavy, one grayish, unreadable eye trained on her as she flopped its too solid body about. A mess of feathers fell to her feet. Blood flecked her forearm and left dark spots on her jeans. The bird's stupid determination enraged her, and she tightened her grasp around its neck and flung its body down like a heavy bag of laundry. She felt its neck snap, as distinct as a pencil breaking. Finally, it was dead, and Kate felt half guilty for the sense of accomplishment killing it had given her. She had overcome the bird. She was the stronger. And this feeling was overshadowed only by her desire to clean herself up, to get rid of the mess, the blood and feathers, of her stupid bird.

That night, Charles opened a nice bottle of Cabernet and prepared a small feast of wild rice, zucchini squash, and grouse breasts,

239

which were thankfully small. Kate's appetite was poor. And though the brightly lit interior of the camper was warm and cozy, she battled a nearly irresistible fatigue that seemed to arrive earlier every evening now. Charles offered a toast to her hunting skills. "To your successful first day out," he said. "We'll do this again."

He was glowing, overjoyed by the success of the day, by the belief that there would be other such days, and Kate felt the urgent need to dim his happiness. But it was already too late to tell him with any justice what he should have already known. "I don't know," she said. "Hunting is a little dirty for me."

It stormed that night, the wind and the rain pounding against the thin walls of the camper. In bed, the darkness was all encompassing, pitch black as it could only be away from city lights. Kate could see nothing in it. No sign of Charles beside her. No sign of her own hand in front of her. And as the wind continued to rage outside the camper's small shelter, Kate thought of the grouse that were out there clenched like fists in the shelter of trees and covered over in the same darkness that seemed to be smothering her. She felt his touch then, his soft fingers settling over the place where her breast was gone. It was not a sexual touch. It was tender. It wanted only closeness. And when Kate tried to remove his hand, he held her more firmly, and soon she let her hand rest over his, let herself be held in a darkness that felt safer now.

In November, Kate found it almost impossible to work through a full day at the bank. She was having pressure headaches that made even light physical activity unthinkable. Her double vision and dizziness had worsened. At times, her left hand stopped functioning. She couldn't make the fingers close, and so for hours at a time she would keep this hand in her lap and hope that no one noticed. To a degree, these signs of her illness relieved Kate. Certainty was good. It precluded hope. It precluded delusion and disappointment. And then, for a day, even two or three, the pain and fatigue would lift and she'd feel remarkably well again. She'd eat large dinners with Charles and make love to him. She'd take long walks with him and stay up late watching rented movies. She'd laugh loudly at his jokes, which were admittedly not so funny. But the pain would always come back, and she had to prepare herself for its return. She had to remind herself that she would die, which she did by handling numerous practicalities with the same dispatch and efficiency she brought to everything else in her life. She prepared her taxes in advance, contacted a lawyer, revised her will, set up a checking account for Melissa, who would turn seventeen in six months, and so would live alone in the year before college. Kate arranged a very brief and affordable funeral, at which, she had decided, no physical remains of her—in a jar or coffin—would be present. Kate found comfort in these tasks. They made death accomplishable, something she could do rather than something that would be done to her.

One morning, after four days of what felt like perfect health, Kate got up from bed and collapsed before she'd gotten halfway to the bathroom. Charles was helping her up when she realized what had happened. She was unhurt, and as soon as she could stand on her own, she pushed Charles away. "Please don't cling to me," she said.

"You just fell."

"I stumbled. I'm fine now." She went into the bathroom, and when she came back out, Charles was sitting on the edge of the bed looking up at her with too much concern in his eyes.

"Is something wrong?" He paused, seeming to realize the danger in his question. "Are you unwell?"

She slammed her underwear drawer, panties and a bra clenched in her fist, and began rifling through dresses in her closet with a physical vigor that was meant to be definite proof of her wellness. Charles flinched when she threw a dress down on the bed. "I am not unwell."

"You just collapsed."

"I tripped."

"Your knees gave out from under you. I saw it. You've been tired lately. I've seen that, too."

She turned her back to him and kicked a stray house slipper into the wall. "I'm dying." She was furious at him for making her say it. But in the long silence after her admission, she felt her fury drain away. "I lied to you earlier. I'm not recovered. I'm sick."

"Dying," he said flatly. "Dying when?"

"I'm dying now."

"When?" he asked again. "How long?"

"Not long." She turned around. Charles was naked save for his boxer shorts. His pale shoulders were drooped in a sad way that made her want to go to him, and through the slightly open slit of his boxer shorts, she glimpsed a small part of his limp penis, the sight of which left her feeling tender and proprietary towards him. He was hers—her lover, her friend, her companion.

"From what?" he asked.

"Cancer."

He nodded.

"It's gone to the brain," she said. "That's why I get dizzy."

"Jesus," he said.

"It'll get worse," she continued, unable to stop herself. "Before it's over, I might not be able to make facial expressions. I might not be able to pronounce words correctly." She stopped. "I'm sorry," she said.

"You didn't tell me any of this."

"We were having a fling," she said. "That was our agreement."

She sat down next to him, but he moved away and then stood up and began hurriedly dressing. "No," she said. She hadn't meant to say that.

He struggled to tie his necktie, finally just letting its ends fall. "I've got to go for a while," he said. He picked his shoes up from the floor, walked out into the hallway in his socks, and closed the door behind him.

She hadn't expected the heartbreak, the thoughts of him, the simple, unrelenting desire for an absent person. She called twice and left messages. In the first, she asked him to please call. In the second, she was blunt. "Call me, Charles. Call me today." She was shocked by her aggression, her outright command. But she was even more surprised by the fact that he didn't call, not on that day and not on the next. The third time she called, Ryan answered with a flat, face-slapping, "Yeah, who is it?"

"Kate," she said softly. "I'd like to speak to your father."

"What did you do to him?" She'd expected the rudeness, but not the defensiveness, the obvious anger in his voice.

"I'd like to speak to him."

"He's not here." He paused. "What did you do to him?"

"I don't think that's really your concern."

"He was crying the other day. He was just sitting at the table crying. I guess you found out just how much you could push him around. I'd say you're an expert at that."

The repressed rage in Ryan's voice made her feel both overwhelmed by guilt and glad that there was some love for Charles mixed in with his son's bitterness. "Please tell him I called."

"Maybe I will," he said, and then hung up.

At the same time, Melissa continued to stay away from home. Kate saw her briefly in the evenings and mornings, before she slipped out of the house with her book bag.

By early November, the beautiful portion of fall had ended. The winds came and blasted the leaves from the trees, and the rains turned them to brown gutter slush. The dark came early, and more often than not Kate woke to gray mornings and the wet sounds of cars driving through water-drenched streets. Kate worked half days now at the bank. She'd told her bad news to her district manager, who was happy to let her work until she no longer could. She spent her quiet afternoons at home re-reading old mysteries and watching stacks of rented movies. She slept. She hoped that Charles would call. And she prepared herself for what would be a quieter, lonelier death than she'd expected.

And just when it seemed things would go on in this way, Kate came home from work one afternoon to find Melissa on the couch hugging her knees. She was in her favorite pajamas—thin yellow cotton with blue polka dots—and her eyes were raw from crying. In the crook of one arm, she held her worn-out teddy bear. Kate sat down on the opposite end of the couch. "Where's Mark?" she asked.

"He's gone."

"Home?" Kate asked.

"Gone," Melissa said. "He dropped me."

Kate felt a rush of guilt. She wanted to go to her daughter, but Melissa made no gesture or sign of wanting her. "I'm sorry, sweetheart."

"I scared him off," Melissa said. "I was too intense for him, or something."

"I don't think it was you," Kate said. "I think it was the circumstances. Sixteen-year-old boys don't particularly want to be around a house where the mother keeps taking to her sick bed."

Melissa shook her head. "I don't want to talk about that."

"OK," Kate said. "There are other boys."

"It doesn't matter," Melissa said, beginning to cry again. "I was just using him. That's what he said and maybe he was right. He was my protector." She looked up at Kate. "From you." She stopped crying then and sat up straight and made an effort, Kate could tell, to be brave. "I'm going to try to be around more."

This news caught Kate off guard. She didn't know what to say, and was just as surprised when she felt the tears come. "I'm sorry," she said.

"I can't be here all the time," Melissa said cautiously. "But I'll be here after school, and I'll be here for dinners."

"I know what to expect this time," Kate said. "I'm going to be better. I'm not going to—"

"You went hunting the other weekend," Melissa interrupted.

Kate nodded. "I actually shot a bird."

Melissa laughed. "I can't picture it."

"I did. I shot it and Charles roasted it and I ate it." Kate and Melissa both laughed at the thought of it.

It took Charles three weeks to call. He left a message on the machine asking Kate to coffee at the café where they'd first met. That afternoon, the temperature fell below freezing, though the sun was out; and people hurried over the sidewalks, bundled in heavy coats. Wanting to look her best, Kate went without a hat and suffered for it, her ears numb by the time she'd entered the warm, mostly empty café. She found him seated in a corner of sunshine where he nonetheless seemed to cling to his coffee cup for warmth. Kate was shocked; after three weeks of not seeing him, he looked different: paler, thinner, slighter than she'd remembered him. His moustache was back, for which she was glad. In truth, she preferred him with his moustache. "Thank you for coming," he said after she'd sat down.

She could hear the fear in his voice and was at first reassured by it. "I've missed you," Kate said. It was a great relief to have said this, to have let it out.

He smiled, but his smile didn't last. "I'm not good at this."

"Good at what?"

"I don't know," he said. "I don't know what I want to say."

Kate already knew from his tone what he wanted to say. "Sure you do. I don't know why you had to make me come out in the cold to hear it."

He shook his head as if he were trying to rid himself of a thought. "I'm very sorry about your . . . about being sick. I wanted you to know that."

"Thank you," Kate said. "I'm sorry, too. About not telling you." But she couldn't make herself sound sorry. And once again, she was surprised by her anger. She wanted to strike out at him now. Instead, she sat back in her chair and waited for him to speak.

"It's nice to see you. I've missed you. That's true for me, too. But I don't think I know you well enough to . . ."

244

He was going to make her finish his thought. He didn't know her well enough to watch her die. "I suppose not," she said. For a moment, she remained silent and fought off an urge to weep. It stung to see this man who had giggled and tumbled in her bed now hold himself at a distance. And when she was sure she would not cry, she laughed. "It was just a fling, right?" Her voice sounded fake, and though she knew this pretense made her ridiculous, she couldn't help herself.

"Sure," Charles said. "I just wanted to see you again." He put his head down, and for a moment Kate thought he might cry. But when he looked up again, he managed to smile briefly. "It was nice," he said.

He wanted her to agree. He wanted her to say something equally fake and cheerful, but she didn't.

Melissa came back to her, as she'd said she would. In the late afternoons, she opened her books on the kitchen table and worked while Kate prepared dinner. One afternoon, Melissa brought dozens of college brochures home from school, and Kate and Melissa paged through them, talking about whether a large or a small college experience would suit Melissa best. Did she want a school with a Greek system? "That's not for me," Melissa said. And Kate, who didn't want to be too influential, was inwardly glad that her daughter would not be a sorority girl. It was far too early to be so absorbed by these questions, but Kate was grateful for any opportunity to talk about her daughter's future, and Melissa seemed to know this and indulged her.

In December, Kate's double vision worsened and she finally left the bank for good. Her doctor recommended that she tape her left eye shut and wear a patch. And so this small part of Kate was already dead. Once or twice a week, she would suffer headaches that were bad enough for morphine. But for the most part, dying was surprisingly painless. More than anything else, it was exhausting, so exhausting that merely standing up was a struggle. At times, death seemed more pleasant than frightening. It promised an end to the fatigue, the brightness of the mornings, the length of midday and late afternoons when she lay on the couch alone waiting for Melissa to come home from school.

Kate still had her bursts of energy, though they'd last now for hours rather than days. When a blizzard descended on Ann Arbor,

Kate and Melissa put on their fattest winter coats, gloves, and hats, and walked for more than an hour in the new snow.

Melissa and Kate almost never spoke of what was happening—and what would soon happen—until one afternoon when Kate was especially sick. She lay over the couch, groggy from painkillers and covered in blankets. Kate had been discussing as lucidly as she could the virtues of Carleton College, while trying to hide the fact that this was the school she would choose for her daughter, when Melissa stopped her with a blunt question. "Does it hurt?"

Kate looked at Melissa for a moment. "You're sure you want to know?"

Melissa nodded.

"Sometimes," she said. "But not as much as I thought it would."

"But it hurts."

"Yes."

"Will it hurt when it happens?" Melissa wasn't looking at her. She was paging through a glossy college brochure.

"No," Kate said. "I won't be awake."

Melissa shook her head. "I don't think I want to be there then. If that's OK."

For an instant, Kate wanted to beg her daughter to be there, to stay with her, above all, at that moment. Instead, she nodded. "I'll be asleep. I won't know who's there."

"Is it OK?" Melissa asked.

"It's OK," Kate said.

It was raining out when someone knocked on the front door. The day nurse had just gone home, and so Kate had to summon nearly all her energy to rise from the couch and answer the door. A cold in-suck of air filled the entryway, and despite the grayness outside, the light had a raw brightness that hurt her eyes. Charles was wet, and the stringy flatness of his hair made him appear desperate. He held a small bunch of drenched tulips out to her, and she managed to carry them back to the couch with her. For some reason, looking at the flowers—their dramatic mess of color—exhausted her. "I got caught in this," he said. Water dripped off his coat and onto her wood floor. "I'm sorry," he said. Then he explained himself: "I just wanted to visit. As a friend."

"I'm tired, Charles," she said. "I won't be able to say much." As usual he was nervous, and for the first time Kate was irritated by his fear rather than touched by it. She knew that he was merely afraid to be in the presence of a dying person. He seemed so reduced: every inch the furniture salesman. She should have offered him tea or coffee, but she could not imagine how she would get up from the couch again. She was in her robe, for God's sake. "Your eye," he said. "Is it OK?" She'd forgotten about her patch until then, and now felt humiliated. She didn't want him there. She didn't want him to see her dying. He had been right: they didn't know each other well enough.

"No," she said. "It's not OK."

"You look good."

She almost laughed but stopped herself when she realized how horrific laughter would sound coming from her. For a time they were silent until Kate finally said, "I'm tired."

He nodded. "I hope . . . I hope I wasn't unkind. I hope I didn't mistreat you. I hope . . ."

So that's why he had come. Kate shook her head, and because he looked so achingly vulnerable, so convinced of his guilt, and because he was so extremely kind that he believed he was in the wrong when he wasn't, she said, "Of course not." And though she was too exhausted to summon the requisite tone of penitence and regret, though she wasn't sure it was entirely true, she remembered her daughter's recent courage and summoned some of her own. "I suppose I used you . . . a little. I didn't want to end up alone. I didn't want to end up"—she paused and let her head sink into her pillow— "like this." She smiled. "It's not as bad as it looks. It's not as bad as I thought it would be. I have my daughter." And now that she had said it, she thought it was true.

His shoulders lifted as if a chain had just come off him. How easily people might push him around. How easily she might have delivered a blow to him right now, had she wanted to. "It was just using me?" he asked.

"Not just. It was more than that, too." The truth of these words was in the sudden enthusiasm and fullness of her voice, and his smile and the lift in his face told her that he had heard it. And for a moment, she wondered if he deserved to be this happy given what would soon happen to her. But the moment passed.

"I'd rather you not come back," she said. "I'm going to get worse, and I'd rather you remember me as the woman you took to bed and not the woman with an eye patch and half a paralyzed face."

247

"Sure," he said. She wished he'd struggled more before saying that.

"I'm tired," she said again. But she was hardly prepared for how quickly he kissed her forehead and then turned around and left.

Her heartbreak continued. When she was especially lonely, in the long hours of daylight, she thought again of his lanky nakedness, his surprising competence at killing, his melancholic voice on her answering machine asking to speak to her. How odd to be heartbroken at this time in her life. How odd to be left with desire. It was a relief and a luxury to know that she did not want the actual man. Not now. She liked him best in her thoughts. He was more vivid, more alive that way. She could spend hours thinking of the soft, contemplative way he'd touched his moustache from time to time, and the way he'd told her, "Always stand behind the shooter," making it clear with his paternalistic tone of voice that her safety was his foremost concern. She would see them making love and be surprised again by his athleticism, his volume, his surprising confidence in bed. She would see years into an imaginary future with him; how annoying his passivity and meekness would become, annoying and also endearing. She would exhaust herself protecting him from those who'd take advantage of him: his son, his business partners, even herself. She would think of him as a hunter, too, a gentle hunter with great respect for his prey. How quickly he got to his wounded bird and snapped its neck. She would think of how he had lifted his wine above their small feast of grouse and toasted to her success, to their many hunts to come; and how he had lain beside her that night, his hand—the same one he had killed with—touching her scar in a darkness that was, for the time, easier to bear.

*Nominated by The Southern Review*

# ROSE OF SHARON

## by BRIGIT PEGEEN KELLY

from THE ORCHARD (BOA Editions)

I loved the rose of Sharon. I would have loved it
For its name alone. I loved its fleshy blossoms.
How fat they were. How fast they fell. How the doves,
Mean as spit, fought the finches and the sparrows
For the golden seed I spilled beneath the bush.
How I threw seed just to watch the birds fight.
And the blossoms fallen were like watered silk
Loosely bound. And the blossoms budding
Were like the dog's bright penis first emerging
From its hairy sheath. And the blossoms opened wide
Were like the warm air above the pool of Siloam.
*Tree of breath*. Pink flowers floating on water.
The flushed blossoms themselves like water.
Rising. Falling. The wind kicking up skeins
Of scented foam. High-kicking waves. Or laughing
Dancers. O silly thoughts. But a great sweetness. . . .
And then it was over. An ice storm felled the tree.
With a clean cut, as if with a hatchet. One year
A whole flock of birds. One year a crop of fruit
That melted on the tongue, a kind of manna, light
As honey, just enough to sustain one. And then nothing.
The breasts gone dry. The window opening onto
Bare grass. The small birds on the wire waiting
For the seed I do not throw. *Pride of my heart*,
Rose of Sharon. *Pool of scented breath*. Rose

Of Sharon. How inflated my sorrow. But the tree
Itself was inflated. A perpetual feast. A perpetual
Snowfall of warm confetti. . . . And now I worry.
Did the bush fear the ice? Did it know of the ice's
Black designs? Did its featherweight nature darken
Just before it was felled? Was it capable of darkening?

*Nominated by Marianne Boruch, Kathleen Hill, Ted Deppe, Diann Blakely,* BOA Editions

# SHOOTING KINESHA

## by DAISY FRIED

from PLOUGHSHARES

"I hate what I come from," says my cousin Shoshana,
22, jawing per always, feather earrings tangling
in her light brown hair. Shoshana hangs on to Kinesha,
her kid, to stop her running off. Our cousin Deb's
wedding just got out; we're standing at the bottom
of the wedding hall steps. "White people
don't have culture, except what they stole
from our African brothers." Shoshana's
wearing black, per always, me too, her in leather,
me in acetate-velour. "Weddings, U-G-H."
Shoshana spells out *ugh* like it's spelled
in books. "I hope yours was cooler than this."
I nod. I always nod at Shoshana, whatever she says.
Shoshana checks, rechecks her watch, watching
for her boyfriend. I'm waiting for my husband too.
I've been a pain in the ass to him all morning.
Shoshana sips cheap California champagne
to hide her upset feelings. Kinesha breaks loose,
veers close to the street and parked cars and traffic,
thrashes her lace anklets and buckle shoes
into a crowd of part-white pigeons.

"In London I only hung out with Jamaicans,"
Shoshana says. "People gave me looks on the bus.
Ouch." She detangles an earring. "Once I ripped
an earlobe on these. Anyway, I want you to meet

251

my boyfriend. He's cool, he's sticking by me.
He says he knew he could when I wouldn't
dime him out after they caught me with his pot
in the Kingston airport. Kinesha's his. He's
the only guy I've loved since, you know, Ken?"
Ken's the one who died beside her
of an overdose in the Motel 6 in Ohio
the time she was 16 and stole her dad's Beamer
to run away. "You heard?" Of course I did,
in this family. "Kinesha's Kinesha
to remember him," she says. "I still miss him."
I nod. I poke Kinesha's belly, her nose.
"U-G-H," says Kinesha, annoyed. I'm bad with kids.
"I'm teaching her to assert herself," Shoshana says.
Her wrist-chains jangle. I twist my wedding ring.
An organ somewhere plays "Ode to Joy."

Here comes the third bad cousin, Christina,
scruff-haired in the pale-pink prom dress
the bride her sister made her wear. $90,000
per year doing something with websites and she
can't even keep her hair in order. "Isn't it awful?"
Christina says, "What do I look like, Gwyneth Paltrow?
You guys look swell." She's good with kids:
Kinesha slams herself for a hug into Christina's
legs. Christina and Kinesha kiss. She says
"Did you like my PowerPoint presentation
on the bride's life? Did you think it was funny?
Go play with the pigeons." She puts Kinesha down.
"Deb wanted a poem, but don't you hate poems?
Was it wrong of me to start with an Eminem quote?"
Kinesha shouts, staggers, stamps at the pigeons;
jaded, they hardly move, only jump-start
halfhearted when Kinesha brandishes
her one-armed naked Barbie above her head,
then turns Barbie into a gun, shoots
at the pigeons. "I feel like we should be
sneaking around back with cigarettes
like we used to, remember?" says Christina.
"Too bad we don't smoke anymore."

Shoshana takes out her Newports, lights up.
I'm remembering we never much liked each other,
only hung together at family gatherings
because we were supposed to be the bad ones.
I hate what I come from. I say "My father
just told me again my poems are 'too full
of disgusting sex.' He said 'Why don't you
write more like Derek Walcott?' I'm sick
of him throwing deep-thinking
genius men up at me." Christina rolls
her eyes, shakes her head, fudges hair tendrils
back into her frizzy twisted updo, vibrates
her lips, blows air out. "Can you tell I'm
drunk already?" she asks. I nod. She shrugs.
"Well, why not, Deb didn't invite single guys
for me like I asked her. Selfish as always."

Shoshana checks her watch. "I'm gonna kill him."
I wish I wanted to kill my husband.
Right now, I hate everything, everybody,
and don't have a friend in the world
except my husband. It's true he dislikes me
more and more these days but at least
he likes my poems and hates Derek Walcott.
Kinesha sprays Barbie bullets at everything,
Barbie's head as bald as her elided crotch.
"I didn't buy her that racist, sexist doll,"
says Shoshana. Christina and I nod.
"She found my old one. I pulled
all her hair out when I was 14
and shaved my head the first time."
Kinesha moves away from the settling pigeons,
turns her Barbie gun on us, shoots.
Rat-a-tat-tat. "Ugh, you got me,"
we say, and "BANG!" I say. We turn
our hands into guns, three bad cousins,
Mother, Bridesmaid, Wife-and-Daughter,
for all our different reasons, shooting the child.

*Nominated by Joyce Carol Oates, Philip Levine*

# SABOR A MÍ

## fiction by ALEX MINDT

from WILLOW SPRINGS

THE SONG SAYS, "So much time we have enjoyed this love." But songs aren't life. What do you do when your grown daughter, a mother of two, comes to you and says she wants to be now with women? I am old, too old for this. So I tell her to leave and I will pray. My whole life I pray and look around, what good has it done? What do I have? My son, my first son Juan, Jr., in Los Angeles, his body found in a car under the freeway. My second son Javier sent back from Vietnam in a bag, for nothing.

In Mexico, you don't lose your family, even after they die. Here, everyone is alone. Loneliness made this country. When you are lonely, you either find some way to kill yourself or you work hard and make money. People here, they either die or they become rich.

When I was fourteen, I waded across the Rio Grande at Ojinaga and saw this country from the back of a pickup truck, picking sugar beets in Minnesota, apples in Wenatchee. In Ventura there were strawberries. In Calabasas, tomatoes. Figs in Palm Springs. Cotton in Arizona and Texas. Now I live in New Mexico. Many years have passed. I saved and saved until I had my own small restaurant and raised my family. I insisted they speak perfect English. Now not one of them speaks Spanish. When I talk to them I have to think about every word.

I do not have a home, I have this facility, in Santa Fe, the second oldest city in America. My youngest boy, Mario, he pays for this place. He owns a body repair shop in Albuquerque. Every month I get a check. But does he come out? Does he take his gringa wife and their kids to see their Papí? Last year, I went down to his big house for Lori's quinceñera. But where was the pan dulce? The dancing? After a few minutes, the kids, they get in their cars and drive off. My son, he just shrugs.

Last week I received a letter in the mail. It was from my daughter. There was a picture of her and a dog and another woman. The dog had long ears. The woman had short hair. Inside was an invitation to a wedding. I had to read it several times.

My daughter, Raquel, wants now to marry this woman. Her first husband was named Charlie; her second will be named Diane. Raquel was so smart. She learned English so fast. And then in school, she learned French and could speak that too. But not Spanish. She went to Paris and became a cook like her father. Only what she makes, with those thick creams, I don't eat so much.

Rosalinda, what do you say to me now? I wait for your voice when the noise fades and the crickets sing. But you are silent. Why won't you speak to me? I live in a facility now, Rosí. For my sadness, the nurses, they give me pills. I still think of that day, climbing down the fig tree. You were at the meal truck, holding a stainless steel tray, the sun shining twice on your lovely skin. I remember your long black hair pulled back tight, and the mark of dirt on your forehead, and how all I could do was smile and look away.

Rosí, I know what you would say. But Raquel wants to love this woman, and I say no. She has a son and a daughter, you remember Stephen and Elizabeth? But who listens to me? She did not ask my permission. Am I not her father? I do not know my own children. They move around me like ghosts.

The food here is hatred on my tongue. Eggs and toast too hard to chew, not even beans have flavor. But I am leaving now. I have eaten breakfast. I have put on my good suit, and now Raquel will hear what I have to say. The gate is open in the back behind the Piñon tree, and outside the cars are rushing. A river of steel and rubber roars past. It is late morning, but the sun is rising fast in the sky. I will walk until darkness, and then I will keep walking if I have to. Outside Santa Fe, the air is dry and sweet from the lavender and poppies. The sign says Taos 78 miles. I will walk 78 miles if I have to.

I do not hold out my hand. Cars will stop. An old man, walking a highway, a slumped, old man, surely someone will stop and ask where I'm going. Gringos are not all bad. They clean up after themselves and act nice, even if they don't mean it.

I need you now, Rosalinda, for I have walked a long time and the sun is pushing down on me. The road is uphill. In a car you don't notice so much. But when the foot comes down, the ground is so much closer than when the foot came up. I have walked almost to the Indian reservation outside of town. Cars and trucks do not see me.

The dirt on the roadside is hard and dry, and the ravine beside me is full of rocks and no water. In this country, rivers and streams, they dry up: The sky takes our lives away. We become clouds. When it rains I see all the people who came before me. Mamí, Papí, and my baby boys. I see Tío Julio on a mattress under an apple tree, playing a guitar with only three strings. There are black birds and rotting apples.

But I don't see you, Rosí, and every time it rains, I ask, what is wrong? What did I do? I would like it to rain now. It is so hot. Sweat is now bubbling up under this wool suit I still have, this suit you bought for me, for Raquel's quinceñera so many years ago. Do you remember Tío Julio and his band playing "Sabor a Mí" in the darkness and how we danced? Do you remember the lovely noise of that night and the sangria, how the neighbors came over and then more and more until our yard was full of dancing?

I need a car to pull off now. My knees are burning with every step. I will stop and wait here until someone pulls over. This is a country made of rushing. Here, no one is anywhere, they are in between places. Only the dead are content.

Voices are singing from the shrubs and red stones. "Tanto tiempo disfrutamos de este amor." Even the cars sing as they rush by. "Nuestras almas se acercaron tanto asi." And I have to sit down. There is a pale rock, a large stone. Its shadow goes down the hill by the dried up river.

Behind me, the wind rises up and a car pulls off the road. It is green, covered in dust, like a fig tree. A gringo gets out and looks at me over the roof, his light hair blowing sideways in the wind. "Hey," he says. And then he says something else. But a truck passes, and I can't hear him. And then he comes around the car and opens the door. He is kind of fat in the chest, with thin, pale legs, and he wears sandals, brown shorts, and a flowered shirt that hangs open over a white t-shirt. "I came by a minute ago and saw you walking," he says.

"Thought I'd double back and see if you needed a lift. You okay?"

He wipes off the seat for me and he tells me to push some buttons under my legs to be more comfortable. But I am fine.

"My name's Peter." He holds out his hand to me.

"I am Juan."

"Juan. That's John, right? In English, I mean."

"Yes." Inside the car, cold air is blowing at me.

"This a little cold for you?" he says. "Here, let me crank this down a bit." He turns a dial. "As you can see, I like my air conditioned." He turns the steering wheel and goes onto the highway. "You want something to drink? Water, beer? You look a little thirsty."

"No, thank you."

Sunlight bounces off the car's green hood and voices come out of a small speaker on the dashboard. "What's your 10-20, Wayward Juice? Wayward Juice, you read me?"

The gringo, Peter, he frowns at the speaker. "This guy's been calling for Wayward Juice all morning. I don't know why I bought this stupid CB, thought it would keep me company, I guess."

The tops of the mountains are white in the distance ahead of us.

"So, where you heading, Juan?"

"Taos."

"No kidding? Well, serendipity-do, so am I. I hope you're not in a hurry, 'cause I was planning on taking the scenic route."

"I have to be there by seven."

"Oh, well we've got some time then." He speaks very fast, this gringo. "So, why are you walking up to Taos on a hot day like this?"

"For a funeral." I do not know why I say it. God forgive me. But how do you tell someone that your daughter is marrying a woman?

"I'm sorry to hear that," he says. "I hate it when people die. Was this person close to you?"

I turn my head and look out the window.

"Well, I'm sorry about that. I'm real sorry." He holds up his can of beer. "How 'bout a toast? To those who've come before, who've paved the way, and showed us how to live." He drinks his beer and places it between his legs.

"Horny Buzzard, we got a Kojak with a Kodak in a plain white wrapper."

Peter chuckles and shakes his head. "You hear that?" he says. "Man, they say the funniest things. 'Kojak with a Kodak.' I don't get half of it."

He turns onto the road that goes through the mountains, the high road, they call it. "I have to go the scenic route," he says. "I just can't stand those freeways. Freeways are just beginnings and endings. You know what I'm saying? You're either leaving a place, or arriving at another place. And really, there's nothing in between. I've been reading some books lately, you know, things I never read in college. Never had any use for them until now, I guess. But let me ask you, Juan, do you think it's a coincidence that the trans-continental freeways were being constructed at the precise time that existentialism had its greatest hold on the American psyche?"

I look out the window. Piñon trees are green spots on the hills around us.

"No comment, huh? I mean, don't get me wrong, America is great, right? The greatest country in the world. But there's something missing, isn't there? That's what I've found, and you know where I found it?"

"The freeways."

"Yes!" he says. "The freeways. They're like an empty stomach, you know, and they just want and want and want." He reaches under the seat and pulls out another can of beer. "You sure you don't want anything to drink? They're getting kinda' warm."

"No, thank you."

"You know what, Juan? This is my first time in the Southwest, and it's beautiful, it's flippin' unbelievable, the mountains, the sky. I know what you're thinking. I'm one of those crazy gringos, right? A car full of crap, driving all over hell? Yeah, well." He smiles and shakes his head. "I got this friend, Gary. Now Gary's a computer guy, you know, one of those coke-bottle glasses type, all hunched over half the time, jerking off three times a day to some porno website, *motherjugs.com* sort of thing. He's got a *shooowing* for old ladies with big *cowangas*, if you get my drift. But don't get me wrong, Gary's brilliant, just like wow, his brain, and he talks about systems, how things work, interconnected grids and all that, you know, overload and whatnot, and the truth of the matter, Juan, is, well, my wife left me a couple weeks ago. Took the kids with her. So I just got in the car and put my foot on the pedal. My mainframe just overloaded, as Gary would say. My firewall, or whatever, was just burning up. You're the first person I've had the chance to really talk to. Lucky you, huh? This CB, nobody wants to talk about real stuff. Just like police warnings or scary sex talk. I mean, some real unpleasant doo-doo." He smiles and blows out air. "That's what Tyler calls it. My son. He's twelve and he still calls it doo-doo."

He is quiet for a while, humming to himself, tapping the steering wheel with his fingers. "Hey" he says, "you know about this church up a ways? What's it called?" He reaches down for some papers. The car begins to swerve. "It's down here somewhere." All over the road, we are swerving. He finds the paper and grabs the steering wheel. "Whoa!" he says. "Ride 'em, cowboy!" He straightens the car out. "Anyway, like two hundred years ago," he says, "or something like that, this friar was digging and he found a crucifix, this miraculous crucifix in the dirt, and then they built a church around this pit, and over the years several miracles have been documented. I don't normally believe in that stuff. But then again, I don't normally just hop in my car and haul-ass around the country."

He keeps talking. He talks and talks, but he is fine. Strangers will say things to you your family would never say. He tells me that he is afraid of heights and the ocean. And then he says, "Have you ever felt so sad that you can't feel anything? Have you ever just done something, just anything, I mean stupid things too, well mainly stupid things really, to just maybe show yourself that you're still alive?"

I don't answer. We drive past a gringo market selling *Native Arts and Crafts*, and a restaurant with a sign that says *Savor the Flavor*. I think of Raquel, and how after coming back from France she told me there's more to flavor than chilé and salt. "Why not use all the spices available to us?" she said. Then she said I was limited, I never opened my mind. I remember all the shouting and yelling, and never knowing why she was so angry at me. "With my limited money," I told her, "I gave you everything you wanted." And now she cooks snails.

Peter talks on and on until we drive through the Nambe Indian Reservation. He goes off the road and stops at a small adobe church, brown and leaning this way and that. "Hey," he says. "You want to take a look?"

"No thank you," I say.

"Okay. I'll only be a minute." He takes a silver camera from the back seat and starts clicking photos.

Raquel is right now preparing for her wedding. The first one, so many years ago, in the church of St. Francis de Assisi, she took my arm, and my whole body shook she was so beautiful. Her wavy brown hair was all up on her head, and her white dress dragged

259

on the ground behind her, like a queen. As I look down now, I cannot believe it, but this is the same suit I wore to her first wedding. And there is the button you sewed on, Rosí, that looks almost like the other buttons. Hush, you said, nobody will notice one silly button. And I was still angry you spent so much on fabric stitched together for me. We cannot afford this, I said. But then you said Raquel cannot afford to have her father show up in picker's clothes.

Peter gets back into the car and says, "That sucked. No one's around, and I couldn't get in." Peter puts the car back onto the highway and says, "Atheists for Jesus!" and punches the roof with his fist.

"10-11 Blutarski! 10-11!"

Peter looks down at the radio and then at me. "I wonder what 10-11 means," he says.

"I said, that's a 10-42 Apache Bob. We got a meatwagon on yardstick 39."

He leans forward and turns off the radio. "A meatwagon. You think that's like a mealtruck, Juan? Cause I'm getting kind of hungry. Maybe they're selling sandwiches or tacos." Peter keeps talking about what he likes to eat, spaghetti, pot roast, what his mother used to make him when he and his brothers and sisters would come in from playing in the park. He talks, this gringo, like no gringo I've met, until we make it to the dusty junkyards of Chimayo, where everything has been left for dead. He stops in the dusty parking lot of the Shrine at El Santuario de Chimayo.

"This is it," he says. "The church I was telling you about, with the pit and the miracles. This is a sacred place." He opens the door. "Come on, I'll buy you something to eat."

There is a burrito stand, a restaurant and a gift shop that sells t-shirts and refrigerator magnets in the shape of the shrine. Tourists bump into each other, looking at postcards and coasters. Peter talks to people he doesn't know, people behind the counter as he pays for postcards and t-shirts. Against the wall, there is a large, stuffed dog wearing jeans and a cowboy hat sitting in a chair with a pistol in his hand. *Cowboy Dog*, the sign says.

In the sacristy of the church there is a small round pit with a mound of dirt to the side. Crutches of wood and aluminum hang on the wall along with rosary beads, pictures of the sick and lame with letters and handmade shrines and crucifixes.

Peter points down to the mound of dirt. "This soil is supposed to be magical. It has healing powers, they say." He looks at me and smiles. "I don't believe any of that crap," he whispers. "But I'm definitely feeling something in here."

I get down on my knees at the pit and close my eyes. I am not praying exactly. But I want to listen, Rosí, for your voice. I spend my days talking to you, my love, but I can never hear you. Maybe your voice will come to me here. I think of those other women. Is that why you are silent? I know I was wrong, but that was so long ago, and I never speak to them, or think of them. They meant nothing, Rosí. I wasn't easy to be with, I know. But what about you? After the children left, and the house was empty, you wouldn't speak to me, and I know why. That was how you did it, Rosí. That was how you punished me. But please, mi amor, please know that I loved you as best I could.

When I open my eyes, Peter is sitting beside me with his eyes closed. He is a funny gringo. The wind has taken hold of him.

He opens his eyes and whispers, "You feeling anything, Juan?"

"Yes."

"Really? What do you think it is?"

"Pain," I say. "My knees. Will you help me up?"

Before we leave, Peter takes a picture of me at the pit and then he asks a gringa to take a picture of us in front of the wall of crutches and shrines. He puts his arm around me and smiles.

Back in the car, Peter eats a burrito while he drives. He says that there is definitely something back there. He holds up his can of beer. "A toast," he says. "To history, to all those who have come before us, to all those searching like we are, Juan."

"Salud," I say.

He drinks from the can. A piece of yellow cheese hangs off his chin.

"If you don't mind my asking," he says. "Whose funeral are you going to?"

I do not know what to say. Whose funeral? I tell him, I don't know why, that I am going to my daughter's funeral. God forgive me.

"I'm sorry to hear that," he says. "I'm sorry. You must be devastated."

"At one time, we were very close."

"What was her name?"

"Raquel," I say.

"She must have been very special."

"She was my baby. And I loved her more than the others. But

everything she ever did, it seemed like she wanted to disappoint me."
I don't know why I say these things.

He nods and then is silent for a while.

"There is cheese on your chin," I say.

We drive through the villages of Truchas and Las Trampas. There are fields of blue flowers. Out my window, a dirt road swerves between Piñon trees, up a distant hill and ends at a large white cross that stands against the pale blue sky.

"You ever been to the Church of St. Francis Assisi, Juan?"

"Yes. Many years ago."

"So, is it as spectacular as the photos and paintings?"

"I don't know."

"I've seen the pictures, you know, Ansel Adams, Georgia O'Keeffe. It's something I've always wanted to see. Some atheist, huh?"

I don't tell him that yes I have made this drive before, that years ago we all drove up to the Church of St. Francis de Assissi, that my wife and sons were in the car with me, and that we were going to my daughter's first wedding.

When he stops in the square in Ranchos de Taos, he sits silently staring out the window at the giant church, at its round buttresses and bulky vigas. There are many cars parked here and many people in work clothes standing outside the church.

"Wow," Peter says. "This is incredible." He gets out of the car and stands by the white cross in front of the church and stares up at the two bell towers.

I remember the irises and columbine, the petunias and roses. It was a spring night, like this. Remember, Rosí? Remember Raquel with flowers in her hair and the church full of family and friends from Texas, California, Arizona? Remember Tío Jorgé, the Garcias, the Tofoyas, little Juan Armijo, Dale Seaver, Renata, Pilar, and their families, José and Felicia, and Charlie's gringo friends and family? Remember the lights in the square and the Mariachi band with the violins, trumpets, bassos and guitars? And the singing! Oh, those voices! How we danced that night under the candles and the string of lights?

Peter comes back to the car and says, "I forgot my camera." He reaches into the back seat. "They're mudding the damn thing. The people, they're all slapping mud on it."

He leaves the car and begins taking pictures of the golden church.

I get out and walk up to the flowerbeds by the white cross and look up at the bell towers. All around, there are people, young and old, gringo and Latino, adding to the church's giant walls. It is like a woman. There are no sharp angles, only curves, and over the years she gets bigger, but only grows more beautiful.

"Hey Juan," Peter says, "turn around. Let's get you in the picture." He snaps his camera and says, "That will be really nice, by the cross, with the bell tower in the background." He points at the people with mud on their hands. "They say they're renewing the church. Everyone gets together and does this renewal thing. They've learned how from the people who came before and will pass it on to those who will come later. Tradition," he says, holding up his can of beer. "Ritual!"

I nod at Peter and then go into the church, where it is quiet and cool. There are paintings on the walls, colorful paintings from the Bible, like I remember it. I begin down the aisle, Rosí. This time I am alone. But it is the same aisle, the same pews, the same church. I am not the same, and Raquel is not the same.

Charlie was young and nervous that night. He was tall, with light hair and blue eyes, in a white tuxedo. And he shifted from foot to foot. And I remember the argument we had, Rosí, the night Charlie came over and asked for our blessings. "Raquel loves him," you said. "And that's what matters."

"All that matters is what Raquel wants," I said. "That's all that ever matters. But what about our family? Why is that not important?"

"You left your family in Mexico, remember? This is your new family, get used to it."

Charlie read her a poem, they said their vows, Father Thomas blessed them, and I had a gringo son-in-law who called me by my first name.

Later, little Juan Armijo stepped in front of the band to sing "Sabor a Mí," and I took you in my arms and you moved with such grace, and everyone stopped to watch. Maybe we couldn't talk too much, especially then, but did that matter when the music started? Tell me, Rosí, weren't we talking then, as we danced, did you not love me then?

"Tanto tiempo disfrutamos de este amor," I sing to myself. "Nuestras almas se acercaron, tanto asi."

I stop and sit in a pew and think I should pray. I do not know why. What do I ask for? I have asked for so much. Maybe God gives only to those who ask for nothing. I get on my knees, and I ask one more time for forgiveness. Please forgive my indiscretions, dear Lord. I was young and foolish. But I always loved my Rosí. Please bring her back to me, please let me hear her voice.

Back in the car, Peter sits like a stone, staring at the church. I climb in and close the door and expect him to say something. The keys hang in the ignition, waiting for him to turn them. But his hands are in his lap, and he is staring down for a long time. Then he looks up at the church. His eyes are shiny. He sniffs and says, "There was something wrong with my son's kidneys, Juan. He had end-stage renal disease. They didn't know what it was exactly, they never found out what was wrong, just the kidneys, they weren't filtering the blood properly." He leans back and takes in a breath. "We had him on dialysis, but that wasn't working. He was getting sick all the time, and they told us that he needed a transplant. My wife, Sharon, well she's diabetic, so she says to me that I need to donate my kidney. But here's the thing, for some reason, I don't know, I hesitated. I flinched. And she saw it, my wife, she caught me. I didn't just step up to the plate."

The church bells begin chiming. The people around the church start cleaning up. Men climb down from the ladders.

Peter wipes his eyes with the back of his hand.

I clear my throat. There is so much sadness, I do not know what to tell him. The bell stops ringing and I say, "We have all done bad things."

Peter looks at me and nods. He sits up and takes in a long breath. "Yeah," he says.

"What happened to your boy?" I ask.

"Tyler? Well, he's doing fine, actually. That's the funny thing, his little brother happened to be a much better match and it all worked out okay in the end. But Sharon and I know the truth. And that's why she left me, and that's why I'm out here. New Mexico is a long way from Cincinnati."

"It is a long way from Chihuahua too. We are both a long way from home."

Peter wipes his eyes again and looks at me. "Chihuahua? Is that where you're from? That's the place where the dog comes from, right? The little dog?"

Peter turns the key and the car starts. He pulls the car out of the

264

parking lot onto the main road and says, "Yeah, those dogs, I don't know, they're always shivering, aren't they? They must be cold or something. Maybe they're scared."

On the road into Taos, he talks about his boys, Tyler and Evan, how Tyler was an accident and was always sick with something. "Evan has always looked out for his big brother, taking care of him and whatnot," he says. "Hell, Sharon's right, they don't need me or my lousy paycheck. Selling fire alarms doesn't get your kids into private school, I'll tell you that much. But they'll be just fine without me. Better, probably."

"You are a weak man," I tell him. "You are weak because you would rather drive a car than do what you know you should do."

"I'm sorry," he says. "I didn't catch that. What did you say?"

"Your family is more important than your pity."

"Let me think about that for a minute." He is quiet, then he says, "Damn. You're right. You're like a sage or something, Juan. See, I knew I picked up the right guy. You're right, you're totally right, pity sucks. I hate people who feel sorry for themselves."

We drive into town, past markets, restaurants, the post office.

He says, "Time has gotten away from us a little bit. I'm sorry about that. What is that address again?"

I pull out the card and show it to him. "Arroyo Seco?" he says. "I thought you said Taos?"

"It is near Taos. Just past."

Peter stops into a gas station and takes the card with him as he gets out of the car. When he comes back, he says, "Okay, no problem. There are directions on the back of this, you know. It tells you how to get there." He looks at the card and says, "Are you sure you're going to a funeral?"

As we drive through Taos, past art galleries and restaurants, Peter tells me that this is where he'll be staying for the next few days. "I'm going to look at some art, do some exploring, see the Rio Grande. Maybe I'll take off my clothes and sit in one of those hot springs I heard about down by the river."

The sun is slipping down into the canyon, and big red clouds are moving in. It is now past seven, and Peter is driving fast. He pulls off the main road and starts heading toward the mountains. We drive through a small town, Arroyo Seco, past a bar with people outside, drinking beer. The road comes to a fork and Peter stops. "This is where we go on the dirt road, I think," he says. "The road less trav-

265

eled." His little car shakes and bounces. "You're wearing a ring there, Juan. Are you married?"

"Yes," I say. "I was. She is dead."

"Oh, I'm sorry to hear that."

"I have two children, Mario and Raquel. My first two boys died many years ago."

"You would have given your kidneys for them, wouldn't you?"

"Quit it," I tell him. "You are not the first man to act without courage."

Out the window, horses eat grass in the dusty red light. They stand like shadows, dark ghosts in the falling sun.

"It's something out here, isn't it?" he says. "I could see just escaping out here. Chucking it all and hiding out here."

"That's what you are doing," I say.

He thinks for a moment, and then says, "You know what? You're right. About everything." He turns the wheel, and we are going down a long, gravel driveway with cars parked along the sides. "I've been running away for a long time," he says.

"Listen," I tell him. "Get some sleep, then go back to your wife and tell her she married a coward. But you have found strength in your heart. Being alone is no good, Peter. In the short time, yes, it may be good, but in the long time you get lonely and for that you may as well be dead."

He pulls up to a large adobe house. "Strange place for a funeral," he says.

"There is no funeral," I say. "My daughter is getting married."

"I know, I read the invitation," he says. "Congratulations. But why did you tell me she died?"

"She is marrying a woman."

"Oh, right," he says. "She threw you a curveball, huh?"

I get out of the car. "Thank you for the ride, Peter."

"Take care, Juan. It was a pleasure." I close the door, and he sits in the car and watches me as I walk up to the house. He honks his horn and then drives away. Dust rises off the ground and floats in the air.

I knock on the door. There is music and voices from somewhere on the other side of the house. I knock again, but no one answers. The dust is now settling on the road behind me, and it is getting dark. Big purple clouds fill the sky.

I walk around the house and music gets louder. There is a stack of wood, Piñon logs and a rusty ax lying on the ground. There is a hole

266

in the ground and a mound of dry, sandy dirt and a shovel leaning up against the house. Beside the hole, there is a bush in a clay pot, waiting to be planted.

The music gets louder with people shouting and laughter.

Through shrubs and around a shed, I move, and down below me on a patio of red tile, people are dancing and clapping their hands. The lights from the house shine down on them. They are mostly gringos trying to salsa, smiling, swiveling their hips. Raquel is dancing with the short-haired woman from the photo with the dog. Raquel's hair is pulled back. Her deep, dark eyes and those full lips and her cheekbones, sharp like a statue, remind me of you, Rosalinda.

The valley below fills with dark grey and pink clouds, and the wind pushes the branches of the trees. The bushes around me shake. The song ends and the gringos clap their hands. Some are on the side with drinks in their hands talking English to each other. Raquel's children, Stephen and Elizabeth, adults now, stand by their father, Charlie, Raquel's ex-husband. What is he doing here, Rosí? This is like no wedding I have been to. It is a small party with a few friends.

Raquel puts her hand up and moves away from the group, saying something to a young man at a wooden table, where the music comes from. Voices can be heard, people talking. Raquel comes back to the woman with the short hair and says something to the other people. They smile and nod and step back, leaving the dance floor for the two women. And then trumpets fill the air. Do you hear that? Those trumpets and that rhythm, that slow rhythm that you loved so much?

Raquel holds up her hand. A man's voice sings out, "Tanto tiempo disfrutamos de este amor," and the woman takes Raquel in her arms, and they begin to dance. "Si negaras mi presencia en tu vivir." She moves like soft wind, and her eyes show only happiness as she spins away from the woman. The man sings those words, those familiar words, Rosí, remember? I sing them out as the woman takes Raquel's hand and brings her back. "Tanta vida yo te di." I want to tell her what the words mean—*I gave you so much life.* If she only knew the language . . . *I do not pretend to be your owner,* the man sings. *I am not in control.* She turns away and then spins back into the woman's arms with such ease that I cannot contain myself. It is like I am dancing with you again, Rosí, the way your fingers touched my palm, with your thumb on my wrist and the wrinkle on your cheek when you smiled. I release you and spin around, with my arms out like a child, and then I pull you close to me, my hand moving from your hip to your back, my lips at the top of your ear.

But then the song ends, and Raquel steps back and says something, and then she puts her arms around the woman and they hold each other. There is clapping, and then the thick clouds above us start to send down rain.

"Did you feel that?" Raquel says. "It's raining!"

A flamenco starts up. Raquel turns and snaps her fingers at her ex-husband Charlie, who walks out and starts dancing. Stephen comes out and dances with his arms in the air. The short-haired woman turns and dances with our granddaughter, Elizabeth. Raindrops come down bigger and bigger, sending down those who have come before. More and more people come out, shouting and clapping. They crowd together, smiling as they dance in the rain, and laughing, these people I'll never know with people I've known forever.

*Nominated by Willow Springs*

# COMFORT

## by ANN HOOD

from TIN HOUSE

TIME HEALS.

She is in a better place.

She is still with you.

You should walk every day; you should write this down; you should go to church, to therapy, to the cemetery; these things will help you.

There is a heaven and you will see her again there.

You are not dreaming about her because you are closed to possibility.

Time heals. Once you have lived through all the firsts, it will get better. The first summer at the beach without her elaborate sand castles; the first day of school, when she would have put on her purple leopard backpack with her collection of key chains—a starfish, miniature Lincoln logs, the butterfly from Japan—and walked into first grade; her sixth birthday and her customary costume / painting / tea party birthday party; the first Halloween without her dressing as something with wings: an angel, a fairy, a ladybug; the first Thanksgiving when her face does not appear among the thirty others eating two twenty-three-pound turkeys in our dining room; the first Christmas that I do not have to hide art supplies in the closet in my study, the bags bulging with glitter markers and crayons and sketch pads and modeling clay and watercolors and fat paintbrushes and gel pens and rolls and rolls of stickers of smiley faces and daisies and puppies and stars; the first Valentine's Day that she does not cut out construction-paper hearts and string them together for me; the first Easter without an Easter egg hunt or a pink basket filled with

Smarties and Sweet Tarts and Peeps, the purple ones; the first anniversary of losing her, when the peonies are blooming in our garden and the air is filled with promise. After you have survived all of those things, it will get easier to live without her.

Are you writing down how you feel? *But I cannot write. I cannot think of anything except her, the way she looked splashing in the bathtub, the way she wiggled her toes against mine, the feel of her sticky hand holding on to my hand good and tight.* Write that down! It will help!

The images of those hours in the hospital, of the doctor's face telling you Grace was not going to make it, the rushing of nurses' feet with vials of her blood, the voice on the intercom announcing that Grace was in cardiac arrest, the way they made you wait outside the room, your face pressed against glass, the sounds of your screams, all of this will fade.

She is with you. She is a rainbow in the sky. She is the butterfly in your garden. She is the cardinal in the mimosa tree. *But I have called out her name to each of these things and they simply fade away.* That is because you don't believe.

You cannot stay in bed every day and watch *Sex and the City* on DVD. You need to get outside. You need to walk.

You will sleep again, an entire night through. *It is when I sleep that I am back in that hospital. My own screams wake me.*

Take Benadryl, Ambien, Xanax, Zoloft, Prozac, Dr. Bach's Rescue Remedy, smoke pot, drink white wine, warm milk, single-malt Scotch.

Go to grief groups and listen to other parents tell how they lost their children. Then you will know you are not alone. *But when I listen to how children are dying, on go-carts and in fires and with guns and falling out windows and from mistakes in hospitals, I only feel more despair.* Then you do not want to help yourself. These people can help you but you won't let them.

God loves you. *If there is a God, why would he have to take my Gracie Belle from me? Why would he do this?* God only gives us what we can bear. *But I cannot bear this.* Yes, you can. You are not trying hard enough.

She is in a better place. *How can a five-year-old little girl be in a better place without her mother?* Heaven is better than here. *But she is all alone. I am all alone.*

Are you writing anything down?

Here is a book by a rabbi who lost his son; by two women who both lost children and have written their stories; by C.S. Lewis, who lost his wife and was Catholic and wise; by a psychiatrist, a sociologist, a teacher; by someone who has interviewed parents who lost children. *But none of them lost Grace. They do not know what it is to lose Grace.*

You need to get out of bed; off that sofa; out of the house. *The world is full of five-year-old girls. They are everywhere I go. The supermarket is full of cucumbers and blueberries and pasta. Target is full of pink dresses and purple shoes and things that sparkle and glitter and shine; the drugstore seems to sell only nail polish and hair ornaments. Out in the world there are only five-year-old girls holding their mothers' hands wherever I go.*

You should walk every day.

Aren't you feeling better? You got through a year of firsts! *I did not go to the beach this summer. I did not park in my usual place at the school so I could avoid watching the first-graders filing outside through the playground at the end of the day. On her birthday I sat outside beside her toy log cabin and ate cucumbers and pasta and drank too much rosé and tried not to think about the feel of her in my arms the night she was born or how her skin was the color of apricots, while my husband talked to her best friend, Adrian Roop, and his mother in the dining room. I did not know what to do with her Christmas stocking, the one with the angel on it and her name sewn in my crooked attempt to use a needle and thread. I did not know how to celebrate a New Year without her. And on the first anniversary of her death, I ran away with my husband and son to Cape Cod and climbed the dunes there and felt the spring sunshine on my face as if these things could make me feel better.*

You look better!

You sound like yourself again.

Grace is sending you white feathers, heart-shaped stones, pennies from heaven.

Have you been writing this down?

I can't believe that after over a year you are still not going out more. You should be walking, taking Pilates, joining a gym. *My body cannot move. I am paralyzed.*

Here is a book about Holocaust survivors.

Did you know Winston Churchill, Abraham Lincoln, Mark Twain all lost children? And look at what they accomplished! *Then I am not as strong as they were. Grief is bigger than I am.*

Time heals.

Grace would not like you to be this way. *How do you know what Grace would like? I believe she would want me to miss her with every cell in my body. And that is how much I ache for her. My arms hurt from not holding her on my lap. My nose aches from not smelling her little-girl sweat and powder and lavender lotion smell. My eyes sting from not seeing her twirl in ballet class. My ears strain every morning for her calling, "Mama!" when she wakes up. My lips reach for her sticky kisses. At night I search for her.*

You need to give her clothes to unfortunate children. *Even her sparkly red shoes? Her pink skirt? Her lei made of paper flowers? Her leopard rain boots? Her two-pointed brightly striped pompom hat?* It is not healthy to keep a shrine. *But there are shrines to lesser things. To Jim Morrison. To pets. To saints who are no longer even considered saints.* But you need to move on.

Are you writing down any of this? *Only the lies people tell me. There are no words for the size of this grief. There are only lies.*

You will see. Time heals.

In time you will sleep again and dream of beautiful things.

In time you will not miss her.

You will see.

Time heals.

*Nominated by Tin House*

# THE FAMOUS WRITERS SCHOOL: LESSONS FROM FAULKNER'S HOUSE

by CYNTHIA SHEARER

from SPEAKEASY

THE FIRST THREE MONTHS I worked as curator of the Famous Writer's house, I had regular nightmares, like deep taproots down into how conflicted I was about the work. The dreams started the first night: I came upon a car wreck on the road between Oxford and Memphis, and the injured party inside had just died moments before. The injured party was Faulkner. There were scores and scores of bystanders, taking out their pocketknives or whatever they had handy, to carve little pieces of the Famous Writer's flesh while it was still fresh, so that they could keep it for a souvenir or sell it for a handsome profit.

In the last dream, I encountered the Famous Writer himself, short and white-haired and sad, on the little landing of the creaky staircase.

"Missy, what are you doing in my house?" he said.

"I'm just trying to help," I said. "It's like the time you shoveled coal in the powerhouse at Ole Miss. I need the work." And I mumbled something about needing a place to write at night, like his kitchen.

He nodded and vanished, and I quit having the nightmares. But I only lasted six years there.

"Missy is what he used to call me," said the Famous Writer's daughter when I confessed these dreams to her one afternoon in Charlottesville. She is short, with beautiful white hair, and she is the spitting image of her father. I had arrived bearing a boxful of family photos that had somehow survived the thievery of tangential relatives in the years after she grew up and married and moved away. They were real treasures, snapped by the Famous Writer himself on his little Kodak he would have had to stare straight down into to see her, an elegant young mother in a strapless black bathing suit and string of pearls, playing with her first baby in a wading pool. The photos were her property, and I was returning them to her. She had never seen them. Nobody had told her they were in the house, over thirty years after she and her mother turned it over to a public university. We had a quiet little laugh about how some professor somewhere would probably not be able to hone his curriculum vitae by publishing them.

Then I told her another story, from the time when I began to know my days in that job were numbered. One day in the house she'd grown up in, a total stranger walked in, bald and wearing some Bermuda shorts that could only be described as ill advised, and sporting a cauliflower nose.

"I just wanna know one thang," the man said. "Is his daughter his *real* daughter?"

"Excuse me?" I said.

"You know what I mean."

"Ever seen a picture of her?"

"I want to know if she is his *biological* daughter. I mean, from what I hear—"

True outrage, when it arrives, is like being touched by something so hot you can't even feel yourself being burned, and you can hardly remember it later. I don't remember my exact words, but I proposed a deal with the man. If he would research whether his own children were truly his and present proof to me, I would become more helpful on the subject of Faulkner's daughter.

On another afternoon a stranger demanded to know, "Was he impotent?"

"I don't know, sir," I said sweetly, through gritted teeth. "I wasn't there."

Those last few months before I left that job, such questions could send me into an ecclesiastical fury. *This, too, have I seen under the sun:* the taxpaying public, whether it is literate enough to read the

274

Famous Writer's books, feels entitled to *access*, in whatever limited manner it can comprehend. There are more readers who know that James Joyce wanted Nora to mail her panties to him than have actually read *Ulysses*, which took him umpty-how-many-dozen years to write?

Faulkner's house was one of the few museums left in America where visitors were not subjected to a canned, rehearsed, scripted "tour." We engaged in conversation with visitors on whatever level they chose to participate. On better days this sometimes could mean a six-hour literary conversation with a Russian or German who'd read the complete works, sitting on the fence by the paddock in the blessed isolation of winter while the rabbits and deer nibbled at the edge of the woods. On the worst days, it could mean a busload of retirees from Wisconsin, surly because their driver had stopped there looking for a bathroom for them.

*The horror, the horror*, if I may steal from Conrad.

"Show me where he drowned his wife in the pool," said one elderly lady one time.

"You're thinking perhaps of William *Shat*ner," said the grad student on duty that day. "This is William *Faulk*ner's house."

"I know, I know," said the Famous Writer's daughter softly, when I described all this to her. She told me that she and her mother had never envisioned their house being open for "tours" when they gave custody of it to a public university. They had meant for it to be something more useful, a roof over the heads of writers who needed a quiet place with some helpful books in it.

Imagine it, brethren and sisteren. Suppose you have become a Famous Writer. A semiliterate old lady staggers off a casino charter bus and squints into the sun in your driveway. She does not kneel and say, "My king," or anything along those lines. She asks in confusion, "Are we still in Alabama?" and announces that she has to pee. She would prefer to actually do the deed under your roof, and seems, uh, *discommoded*, that there are no public accommodations for her. She has, by God, paid her church tithes, her taxes, her cable TV, and garden club dues, and she wants *access*, baby, to the great lives that have been lived in her great republic. She is not what you'd consider a reader, but she's not averse to standing meekly behind a red velvet rope and surveying what others have deemed greatness.

And once inside your house, she can barely contain her disap-

pointment! The wattles of her neck are wobbling. Where are the liv-
eried servants? The plasma television? What kind of crib is this, anyway? I mean, your discount store chandelier is exactly like her baby
sister's in *Weehauken. My God*, your ironing board is the same identical one as her own. And there are entirely too many books in the
place. And what, please, is that bucketful of muddy sneakers in the
garage? She can hardly wait to get back on the bus, onward to the
casino where there will be, *yes ma'am*, brothel-sized chandeliers
worthy of Scarlett O'Hara and gold-plated public pissoirs the size of
steamboats, biggie-size. There she can feed coins into the slots, and
rest assured that, in due time, the biographers and filmmakers of the
republic will make their own fortunes when they visit the same house
feeling fully entitled to gain access to your correspondence, your
medical records, your underwear, your empties, your recycling bin.

The word *scandal* comes to us from the French, who got it from the
Romans, who got it from the Greeks. In Greek, it meant to snare or
trap, as one might capture a witless goose. Scandal's not so much
about whether the goose is caught in flagrante delicto—it's all about
how well the goose is cooked in absentia, in effigy ad absurdum, and
the relative juiciness of the results. Some linguists even relate the
word to the Latin verb for climbing, *scandere*. The goose may fall
into the cookpot, but those who stir the pot can social-climb to a
whole new level of prominence. Information is power. No information? Not to worry. That, too, is power in some quarters. You can always make veiled allusions to faulty intelligence later.

Somebody asked Flannery O'Connor why Southerners wrote
about freaks so much, and she said, sweetly, that it was because they
could still recognize one when they saw it. The same principle ap-
plies to scandal. A real writer can still recognize real scandal, which is
usually whatever is going on under the big table the general public
likes to belly up to when it smells cooked goose.

---

**Here's a little test to see if you know a scandal when you see
one. Mark an X beside each statement below that constitutes
a genuine scandal.**

\_\_\_ F., a Nobel laureate, is believed to have committed adultery with
J., an unknown.

\_\_\_ S., also an unknown assumed to be an educated woman, is said to have knelt and murmured, "My king," when F. entered a New York party in the 1950s, and it is generally believed she committed adultery with him.

___ B., temporarily a young nobody in the 1950s, would probably have happily committed adultery with S. but, alas, was not yet a Nobel laureate.

___ Therefore S. wouldn't have had the time of day for B.

___ There are human beings who've earned their living assembling such facts and selling them to publishers.

___ Eudora Welty was never a Nobel laureate.

(Answers: If you didn't mark the last statement as *absolutely scandalous*, you fail.)

---

**Put an I, for *incredible*, in any of the blanks below. Put an A beside any that strike you as *admirable*.**

___ Faulkner once observed a prominent literary scholar picking through the garbage behind his, Faulkner's, house.

___ Faulkner thereafter sometimes spiked his garbage with carefully typed gibberish.

___ F., the Nobel laureate, had an affair with the single M., in Hollywood.

___ Years later, when M.'s abusive husband had beaten her, F. wired her the trainfare to get away from him.

___ F. and M. loved each other, distantly, until the days they each died.

___ Not long before F. died, J. (remember her?) walked up to F.'s antebellum house in Mississippi, and his wife graciously said something close to, "He's inside, please go in and see him."

___ Within a year of M.'s death, her agent rolled up to F.'s antebellum house in Mississippi, by then a public museum, in a black Mercedes with California license plates, and offered to sell her most intimate and private papers, which were in the trunk. This was done in a manner somewhat reminiscent of cartoon figures with Swiss watches sewn into the linings of their coats.

___ I declined the offer.

(Answers: If you find it scandalous that F. and M. loved each other so deeply and for so long, while married to others, you need to grow up.

If you marked the last statement as *absolutely scandalous*, you may have missed your true calling. In your heart of hearts, you are a librarian, not a writer. If you were scandalized by Faulkner's spiking his garbage, you are a critic, not a writer. If you were scandalized by the agent, you probably are a writer. If you are outraged by the agent but would have purchased the papers in a heartbeat, you are probably already a Famous Writer, and you could perhaps have yet another, additional future, namely, insider trading.)

---

**In the blanks below, put CC for *crass commercialism*.**

___ Faulkner's nephew offered to sell me the car, the *very* car, in which F. had made his last trip to the sanatorium south of Memphis, the time he didn't come home alive. The car didn't run, of course, and would have to be put up on blocks, but it was the *very one*. For the low, low price of fifteen hundred dollars, take it or leave it.

___ I declined.

___ A descendant of staff at the sanatorium offered to sell me F.'s medical records.

___ I declined.

___ Some outfit up North offered to make refrigerator magnets and little replicas of the house to sell in the gift shop.

___ Faulkner's house did not have a gift shop for tourists.

(Answers: If it bothers you that there was no gift shop, you obviously have not read Faulkner, and you've missed your calling. You were not meant to write; you were meant to hawk tomatoes and birdhouses by the side of the road to tourists on their way to the alligator farm.

If you had sudden insights into where "Spotted Horses" came from, and your fingers itched to write some howlingly funny story about old 'fifty-something Fords that suddenly acquire the status of the Shroud of Turin, you've got real possibilities.

If you see similar situations in the lives of close writer friends that could be parlayed into tangible income for yourself, you too could become a Famous Writer, with perseverance and a good agent.)

---

**Put an O for *outrageous* in the appropriate blanks below.**

___ F. consumed prodigious amounts of alcohol.

___ When his daughter asked him not to get drunk on her sixteenth birthday, he looked down at her from the promontory of the Nobel laureateship and said, "Nobody remembers Shakespeare's daughter."

___ During these same years, Faulkner was employed by the Department of State, who wanted certain Famous Writers to travel abroad and "explain" the United States.

___ Faulkner wrote letters in response to what he'd seen on his travels. In the midst of the cold war, he observed that Russians were possessed of souls grown immense from their collective suffering, and that the Berlin Wall was a stupid idea and needed to come down.

___ His letters were filed and basically ignored. The functionaries at State made sly jokes with each other about how you just had to keep the liquor and the young ladies present to keep him comfortable.

___ In this same decade, his publisher, Bennett Cerf, playfully mailed him brochures and application forms from some outfit up North billing itself as the Famous Writers School.

___ The Famous Writer who got famous for his long hallucinatory passages about the nightmare of nations and history and race, drank so much one night in New York he passed out and burned himself badly on a radiator.

___ I once asked a doctor to tell me what the big white pills were in the silver cylinder from the Stockholm apothecary. "Codeine," he said, after one sniff. "Probably for his back pain."

___ In the film *Barton Fink* Faulkner is presented as a cartoonish drunk in Hollywood.

___ Faulkner's daughter was deeply grieved by that presentation, because it ignored his greatness.

___ A young French filmmaker wanted to foreground a whiskey bottle in front of the 150-year-old house and shatter it with a bullet, something about "cinema verité via symbolism."

___ I declined. No live ammo on National Historic Landmarks, sorry. To do so would be a felony.

___ Then the young French filmmaker wanted me to give him a framed photo of Faulkner's wife so that he could make it fall off the wall, to shatter it.

___ I declined.

___ I once threw two guys who said they were filmmakers out of Faulkner's house. One had tried to distract me while the other jumped the plastic barrier and was reaching for the sacred Underwood typewriter. I asked them to leave. They left. A good thing. The

279

typewriter was wired into the security alarm system. They got out just in time.

___ Within weeks, a rumor was sweeping town, out of the mouths of otherwise reasonably educated folk, that I had thrown the Coen brothers out of Faulkner's home because they'd portrayed him as a drunk.

___ Years later, after seeing *O Brother, Where Art Thou?*, I wondered aloud if the two had been the Coen brothers.

___ I sometimes lie awake at night, wondering if it really was the Coen brothers I threw out of Faulkner's house.

___ I sometimes hope it was.

The Coens, had they bothered to do their research, could have found much "material" in Faulkner's life and his death. There is one wildly funny story his nephew used to tell. After Faulkner died, his body was brought home, as per his request, in an inexpensive coffin, and placed in the parlor for viewing. His sister-in-law, thought to be something of a meddler, felt it was incommensurate with his station in life, so she ordered the funeral directors to retrieve him and install him in the best one they had in stock. (You'd have to see that long, curving driveway to fully appreciate the effort this order entailed.) After the body had been whisked away, the nephew came downstairs and saw that it was gone. "I thought somebody had taken Brother Will for a souvenir," he says. After the coffin swap, Faulkner was placed back in the parlor for viewing in his resplendent coffin, the one that showed up in the *Life* magazine photos, much like the one John F. Kennedy would be buried in. Then Faulkner's daughter arrived from Charlottesville, took one look at the coffin, and said, "Who in the hell picked that out?"

---

**Is it true? Who cares anymore? This is the price of immortality, friends and neighbors.**

___ A woman came into Faulkner's house, pointed to his office, and said, "Take me into that room. I want to show you something."

___ I took her past the plastic barrier into the room.

___ "My daddy was the bootlegger from Water Valley," she said. "We used to come here on Saturdays, and this hand would come out the back door and take the bottle, and then it would come back out again with the money. That's all I ever saw, just that hand coming out."

280

___ This was about the same time a restoration architect had found piles of empties, both licensed and bootleg, in the attic of an outbuilding. Some went back to the 1930s.

___ Out in the vast hinterlands and alleys of our great republic, there are, apparently, legions of young men who consume vast quantities of alcohol and say hurtful things to their loved ones, part of the territory if you want to be a Nobel laureate.

___ Some probably will be.

Answers? You still believe in answers?

If so, you fail.

Forget Shakespeare's daughter. Remember Faulkner's. She had the ringside seat at the Famous Writers School.

"I don't read much literary fiction," she said quietly that afternoon in Charlottesville. "Life is not that sad."

*Nominated by Speakeasy*

# YOU PEOPLE

## by NANCE VAN WINCKEL

from POETRY

People, don't ask me again where my shoes are.
The valley I walked through was frozen to me
as I was to it. My heavy hide, my zinc
talisman—I'm fine, people. Don't stare
at my feet. And don't flash the sign of the cross
in my face. I carry the Blue Cross Card—
card among cards, card of my number
and gold seal. So shall ye know I am of
the system, in the beast's belly and up
to here, people, with your pity.

People, what is wrong with you? I don't care
what the sign on your door says. I will go
to another door. I will knock and rattle
and if *you* won't, then surely someone, somewhere,
will put a pancake in my hand.

You people of the rhetorical *huh?* You lords and ladies
of the blooming stump, I bend over you, taste you,
keep an eye on you, dream for you the beginning
of what you may one day dream an end to.

The new century peeled me bone-bare
like a first song inside a warbler—that bird, people,
who knows not to go where the sky's stopped.
Keep this in mind. Do you think

the fox won't find your nest? That
the egg of you will endure the famine?

You, you people born of moons with no
mother-planets, you who are back-lit,
who have no fathers in heaven, hear now
the bruise-knuckled knock of me. I am returned.

From your alley. From your car up on blocks.
From the battered, graffitied railcars that uncouple
and move out into the studded green lightning.

Dare you trust any longer the chained-up dogs of hell
not to bust free? Or that because your youth's
been ransacked, nothing more will be asked of you?
If a bloody foot's dragged across your coiffed lawn—
do not confuse me with dawn.

Now people, about the shoes: the shoes
have no doubt entered the sea
and are by now walking the ramparts of Atlantis.
I may be a false prophet, but god bless me, at least
I have something to say. I lay myself down
in a pencil of night—no chiseled tip yet,
but the marks already forming in the lead.

*Nominated by Stephen Dunn, Dick Allen, Henry Carlile*

# PEARLIE TELLS WHAT HAPPENED AT SCHOOL

by DIANE GILLIAM FISHER

from KETTLE BOTTOM (Perugia Press)

Miss Terry has figured since we are living
in a coal camp, we ought to know geology,
which is learning about rocks. Every day
we got to bring in a different rock
and say what it is. Even our spelling words
is rock words, like *sediment* and *petrified*.
Yesterday, Miss Terry says, *Who can use
"petrified" in a sentence?* and Walter Coyle
raises his hand, which, he don't never
say nothing. He's a little touched, Walter is,
ever since his uncle Joe—he was the laughingest,
sparkliest-eyed man you ever seen—ever since Joe
got sealed in at Layland and they ain't never
gonna know if he got burnt up or gassed
or just plain buried. So Walter says,
and he don't never look up from his desk,
he says, *Miss Terry, can a person get petrified?*

Miss Terry thinks he is sassing her, 'cause she
don't know about Joe Coyle, and about
how Walter don't never sleep no more
nor hardly eat enough to keep
a bird alive, as his mama says.

284

Miss Terry sends him to the cloak room
but Walter, he just walks on out. I reckoned
that was the last we'd see of Walter.
He come back this morning, though, pockets
filled with rocks, and with a poke full of rocks.
Spreads them all out on Miss Terry's desk
'fore she even asks. *Well, alright*, she says,
*suppose you tell us what these are.*
Walter stirs the rocks around a bit, so gentle,
picks up a flat, roundish one and lays it
agin his cheek. *This here*, he says,
*is the hand.*

*Nominated by Eleanor Wilner, Perugia Press*

# SAD COINCIDENCE IN THE CONFESSIONAL MODE AND WITH A BORROWED MOVIE TROPE

by LUCIA PERILLO

from TRIQUARTERLY

. . . and then there is the idea of another life
of which this outward life is only an expression,
the way the bag floating round in the alley
traces out the shape of wind
but is not wind. In the fleabag hotel
in Worcester Mass., a man is dying,
muscles stiff, their ropes pulled taut,
his voice somewhere between a honk and whisper.
But float down through the years, many years
& it's us, meaning me & the man
as a boy who's upstairs in the house
where I've finagled my deflowering.
Maybe finagled. Hard to say if it's working.
It reminds me of trying to cram a washrag

286

down a bottleneck—you twist and twist
to make it reach, but it does not,
and in the end the inside of me
was not wiped clean. Oh I was once
in such a hurry. The job had to be done
before the pot roast was, his stepmother
thumping the ceiling under us: *Whatever*
*you're doing, you better get out*
*of your sister's room.* But her voice
carried more of the wasp's irritation
than the hornet's true rage, so we forged on:—
while our jury of busty Barbies perched
on their stiff toes, their gowns iridescent,
a sword of gray light coming through the curtain crack
& knighting me where I contorted
on the rug. And it's clear to me still,
what I wanted back then, namely my old life
cut up into shreds so I could get on
with my next. But the boy was only
halfway-hard, no knife-edge there,
though the rest of him looked like it were bronze,
with muscles rumpling his dark gold skin.
Meaning this is a story about beauty after all.
And when his roast was ready, I slipped outside,
where November dusk was already sifting down
into the ballrooms underneath the trees.
It was time to go home to my own dinner,
the ziti, the meatballs, Star Trek on TV,
but how could I sit there, familiar among them,
now that I was this completely different thing?
Sweat was my coat as I flew from his house
while the brakes of my ten-speed sang like geese.
But now it's his voice that resembles a honk
in a room where the empty amber vials
rattle underneath his narrow bed. Meaning
he's trying hard to take himself out.
And while I have as yet no theory
to unlock the secret forces of the earth, still
I think there's a reason why the boy & I,
when we grew up, both got stuck

with the same disease. Meaning the stiffness,
the spasms, the concrete legs—
oh I was once in such a hurry. Now
my thighs are purple from all the drugs
I'm shooting in, & I don't even want to know
how the boy looks wracked and wrecked.
Sometimes in the midst of making love
that kind of body will come floating in,
but quickly I'll nudge it away in favor of
the airbrushed visions. But not him,
the young him, the brass plate of whose belly
would be more lovely than I could bear,
though in chaster moments I will visit
that alcove of me where his torso is struck
by all the dark gold light that still slants in.
Oh we are blown, we are bags,
we are moved by such elegant chaos.
Call it god. Only because it is an expletive that fits.
His body, his beauty, all fucked up now.
*God*. Then the air cuts out, & then we drop.

*Nominated by Bruce Beasley, David Janss, William Olsen, TriQuarterly*

# HEAVENLY CREATURES: FOR WANDERING CHILDREN AND THEIR DELINQUENT MOTHER

fiction by MELANIE RAE THON

from THE PARIS REVIEW

## I. FATHERS

Didi Kinkaid and her three children by three fathers lived in a narrow pink and green trailer at the end of a rutted road in Paradise Hollow. One wintry November night, fifteen days after my father died, eleven days after he was buried, Didi's only son climbed the hill to our house, leaped from our bare maple to a windowsill on the second floor, shattered the glass above my mother's bed, and burst, bleeding, onto her pillows.

The house was dark, all his—Mother and I had gone to town that night to eat dinner by the hot-bellied stove in my brother's kitchen.

Evan Kinkaid helped himself to twenty-two pounds of frozen venison, a bottle of scotch, six jars of sweet peaches. The boy carried away my down comforter, a green sleeping bag, our little black and white television. He found Mother's cashmere scarf, rolled tight and tucked safe in a shoebox full of cedar chips, never worn because it was too precious. Now it was gone, wrapping Evan's throat, a lovely gift, something soft and dear for him to wear home and offer Didi. The starved boy crushed chocolate cookies in a bowl of milk and sugar. He stopped to eat, then slipped his hands in Daddy's gloves: deerskin dyed black, lined with the silky fur of a white rabbit.

In exchange, he left his blood, his dirt, his smell of bonfire smoke everywhere.

On the playground the next day, I saw the little wolf in sheep's clothing: Evan Kinkaid dressed in red wool and green flannel, my father's vest and shirt—both ridiculously loose, two sizes too big for a skinny child from the Hollow.

Why should the hungry repent? Evan Kinkaid wanted me to betray him. I stared, defiant as he was. *Mine*, I thought, *one holy secret*. Mother didn't deserve to know the truth, she who had sent me to school that day, against my will, against what I believed to be my father's deepest wishes. He would have wanted me home, with her, waiting till dawn to fold the clothes Evan tossed and trampled in their bedroom. Daddy would have wanted me to crawl under their bed, to find every stray sock, to lay my little hands on each one of his tattered undershirts as if cloth, like skin, might still be healed. Neither he nor I wanted to lie in the dark, listening to Mother scour and scurry.

By the mercy of morning light, Daddy hoped I would discover his last words, a note to himself still crumpled in the pocket of his wrinkled trousers: *Don't forget! Honey Walnut.* A loaf of sweet bread for me or a color of stain for a birdhouse?

The dead speak in riddles and leave us to imagine.

Face to face with the righteous thief, I made a vow to keep my silence. I was ten years old that winter day, arrogant enough to feel pity for this failure of a boy, Evan Kinkaid, stooped and pale, a fourteen-year-old sixth grader who had flunked three times, Evan Kinkaid who would never go to high school.

Less than a year later, Didi Kinkaid's pink trailer burned so hot even the refrigerator melted. By then, Didi lived in the Women's Correctional Facility in Billings, and Evan at the Pine Hills School for Boys in Miles City. Meribeth, seventeen, the oldest Kinkaid, a good girl, a girl who might grow up to be useful, lived in Glasgow with foster parents and eight false siblings. Fierce little Holly, just eleven—the dangerous child who once stole my lunch and slammed me to the wall of the girls' bathroom when I accused her—had become the only daughter of a hopeful Pentecostal minister and his barren wife in Polebridge.

So nobody was home the night the Kinkaids' trailer sparked, nobody real, though on any given night there night have been six or ten or twenty-nine tossed-out, worthless, wild kids crashing at Didi's, wishing she would return, their darling delinquent mother, dreaming she would appear in time to cook them breakfast, hoping to hear the roar and grind of her battered baby-blue Apache.

What a truck! Dusty, rusty, too dented to repair—you could squeeze thirty stray kids in the back and whoop all the way to Kalispell—you could pad the bed with leaves or rags or borrowed blankets, sleep out under the stars, warm and safe even in December.

*Oh, Didi*—slim in the hips, tiny at the waist—she might have been one of them, the best one, if you didn't spin her around too fast, if you didn't look too closely. The lost children built shelters of sticks and tarps in the woods behind her trailer. She let them drink beer in her yard. She gave them marshmallows and hot dogs to roast over the bonfire where she burned her garbage.

No wonder they loved her.

Any day now, Didi might honk her horn and rev the engine hard to wake them. *Sweet Mother of God!* Didi, home at last with four loaves of soft white bread and a five-pound tub of creamy peanut butter.

In half-sleep, the throwaway children kept their faith, but when they woke, they remembered: Mother in chains, Didi in prison. Of her seventeen known accomplices, three were willing to testify against her. *Three of them!* Sheree, Vince, Travis. *Traitors, snitches.* Three who still believed in real homes: mothers, fathers, feather pillows, fleece blankets.

Every night, these three lay alone between clean sheets, trying to be good, trying to be quiet, taking shallow breaths, hoping their clean and perfect mothers might slip into their rooms, kneel by their beds, and with tender mouths kiss them, kiss them, kiss them.

But only Didi came, in dreams, to mock and then forgive them.

Didi Kinkaid was made for trouble, slender but round, lovely to touch, lovely to hold, and mostly she liked it. To Didi Kinkaid, any roadside motel seemed luxurious.

What she liked best was the bath after, when the man, whoever he might be that night, was drowned in sleep on the bed and she was alone, almost floating, warm in the warm water, one with the water—not like the trailer where there was only a cramped closet with a spitting shower, three kids and twelve minutes of scalding water to share between them.

Any night of the week Didi might be lucky or unlucky enough to glimpse the father of one of her children—one good ole boy pumping quarters in the jukebox to conjure Elvis, one sweet, sorry sight for sore eyes slumped on a bar stool—and a feeling long lost might rise up: pity, fear, hope, desire.

There was Billy Hayes, Meribeth's father, and she'd loved him best, and she might have married him. But Billy was too young for Didi even when she was young—just sixteen when she was twenty—a skinny golden boy with a fuzz of beard and long flowing hair. Billy got sad when he drank and started looking like Jesus. She didn't have a chance with Billy Hayes, a boy still in high school, a child living with his parents. Didi knew from the start a woman from the Hollow could never keep him.

Now, the taxidermist Billy Hayes was old enough, and the years between them made no difference; his hair was thin and short; he had four kids and a wife named Mary. Mary Patrillo's patient parents had taught Billy Hayes to stuff the bodies of the dead and make the mouths of bobcats and badgers look ferocious, but the place he'd opened in Didi Kinkaid stayed empty forever.

When she told him she was pregnant, he never seemed to imagine any choice for them but having the baby—*I'll help you*, he said. And so it was: Meribeth came to be; and though Didi thought she'd loved Billy as much as she could love anybody, the child was her first true love, her first true blessing.

Billy helped her steal a crib and a high chair, booties and bibs, disposable diapers. *Shopping*, he called it. One night, their last night, he came to the trailer with a blue rubber duck and seven white rubber ducklings, toys to float in the tub Didi didn't have, so they put Meribeth in the kitchen sink with her eight ducks, and Billy, Sweet Billy Boy, hummed lullabies while he washed her.

Evan's dad was a different story, a mean sonuvabitch if ever there was one—Rick McQueen, Mister Critter Control, who was kind enough in the beginning, who rescued her at two-thirty one morning when she came home to discover pack rats had invaded the trailer. It didn't occur to her that a man willing to drown rats and feed cyanide to coyotes might harbor similar attitudes toward his own child. Evan swore to this day that he remembered his first beating. *Before I was born, when I was inside you.*

He banged his head and bruised his eye. Even now, when he's tired or mad or hungry, that place around the socket still hurts him. He traces the bone. *You have hard hips,* he says, and this much is true, so what about the rest of it?

Didi remembers how Evan kicked and punched, twisting inside her womb for days after the pummeling. She thought he'd choke, furious and desperate enough to strangle himself with his own umbilical cord. Maybe Evan truly remembers the beating, and maybe he's only heard Didi's story. Truth or tale—what does it matter in the end if a boy believes he felt his father's fists hammering?

*You saved me,* Didi says, and this is fact. The baby fought the man. If she'd had any inclination to forget, if she'd been tempted by Rick McQueen's tears, scared by his threats, or lulled by his promises, the baby unknown and unnamed reminded her night and day: *You let him stay, I'll kill him.*

Holly's father could have been any one of three people—it was a long winter, too cold, so it was hard to keep track of who was when, what might be possible. There was Didi's cousin, Harlan Dekker, and a fat man by the river whose name she's blissfully forgotten, and a third man too thin, like a freak, like the Emaciated Marvel in a cage at the carnival. *Half my life behind bars,* he said, *a guard, not a prisoner.* Now he lived on the road, *free,* he said, in his rust-riddled Mustang.

The man who could suck his belly back to his spine didn't have the cash for even one night at a motel, so Didi, in her kindness, in her mercy, brought him back to the trailer, and they made love right there with three-year-old Evan and five-year-old Meribeth wide awake, no doubt, and listening. He had a pretty name, *Aidan Cordeaux.* The last part meant fuse, and the first was the fire, so maybe the flickering man did spark inside her.

Strange as it was, she often hoped the starved prison guard was Holly's father, that the night she'd conceived her youngest child, Evan and Meribeth had been there with her. *Little angels!* She felt them hovering all night, close and conscious, her darlings lying together in the narrow bunk above the bed where she and the Living Skeleton made love, where she touched the man's sharp ribs and knotted vertebrae, where she prayed, *yes, prayed,* for God to give him flesh, to restore him.

293

She heard her two children breathing slowly afterward, asleep at last, and the man was asleep too, up in smoke, and so she was alone, yes, but safe unto herself, blessed by her children, and the sound of their quiet breath was so sweet and familiar that she felt them as breath in her own body, as wings of sparrows softly fluttering. *God, she thought, his messengers.*

She was drunk enough to pretend, drunk enough to imagine. Later, the cries of feral cats in the woods sounded half-human, and she had to laugh at herself. What a hoot to think God might send angels to Didi Kinkaid in her trailer. *Just my own damn kids, but Christ, it was comforting.*

Her cousin Harlan was probably Holly's dad. It made the most sense: Holly and Harlan with that bright blond hair, those weird white eyelashes. Harlan's wife lived in Winnipeg all that winter, following her senile mother out in the snow, lifting her crippled father onto the toilet. Harland and Didi met four times at the Kozy Kabins: twice to make love, once to watch television, once to be sorry.

More than anything, Didi wanted to believe Holly's father wasn't the fat man in his truck who passed out on top of her. She'd escaped inch by inch, hoping his cold sweat wouldn't freeze them together. She walked back to the Deerlick Saloon, to her own car, a yellow Dodge Dart that year, lemon yellow, a tin heap destined for the junkyard. She thought she should tell somebody he was out there alone at the edge of the river. She pictured him rolling off the seat to the floor, pants pulled down to his ankles, ripe body wedged underneath the dashboard. He could die tonight, numb despite all that flesh, and Didi Kinkaid would be his killer.

But the bar had been closed for hours, and her fingers were so stiff she could barely turn the key in the lock of her car door, arms so sore she could barely grip the wheel. Didi didn't feel sorry for anybody but herself by then, so she didn't stop at the all-night gas station, and she didn't call the police when she got home—she didn't even tell Rita LaCroix, her neighbor, the babysitter—she just dropped into bed, shivering, and the truth was she was so damn cold she forgot the man, his flesh and sweat, his terrible whinny of high laughter.

In the morning, she smelled his skin on her skin and she used every drop of water in the shower, all twelve minutes, and she drank bright green mouthwash straight from the bottle and she listened to the news on the radio. There was no report of a dead man gone blue as ice by the river. She figured he'd been spared and so had she, but when she thought of it now, she hoped to God she hadn't been cruel or stupid enough to abandon the one who was Holly's true father.

When Didi Kinkaid's child splintered the window above my mother's bed and entered our lives, her story became my story—her only son burst in my heart, her bad boy broke me open. My father was dead. Eleven months later, the second night of November, the night Didi's pink and green trailer burned and melted, I knew my mother was dying.

Didi had been in prison since August. When I imagined her children—the desperate ones she'd borne and the wild ones she'd rescued, when I imagined all the sooty-faced, tossed-up runaways left to wander—I understood there are three hundred ways for a family to be shattered.

Soon, so soon, I too would be an orphan.

## II. FIRE

The fire was revenge, intimate and tribal. We came to witness, we people of the hills and hollows, lured up Didi's road by smoke and sirens. Through the flames, I saw the glowing faces of Didi's closest neighbors: Nellie Rydell and Doris Kelso, Lorna Coake and Ruby Whipple. I thought that one of them must have sparked this blaze—with her own two hands and the holy heat of her desire.

Who poured the stream of gasoline, who struck the match, who lit the torch of wood and paper? *Tell me now. I keep all secrets.* Was it one of you alone, or did all four conspire together?

For the small crime of arson, no respectable woman ever stood trial. The trailer was a temptation and an eyesore, a refuge for feral cats, a sanctuary for wayward children. Now Didi's home could be hauled away, a heap of melted rubble. *An accident,* Ruby said. *A blessing,* Lorna whispered.

Who can know for sure? Maybe the small boy called Rooster lit a pile of sticks to warm the fingers of his twelve-year-old girlfriend Simone so that it wouldn't hurt where she touched him. Maybe cross-eyed Georgia squirted loops of lighter fluid into the blaze just to see what would happen, and all the children danced in the dark, hot at last, giddy as the fire spread, too joyful now to try to smother it.

But I will always believe those four women in their righteous rage burned Didi out forever.

Didi Kinkaid trespassed against us: She harbored fugitives; she tempted boys; she tempted husbands. She slept with strangers and her own cousin—and despite all this generous love; Didi Kinkaid still failed to marry the father of even one of her children.

Compared with these transgressions, the crimes named by Country Prosecutor Marvin Beloit—the violations for which Didi Kinkaid was shackled, chained, and dumped in prison—seemed almost trivial: receiving and selling stolen goods, felony offenses, theft of property far exceeding $1,000. To be precise: forty-one bicycles snatched by children and fenced by Didi over a thirteen-month period.

Forty-one, including the three treasures in her last load: a black and yellow 1947 Schwinn Hornet Deluxe with its original headlight, worth an astonishing $3,700; the 1959 Radiant Red Phantom, a three-speed wonder with lavish chrome, almost a motorcycle—and radiant, yes—worth $59.95 new, and now, lovingly restored by Merle Tremble's huge but delicate hands, worth $3,250; finally, the lovely 1951 Starlet painted in its original Summer Cloud White with Holiday Rose trim and pink streamers, worth only $1,900, but polished inch by inch for the daughter Merle never had. To him, priceless.

In court, Merle Tremble confessed: The jeweled reflector for the Phantom cost him $107. *A perfect prism of light, worth every penny.* He found a seat for the Hornet, smooth leather with a patina like an antique baseball glove, worn shiny by one particular boy's bones and muscles. *No man can buy such joy with money.*

For six years, Merle Tremble had haunted thrift stores and junkyards, digging through steaming heaps of trash to recover donor bikes with any precious piece that might be salvageable. Under oath, Merle Tremble swore to God he loved his bikes like children.

No wonder Didi laughed out loud, a snort that filled the courtroom. A man who believes he loves twisted chrome as much as he might love a human child deserves to lose everything he has, deserves fire and flood and swarms of locusts. But Didi's lack of remorse, her justifiable scorn, didn't help her.

For crimes named and trespasses unspoken, Didi Kinkaid received ten years, the maximum sentence.

*Ten years.* More than any man gets for beating his wife or stabbing his brother. More years than a man with drunken rage as his excuse might serve for barroom brawl and murder.

Didi's transgressions wounded our spirits. She fed the children no mother could tame. She loved them for a night or for an hour, just as she loved the men who shared all her beds in all those motel rooms, and this terrifying, transient love, this passion without faith that tomorrow will be the same or ever come, this endless offering of the body and the soul and the self was dangerous, dangerous, dangerous.

If she was good, then we were guilty. Exile wasn't enough. We had to burn her.

When Didi heard about the fire, she knew. *Busybody dogooders*, she said, *always coming to my door with their greasy casseroles and stale muffins, acting all high and holy when all they really wanted was to get a peek inside, see if I had some tattooed cowboy sprawled on my bed, find out how many kids were crashing at my place and if my own three were running naked. Kindhearted ladies benevolent as that did the same damn thing to my mother. Ran her out of Riverton in the end. Killed her with their mercy.*

The bikes were just an excuse. *It could have been anything*, she said, *but in the end, I made it easy.*

### III. BICYCLE BANDITS

Didi never asked the stray children for anything. Rooster and Simone brought the first bike to her doorstep, a silver mountain bike with gloriously fat tires, tires nubbed and tough enough to ride through snow and slush and mud and rivers, a bike sturdy enough to carry two riders down ditches and up the rocky road to Didi's trailer. A small gift, for all the times she'd fed them. Rooster said, *I've got a number and a name, a guy willing to travel for a truckload.*

Stealing bikes was a good job, one the children could keep, without bosses or customers, time clocks or hair nets. They loved mountain bikes best—so many gears to grind, so many colors: black as a black hole black, metallic blue, fool's gold, one green so bright it looked radioactive. Rooster had to ride that bike alone: His Kootenai girlfriend was afraid to touch it.

There was a dump in the ravine behind Didi's trailer, *The Child Dump*, she called it, because sometimes it seemed the children just kept crawling out of it. They glued themselves together from broken sleds and headless dolls and bits of fur and scraps of plastic. Their bones were splintered wood. Their hearts were chicken hearts. Their little hands were rubber.

She expected them to stop one day—she thought there might be nine or ten or even forty—but they just kept rising out of the pit. In court, the day three testified against her, County Prosecutor Marvin Beloit said he had reason to believe more than three hundred homeless children roamed the woods surrounding Kalispell.

They slept in abandoned cars and culverts. Busted the locks of sheds. Shattered the windows of cabins. Desperate in a blizzard last winter, two cousins with sharp knives stabbed Leo Henry's cow in the throat, split her gut with a hatchet and pulled her entrails out so that they could sleep curled up safe in the cave of her body.

*Three hundred homeless children.*

Sleep was good, was God, their only comfort.

Nobody in court wanted to believe Marvin Beloit. *Not in our little town.* Didi pitied him—her brother, her prosecutor—a man alone, besieged by visions. She knew the truth, but couldn't help him.

*Ferris, Cate, Luke, Scarla—Hansel, Heidi, Micah, LaFlora— Dawn, Daisy, Duncan, Mirinda.* These children offered themselves to Didi in humility and gratitude. Joyfully and by design, they became thieves. They'd found their purpose.

Sometimes when a child stole a bike, he stole a whole family, and they lived in his mind, a vision of the life he couldn't have: They pestered, they poked him. Nuke was sorry after he took the candy-striped tandem with a baby seat and a rack to carry tent and camp stove. That night he dreamed he was the smiling infant who had no words, who knew only the bliss of pure sensation. Wind in his face carried the scent of his mother: sweet milk and clean cotton, white powder patted soft on his own bare bottom. Daddy peddled hard in front, and the sun seemed so close and hot the baby believed he could touch it.

But Nuke woke on the hard dirt to the spit of his real name, *Peter Petrosky*, his mother's curse: *Not in my house, you little fucker.* Then he was an only child caught smoking weed laced with crack in his mother's house, in his father's shower. Doctor Petrosky was a genius, an artist with a scalpel who could scoop a pacemaker from a dead man and set it humming inside the chest of a black Labrador. Peter didn't wait to receive his clever father's pity or redemption. Sick with sound and light, the boy lay under his bed for an hour then climbed out the window. Now he was Nuke the nuke, a walking holocaust, sending up mushroom clouds with every footstep.

*Wendy, Wanda, Bix, Griffin.*

Tianna found a smoked chrome BMX with a gusseted frame and scrambler tires. She could fly on this bike, airborne off every mogul.

Indestructible. *Tianna!* Thirteen years old and four fingers gone to frostbite last winter. *No more piano lessons,* she said, *no flute, no cello.* Tianna imagined sitting at the polished mahogany piano in her parents' cedar house, high on a hill, overlooking the valley. Oh! How strange and lovely the music would sound, true at last, with so many of the notes missing.

She might lie down, *just for a moment,* and fall asleep on her mother's creamy white leather sofa. Sleeping outside was torture. Tianna sucked and bit her stumps. The fingers she'd lost itched in the heat and stung in the cold. *They're still there,* she said, *but I can't see them.*

*Naomi, Rose, Garth, Devon.*

Angel Donner bashed into his own basement and stole his own bike, a black and orange Diablo Dynamo that any kid could see was just a pitiful imitation of a Stingray, worth less than fifty dollars new and now worth nothing. He remembered it under the Christmas tree, his father's grin, his mother's joy, his pit of disappointment.

*Laurel, Grace, Logan, Nikos.*

There was the one who called herself Trace because she'd vanished without one. *Idaho, Craters of the Moon, family vacation.* Cleo Kruse climbed out the bathroom window while Daddy and his new wife and Cleo's two baby stepsisters lay sweetly sleeping. *Knew I was gone before it was light, but didn't start looking till sunset. I read about me in the paper. Daddy thought it was just my way—doing all I could to cause him trouble.*

Trace was the little thief who jimmied the lock of the garage where Merle Tremble had laced each spoke of his Hornet Deluxe, his Starlet, his Phantom. Cleo disappeared at eight, and now the girl gone without a trace was barely eleven. *Too big for your britches,* Daddy always said, but anybody could see she was puny. She wore loose T-shirts and baggy jeans, chopped her hair short, turned her baseball cap backwards. *I'm a boy,* she said, *halfway. That's the real problem.* She could never mind her p's and q's, never cross her legs in church, never sit still like a lady. Cleo Kruse was a six-year-old bully, suspended from first grade—two months for pinning and pounding a third-grade boy who called her *Little It,* who pulled her from the monkey bars, flipped up her skirt and said, *If you're a real girl, show me.*

Boy or girl, what did it matter now? Out here in the woods, down in The Child Dump, everybody was half-human. If you stole groceries to eat in Depot Park, you could convince yourself you might

299

go home someday, scrub yourself clean, eat at your mother's table. But if one day in August you got so hungry you ate crackling bugs rolled in leaves, you had to believe you'd turned part lizard and grown the nub of a tail. Cleo had eaten bugs in leaves so many times she decided she liked them.

*Jodie, Van, Kane, Kristian—Faith, Finn, Trevor, Nova.* They broke Didi's heart with their gifts and their hunger.

Sufi wanted to twirl like a dervish, spin herself into a blur, turn so fast the back became the front, the air the breath, the girl nothing. She wanted to stop eating forever, to grow crisp and thin, to see through herself like paper.

She didn't believe in theft. If nothing belonged to anybody, how could anything be stolen? Objects passed, one hand to another, and this was good, what God wanted, so she was glad to ride the Starlet out of Merle Tremble's garage, grateful to be God's vessel, perfectly at peace as she watched Cleo buzz ahead on the Hornet, and Nuke disappear on the Phantom.

*Caspar, Skeeter, Dillon, Crystal—Renée, Rhonda, Bird, JoJo— Margot, Madeleine, Quinn, Ezekiel.* Swaddled in her narrow prison bed, Didi counts the lost children as she tries to fall asleep—so many came to her door, and now she wants to remember. *Cody, Kira, Joyce, Jewell.* If ninety-nine were found and one missing, she wouldn't sleep: She'd search the woods all night, calling. Nate carved his own name into his own white belly, a jagged purple wound that kept opening. *If my head's smashed flat, my mother will still know me.* Ray taught the others to make beds of boughs. Cedar is soft enough, and young fir with blistered bark smells of balsam, but spruce will stab your hands and back: a bed of spruce is a bed of nails.

Didi tries to rock herself to sleep, but the rocking brings the children close, and she sees their lives, so quick and sharp, one dark cradle to another.

*Dustin, Sam, Chloë, Lulu—Betsy, Bliss, Malcolm, Neville. Oh, Didi, you sing their names. Mercy, Po, Hope, Isaac. Let them all join hands. Here is your ring of thieves. Let them dance like fire around us.*

IV. THE LOVER

When Didi Kinkaid was good, she was very very good. She fed the poor. She sheltered the homeless. She lived as Jesus asks us to live: turned only by love, purely selfless.

But when Didi Kinkaid was bad, she abandoned her own three children, deserted Evan and Holly and Meribeth for nine days one January while she lived with Daniel Lute in his log cabin, perched high on a snow-blown ridge above Lake Koocanusa. Later, she swore she didn't understand how far it was, how deep the snow, how difficult it might be to find a road in the grip of winter.

She slept fourteen, sixteen, twenty hours. She woke not knowing if it was morning or evening, November or April. Daniel Lute's cabin whistled in the wind at the edge of outer darkness.

He fed her glistening orange eggs, the fruit of the salmon, its smoked pink flesh, his Russian vodka. Ten words could fill a day, a hundred might describe a lifetime.

They made love under a bearskin, *a Kodiak from Kodiak,* and the bed rocked like a boat, like a cradle, and the cradle was a box, sealed tight, sinking to the bottom of the lake far below them.

Daniel was a bear himself, tall but oddly hunched, black hair and black beard tipped silver, a man trapped in his own skin, condemned to live in constant hunger until a virgin loved him. Didi couldn't break that spell, and for this she was truly sorry.

On the seventh day, Daniel dressed in winter camouflage and left her alone while he stalked the white fox and the white weasel.

In utter silence, all the skinned Kodiaks walked the earth, bare and pink, like giant humans. Didi woke drenched in sweat, the skin of Daniel's bear stuck to her.

His fire flickered out. She'd never been so cold. She thought she'd die here, the stranger's captive bride, her face becalmed by hypothermia. But her children came to drag her home. Their muttering voices surged, soft at first, then angry. She tasted Holly's black-licorice breath and smelled Evan's wet wool socks. Meribeth said, *It's time, Mom. Get up.*

The children sat on the bed. Didi felt their weight, but never saw them. Tiny fingers pinched her legs like claws. Two little hands gripped her wrists and tugged. Six tight fists pressed hard: chest, ribcage, pelvis, throat.

The basin by the bed was full. It took all her strength and all her will to rise from this bed of death and go outside to piss in the snow. Her clamoring children had grown furiously still, unwilling to touch, unwilling to help. She ate pickled herrings from a tiny tin. They tasted terrible; they filled her up. She pulled Daniel Lute's wool pants over her own denim jeans and cinched them tight with his leather belt. Though the bearskin was heavy, she took it too, just in case she couldn't make it off the mountain, just in case she needed to lie down and sleep inside the animal.

She returned with gifts to appease her children: $309 in cash, two pounds of smoked salmon, a silver flask with a Celtic cross, still miraculously full of Daniel's brandy.

She came with a preposterous tale, the truth of sinking thigh-deep in the snow as she climbed down the ridge, the luck of finding the road around the lake before dark, the blessing of hitching a ride with an old woman driving herself to the hospital in Libby. Adela Odegard had crackers in the car, five hand-rolled cigarettes, half a thermos of coffee. *The gifts of God for the people of God: Body, Blood, Holy Ghost.* Didi ate and drank and smoked in humble gratitude.

Adela Odegard looked shriveled up dark as an old potato, a woman so yellow, so thin, Didi thought she might be dead already, but her wild, white hair glowed and made her weirdly beautiful.

In Libby, Adela delivered Didi to her nephew, Milo Kovash, and Didi slept on his couch that night. In the morning, Milo gave her ten dollars and dropped her at the truck stop diner. He knew a waitress there named Madrigal, and the waitress had a friend named Fawn who had a little brother named Gabriel, *Gabe Lofgren*, sixteen years old and glad to skip school to drive Didi Kinkaid down to Kalispell.

A story like that could turn the hard of heart into believers, or the most trusting souls into cynics.

### V. HOME

Didi's children chose to believe. *Mercy*, she thought, *who deserves it?* She smelled of creosote and pine, pickled herring, her own cold sweat gone rancid. She had Daniel's pants and belt as proof—so yes, some of what she remembered must have happened.

After her shower, Didi wore the bearskin around her naked self, his head above her head, and her children stroked her fur: their own mother, so soft everywhere. The Kodiak had a face like a dog's. He might be your best friend. *From a distance.*

Didi told her children that the cabin above the lake was dark as the inside of a bear's belly. *Swallowed alive*, she said, *but I had a silver fishing knife; I stole it from the trapper.* She showed them the jagged blade. *I cut myself out when the bear got sleepy.*

Now the Kodiak's skin was her skin, the gift of the father she never had, Daniel Lute: She could wear him like a coat, pin him to the wall, use him as her blanket.

Didi and her children drank Daniel's brandy, and the ones who wanted to forget almost did forget how they'd lived without her.

Two nights before Didi returned, little mother Meribeth, not yet thirteen, had made soup with ketchup and boiled water, crushed saltines and a shot of Tabasco. Every morning of the week, she got her ten-year-old brother and six-year-old sister to the bus on time— so nobody would know, so nobody would come to take them.

Though Evan might pull Holly from her swing, though Holly might bite him, though Meribeth might scold them both—*You little shits*, might cuss them down, *I'm so damn tired*—they belonged to one another in ways that children who live in real houses never belong to their brothers and sisters.

Only Holly stayed hard now, refusing to eat Daniel's fish, loving the pang of her hunger, the fishing knife stuck sharp in her belly. Brandy burned her throat and stomach, and she loved that too, the way it hurt at first, then soothed her. *Mother in a bottle, the slap before the kiss, the incredible peace that comes after.*

What do I know of Didi's grief? Who am I to judge her?

The day I became a twenty-two-year-old widow, the day my husband who was a fireman died by fire—not in a trailer or a house, not as a hero saving a child, but as a father driving home, as a husband who dozed, as a man too weary to turn the wheel—that day when my husband's silver truck skidded and rolled to the bottom of the gully— when three men came to my door to tell me there was no body for me to identify—only a man's teeth, only dental records—that impossibly blue October day, I began to understand why a woman might refuse to dress and forget to wash, how a mother might fail to rise, fail to love, fail to wake and feed her children.

*Didi, I know what it means to melt away, to repent forever in dust and ashes.* My daughters lived because my brother found us. My children ate because my brother in his bitter mercy stole them.

*Lilla, Faye, Isabelle—most darling ones, most beloved—though I lay in my own bed, I deserted them in spirit.*

In the days after the trailer burned, in the months after Didi Kinkaid went to prison, people said she got what she deserved. *But Didi, what about your children?*

One Friday night, as Didi lay rocking in the cradle of Daniel Lute's bed, Meribeth and Holly dressed up in her best clothes—a slinky green dress, a sparkly black sweater. The little girls teetered on their mother's spiked heels. Evan let Meribeth paint his nails pink and glossy. Holly rouged his cheeks and smeared his mouth red while he was sleeping. In the morning, the boy glimpsed the reflection of his own flushed face and soft lips, and before it occurred to him to be ashamed, he thought, *Look at me! I'm pretty.*

*Didi, no matter what we deserved, our children deserved to stay together.*

## VI. MOTHER

After her nights under the bearskin, Didi made a promise to always get herself home before dawn, to never again let her children wake alone in daylight.

She vowed to love her work. That's where the trouble started. She'd spent the whole dark day hunched over her sewing machine, drinking and weeping like her own pitiful mother. *Oh, Daphne!* Seven years gone, ashes scattered to the wind from a high peak in Wyoming, and still, after all this time, she could blow through a crack under the door and make her daughter miserable.

They were ashamed together, mending clothes for the dead who can't complain and don't judge you. Didi saw Daphne's crippled hands, each joint twisted by arthritis. Mother needed her Whiskey Sours, her Winston Lights, her amber bottle of crushed pills—though the killers of pain made it hard to sew, and the smoke made her bad eyes blurry.

Seeing her mother like this made Didi wish for the father she didn't have. Murmuring beekeeper, Jehovah's Witness, busted-up rodeo rider with a broken clavicle—who was he?

*Be kind,* Daphne said, *any man you meet might be your daddy.*

Didi's real father was probably the hypnotist at Lola Fiori's eighteenth birthday party, the Amazing Quintero, who chose Daphne because, he said, *Pretty girls with red hair are the most susceptible.*

Under his spell, Daphne was an owl perched on a stool, a wolf on all fours, a skunk, a snake, a jackrabbit, a burro. She hooted and howled. Quintero made her ridiculous.

Alone, in Quintero's room, the hypnotist blindfolded her with a silky cloth, its violet so deep she felt it bleeding into her.

Didi imagined her mother on her hands and knees again, not hypnotized, the scarf tied around her head like a halter. If this was the night, if Quintero was the father, if her mother hooted and howled and bucked and brayed the night Didi was conceived, the whole world was horrible.

As Didi sewed, as Didi drank whiskey and water, as her own fingers ached, as her own seams grew crooked, she thought, *There you are, Mama. I'm just like you.*

At dusk, she delivered the pressed clothes to Devlin Slade's Funeral Home: a gray suit for a handsome young man and a white christening dress for a newborn baby.

She meant to drive straight home. Rain had turned to sleet, and all the dead were with her. She was almost to the Hollow, almost safe with her children in the trailer, and the sleet softly became snow, and she thought God must love her even now, despite her fear, despite her sorrow. In the beams of her headlights, He showed her the secret of snow: each flake illuminated.

*Each one of them, each one of us, is precious.*

Mesmerized by snow, Didi didn't see the deer until the animal leaped, with astonishing grace, as if to die on purpose. The doe bounced onto the hood and crumpled on the slick pavement, but she didn't die, and Didi stopped and got out of the truck and walked back down the road to witness the creature's suffering. The animal lay on her side, panting hard, legs still running. Frenzied, she tried to stand on fractured bones. They'd done this to each other.

A man appeared, walking out of the snow, a ghost at first, then human. He'd seen it all, before it happened. The stranger had a gun in his glove box to put Didi and the deer out of their misery. The blast of the bullet through the doe's skull made Didi's bones vibrate. She felt snowflakes melting on her cheeks and was amazed again: this mercy in the midst of sorrow.

The man dragged the limp animal toward the woods, then knelt to wipe his hands in the snow. She would have gone anywhere with him. That January night, Didi Kinkaid considered Daniel Lute her personal savior. *Heading to town*, he said. *Need some medicine.*

She ditched the Apache less than a mile from the trailer, and slid into Daniel's El Camino. She told him: *One drink, that's all, three kids home alone*; and Daniel said, *No problem.*

If Didi learned to work with love, nothing like this could ever happen again. She had small hands and a good eye for the eye of the needle, a mother's gifts, both curse and blessing. Self-pity led to betrayal. Any work done with dignity might become holy. Sometimes, as you sewed a frail woman into her favorite lavender dress, as you stitched the seams to fit close where she'd shrunken, you touched her skin and felt all the hands of all the people who had ever loved her.

After Didi Kinkaid came home to the children she'd abandoned, she saw every filthy, furious, half-starved stray who rose out of The Child Dump as her own. Their mothers had failed to love them enough, and now they hated themselves with bitter vengeance.

*Mine*, she thought, *each one. I was that careless.*

When she cut gum out of Holly's hair, or bandaged Meribeth's thin wrist, or touched the sharp blades of Evan's narrow shoulders, she couldn't believe she'd done what she had done; she didn't know how she'd survived one day without them. No man could save her now. No tub was deep enough to tempt her. She sewed with faith. She loved her children. She never stayed out till dawn. She kept these promises. She offered herself to the strays, and the ritual of love made her really love them.

### VII. THE ROAD TO PRISON

Between March 1989 and early April 1990, Didi borrowed her cousin Harlan Dekker's white van three times to deliver bicycles to Beau Cryder who agreed to meet her just south of Evaro. For testimony against her, Beau walked free. *Flesh peddling*, the lawyers called it, not in court but to each other.

Nobody wanted Cryder, twenty-five and still a kid, a bad luck boy, out of work seven months, with a pregnant eighteen-year-old wife and a two-year-old son. Nobody wanted to trace the bikes to Liam Jolley, Beau's uncle, a once-upon-a-time hero in Vietnam and now just a crippled ex-cop in Missoula. Nobody ever wanted to hear how Liam's devoted daughter Gwyneth had ferried the bikes—sometimes whole and sometimes in pieces—to dealers in Butte, Boise, Anaconda, and Bozeman.

They were the victims of Didi's crimes. Her body could be exchanged for theirs, her breath for their freedom. Nobody in or out of court objected.

When Didi learned the value of Merle Tremble's bikes, she understood she'd been both betrayed and cheated. Beau paid two hundred for the set, three-twenty for the load: At the time, it seemed a fortune. Didi planned to stop in Kalispell on her way home. She wanted to buy her raggedy band of thieves two buckets of fried chicken and a tub of buttery mashed potatoes. They needed brushes and tooth-paste, calamine for poison ivy, gauze to wrap their cuts and burns, ar-nica for bruises. She intended to bring gallons of ice cream: *Fudge Ecstasy, Banana Blast, Strawberry Heaven*. She wanted the children to know there was enough: They could eat themselves sick tonight and still eat again tomorrow. Sooner or later, she'd spend everything she'd earned on them. She didn't care about her profit.

Didi took Evan on her last trip, to help her load the bikes, to help her deal with Cryder. She promised to pay him fifty. *My best boyfriend*, she said, *my partner*. In truth, she'd made him her ac-complice.

They might have gone free for lack of evidence, but Beau Cryder refused to take Angel Donner's Dynamo and a cheap BMX with popped spokes and a bent axle. Didi headed back across reservation land, through Ravalli, Dixon, Perma. She thought she was safe here, outside whiteman's law, protected by the Kootenai and Salish. She planned to dump the bikes before she got to Elmo.

They stopped at Wild Horse Hot Springs, *to celebrate*, she said, and they left the bikes in the van while they soaked for an hour, naked together in one room, immersed in hot mineral water.

She never figured on a raid. Never contemplated the possibility that Travis Poole might become a snitch, might want to go home, might tell his father, who would tell the police, who would tip bounty hunters—two trackers who lived outside the laws of any nation, who were free to bust down the door of a private room and drag a kicking woman and her biting boy from sacred water. The men shoved Didi and Evan out the door barefoot and naked, wrapped them in stiff wool blankets, bound them, gagged them, and stuffed them face down in the backseat of their beat-to-hell black Cadillac.

At precisely 3:26, back on whiteman's time, the fearless hunters delivered two fugitives and their stolen bicycles to the proper au-thorities in Kalispell.

## VIII. THE KINGDOM ON EARTH

Didi never caught a break for good behavior. If a guard spit words, she spit back. She was disrespectful. She stashed contraband: twenty-seven unauthorized aspirin, ten nips of tequila, and one shiny gold tube of coral lamé lipstick. Lipstick inspired vanity and theft, dangerous trades and retribution. Twice denied parole, Didi Kinkaid served every minute of her 3,653-day sentence.

Now, four years free, she sews clothes for the living and the dead in Helena. She could start a new life with a new name and a grateful lover in Vermont or Texas. But she stays here, close enough to visit Evan once a week in Deer Lodge. Her boy lives in a cell, down for fifty-five, hard time, attempted murder.

Evan was twenty years old and out of the Pine Hills School for Boys just thirteen months when he hit the headlines. A weird tale: hunting with a forbidden friend, Gil Ransom, thirty-nine and on parole, a known felon—dusk, out of season—Gil's idea, *just a little adventure*. They fired from the windows of the car—dumb beyond dumb and highly illegal. Any shadow that moved was fair game: deer, dog, rat, chicken. They smoked some weed. They split a six-pack. Evan saw trees walk like men through the forest.

An off-duty cop who recognized the roar of Gil's Wrangler followed them up a logging road, bumped them into the ditch, and tried to arrest them. Gil shot Tobias Revell three times: *Just to slow him down, nothing serious.* They left him crawling in the snow, wounded in the leg and neck and shoulder. He could have bled to death. He could have died of shock or hypothermia. But he was too pissed off to die. He lived to speak. He lived to bring those men to justice.

*Justice?* Evan learned that it didn't matter who pulled the trigger. For the abandonment of Tobias Revell, for the failure to send someone out that night to save him, Evan Kinkaid shared Gil's crime: the gun, the hand, the thought, the bullets.

Meribeth does not visit her brother. She teaches in a three-room school and lives without husband or children in a two-room shack up a canyon west of Lolo. I picture her as she was: flat-chested and gangly. She speaks softly. She walks swiftly. She never looks anybody straight in the eyes, but she never looks away either. She seems humble and kind, dignified even when she wears a dress sewn from an old checkered tablecloth. Meribeth Kinkaid, a princess in rags, mysteriously moving among peasants who scorn her.

Meribeth's worst fear is that one day her mother and brother and sister will knock at the door of her secret cottage in the canyon. Meribeth's deepest desire is that Evan and Holly and Didi will one day sit at her table to share a meal of bread and fish and wine and olives, that they will all sleep that night and every night thereafter in one bed in the living room, on three mattresses laid out on the floor and pushed close together, breathing as one body breathes, heart inside of heart, holy and whole, miraculously healed.

Eight months after she was adopted, Holly Kinkaid escaped Reverend Cassolay and his good wife Alicia. She didn't want to be saved. She'd been baptized by fire. If she couldn't live with her brother and sister, if the trailer was burned to rubble and gone forever, Holly wanted to live alone in a junked car or a tree or a culvert.

I am a mother now, an orphan, and a widow.

Sometimes in the early dark of winter I feel Holly at my window watching my daughters and me as we eat our dinner. She won't come in. The cold no longer feels cold to her. The cold to her is familiar.

This morning—a deep gray November morning, woods full of damp snow, light drizzle falling—I followed the school bus to town, twenty-three miles. My daughters Lilla and Faye, nine and six, sat in the far backseat of the bus to flap their hands and wave furiously, to smash their lips and noses flat against smudged glass. Their terrible faces scared me.

Isabelle, my youngest, my baby, slept in her car seat. I heard every wet sound: wipers in the rain, melting snow, dripping trees, the murmuring woods closing around us.

I saw flowers in the rain: boys in blue and girls in yellow, a tiny child in a pink fur coat, and another dressed in bright red stockings—all the pretty children waiting for the bus in bright pairs and shimmering clusters. Sometimes a mother stood in the center to shelter them beneath her wide umbrella.

In this rain, in this dark becoming light, I began to see the ones who won't come out of the woods. *Griffin, Bix, Wanda, Wendy.* They wear olive green and brown and khaki, coats the color of fallen leaves, jeans stained with blood, boots always muddy. They steal the skins of wolves and wings of falcons. The red fur of the fox swirls down Tianna's spine, and her teeth are long but broken.

*Hansel, Heidi, Micah, LaFlora.* They never grow up or old. They starve forever. Cleo Kruse who vanished without a trace, who could never be just one thing or another, has the body of a lynx and the eyes of a hoot owl, the legs of a mule deer, and the hands of a child.

*Faith, Bliss, Trevor, Nova.*

Vince Lavadour who betrayed Didi Kinkaid, who testified against her, has lost his arms and legs, has found instead his fins and tail. The boy slips free at last, a rainbow trout, gloriously striped and speckled.

309

*Nate, Ray, Grace, Laurel.*

Angel's skin bursts with thirty-thousand barbed quills. Bold in his new body, Angel says, *Only fire will kill me.*

*Dustin, Rose, Lulu, Chloë—Georgia, Sheree, Travis, Devon.*

Rooster knows that if he eats as the coyote eats, he will live forever. And so he does eat: snakes, eggs, plastic, rubber, sheep, tomatoes, rusted metal, dead horses by the road, dead salmon at the river.

*Simone, Nuke, Duncan, Daisy.*

Last summer, Sufi flung herself fifty feet into the air at twilight. Flying heart, vesper sparrow, she sang as if one ecstatic cry could save the world. Now she lies broken under dead leaves. She smells only of the woods—pine under snow, damp moss, a swirl of gold tamarack needles. Her wish comes true at last: She is one with God, one with mud and air and water. But if Didi called her name tonight, from death to life she might recover.

*Naomi, Quinn, Madeleine, Skeeter—Rhonda, JoJo, Neville, Ezekiel—Finn, Scarla, Luke, Jewel.*

How quickly the night comes!

I am home at dusk, so many hours later, my three girls safe this night in the house their father built before he left us. Birds cry from the yard, and I go to them, a mother alone in the gathering dark. A flock of crows whirls into the gray sky. *Didi, there must be ninety-nine, there must be three hundred dark birds rising on their dark wings.* When they land, the crows fill a single tree, every branch of a stripped maple.

*Your children are my children. They are dangerous. They are in danger.*

One by one, each black-eyed bird falls to the ground, brittle and breakable, terrible and human.

*Oh, my children, all my little children, I knew you before you were in the womb. Love is the Kingdom on Earth. As we fall to earth this day, let us love, let us love one another.*

*Nominated by Erin McGraw, Michael Martone*

# THE MECHANICS

## by PAUL ZIMMER

from GREAT RIVER REVIEW

An EYESORE, my mother called it. Neighborhood legend had it that the building was originally a bootleg operation disguised as a pickle factory; but in the late 30s Art Saunier acquired it and changed it into an auto repair shop. I was a child, and hence Art's Garage seemed to me a place of true significance when I played near it in our quiet neighborhood. It was a long, tan stucco building in the middle of our block of tidy frame houses, extending all the way back from McGregor Avenue to the alley called Rose Court, and it seemed like a cave through the summer brightness.

When the world war started, Art closed it down and went to serve in the army paratroopers. He was severely wounded in Sicily and received an early discharge. He came home walking with a limp, his right cheek and jaw mangled, and his eye drooping in a perpetual wince. I remembered almost nothing of Art before he went away, but my father said he had been steady and strong. Now he talked with a lisp and sometimes his hands shook.

Two large, sagging doors hung at the entry to the garage, at the end of a concrete ramp running up from our street. There were glass brick windows along each side of the building with hinged prop panels in the middle. Inside, the long building was divided into three large, open rooms. The front part was Art's work area—benches, jacks, pull-lights, heavy wrenches, screwdrivers, rubber hammers. In the middle bay Art parked junked vehicles that he stripped for parts, and the back room was where he discarded useless, impossible junk. Art never threw anything away. He kept a space open in the middle of this third room, and all around the walls he piled greasy, mechanical flotsam and jetsam. "You never know," he would say.

He was a messy, eccentric mechanic. There were pools and smears of oil on the filthy cement. Broken gearwheels, shafts, and piston rods were tossed into corners until he had time to transfer them to the back room. But apparently Art knew his stuff. Our neighbor, Ron Flynn, said, "He's good. That man can zip a busted motor back up and make it sing again." Art's business was brisk, and often he worked late into the night.

My father took a stroll each evening after supper to smoke a cigar, and usually I walked with him. We often stepped into the garage on our way home to chat with Art as he worked. He kept a heavy, oil-stained wooden bench in his repair area for visitors. As a rule there were two or three neighborhood men hanging around or playing poker. Art was under a jacked-up car or had his head under a hood, and rarely joined in these conversations, but he seemed to enjoy having his garage serve as a kind of neighborhood evening men's club.

Art's war wounds seemed frightful to me. On summer days I would sometimes wander into the garage to say hello to him, and find him slumped on the sitting bench with his head in his hands. He was very lean and when he raised his head in the dim light from the glass brick windows, the shadows were deep in his eye sockets and across his wounded cheek. He wore a filthy engineer's cap on his unwashed gray hair. He sighed often, and did not look at you when he talked. My father said that Art had a girlfriend when he went away to war, but she married someone else while he was gone. Now that he was so badly hurt, it didn't seem possible that a woman would have him. I never saw him smile. Occasionally he would fake a cackle when one of the men told a joke, but he kept his mouth rigid when he laughed.

When I looked in on Art during the day, if he had a moment and was in the mood, he would try to explain some of the work he was doing. He asked me to help him by turning a screw or bolt. As I did this, he carefully explained and assured me that what I was doing made a difference, holding two parts together or tightening an important connection. With his greasy fingers he would draw pictures and diagrams on the back of old bill forms to illustrate connections and working parts.

But I was a small boy and I never understood how the engines worked. He could see this, but he kept trying to instruct me, and he was a good, earnest teacher. Finally, I would say, "Mr. Saunier, I've got to go now."

On one side of Art's Garage building was a house, but the other side faced a vacant lot full of tall grass and weed trees. This was sacred ground to me. I had buried my pet rabbit, Mortimer, in this soil. I knew a stray cat who hunted the weeds. She was very strange and skittish and accepted only me as her friend. One summer I cleared a patch of weeds and constructed a wooden hut from orange crates I purloined from Volzer's Grocery. I built it beneath cooling ailanthus trees, propping it against the garage under one of the glass brick windows. I kept it stocked with comics, forbidden matchbooks, and candle stubs I had pocketed from the wastebasket in St. John's sacristy when I served mass. I thumb-tacked a picture of Jim Hegan, the Cleveland Indian's catcher, on the rough boards. It was my secret place. I could hear Art inside, talking to himself and clanking his tools.

I got into a scrap with my playmates one August afternoon and retreated to my secret hut. My mother had given me a worn-out bed pillow, and I propped myself up, nibbled some Good 'n Plenties from a Mason jar, and lit one of my candle stubs. It was very quiet in the semidark with only grasshoppers grating the summer heat in the field and the stray cat purring as I stroked it. I had just begun turning the pages of a Boy Commandos comic when I heard a sound that began like a pennywhistle, descending abruptly to a growl, trailing off into a wail, then breaking into sobs. It came once more, the pattern repeated—then again, this alarming sound like a great angry bird, again, then again. I bumped my head as I tried to stand up, then scrambled out of the hut. I stood in the high sunlight of the field, knee deep in broomgrass and cheat, rubbing my head. The wailing went on and on, echoing from the window of Art's Garage, the sound making me feel desolate and frightened.

I ran through the weeds to the front of the building and peered into the big open doorway, into the long darkness extending through the three rooms all the way back to Rose Court. The howling was coming from the rear of the building.

I thought to go for help, but this would take time. There was an urgency in the calling. I stepped into the dank light of the garage and crept back and back, through the work area, the stacks of worn tires, criss-cross of greasy shafts and gears, tools scattered about the pitted cement, the smell of ancient engines and burnt-out gears.

Into the next room of stripped-down cars, shells of derelict Fords, Chevrolets, and Dodges that Art had stripped down for parts. Then into the last room, the room of chaos, the space where abandoned, totally useless things had been thrown into corners, smelling of rust, encrusted carbon, and rotting rubber.

Art was in the open space in the middle of the junk piles, pacing with a violent motion, holding his head as he reeled back and forth in the light coming through the glass block window. His howling had not varied, the shrill cry, grinding into a coarse growl that ended in a wail. His mouth stayed open, his eyes seemed lidless as he limped back and forth. I thought he might be trying to kill himself with his squalling.

I wanted to bolt from this room of anguish; more than anything I had ever felt—I wanted to flee. But if I ran, who would help Art? I cannot say why I held my ground. A small boy. Perhaps I felt pity—an obscure thing for a child to feel—but it was a concern that overcame my uncertainty and terror.

"Mr. Saunier," I said tentatively. He did not stop his wailing.

"Mr. Saunier, are you hurt?"

He paused then, lowered his hands from his head and looked about. When he saw me he looked away. His mouth loosened. He wrung his hands and blinked. "Oh," he murmured. He closed his eyes, but he was quiet.

"Are you okay?" I asked.

He looked at me again; then his eyes rolled up into his head. "Oh."

I thought he might fall. I took a step toward him and reached out. "Have you hurt yourself?" He saw my hand and took hold of it with his heavy, blackened fingers. "Can I do anything?" I asked. He did not squeeze my hand, but held it almost greedily and breathed hard with his eyes shut. The scars were stark and jagged on his face.

"Is everything okay?"

He nodded his head, then let go of my hand.

"Can I get something for you? Should I get help?"

He shook his head. He said nothing, but I felt that he was all right now. He would be able to go on. Somehow I had helped him. I knew this. I started backing toward the big open doorway. But before I could bolt, he held up his stained hand, flat toward me, and moved it back and forth, like a priest giving a blessing. He opened his eyes wide and looked at me, shook his head gently, as if pleading.

I knew what he wanted. I never told anyone—not my parents, my friends, my schoolmates. Like the secret grave of my dead rabbit, this episode became part of the arcane life I led sometimes in the field beside the garage. The image of Art's soiled fingers on the paper as he drew diagrams, and his words of instruction remain in my mind.

But I have never been able to repair my own engines; their workings have remained a mystery to me. Years later I was a desperate young man when a feverishly enthusiastic woman at a San Francisco employment agency called me about a position she had just listed. "Here it is, Paul. Your writing job. Go get it!" Her zeal was understandable—if I was hired I had promised her agency half my first month salary. I could little afford this, but I had been drudging for a year as a clerk for a stockbroker after leaving college and my boredom was comprehensive.

At the job interview, Roland Persons peered at me over the top of his glasses. "The writing we do is not very creative. I was an English major, too. This isn't poetry; it's more like laying bricks."

"But I want a job where I can work with words."

"Do you know anything about cars?"

"A little," I lied.

"We don't exactly write about elysian fields here."

But I was young, and possibilities seemed unlimited. I figured I could make it work. Poets have special powers. I would apply my talents to the gears.

National Automotive Services published a basic car repair manual and a subscription service to annual supplements for new model cars as they were produced. Their offices were in a derelict building in a cheap rental district near the docks, where the air smelled of sour wine and spoiled French fries. When we came to work in the morning, we often found winos sleeping it off on the front steps of the building. Sometimes they tried to enter our office, and it was one of my duties to usher them back to the street. "Brother!" they would say to me as I moved them toward the door. "A cigarette. A quarter."

Roland Persons was a kind man, but he had his own responsibilities, and there was work to be done. Very quickly he realized that I did not know the difference between a camshaft and a sparkplug. My mechanical obtuseness had appeared early in life and it was unlikely that I would ever be able to make the connections. Sometimes the owner lost patience with me, but Roland would cover for me, giving reassurances that I was making progress. He tried to nurse me along. He drew pictures and diagrams for me and tried to hone down my florid, ambitious prose. We gleaned and standardized our repair copy from the new model manuals issued by the manufacturers. Roland was right—it was like masonry with words, but I could never quite get things to line up plumb.

When I worked at National Automotive there must have been mechanics in Peoria and Albany and San Luis Obispo and Macon tearing out their hair. Sometimes the office received outraged phone calls. Finally Roland called me into his office. "The heat is really on," he said. "Don't quit until you have another job, but don't take more than two weeks to find one."

Since those days, I have had even greater respect for the work of mechanics, and I regard their mysterious rituals as blessings. I have benefited from these mercies in some very remote places.

It was an alien scene at dusk, like driving on a moonscape, halfway between the Atomic Energy Commission base at Mercury, Nevada and the checkpoint at the border of the test-grounds, before the road went on across the desert to our army camp called Desert Rock. I was returning from a briefing in Mercury when my open jeep suddenly wheezed and started missing. Then it went ping, and something snapped. I steered it to the shoulder and sat hunched over the wheel, listening to the silence. The sun was almost down and a chill wind lowered with the darkness, blowing off the snow-patched desert hills in the distance. I was wearing only a lightweight fatigue jacket. The temperature had been warm when I left Desert Rock that morning, but the briefing had gone on and on through the day.

I climbed out and threw up the hood, staring numbly at the cooling motor. There was nothing I could do. Nothing. I sat down on the bumper and cursed.

These had been strange, challenging months for me, an ongoing phantasm of fear and absurdity—fireballs and mushroom clouds, shock waves burying me in trenches, my bed blown away by violent sandstorms, my ears set permanently ringing by huge explosions. I had been alternately bored by soporific duties and frightened to my limit.

Now here I was in the middle of another nightmare, broken down and alone as stygian darkness advanced across the desert. I looked each way up and down the road, and saw some lights in the distance.

316

There was nothing to do but button my jacket, pull my cap down to my nose, jam my hands into my pockets, and hoof it down the packed macadam toward the glow. Whatever these lights might be, they were my best hope, an extraordinary piece of luck, because for forty-five minutes as I drove the road, I had not passed another vehicle nor seen anything along the dismal way but sand, brittle-bush, yucca, and violently authoritative warning signs posted by the AEC.

By the time I reached the lights several miles down the road, I had almost turned blue. But I was relieved to find that they came from the camp of a small army engineer unit, stationed on the test-grounds to prepare and maintain military viewing areas. The top sergeant took me to a motor pool and introduced me to a mechanic who had just finished his evening chow. I have not forgotten that mechanic's name—it was Danny Winiarski. He was grease from head to toe as he shook my hand; only his teeth were white as he smiled, but to my cold, weary eyes he looked as neat and efficient as an English butler.

"Whatsa trouble?" Danny said. When I told him, he revved up a tow truck and we drove back down the road, hooked up my afflicted vehicle and pulled it back to his repair tent. He threw the hood up and stuck his head under.

"Holy shit!" Danny said. My weary nerves jumped. I had to sit down on an oily stool in his work tent. What Danny said then made no sense at all to me. It was mechanical rant, an automotive litany that sounded something like: "Oh man, the piston's cranked into them fuckin' pipes; it's in the upper manifold. It got throwed against the rods. She's stroking the gears off the intake valve. She's pushing a cylinder into the carburetor. We got to come through the throttle. We got to shim the drive wheel to the spark plug. I ain't got the right fuckin' coil spring. But I think we can persuade her."

"Jesus!" I said. "I hope so."

"We'll get her," Danny said. He had a kerosene heater in his garage tent and I huddled near it as he tied into the job with his tools. I noticed he kept a can of beer going, which he hid in a coffee tin in case the sergeant walked in. He ran a monologue as he worked. "The fuckin' engineers who dreamed up jeeps had brains made out of pinto beans. There ain't no wrench made that can get to some of these nuts, and then you got to have an arm shaped like a Z. You can't even get the hood up without skinning a knuckle. What you need is dynamite and glue to repair these things."

317

"I sure do appreciate your help," I said.

"If we can't help each other out here in this shit-hole, what can we do? This ain't no place for a human being. You got sand everywhere, in your eyes, between your teeth, up your asshole. Then the sun goes down and you can't even tune in a radio. At least you guys got a PX at Desert Rock. All we got at night here is beer and cold stars. I ain't seen a movie in six months. And girls! What are they? I got into Vegas a couple of times and I got so excited I couldn't get near the tables because I got a rod on the whole time, looking at the women. You want a beer?"

"I don't mind if I do, if you've got enough."

"Beer, I got," he said. "Pussy, I don't." He took an opener out of his toolbox, and punctured a can top for me.

"I stay about half-lit most of the time," he said. "It's the only way you can get through this place. When they test them bombs, they got to move us out of here because our camp is so close. Sometimes they make us go into the trenches with you Desert Rock guys."

He started hammering on a ratchet handle and I couldn't hear him for a while, but he didn't stop talking. Finally he got the nut to turn.

"Them bombs come from hell," he was saying. "I never thought I'd see anything like that in my life. Them things were thought up by the evil brothers of the engineers who dreamed up jeeps. Them bastards are going to burn down the whole world if we give 'em half a chance. They don't give a shit about anything but their brains. I bet they all look like pissed-off Frankensteins. What do they care about guys like us? They'd blow our fuckin' heads off, if they thought it would get 'em ahead. I'll never get used to them explosions. Hell, I don't even like to watch fireworks. If I had known this was going to happen to me when they drafted me, I'd of volunteered for the 82d poopy-troopers and jumped out of airplanes. It would have been better than crawling around in trenches waiting to get your ass blowed off. Some of the guys in this outfit pretend they ain't scared. Tough guys. Hell, I don't mind saying that them things make my balls turn cold. What kind of a fool are you, if you can't admit being scared of hell's fire? If I get out of here alive, I'm going to start going to mass again."

After a while I nodded off. Danny poked me awake.

"Go over there and lay down on top of my cot," he said. "Use the extra blanket."

I awakened from time to time to hear him mumbling and clanking

318

his tools. It was first light by the time he finished. He took me by the arm and led me to my jeep, proudly turned the ignition on, and revved the motor for me. I had slept through most of his angelic night ministrations.

"You're on your way," Danny said.

"Listen, man. How can I thank you?"

"Don't worry about that, pal. The U.S. Army is paying for it."

"Let me give you some dough."

"Put that away! I'll tell you what. If you come through here again, bring me a six-pack of Regal Pale."

"Hey! You worked all night while I was sawing logs on your cot. I'm not even in your outfit."

"Pal, we are in this thing together. They stuck us in this shit hole to see how we would stand it. If we can't help each other, what the fuck have we got?"

I did see Danny Winiarski again a month later. It was late morning after we had been brought back on buses to Desert Rock from a dawn test shot. Weary and dazed, we were assembled for a final roll call and briefing. There was Danny, stomping around in the cold with his engineer mates. I went over and touched his shoulder.

"Hey!" he said. "It's the sleeping beauty."

"I owe you something," I said.

"Will you stop that shit!"

"Don't go anywhere until I come back."

The P. X. had opened and I bought a full case of Regal Pale talls, hustled back to the gathering, and put it on Danny's shoulder.

"What are you doin'?" Danny said. He was embarrassed in front of his buddies. "I don't know this guy," he assured them. He tried to hand the case back to me, but I pushed it back.

"For the cold stars," I said.

"This guy is a stranger," he told his mates. "I don't know him." But he kept the beer.

I remained a mechanical stranger for many years. When I retired to rural Wisconsin and took up grass-cutting and gardening, I still had to rely on others to maintain my equipment. Ted Magnuson was a considerate and understanding machinist. The benches and shelves in his repair shop were always lined with torn-down motors that he was resuscitating and bringing back to life. At one time or another

319

Ted had helped everyone in the community through some very tough spots.

I was a short-timer in rural southwestern Wisconsin, and I needed Ted's help more than anyone else. I had learned to do some maintenance and occasionally made simple repairs, but I relied on Ted when my Bolens tractor really started biting back. He even made house calls when I was in particular trouble.

Ted Magnuson had not finished high school, but he was an accomplished man. Sometimes I sat on his bench and hung around just to watch him work. Good mechanics are usually methodical, but Ted went beyond this. He didn't think of shafts and bolts and cogwheels as objects to be lined up and reinstalled in one-two-three order. When he worked on a motor, his eyes deepened and he seemed to shift into another dimension, an abstract area of matrices, connections, and prototypes, where the parts floated in a loose plane of possibilities, until they came together in his mind and through his agile hands.

He kept a small grease-thumbed portable radio at hand as he worked and tuned it in to the classical station from Madison. One day I walked into his shop as a Mahler symphony was resounding into its second hour, and Ted was under the tractor humming and whistling along with the melodies. I had always hesitated to ask him about his musical preferences, but now I could resist no longer.

"That's interesting music," I said. Ted kicked his heels and rolled out from under the tractor on his flat cart to see who was talking to him, then he gave me his good smile. "Some of my customers say I listen to ghost music."

"Do you play an instrument?"

"Just this radio. I got tired of listening to country when I was a kid. They keep telling the same stories, and I always know the endings. I finally figured music could just be music. Just the sound. Mozart lets me do my own thinking."

Ted was a man of wit, too, a master of the pun and the straight face. His laughter came without reservation. He loved to banter with me. Once I purchased a set of bright orange ear guards to wear when I was running my chainsaw. A week later I took them back to his shop.

"Ted," I said, faking perplexity. "I can't get any music to come out of these buggers. I've tried everything."

"Let me see them things," he said. He turned the head set in his

320

hands and deliberated. "I see the trouble. You got to tie a rope to it right here and run it to a tree if you want to get the Mozart."

Sometimes my Bolens defies me, whining and choking off in the middle of a job like a stolid, exasperating child. I dismount and circle it, at first hopeful that the trouble might just be an empty gas tank. I have no compassion or patience for faltering mechanical things. If they break down, I hate them. Failure is unacceptable. As the recognition of real trouble grows, I begin to feel sorry for myself. Why should this idiot thing disappoint me like this? Then I grow angry and kick the fat tires. Stupid, God damned thing!

Already I sense the grass growing out of control. I must do something before we disappear in a sea of green. I used to dial Ted like an hysterical patient calling a doctor. I once suggested that he get on the 911 emergency circuit. "You're more important than the fire department," I told him. Ted grew to recognize my symptoms and, like a good doctor, did his best to comfort me. Eventually I'd see his pickup coming patiently over the rise.

"What's wrong with her?" he'd ask.

"She won't run."

"I can see *that*. Did she kick up a fuss or make a noise when she was going down?"

"She sounded like she was going to throw up. Then she farted, screamed once, and just stopped."

"Whoa!" Ted exclaimed. "Oh-oh." He walked around the Bolens and toed the tires as my anxiety rose. "Sounds like the green fantods to me."

"What?" I said in alarm. I was always terrified of some new mechanical plague that might befall my equipment.

"She's got indigestion," he said. "Too many dandelions."

"Come on, Ted! I'm half out of my mind."

"I know that," he said. "I'm just trying to keep you loose." He pulled his tool-chest out of the truck bed, got his greasy little radio from the cab, tuned in the Madison classics, and set to work.

Ted's son, Luke, has the shrouded eyes and bashed-in nose of a parking lot fighter. He is brawnier than his father, but he has the same scuffed mechanic's knuckles. He also has Ted's unqualified laugh—but it comes rarely. Luke seems to be the antithesis of his gentle father. He started hanging around the garage when he was ten, and Ted was a good teacher. But Luke's temperament and approach to the work is different than Ted's. He takes on repairs like he challenges everything else in his life, attacking a broken-down motor as if it is his adversary, flinging tools around on the gummy, black cement, and cursing when he can't make things fit.

Ted Magnuson died one summer of a brain tumor. Suddenly he was gone, and the whole community went into mourning. I went to his crowded funeral and gave my condolences to Luke; but I did not have the heart to go to the shop for a while. I knew what I had lost and could only imagine how Ted's family felt. But finally I drove to town to see how Luke was doing. The shop door was propped open, but there was no one around. I ducked under the counter and walked through the work benches and parts bins. No one answered my calls. At last I found Luke in the back of the stock room, slouched behind some shelves on a stack of tractor tires.

He would not look up and could barely respond when I talked to him. I saw how deeply he was mourning—almost beyond the normal grief of a young son for his father. I realized that Ted had not only kept our engines running, he had kept young Luke in repair as well. Now Ted was suddenly gone before the job was completed.

I put a tentative hand on Luke's shoulder and spoke gently. He lifted his head and looked at me squarely. I took a step back. I quickly realized where I stood. I needed Luke now, but Luke did not need me. Luke needed his father—and his father was gone. He didn't want anyone else trying to be fatherly. His father was irreplaceable. I was going to have to remember this. Luke did not want to banter with me; I wasn't even in his range of vision. He played loud rockabilly on a boom-box when he did repairs. He drank beer in the evenings and got into fights. His work area looked like a battlefield. He also recognized more readily than I did that there was almost fifty years difference in our ages. He had no intentions of trying to close this gap himself. It was up to me.

I had three options: Find a new mechanic, sell the farm, or learn to communicate with young Luke. I chose the latter. There was a possible fourth option—to attempt my own repairs—but I did not allow for this.

I had to learn to speak to Luke. It did not begin well. My tractor broke down two days after I had found Luke brooding in the parts bins. It snarled, choked asthmatically, went bang, and died right in the middle of a field of grass. I went to our house and spent some time on the couch, looking out the window. Suzanne and Sheba the dog gave me wide berth. Finally, I gathered my resolve, went out to the tractor and stood staring at it. I considered fetching my toolbox. It was a helpless, fretful feeling. I went back into the house, knowing what I had to do.

Luke didn't answer the phone right away. When he finally did, after a half dozen rings, he sounded more like a badger than a mechanic, but he agreed to come out to the farm. I waited a week for him to appear, my tractor perched forlornly under a tarp in the field as the grass grew around it. Finally, I dialed Luke's number again and held the phone away from my ear, but he didn't answer.

September 11, 2001 happened in the meantime. For a while, I did not care if the grass grew over my head. Finally, a week later, I was able to tear myself away from anguish and drive to the shop in town. The bell on the door rang as I walked in, but no one came to the counter. I could hear loud country rock from the workroom in back. Luke wasn't listening to the news. I pulled the hinged gate up on the counter and walked through. Luke looked up from the motor he was repairing. Then he put his head back down. He said something, but I could not hear him.

"What?" I said.

He did not turn the music down. "I'll be out tomorrow after supper," he shouted. There was a deep cut over his eye and his face was red.

I drove home in despair, listening on the car radio to the agonized reports from the Trade Towers scene. It was disorienting to be out on the road; it even seemed fearful to be traveling in gentle, bucolic Crawford County. The news people, who normally act as if they know all the answers, seemed distracted and frightened. Everything large and small in the world seemed askew. As I came over the rise to our house I saw my Bolens broken down in the field, but now it seemed like an annoying fly. Whatever difficulties I had were absorbed by the world's greater troubles. But like everyone else, I had to go on with things. It was the best thing to do.

Luke came the next day. He got out of his pickup, put his head under my tractor hood and did some things. Then he slammed the hood down, turned the key switch, and the tractor ran again. I felt almost guilty to feel so relieved.

"What do I owe you?" I asked.

"A bottle of beer," Luke said.

"I'll do better than that," I said, surprised and pleased that he had made this congenial sign. "But come on, let's go up on the deck."

I opened two Leinenkugel lagers and we sat together gazing down into the farm valley below, wondering what to say to each other. Luke guzzled his beer greedily, and I got him another.

"Tough times," he said finally.

"I can't remember feeling worse about things."

"The bastards!" His anger was quick-rising and genuine. He stood up and I thought he was going to heave his bottle down into the brush on the hillside. He began pacing the deck.

"Luke, take it easy. Sit down," I presumed to say.

His eyes flared when he looked at me, but then he sat back down in the deck chair. "Did you see those buildings going down?" he said. "I never thought I'd see anything like that in my life. The filthy sons of bitches! Somebody's got to pay."

"We don't even know for sure who's responsible."

"When we find out, I want a crack at them."

His hands trembled as he picked at the label on his bottle. I tried to get his mind onto something else. "Are you staying busy?"

"Oh, I'm keeping up. But I'm going to have to hire some help pretty soon. Dad knew a lot of things. I miss him." I could see his sorrow rising over his anger now, and knew he would not want to grieve in front of me.

"Of course you do. We all do."

"I wish I'd paid better attention. He could fix anything." Luke took another pull on his beer and steadied himself.

"If we get into a war and this thing goes on," he said, "I'm thinking I might close the shop down and join up. I'd like to get into the airborne." Luke is a very young man, but when he said this, even in the sunlight, his face grew shadowed and aged.

"That's mighty tough duty."

"Dad was in the marines in Vietnam," Luke said.

I had not known this. Gentle Ted.

"I never thought much beyond this town. But if there's a fight, I want to be in it."

"What will I do if my Bolens breaks down?" I was trying to tease him, see if I could get him to ease up and banter with me.

Luke peered at me carefully. "You could go write a poem," he said, and stopped me in my tracks. He wasn't smiling, he was giving me the old Magnuson straight face routine.

How did he know I was a poet? Ted! But how had Ted known?

"Dad told me you like ghost music, too." Then he gave me one of his unrestrained laughs.

"It's not fair. You know *all* my secrets."

"I'll bet dad told you a few of mine, too."

"No. He never did. We had our own business."

Luke's cheeks were flexing as he looked off at the silos on the ridge across the valley. "I don't know what dad would have wanted me to do. But I can't just stay around here turning wrenches if there's trouble."

Well, we won our war quickly with shock and awe. We still seem to be surrounded by adversaries old and new, covert and outright, but Luke did not have to go off and join the paratroopers.

He has an answering machine on his shop phone now, but he does not return messages. If I stop by, he waves to me congenially from under a tractor, and says some words, which I cannot hear over the bombinating rockabilly. He has written up a work order for me. He will come eventually, but I must take my turn, and my needs are generally more urgent than his availability.

So I am learning to prostrate my sixty-nine year old body. My back and knees and arms are serious liabilities, but I am learning. It is late, but not too late. I go down on my own cold, oil-stained cement, down where everything hurts; a Schubert lieder romps elegantly from the cheap, little stereo on the steel shelf beside the cluttered work bench as I utter the vile words that men speak to cold, indifferent machines.

Last week I changed the oil in the Bolens. In describing this process, I will attempt to display the skills I acquired at National Automotive Services all those years ago: Changing the oil on the Bolens requires an almost hopeless, heartbreaking maneuver, performed while one is lying on a sore shoulder on a cold floor. With your free arm you reach around the hydraulic lift arms, over the drive shaft to the small oil plug, which is remotely located in dark obscurity between the engine and the mower deck. It is easiest if you can shape your forearm like a Z.

Only the smallest crescent wrench can be maneuvered into this limited space to eventually, and with considerable difficulty, be fitted over the plug head. When this is accomplished, there is perhaps a half-inch of space in which to turn the wrench before it has to be laboriously reset on the plug. All this must be accomplished by touch alone, because your aching arm, reaching into the machine, obscures any view.

I was in the midst of this agony when I suddenly realized that I had not remembered to set the foot brake on the tractor. If the tractor rolled by accident, my arm would have been pinched between the motor and the deck. My only option then would have been to call forlornly for Suzanne, who was far away in the house, and would not know how to extract me if she did come.

And so, joint by painful joint, I struggled to my feet and wavered around the tractor until I could stand straight. I climbed up on the seat and pushed the brake down with my left foot while reaching down to set the holding lever with my hand. This lever sets into a groove and is held in place by a strong spring. I eased the lever into its notch and started to let up on the pedal—but the lever snapped up from its groove and the pedal gave me a resounding whack on my shin. My shoulders and the top of my head froze with shock as the pain arced up my leg.

I have a blood condition, a shortage of clotting agents which sometimes causes deep discoloration and bleeding dangers. I was going to have a midnight-colored bruise all the way up my leg, and I hoped the skin had not been broken.

Besides, it hurt. My God, it hurt like hell! I struggled off the tractor and began pacing back and forth on the gritty concrete. I heard a sound, beginning like a pennywhistle, descending abruptly to a growl, trailing off into a wail, then breaking into sobs. Over and over.

I realized, it was me. I was howling. Oh. And it hurt. It was me. Over and over.

*Nominated by Marvin Bell, Great River Review*

# LUCIFERIN

## by DEAN YOUNG

from POETRY

"They won't attack us here in the Indian graveyard."
I love that moment. And I love the moment
when I climb into your warm you-smelling
bed-dent after you've risen. And sunflowers,
once a whole field and I almost crashed,
the next year all pumpkins! Crop rotation,
I love you. Dividing words between syl-
lables! Dachshunds! What am I but the inter-
section of these loves? I spend 35 dollars on a CD
of some guy with 15 different guitars in his shack
with lots of tape delays and loops, a good buy!
Mexican animal crackers! But only to be identified
by what you love is a malformation just as
embryonic chickens grow very strange in zero
gravity. I hate those experiments on animals,
varnished bats, blinded rabbits, cows
with windows in their flanks but obviously
I'm fascinated. Perhaps it was my early exposure
to Frankenstein. I love Frankenstein! Arrgh,
he replies to everything, fire particularly
sets him off, something the villagers quickly
pick up. Fucking villagers. All their shouting's
making conversation impossible and now
there's grit in my lettuce which I hate
but kinda like in clams as one bespeaks

poor hygiene and the other the sea.
I hate what we're doing to the sea,
dragging huge chains across the bottom,
bleaching reefs. Either you're a rubber/
gasoline salesman or like me, you'd like
to duct tape the vice president's mouth
to the exhaust pipe of an SUV and I hate
feeling like that. I would rather concentrate
on the rapidity of your ideograms, how
only a biochemical or two keeps me
from becoming the world's biggest lightning bug.

*Nominated by Philip Levine, David Wojahn, Ralph Angel, David Rivard*

# AMERICAN SPEAKING

## by DAVID RIVARD

from AMERICAN POETRY REVIEW

Pressure of what you'd hear
if you really heard
the findable pressures
of finite things—

you'd be concussed, actually,
by the carpenter
a Catalan or South Miami Cubano
60-something years old

and carrying a ladder
with inordinate care while complaining
in curses yelped
Spanish-style about the

hardening of his arteries,
his legs ready for the go-round
still, being on the make—
only, in this country

it's your money or your life,
and we don't want any
of those who slide into the pew these
Sunday summer mornings

to think the bedmaker
we call Jesus
has really died—after all, the sheets
so neatly & finally tucked-in

on all our beds
are clean, are they not?—so speak
American, says the crew boss,
speak American, OK?

and then shut the hell up.

*Nominated by Stuart Dischell, David Wojahn*

# THE WIDOW JOY

fiction by ROSELLEN BROWN

from SPEAKEASY

IT WAS HARD TO DECIDE what was the worst thing about being a widow—missing Stan, worrying about money; there were lots of what her son callously called "downsides"—but Joy thought, sometimes, that the worst was that now she was "a widow." A thing, a category, something that began with an indefinite article. She had been an English teacher before the children were born and still tended to think in terms of parts of speech, which she knew was pedantic but couldn't help. It was one of those traits, she noted bitterly, that was far more pathetic in a widow than in a woman with a man around the house.

"Well, before you were, I don't know, a wife," her daughter Stacy said. "A married woman. That was a 'thing.' "

"Different. Wives can be all sorts of kinds of people. Widows are first and foremost pathetic. I'm not the first person to think so."

"God, Mom, you make it sound like it's your fault Daddy died. I don't know why that makes you pathetic. Do you think people *blame* you that he died?"

Joy waved her hand, which she seemed to be keeping notably well manicured these days, one of the many parts of her person that needed extracareful maintenance because she felt herself under scrutiny. That horrible ugly-syllabled term, just listen to it, like some kind of punishment you got in prison, secretly, in a hidden room under glaring lights: "I'm sorry, but you can't see her right now. She's *under scrutiny.*"

"Nobody blames me for his heart—though come to think of it

there might be some food police types who'd like to get me for murder by cholesterol or, you know, not enough antioxidants. No, I mean—" But she stopped. Stacy was twenty-four. She was still dazzling, open to anything and anything had yet to happen. Why even bother trying to explain the hopelessness of it to someone mired in hope? Joy felt shelved, like a book nobody intended to read anymore.

This conversation had not taken place until well after Stan's sudden disappearance. Joy tended to think of it that way, not quite as a death, which was a heavy, frightening word that seemed to demand preparation, but as a mysterious, almost casual withdrawal of himself from her presence, as if he had just, on a whim, stepped out of sight.

He had been, in fact, already out of her sight. He had gone out to the deck above her garden to sit in the mild sun with his newspaper, and since she was used to seeing him slip into a doze—he was a urologist; he worked hard all week, fixing the plumbing, he liked to say— she waited a long time before she called him in for lunch and discovered that he was gone. Just like that, this large, complex, talkative, sweet, skillful man had somehow escaped, or been kidnapped, across the border into the other world while she was rolling out a double pie crust. They were having company that night, and she had found a sale on the perfect pie apples, sweet-sour, tough, easily peeled. She had gone outside to announce lunch and to show him proudly the endless ruddy peel she held between her fingers like a tapeworm, the best she'd ever made.

People said, months later, that she didn't show enough evidence that she'd lost her husband but that—*that*, she said, exactly *that*— was the problem: he only felt lost, mislaid, temporarily missing. Death that comes so casually, so surreptitiously, is hard to take seriously. She begged his forgiveness for not believing he no longer existed.

But the months went by, she turned fifty, and Stan didn't reappear. Aside from the loss of him, poor dear man, she finally feared the loss of herself. She wasn't Joy first anymore; she was a widow. She had been abducted, too.

They had had a comfortable life full of what she was occasionally embarrassed to call middle-class pleasures: the large house with its more-interesting-than-most paintings and dustables; the travel, sometimes to the appealing places where Stan's medical conferences were cannily set—Helsinki, Tokyo, Honolulu. (Nobody had ever adequately explained to her why the American Renal and Urology Association had to meet in distant countries, in the finest hotels, as if its members couldn't concentrate anywhere closer to home and the English language. But since she got to go along, she wasn't asking.) They entertained not lavishly but generously. Stan loved his work, he still got excited about diagnosis and surgery. Joy loved her combination of mothering (though that would soon give out) and community volunteering, which she could do when she felt like it, and not do when she didn't. Her friends purported to love her for her high spirits, her taste, her sense of absurdity that was not so profound as to make her too critical of them.

And this was absurd: it had begun to look as if she would be alone, manwise, for the rest of her life. Why? Why? She liked herself. She was a good companion. She wasn't enough to keep herself company, was all: she needed somebody to ask and answer and agree and disagree. It had nothing to do with not being sufficiently competent, nothing to do with patriarchy or subservience. It was much simpler: she would never get used to so much silence.

So she was heavy. Zaftig, if you liked flesh broad and round as a Renoir. Stan had called thin women stringy chickens and luxuriated in her. She was still funny, still described as "lively," whatever that meant—she could hear her friends repeating the word to their few unattached male friends: "Lively, friendly. Comfortable." Which translated as "heavy." *Comfortable* meant built like a couch, soft as a beanbag chair. The personal ads, if you dared to read them, all asked for "slender." They liked personality, they went for financially independent, but first and foremost these nervy searchers, who could be ugly as the bottom of your boot, and fat and sloppy or scrawny and underbuilt, what they were looking for, to a one, was slender.

The dirty secret was that there were no men out there, not men anybody would be caught wanting. Not exactly a surprise, but when you don't have to notice it, you don't. She felt as if she'd been willfully blind while a disease raged outside her window: the peculiarly bereft loneliness of the once-coupled spinster who dared to ask for good luck another time around.

Spinster? Who spins, who knits, who weaves? The widow.

Stacy said there were no worthwhile men at her age either, but that was a lie, or at least a friendly exaggeration. And Fort Worth was not—whatever the opposite of Fort Worth was. New York? L.A.?

The first likable man she met, five years after Stan's unanticipated evaporation, was dying. He had started a conversation at the drug store prescription station where she was renewing (it was too funny to be true) her estrogen replacement pills. He had said to her, amiably, "We all end up here, don't we? Remember when you used to meet your friends at the soda fountain and keep your back to the old geezers at the pharmacist's window?"

Later she told him that was the most unpromising opening line she'd ever heard.

Charles, called Chas by those who were fond of him, was dying in a more drawn-out and less sensational way than Stan had, of leukemia, which gave him good periods and after a while subtracted them, leaving him stranded like a fish on the beach of his life, then kindly wet him down again as the tide turned. And then again. And still again.

He was a widower, so, even without discussing it, they shared certain feelings. They knew the faint brush of condescension from the fixer-uppers, who arranged dates with shockingly inappropriate "singles" with whom they had nothing in common but their loneliness. They felt their children's sighs, whether sighed or not, over the difficulty they presented; felt the children's guilt at seeing them unhappy and their helplessness to do anything about it, which at best makes for false cheer and at worst for anger. Impotence was what parents of grown children tended to feel; it was unnatural the other way around.

She and Chas would have surprised anyone who saw them together, though no one did: they had houses, they didn't need to skulk around looking for privacy. They did not exactly have what would have been called sex, but they had everything that usually came before and after it: hugging, kissing, tender speech, ecstatic sound, then a surprised and urgent clinging that was nearly—not quite but not unlike—the actual pleasure of consummation; and then the sweet falling away, the luxuriant side-by-side stretching out or curling up, front to back, her ample breasts pushed against his wasting spine and shoulders. His medications, uncountable—the day they met at Walgreen's she saw his bill and was staggered by it—made him incapable but not, as he put it, unwilling. Willingness, she laughed, was what sex was really about, wasn't it? Wanting each

334

other, which became a kind of having. Remembering, imagining. "It's all right," she told him the first time. "The part of me that's empty isn't the part down *there*."

He had kissed the tops of her ears when she said that, tiny, fluttering, grateful kisses, and she felt the electric connection so deeply her chest flushed red and her heart beat noisily as though she'd gone everywhere with him and back.

The other thing that interested her in her miniromance with Chas was that so much that had mattered to her all her life, and deeply, seemed distant and very nearly irrelevant when she was with him. Old people got like this, she knew: her own mother, after eighty, had stopped criticizing Joy's failings, her weight, her hair, her clothes. She had turned all her fading vision in on herself, which, given the encroaching darkness, took so much out of her there wasn't any left for her carping habit. Joy was glad and sorry to be exempt; unexamined, she was lonelier still. Now, was desperation doing to her what weariness had accomplished on her mother?

The things that seemed to be fading in importance: that she was Jewish, volubly, commitedly so, and he was some anonymous form of WASP, the kind that hardly knows which denomination it is, let alone cares. "Whatever church was nearby, that's where we went. Except Catholic, of course. You don't just *stop in* at a Catholic church!"

She liked concerts, museums, grand or subtle things on her walls but something original, something genuine, while Chas's idea of culture tended toward the rodeo ("Actually," he instructed, "it's rightly called the Fat Stock Show") and the kind of music you went to Las Vegas for—he and his wife had done this more than once—or to Branson, Missouri, to hear Wayne Newton and Johnny Cash and Amy Grant, that white gospel girl. Give or take an Amy or two, guys with suits that reflected light, and big big cuffs. This made her put off introducing him to her friends. It was craven, she knew, but there was too much explaining involved.

But in spite of his macho heroes Chas was a gentle man, and he thought Joy was a goddess. His wife, dead only a few years, had been, she surmised, a frail birdlike woman in stature and personality— "delicate" is how Chas delicately put it—and he feasted on Joy's body like a man who'd been pent up in a small place suddenly let free to leap and frolic. He did more than he should have to please her, and her delight was his delight. He gave her touching gifts, too: a small, bubbled-leather book of love poems beginning with Sappho, with a cloth bookmark sewn in, "like in the Bible," he said abashedly. A box of chocolates that said "Eat me" on the front. A glass unicorn. His own house, or rather the house his wife had furnished, heavy with beige drapery and shiny surfaces, tended toward coverings: an extra roll of toilet paper sat on the formica sink cabinet under a frothy plastic cap, like a lady about to step into the shower; the hall rug was protected by a plastic runner—you could not track mud in if you tried. Their bedroom was cluttered with toadstools, porcelain dogs, and other small objects. In another time and culture, Joy thought, these would have gone to decorate his wife's grave.

But the thing that moved her most, of course, was that he was dying and didn't try to turn away from it. He spoke with stunning matter-of-factness about "then" and "after." These lean, honest-eyed Protestant boys, she thought, not brought up to be histrionic, might lack a little pizzazz in certain respects, but there's useful, sharp-sided grit in their souls. He'd been a mining engineer; he'd worked with oil and stone and earth, the whole physical world like a body laid open to prodding and the removal of its parts. And now he talked about himself as though he were only another element to be thrown into the eternal mix—he wanted cremation and an unceremonious fling, by the practical hands of his three grown daughters, into his favorite trout stream.

"The girls" and their husbands had met her once in their father's house, over a tense meal of dry turkey and cranberry sauce still shaped like the can that left all her appetites unsatisfied. They looked at her suspiciously, as though she might be a gold digger or a floozie, searching, searching for their proper father's possible motives for involving himself with a broad-bosomed woman with tinted highlights in her hair, who opened her mouth wide to laugh and somehow did not seem—well . . . she knew a euphemism when she felt one coming up behind her—*Texas*.

But all that was neither here nor there: Chas was beyond the need for his family's approval, not because he might not be hurt by it but because only a week or so after that dinner, without warning, his dying began in earnest. Suddenly a transfusion could no longer pull him back from the brink. Almost overnight he went from man in possible danger to man in dire straits, uncomplaining, wearing an expression of mild surprise but not fear and certainly not the anger he deserved.

Joy found herself studying him as if he were another species, this second love who was about to slip out of her hands. She was there to see him go, standing beside two of the daughters, who ignored her as if she were invisible, which was fine since this wasn't about any of them. He blinked out gradually and silently, like a lightbulb dimming. And like a bulb, he flared once at the very end, another gift to her. Staring straight ahead where she was not, he cried out "Joy!" as if, astonished, he was calling out to show her something. As if Joy were an emotion, not a name. She had always thought her celebratory name silly, but she forgave her parents then and there for their hopefulness and prescience.

She didn't allow herself to cry for Chas, though it took a terrible effort. But he would have been very uncomfortable with her tears, and if he could be disciplined, so could she in his honor. She wished he had a gravestone instead of an empty urn. If she'd had any say in the matter she'd have written COMPLETED and meant it for both of them. He had taught her a few things. But no, on second thought, she wasn't finished, not yet, though she had no idea what to do next. Why did all of them, finally, go off by themselves and leave her alone?

Years later, Joy spent a month in Umbria in a stone farmhouse she had rented with a girlfriend, Max—they were still and forever girls— whom she had met as a docent at the Metropolitan Museum. She had left Fort Worth behind, left her children with their blessings and yielded to a desire for a fast-moving city that she hadn't known she possessed. When her friends back home asked if New York weren't too full of distractions, she had to ask them, distractions from what? This, she said, is not the appetizer, it's the main course.

The morning she and Max met they were standing, smitten, in a newly assembled roomful of poignant portraits on something like wood that had adorned mummy cases a few millennia ago. The faces were so contemporary, so rich with feeling, both women confided that they suspected a daring fraud. Could these people truly have lived and died when the world was young—that curly-haired young man with the depressive, down-turned mouth of a dozen teenaged sons she had known; a shy-looking girl with ringlets, the shoulder of her pleated gown not entirely modest in its arrangement. Someone, friend, lover, or mischievous artist in possession of gossip, had helped her slip into eternity looking slightly naughty! Joy and Max shook their heads in unison, full of wonder and confusion.

337

Did all the mummies have tombs to accommodate these gorgeous likenesses, and their papier-mâché sarcophagi? She loved graveyards, which somehow she put in a category unrelated to the cheerless cemeteries—memorial parks, so called—like the kind into which Stan had disappeared beneath a cold pinkish granite slab with his Hebrew name inscribed above *Beloved Husband, Father, Physician*. Chas, in the possession of his daughters, had indeed become food for the fishes he had menaced with those fluttering flies he'd spent a thousand hours of his life creating.

Now, July in Castello Falignano, the two friends made it a habit to stroll like wanderers in a garden through the hill town's *cimitero*, where life—represented by fresh flowers renewed with awesome frequency—trumped death, no contest. Women in housedresses stood wet-eyed, still, before the tombs of parents who had died forty years ago; they wielded brooms and kept blood-red glass-enclosed candles lit. Time was layered in Castello: the Etruscans, the Greeks, the Romans, and only lately the Christians, had surged up its hills and down again, sometimes in pursuit, sometimes in flight. Manhattan, Joy thought, was just a moment's cinder in the eye of eternity. Blink once and it will be covered by some civilization not yet invented.

She and Max, replete with their morning cappuccini and cornetti, made up stories for the stones, using a dictionary when the going got rough—though *caro italiano* was generally so forgiving of their illiteracy it seemed enough to read English, once you got through the intricacies of conjugal code: *ved* = "widow of" and *in* = "married into the family." The women were most often represented first by their maiden names, then by those veds and ins; she liked that. (The Spanish excelled at respect for matriarchal naming too, though from her experience, neither culture was particularly thoughtful, thereafter, of its women's comfort.)

Little oval portraits in porcelain clung to most of the stones, and these were the provocations that set them off on melodramatic scenarios: oh, the baby dead in 1882 in what appeared to be the rage of a "sudden torrent" that tore her from the bosom of her grief-shattered parents! Joy's eyes welled with tears. Except for the creeping lichen at the edges of her photograph, the baby, like those mummy faces, looked unsettlingly contemporary. A few young men posed in full color beside the motorcycles and cars in which they had likely perished.

But what stopped her, time and again, were the pictures of husbands in their youth—wavy hair, dark suits and bow ties, innocence still rounding their cheeks and brightening their eyes—and beside them (ved!) the ancient crones who outlived them by generations. *Coniugi, Mario Gandolfi 1894–1921*, on the left and, as if in their marriage bed, on the right *Maria Zanardi in Gandolfi 1899–1976*. Joy was off and running: he had the looks of a poet and the soul of an arrogant idler, the soft-voiced serpent kind. He must have liked being a dandy; there were no dandies his age around here, so he got a lot of attention. And that beautiful girl, Zanardi's youngest, fell for him so fast she seemed possessed. A glorious couple, blessed, Mario in a state of grateful reform until consumption invaded his chest and took him in a flash, just after the birth of their second son. Why not? Such stories were a better sport than knowing the truth, which was passive. Flat.

Handsome Mario's was a studio portrait. Maria, staring straight ahead, was the *nonna* in a family snapshot by the time everyone owned a brownie, her eyes like the olives in Greek salads, the tiny ones. Wizened, warped, she had the face of one of those stray apples that gets lost in the back of the fridge and rolls out wrinkled, winy as yeast, hollow inside.

Max had been out of sight for a while, inspecting a mausoleum adorned with what looked, at a distance, like statuary worthy of the Uffizi. She came toward Joy with her arms out as if to say, "Can you believe this?!" She was a broad-shouldered, large-boned woman whose flowing denim skirt and jangling bracelets made her the least Italian-looking person on any Umbrian street, yet she seemed perpetually surprised that no one took her for a native. She made Joy feel delightfully small. "And there are mosaics down at the end of the row that you won't believe! Lots of gold leaf. You hock Mary's halo, you could probably buy yourself a Lexus." She turned her head from left to right, to take in the terraces of tombs, and at the top a pure-lined little Roman church. "I wonder if all this is devotion to, you know, the dead, or maybe just competition with the neighbors."

Joy shrugged. "You'd have to know a lot of local sociology to have a clue." Tranced before the grave of Zanardi in Gandolfi, she was reluctant to move on. "Look at this one, Max."

Max bent to read the dates on the stone. "Wow." She frowned. "Why do I find that sort of grotesque? I'm picturing them showing up together at a party, the beautiful boy with his ancient wife on his arm." She shivered. "It isn't really funny, actually."

"No, it isn't," Joy agreed, bemused and a little shaken. Long widowhood seemed, right here, like a cruel jest, an odd-smelling black flower.

But Max was not the one to sympathize. She had been married for a few years right after college but claimed to remember nothing of her marriage except sullen, silent mealtimes and the humiliation of ducking a plate her husband threw at her one evening at a dinner party. Her sentiment for permanent liaisons seemed to have disappeared around the time the dish hit the wall behind her head. "At least it was before dinner, so the plate was still clean. It would have been ghastly if our friends' carpet got a mess of coq au vin to show for inviting us. In addition, of course, to a really fun evening."

Joy hadn't intruded on Max's cynicism to defend marriage; there seemed no point in generalizing from her own case, though her friend so cheerfully—mock cheerfully—did so. But the Zanardi-Gandolfis deserved defending. "Do you think she remembered him—you know—after all that time?"

"She's staring straight at *something*, isn't she? She looks like she hasn't smiled for fifty years."

Joy considered the group portraits of her own family in the old country—everyone had one. "People never used to smile for their pictures. If you're old enough it probably never occurred to you to make yourself look ingratiating."

Maria's was a snapshot, though, taken, perhaps, by one of her children. Her sons would have been older than their boy-father forever! Probably she confused them, all those men, by the time she died. Though she hardly looked confused; she looked formidable.

"Well." Max laughed and started up the path. Her shoes on the pebbles sounded like someone chewing. She looked back over her shoulder. "Did you notice, most of these old gals don't seem to have gotten married again or they'd be buried with the new family, right? We all figured once was enough!"

Her bitterness was delivered, as usual, with a laugh. Joy forced herself to follow, but her mind was back in the cemetery in Fort Worth. On that pinky-gray stone, Stan's face in a black-and-white oval on the left, as he always stood and as he lay in their king-sized bed, looking sound and avid and engaged, not prepared for the ambush that overtook him. And she—a few more decades and her face would be in collapse, as everyone's was, given the luck to outlive tight skin and bright eyes—and there she would be, looking like his grand-

340

mother. And? And? What could she summon up besides affronted vanity?

She thought about it as she walked, passing some magnificence and some absurdity—this certainly was a playground for the living, who flexed their power over the dead bodies of their departed. Again, she pictured herself and Stan, what they would look like, their middle-aged and old-aged faces separated by a few inches of cold stone. The space between them would vibrate with all the things she wished she could tell him—all she had learned since his vanishing! All she had seen! The paradox was that they were the result of his not being with her, but he would appreciate them if only she could convey them. She hadn't, like Max, lost faith in—well, there was no permanence, was there? But there was long-term affection. She supposed she had Stan to thank for that. And Chas, with his innocent enthusiasm. She could have been broken along the way, but, however chipped, she was still whole. She pictured the sun striking their stone and heating it up. She was, peculiar as it seemed, envious of no one but herself.

Max was hidden, again, behind a tomb, but Joy followed the sound of her bracelets and found her shaking her head at an A-frame with an altar inside its glass doors. On a marble ledge gold-framed photographs stood at stylish angles, shadowed by fresh orange gladioli. A broom and a watering can leaned, tucked not quite out of sight, in the corner.

Invigorated by this challenge of death by the routines of daily life, they began their ritual negotiation over which trattoria deserved their business for lunch, and then—she did look forward to it as much as she looked forward to eating—*il riposo*, the shutters closed, Joy's imagination quelled, unloading the wonders of the morning, readying for what would come next.

*Nominated by Speakeasy*

341

# D/ALTERED

## by JAMES MCKEAN

from THE IOWA REVIEW

THE RED LIGHT MEANS you're ready to go. It's on top of the
starter's Christmas tree. Ominous and ironic. In this world, red
means you're staged, your front wheels having entered the timing
lights. If you ask what drove you here or if you'll drive away, consider
it a bad joke. On second thought, maybe it's a good question. How
did you get into this—strapped in and petrified? Think about it.
You're straddling three hundred cubic inches of six-cylinder in-line
Hudson Hornet engine and its two speed dynaflow transmission
bolted to a chrome moly tubing heliarc welded shortened sling shot
dragster frame with a fiberglass roadster body. If you're knocking
your helmet-encased head against the Kandi blue metal-flake roll
bar, it's because the lights on the Christmas tree have fallen to yellow; you've got the engine revved to stall speed against the brakes,
and in the pits and on the sidelines Steve Henshaw and all your
dubious partners expect you to smoke the slicks the whole quarter
mile in your very own, hand-crafted, scavenged and jury-rigged,
D/Altered dragster.

The Puyallup Raceway in the summer of 1965. I'm nineteen. I
should be shooting baskets at the "Y." Instead I've shoveled half my
asphalt laborer's summer wages into a machine the purpose of which
is simply hormonal—all adrenalin and acceleration, all held breath
and grunting and explosion, all noise and smoking tires. It's fireworks
you can ride. It's impatient and absolutely self-centered sex, the
point of which is to get it over with as quickly and with as much enthusiasm as possible. It's testosterone renamed alcohol or high-test

injected or nitromethane supercharged and blown so that ten-foot acetylene hot flames rocket from those sling-shot top-fuelers four out each zoomie header like a brilliant blue-white diabolic candelabrum. Cover your ears it hurts that much. Even fifty feet away the sound whaps your body like a broom against a carpet.

Another yellow. Admit it. Come on. Think. It's more than a twelve-second ride. It's more than my weight tripled in Gs or the redundant maniac with his starter's flag down on his knees, ready to swat flies. I don't need his OK. Fess up. There's something to love in the language of all this, though I'd never tell my crew that—Henshaw up to his elbows in oil, knuckles busted, or Billy with his grinding tools, near tears at the prospect of dismantling the largest six-cylinder flathead cast after World War II, the 1953 Hudson Hornet 5,047 cc behemoth that Henshaw found in a junk yard and convinced me to haul in my father's Ford station wagon—its leaf springs were never the same—back to Billy's shop so he could stroke and bore and port and polish. The assonance and alliteration sold me, as if the engine would breathe again, as if the very words themselves greased the bearings.

Or how the holy catalogs turned my head, their gospel the text I pored over column after column. Salvation lay somewhere in the Moon Equipment Co. inventory, its stock of manifolds and magnetos. And Honest Charley, the graffiti man and car parts huckster "hisself" pointing in his ads like Uncle Sam or Elmer Gantry, freed you from the conventions of grammar in his "Honest Price Catalog." As long as I kept turning the page, a litany of names and parts echoed in my ears like a roll call of saints: Iskenderian the cam grinder, Mallory and his magnetos, Edelbrock of the manifold, Jahns forged pistons, Hurst of the spring-loaded four-on-the-floor, Hedman Hedders, Halibrand of the rear end and mag wheels, Hilborn the fuel injector. Offenhauser and Eelco, Grant rings and Getz gears. Traction Master and Cal custom. Oh, how they moved me, these names all sibilance and repetition, a revving of consonants and chrome. Headlong, full speed, bustin' loose, the euphony wound you clear to imagination's red line.

And it cost nothing to say these names, as if speaking would qualify me to stand before drag racing's pantheon, a kind of incantatory pit-pass so that I might enter into the presence of "Big Daddy" Don Garlits and Don "The Snake" Prudhomme and Rick "The Iceman" Stewart, drivers so fast only their nicknames kept up with them. Mickey Thompson, Brooks and Rapp, the Northwest's own Jerry

Ruth, the Baromas brothers, Danny Ongais, the Sandoval brothers, and Warren, Ferguson, Jackson, and Faust. Said all at once, they sound like latter-day gunslingers who listen to rock & roll and make pacts with the nitro devil.

Piece by piece, however, our D/Altered cost plenty. Woops. Another yellow light for the heart. We painted Henshaw and McKean on the back of our catalog-special, Acme Freight-delivered model "A" ersatz fiberglass coupe body, because we wanted to drive our names as fast as we could into hot rod recognition. We asked Tacoma's Thane Porlier to build the frame. Who else? Sculptor Thane. An artist in chrome-moly. Baron Thane. Thane of Cawdor. Holder of the welding torch. Who sat me on his workbench to measure me butt to brow for the enormous roll bar. The frame all steel tubing and heliarc welds, the junkyard Olds rear end and axle chopped and narrowed, as if this car were a tailored suit of armor. Thane cut and welded the steel headers. He built the axles and radius rods and kingpins and set the spindles and caster and bolted in the drag link and steering box.

The steering wheel we lifted from Billy's go-cart. We ordered a two-gallon polished aluminum gas tank from Moon auto, round chrome filter caps to sparkle atop the dual single choke "Twin-H Power" Hudson carburetors, and a pair of steel rims to fit the used ten-inch slicks that Henshaw found at a hot rodder's yard sale, and a new aluminum head and gaskets for the Hudson that Billy had ported and polished to perfection. A new cam, valves, plugs, metal-flake paint job, junkyard front rims and on-sale six-dollar black-walled tires. Fasteners and tubes and fittings and firewalls. Scavenge and search and toil and trouble.

Yellow. There's someone in the lane next to me but I haven't got the nerve to look. Too late to turn my head, sitting in my purloined plastic lawn chair bolted to the frame and bound by shoulder straps and seat belts over my borrowed aluminum and asbestos-lined safety jacket, my helmet full of sweat, the visor fogged, the Hudson six spasmodic, epileptic, groaning against the brakes, the brake lever tight in my right hand, my left on the wheel. Hold it. Hold it. Too late to add a Moon foot-shaped gas pedal. Too late to add spoke wheels. Too late and no money to add a magneto—a Rube Goldberg Ray-o-Vac tied-to-the-Hudson-with-hemp-rope ignition system standing in, a spark from the profane for the finely tuned and chrome-plated sublime. . . .

344

Green. Oh, god. Brake off. Foot down. Hands on the wheel. The Hudson sucks the air blue, growling like a diesel, the whole D/Altered hunching as if jabbed in the rear, smoke billowing from the tires, your head popped back, helmet clanking against the roll bar. Whining. Point it straight. Higher. The RPMS vibrating your teeth, the crowd left behind, the track before you all vanishing point, trees a green blur. Wait, wait. Shift once. Left hand down. Right on the wheel. The dynaflow thumps into drive and the big six settles into its shoulders and back muscles and growls and stuffs you into the seat, wind filling your collar and flattening the face shield, the finish line, the timing booth, the black and white finish banner growing larger faster, faster and faster. Heart thumping, mouth open, you think you're a driver, that you'll make one small steering adjustment, the car drifting, the run still accelerating, just a little turn on the wheel back toward the middle of your lane and clank.

Then nothing.

How suddenly the world goes metaphoric. How curious and calm such moments seem. My first thought is sentimental—the little red car on its pedestal outside the Safeway store. How my mother stood next to me and plugged dimes in the slot so the car rocked back and forth and I could steer frantically nowhere—I knew even then—the wheel turning round and round and round. And then I remember the awful wreck of the Baromas brothers' supercharged hemi Anglia, so overpowered and souped up it looked like a Jerry Roth "Rat Fink" hyperbolic cartoon, how the driver goosed the car sideways, let off, goosed it again twice as hard and the car leaped straight up, pitched onto its nose and dove into the asphalt, disintegrating half-way up the track right in front of you. Remember the ambulances and red lights, the engine broken loose, upside-down and leaking its oil, the driver lying next to it, moaning, his helmet ripped off, still alive though his right leg bent under him four different ways. Oh, man, Jim, think about this—your steering is gone.

Next week, Thane Porlier will admit that he should have sleeved the rod connecting the steering box and the lever gears. That butt weld just couldn't stand the torque. But I don't know this yet. All I know is that the wheel spins free. All I see is the finish line here and gone. All they see in the booth is a D/Altered flashing by, its crazy driver with both hands on the brake lever bending it by his right ear, the engine sighing and backfiring and decompressing.

No one seems worried, although Henshaw and Billy in the towcar had to search to find me. I have rolled far past the finish area down a dirt road and into the pine woods, both of my hands still yanking on the brake. But I have a new understanding. Shut off, the engine steams and tinks, heat waffling the air. Henshaw unbuckles me and slaps my shoulder for the time and speed. "Twelve point nine," he says. "Terrific. And 124 miles per hour."

"Well, I didn't have a hand in it," I say but no one gets it. My knees wobble the rest of the day. My thinking wobbles a lot longer than that.

When Thane asks what's the worry and says, "Hey, we designed it to go straight," and explains the physics behind fifteen-degree axle tilt and kingpins and the gyroscope effect and wheel flop, all I hear are the puns. I need to think about this and beg off drag racing for the next few weeks. Then I beg off for good, playing basketball instead three nights a week at the "Y" and lifting weights, my sophomore season at Washington State University only months away. I reread poems from my English classes, the language now more poignant than ever. Grasping the obvious, I discover words really mean something. Roethke says, "I learn by going where I have to go," and Stafford negotiates the dark, his exhaust red. Words such as "headlong," "steering," "acceleration," "full speed," "brakes," and "deep woods" spark and roll and rumble.

And when I rediscover Robert Creeley's poem "I Know a Man," the summer compresses itself into his lines

. . . the darkness sur-
rounds us, what

can we do against
it, or else, shall we &
why not, buy a goddamn big car,

drive, he sd, for
christ's sake, look
out where yr going.

I copy the poem and carry it in my wallet, admonished by word and circumstances—and my father, who mentions my dangerous quarter mile in passing, eyebrow raised, just once.

It's 1965. I try to look where I'm going in an impetuous time accelerating way too fast. Rock music. Riots. Vietnam. I go to school. I play ball. I read and love words and try to write poems with speed and rhythm. There are language wrecks galore but each is survivable. And when I look over my shoulder, it's to be thankful again that I made it through my wild run—twenty odd seconds with no steering—and to see what kind of times Henshaw and Billy are posting, to write them letters, and then to wonder what they'll do after the Hudson throws a rod and Henshaw gets drafted and Billy joins up. And for months, I hope they make it back from their over-revved, fully blown and flat-out tours in Vietnam—Steve Henshaw, race car driver and welder, who does, and Billy—I hear one day—sweet Billy, artist of the port and polish, who doesn't.

*Nominated by Fred Leebron, Iowa Review*

# THORNS. THISTLES.

## by DANIEL ANDERSON

from THE KENYON REVIEW

The finches jig and sprint.
They tease the sprinkler's oscillating spray
That pulses like a sterling macramé
Of water on the lawn.
*If actuaries are to be believed,*
*Barring unforeseen circumstances,*
*I have, roundly, two thousand Saturdays*
*To live. Four hundred waning crescent moons,*
*Some thirty-seven more Thanksgiving meals,*
*And nine elections for the President.*
In the rich, blue, waxing alp of shade
The gabled roof has laid,
The lilies cool. The lilies bruise.
*Now, by my own accounts, I'd guess*
*Almost twelve thousand shaves,*
*Six thousand hours, more or less,*
*Of watching televised athletics,*
*And five hundred ventures—give or take—*
*To haul the empty bottles to the dump.*
In five o'clock's thin light,
All multiples of green begin to blur.
Mulberry bush. The buckeye. The ivy vines.
A nearby power mower whines
In Doppler modulation, like locust-song.
It floats this precinct of the middle class

With the sweet, cut scent of grass,
And nothing, nothing now, seems wrong.
*Three hundred thirty books of stamps,*
*Two hundred airline flights,*
*Ninety dental appointments,*
*Seven timing belts and three more dogs.*
*Two times a year, or so,*
*(Which roughly comes to seventy in all)*
*I'll cry myself to sleep.*
My, how our silver willows weep.
The tulips lift their chalice heads
As in a crimson toast.
*L'chaim!* they seem to say, or *Skoal!*
I have, I'd speculate,
One hundred sixty-five of these
Late afternoon harmonic moments left—
Of iced tea and the Adirondack chair,
Of pure and undistracted ease,
Until a car horn's blare,
Or the gun-crack slamming of a back-porch door,
The day's commotion coming home at last.
*One hundred sixty-four.*

*Nominated by Erin McGraw*

# MEDITERRANEAN

## by ROSANNA WARREN

from POETRY

—when she disappeared on the path ahead of me
I leaned against a twisted oak, all I saw was evening light
                               where she had been:

gold dust light, where a moment before
and thirty-eight years before that

my substantial mother strode before me in straw hat, bathing
                           suit, and loose flapping shirt,
every summer afternoon, her knapsack light across her back,

her step, in sandals, firm on the stony path
as we returned from the beach

and I mulled small rebellions and observed the dwarfish cork trees
with their pocky bark, the wind-wrestled oaks with elbows
                                    akimbo,

while shafts of sea-light stabbed down between the trunks.
There was something I wanted to say, at the age of twelve,

some question she hadn't answered,
and yesterday, so clearly seeing her pace before me

it rose again to the tip of my tongue, and the mystery was
not that she walked there, ten years after her death,

but that she vanished, and let twilight take her place—

*Nominated by Alan Michael Parker, Sherod Santos*

350

# JESUS WEPT

fiction by R. T. SMITH

from THE SOUTHERN REVIEW

W HEN LIGHTNING STRIKES THE OUTHOUSE IT IS ANOINTED. Haloed and shaken and char-dark, it is God-glad but not set aflame like the overhanging mulberry tree, and from that day it always smells like buttermilk and dead roses. We call it the Light House now and offer up our prayers there because Daddy is full-circle converted. He has nailed up the dump hole and propped in the seat of a '64 Dodge pickup. We keep a Testament on a shelf where the scroll paper was, but the black book isn't much use, as anybody with their mind on the holy can feel the scripture scorched into the boards. That's what Daddy says. The quarter-moon slot in the spruce door lets sunlight bleed in, but it's God Redeeming that makes every splinter glow. That's where Daddy's shout sermons come to him in a startle, so he should know. He also has hung up a half-moon hubcap losing chrome, which he says is rusting toward the outline of the Jesus face with its crown of thorns. We'll see.

We is my daddy John Crow Epps and my brother Jester. Also myself, Dock.

There was never any symptoms of flight in our family before, but now Daddy, whose black hair made him Crow, hardly scuffs the ground when he steps. He's that lifted.

I wish Jester and me could rise up and float about. We have to work the sunflower rows on normal legs while Daddy preaches around or witnesses down at Sentry Park or some close-by camp meeting. When the spirit is on him, Daddy hot-wires the possum-colored rattletrap truck and's gone most all day. It is not so easy for a

351

pair of boys thirteen and twelve to run a flower farm alone. We have to stake some and string them, have to cut the suckers and cull the puny, spray against the aphids, whiteflies, and Apollo moths. They are also prone to rust and mildew, so we boys hover close to home, doctoring plants, killing bugs, staying all sweaty and weary while the Word is spread far and wide. Every day here this summer we have to choose what goes to market with El Louise Swofford, who stops by everybody's house who has a whisper crop. The cotton folks with big spreads by the river have their own rigs, and we gawk at them whizzing down Governor Toombs Road, which since the lightning Daddy says we should call Miracle Way. When Uncle Pre asks Daddy do you call yourself farming, he says just a whisper. So that's us.

Even Jester knows the short bus El Louise drives is for the lame and halt, but in midmorning she totes beans and peaches, salt hams and yellow vegetables, red peppers, some food stuff in hulls, some tasseled. Eggs, too, and sometimes chickens. For us it's just bouquet sunflowers and a few scuppernongs when they come ripe. We do all right.

El Louise is a hefty woman with cigarettes, using state gas to haul produce and fill her pocket. Her hair is hived up tall. I say, Jes, let's catch some wasps on sticky paper and fill a poke. We'll set them in the bottom of a scuppernong basket and see will they escape out to mess with El Louise. Jester says Our Savior wouldn't. He has been in the Light House too often to suit me, so I play-slap him and run off giggling into the crown rows of King Red Streaks. I know I'm marked out to be more responsible, but it's hard.

Our mother hails from Woolwine, Virginia. She first came down here for Bessie Tift Women's College over in Forsythe, and I reckon she was happy once, but everything started going to the dogs a couple of years back. Then she didn't take to the Lord setting up shop in the piddle shack. From the day of the lightning bolt, she was sour and riled, sat half the day just gazing out at flash-by highway traffic. Wasn't much go left in her, but Mama and Daddy took to scuffling even worse come evenings.

I don't know what he sold, the Hudson man with travel cases and eyes slick as a cold sky, but she climbed in with her lima-green valise at dusk about six weeks back and was gone in a swirl of dust. Not so much as a word.

Back before his being washed in the Lamb, when I guess Daddy used to smack her on the sly, I'd see Mama's face red as a blister burn, arms bruised church purple and gold. One night I was up to spill my water on the yard where I'm salting a dandelion to death, and I saw her in the kitchen working the blue pump by the sink. It has a curved handle which seems like it's too beautiful to be a tool, and 3-in-1 keeps its iron parts from owl-screeching. I always love to watch that pump work. On that particular night the water gushed out silver, and I tell Jester about what I saw when she stepped clear of shadow, her whole back and shoulders that yellow of a new bruise dawning.

Jester's so riled he says, we'll have to kill him, but two weeks later we're still plotting—lye soup or a gas jacket?—when the storm blazes and the Light House is born. Not long after, she rescues herself in the Hudson.

Now Daddy is down at Jesus Wept Chapel thumping the pulpit against hell-bound sinners and unworthy women. He says plagues are coming, monsters about to be unleashed. He says there will come a swarm of weevils and a flood or maybe no rain ever again and sand whirled into a deadly rose. God has told him there will be suffering and gnashing of teeth and bloody sores. They all amen and raise up a hand. They writhe about shouting Kaluja! or Yes, my shepherd! and pass the plate with a flannel pancake in the bottom to hush the coins.

We have eaten our egg sandwiches and have shucked our gloves off in the shade. I am poking at a chinchbug hole with my weed. Jester has made a creel of wild grapevine and put his wood soldier doll inside with a swaddle dishrag.

Lookee. Moses in the bullbushes, he says, all innocent in the face.

It makes me slap at him again and stomp his Bible story into a mess. I just do some things. I don't know why.

Daddy comes back still cloud-walking from his Jeremiah trance, intoning on Og the King of Bashan and such, and wants to look at the Blue Horse notebook where I keep receipts from El Louise and all the running figures—profit and loss, halfs and carry-overs, spend-outs and owed. The Owl Producto cigar box hiding sunflower money sits under the roll top amongst the cubbyholes and pigeon slots with a mess of bill papers. He says money is the root of evil and keeps a mummy-dried bat on top of the bills to warn off any man jack with selfish notions. Daddy says God Himself needs cash in a steady river to further the Work, but I know he is drinking it. I found an empty Ancient Age bottle in the Dodge springs. It had the old smell all right. I've seen other signs. Even if he has us get up with the rooster

353

and cite the Green Pasture Psalm, he is deep into what Mama used to call "the medicine." It don't speak well for religion, I don't care if he can step on air.

We stack them in a wagon, careful not to bend the ray petals. Jester sloshes the cut stems till we can tote them back to the cooling cans. Even the Shy Brownies and Oxblood brand look like somebody's faces. Some are bright lion heads with star-point manes. Some are just beaming children. Daddy says Jesus is a sun god. You have to respect their joyful no-noise of soft color. They follow the sun path and are all helio-something-or-other, the Silverleaf and Primrose, Icarus and Evening Sun, the Ring of Fire and other soaring solos, as well as the polyheads like little Tom Thumb, which are yellow as store-bought butter. I don't see myself why anybody with such plants like the eye of God over six flat acres should need a Light House.

What I want is a baseball, a crate of Co-Colas, one ride on the Ferris, a little pet birch tree so its bark will hold on to light from the moon. A deep well and good furrows ain't enough to keep a chap like me smiling forever. I've got calluses on my fingers and lots of nicks. My shoulders stay slump-sore, and the stalks make an itch burn, but Daddy says just to use bag balm at night. I'd enjoy to have a beagle pup and a glass-top showcase for my arrowheads. A bullwhip to crack at rats. Jester wants a *Have Gun Will Travel* cowboy kit with the horse head and some floss candy on a stick. We both want a book of fairy stories and a bike. Pan of fried chicken. Daddy says we are pagans. Remember the poor, he says, the miseried and starving. We should be ashamed.

It is after dinner, and we are sick of souse and butterbeans, boiled okra, collard greens, hopping john that tastes like mush, pone cakes, tomatoes, and Luzianne water with no sweetening. It's our mama's cooking we yearn after. Fried drumsticks and pies, the sunflower loaf with black strap and fig bits. She could make a chicken that would put manna in the shade. He says we're ungrateful and stomps out. Says we are heathens who wouldn't be happy with ginger beer and butterfly pie, says we are the kind that drove the nails in and stuck the spear.

Now clean 'em up, Epps, no idle hands, choppy-chop! He means the vittle dishes. The vein in his right temple is a blue snake.

Now he's holed up out in the Light House again, most likely with a pocket bottle, whipping up a new scare-'em sermon to reap any stray dollars that might happen along. He stomps and raises his voice in the holy closet. I would like to see the lightning come back and miracle again, so I am listening hard for thunder booms upstairs, but now all I hear is his tambourine bottlecaps shivering like a rattlesnake, mad.

Then one night he catches Jester peeing in the washtub, and we have to start trailing along to Jesus Wept to get our lesson in Good. Spending so much time pew-cramped and dozing upright, it's hard to keep the farm on calendar, and some flowers are stooping, begging any Samaritan passerby to cut a bunch. Ducking work. Is that what they mean by revival? We should feel lucky to get the rest, but I'm antsy. Pretty soon we'll be wanting to start barning the runts and other wounded flowers. About Christmas we always sell the seeds for bird snacks and roasting, the worst mealy ones for sow mix. Only Daddy has the trained eye for what we pour into the press and crank the handle to make helio oil, but me and Jes'd have to learn it ourselves, if there was enough time we weren't down at the chapel. Daddy read the flower book cover to cover by himself and has been in it since before Jester was born. Before that it was dusty goobers, which will stoop a man bad and have no self beauty. Sunflowers were his plan to make Mama happy, a pretty crop against all the dirt and bland, but now he is just a prophet and a lily of the field. He is worshiping us straight to ruin.

Then Daddy brings home a soiled dove from Macon, says we should make her welcome. Pandy Cleave. She is a natural slattern—tassel blonde out of a bottle, a long jaw, eyes gray as gravel, and can't cook any better than me, but she has a Sears guitar, which is the beat of a tambourine any day. Now me and Jes get to stay home and do our job again. She sulks around the house and is no use, paints her nails and writes silly songs, and after supper it's jibber-jabber, jibber-jabber, jibber.

Jester says Daddy thinks he can save anybody he wants. That man ain't got the sense God gave a goat. I'd get a hiding if he knew I said that, or most anything that crosses my mouth when he's out Bible beating. We're trying to get used to her, but she favors those peculiar old Carter Family songs ands sings "The Storms of Jordan" tangled up with a murder ballad about Blackie. Me and Jester know better, as we had the plum-colored Philco, but I think Hudson Man thiefed it off. We didn't miss it for days, but who else?

It all comes to a head now like a boil on your scruff.

First off, Pandy has taken to touching Jester on the gizmo. It starts when she is washing him like pretending to be our mama, and she tickles him and gets him all wiggly, but pretty soon it's the middle of August and she ain't adding to the work crew or giving much help in the kitchen. Just lazing. Daddy says she'll gallop on down to Jesus Wept fast as a thirsty jennet on the day when the Holy Ghost surprises her, but till then she can just hang about and be what he calls available. The Holy Ghost is like something in a wedding dress you can't quite see. It will jump you from behind. That's why there's no point looking out for it. I wonder would she hear the call if it was to come.

I already don't trust her. Things she does. Pandy thinks it's fun to sneak up on most anybody, but she creeped behind me once in the coop and made me drop a handful of Dominecker eggs where they smashed and ran, three useless suns.

Mess with me and I'll cut you. I have it out already, bright with the morning's fifty stone strokes. Daddy said a dull knife ain't no knife at all.

I'll tell John Crow, and he'll whup the tar out of you.

You won't tell him a thing. My eyes and the Barlow give her every reason to believe. Gleam.

But she has a hanker to fool with Jester. I don't know it yet, but then I do. We are out in the hillside rows, cutting a bunch of glory circles for a cash windfall order over from the Senoia Methodists, and I am trying to daydream butterfly pie. It must taste like slap-happy colors with sugar, food in a dream. A wind is breathing, and a hawk goes over, his X sky-sweeping over the leaning rows. Then Jester behind me breaks out crying and says Hell might be coming for him.

You never done nothing worth notice.

The harlot has me. I can see tears streaking the dirt on his cheeks.

Talk sense, Jes. What?

So he tells me she rubs him, and his gizmo swells up a little, he can't stop it. She gets him once when Daddy and me are cleaning the seed press and once when I'm in front trying a cigarette and haggling with El and Daddy's as usual out Lording somewhere. Broad daylight. Now he's afraid to go into the Light House.

He says, I thought she wanted to cuddle like a momma. She has a sweetness in her voice. You know that blue train-yodel she has like Jimmie Rodgers. I was took in, and she gives me pennies. Now I can feel the Devil crawling on my skin.

He reaches into his coverall bib and brings out a clutch of coppers. I be damn.

I'm about to explode, but I don't hit him. I hold it in, knowing who's to blame. Then I say we need to get something else on her. We need to blacken her name.

For three evenings we give off work early and use the tall stalks of Gold Giants to hide our way back to the house. We are like Crock-etts—field edge to the crape myrtles, run run run, the abelia shrub where our Joshua cat likes to doze, then up to the house, flat as shadows on the board and batten. Inside the front door I can see his coat peg is empty, so she's alone, like usual. No Sears Roebuck music. No supper sizzling. I don't know what she does all day. Then the third evening we find out.

She's in Daddy's and her room at the roll top, so Jester fetches the hubcap, and he's on my shoulders, reflecting through the window, I know the room is mirrored up funny in the chrome, but he can make her out and motions me to set him down. The Jesus rust hasn't much shaped up.

Pandy's got the books, and she's changing my figures with a pencil rubber. She has the Owl Producto box. Dock, he whispers, she is filching our cash. It's on her lap over the rose print dress. I think she is robbing us. The bat is on the floor.

We crouch there and figure. She can't make letters like me. Nobody can, as I write a peculiar tilty hand and cipher a lot on the edges. How's she going to fool John Crow Epps?

She'll get caught, Dock. He won't let her. He won't keep her on if she's a pilfer. Anybody can see that. Could she really be that stupid?

Not for long.

What we don't know is she's got a scissor lock on him. That's what Uncle Brinson used to call it. Her night work has smoked his judgment. I find out when I try to tell him, and what I get is the wrath side of God's message, the back of a hand. Blood leaking out my nose.

You've got your momma's demon in you, boy. You're a born heathen. If there's flower money missing, I'll know who to look to. That vein again, beating.

He storms out the door and walks to the yard swing, where she is looking at the moon. Pretty soon they are giggling and drinking from a sack. It don't occur to him to ask where she got cigarettes and a fresh hair ribbon. Jester and me lie abed and wonder how to bring

357

him back to solid ground. We toss about and scheme till their spring squeak comes under our door and through the walls, but then sleep comes on us, and then it's time to perk coffee and hit the fields. I hear her in the back bedroom strumming chords while she pops her gum, and the Ford truck is gone. I don't know if he's told her I have borne witness. I don't much care.

While I make us lunch buckets Jester taps the table in time with the coffee spurting up into its little glass bubble.

We have a hard day, Jes, lots of bunches to tote over, and a sight of watering.

I know, D, I know, but I don't care for it now. I can't understand. Why do we have to work while Daddy plays Jesus? It's the Light House's fault, that's what it is.

I say don't forget your round hat. I can feel a scorcher coming.

When we trot down the steps, I can hear there's no noise from her and Daddy's room. I would like to see her chewed and spit out by God. Daddy says it's a rule not to suffer a witch to live, but he wouldn't know a witch if she was cackling and stirring afterbirth and rabbit crap in a kettle.

It's a rough one all right, a brain burner, and we have split hoses and a slow sputter pump to work with. The pump at the field heart ain't a patch on the blue kitchen one, and we have to ram a hoe handle in so we can work it together sucking the water from a deep spring nobody has ever seen. At the spit head I have some stripped threads to fight with on a joining. The way the pipe wrench opens its jaws puts me in mind of the Godzilla, and that's my idea of a God, I think, chomping up the doers of evil, even if it means you-know-who in my own family tree.

We break off to load up for El Louise, and she grins like a gator handing me a big fold of money to settle for the month. I stuff it in my bib so we can get back to what Daddy calls appointed toil.

Like always, I eventually get some thread cuts from twisting new pipe steel on, and like I say, it is a hard one. By noon I see Jester is flagging on me, so we take our tea water and biscuits with black bananas and boiled eggs in the shade of the flowers. I love to stretch on my back and look where the sky is blocked out by our giants. We have some tree helios out of rogue seeds, and the blooms are bigger than our straw hats. You could almost believe yourself safe from anything in the sky down here, like the world can't find you. It's like sunflowers are your army of mighty shields. The highway is zooming by, but I can't see it. It can't see me, neither.

After I figure out Jester has got into poison oak and is scratching like a flea terrier, we head back to the house for calamine, but when we get there, something feels wrong. I holler out for Pandy, but no answer. Then it's up the steps and through the house calling her name. It's just an echo, and I'm not surprised much, just like a hollow log, but I know where to go, and sure as Judas, there's the cigar box and bat on the bed, not a dollar in sight. I'm in a frazzle. If he thinks it was me, he'll be dangerous as a runaway crop duster. Still, I don't have much choice. Where would we go?

So I tell Jester, and it sinks the heart out of both of us. We chip ice and make big glasses of water to sit on the porch swing and watch for cars and trucks passing. He'll be home, we reckon, in time for something to eat. We sit quiet as bird eggs. The Bible says for everything there's a season, but I'm not ready.

When he comes, he bounds out the truck cab again smiling and giving out hosanna. I can see he's got that air-walking gait again, but I hold up the box. All gone, I say. She's done struck out.

She what? She what? The vein swelling.

He gets red as a pickled beet and, snort breathing, runs inside shouting her name. He must be thinking: just like Mama. Hudson Man. His usual angle of wrong.

Now he runs out the back and around the sheds yelling no-words and also screaming he has been touched by the she-devil. Jester and me just sit there, nothing else to do. She has loosed all the sins and horrors on the world. We just hope he won't turn it on us.

Then he's back in the house again throwing fury fits. He is pounding walls and snarling, kicking chairs and stuff about. Fling and hurl. The flatiron comes out a window, and me and Jester decide to get some distance. It's like a tornado has set down in the house, and the smashing and splintering is like a twister, so we drag the ladder over and climb up top of the house, where it might be some safer. Pull the ladder up, just in case. We are still in the frazzle. We want to be calm, but we're too scared.

When he comes out, he has his own daddy's war pistol and is raving, Heathens and pagans, anathema the bitch scourge of God! Kneel with me, sons, he says. Kneel and raise our mighty plea. We crouch down and don't feel too safe, but he looks up at us perching and says boys, I'll bring her back, I'll get our money, I'll smite and venge, oh abomination! and a laugh like somebody plain crazy.

Then he is in the truck and gunning the engine. Coming to Miracle Way, he stops like deciding east or west. It's west, and we watch him heading after the sun that's going down like the king of the flowers. He leaves a swirling trail of rusty dust. From up here I can see our thousands of flowers in their careful rows, holes where the cut ones are missing, lanes for the sprinkler that's spitting water feeble like a cricket. Out beyond, our crops—the acres of flowers waving, refreshed—give way to sweet corn ready for its last picking and then soybeans still growing. Farmhouses, yards, and the road seem like they're glowing till everything in every direction just blurs with twilight and the worn-out day's haze.

Jes is slowly turning, shading his eyes like an Arapaho scout.

Do you reckon we'll see him again, Dock?

Come sleet, come gray wind, the world turning like it does, I expect he'll show up with his tail tucked. Maybe he'll come back wrung out, unsmitten, whole. If he don't show, we'll keep the farm ourselves if we can.

Before long we figure it's safe and run the ladder back over the edge.

There's no weather clouds flocking up there, so I halt my steps on a middle rung and say up to my brother, I have me an idea. Let's torch the Light House and be done with it. Kerosene in the barn. We'll say lightning again if Daddy comes back. I don't care one way or the other. I've got eighty dollars in my chest pocket, and we've got a heap of orders.

Then Jes says can we have fried dinner now, D? Can we sacrifice a chicken?

Pagans like us, you know. Jesus wept. I lock my eyes on a fox-colored hen, and we climb on down.

*Nominated by The Southern Review*

# SKIN TEETH

## by NEISHA TWEED

from POETRY

One good Friday night I come home—
tired bad—and I can't find me children
or me husband. The house quiet like somebody dead.
I call up he best friend. He say the children
wid the woman up the road, but he don't know where
    they father be.
Or maybe he just don't want to tell me.
So I jump in me car and drive up Monkey Hill.
I gon catch him, the bastard. I park behind he jeep
and take me blessed time an let the air
out of one—two—three tires.
Then I walk in the stupid lickle rum shop
as if is me who lay down the foundation
and is me who pay the rent. And I see him
holding some girl hand. Laughing like the world can't end.
As soon as the little squeng see me
she up like she ready for war.
But I is a big woman—can't bodda fight
wid pickney who don't understand what is mine is mine,
I smile broad wid alla them.
Then I pour he drink over he head, an tell him never
leave me children with nobody again.

*Nominated by Sherod Santos*

# ON THE REALITY OF THE SYMBOL

## by GEOFFREY HILL

from LITERARY IMAGINATION

1

That he feared death—Karl Rahner—unrevealing.
Fine theologian with or against
the world, in senses that are not the world's,
his symbolism, both
a throwback and way forward, claims its own
cussedness, yet goes with the mystery.
Parturition of psalm like pissing blood
I múst say, the formal evidence
so much an issue. Though not painful
pain's in the offing, somewhere signifies
its needled presence. Plus, the prostate's
a nasty beast even at the best of times.
But for translation the old linguaduct
works not too badly. This is a translation.

2

So? Say it again: ephemeralities
ever recurring. There are numerous
things you can't speak or think. Must confess I
sometimes rape her ghost? The olive trees
oblige with well-reft branches. Scapegoats are not

hunted but driven out. There yet remain
impassioned and strange readings: a remote
cry of the blood sugars.
Try *melos* for desired numbness of breath.
And you a poet in all justice. Too
many signs: call scourings from fouled pipes
purification. There! the white dove plumps
her spectral finery. Building my ark begins
late in the terminal welter of the flood.

3

Pity love could not act us. No scarcity
of drama schools where I live. In some of them
refusal's not much worse than other failings
I won't elaborate. We refused each other:
loss is what we are left with. Re-audition.
They'd take us back, instruct us to be old.
Here's bargain-gelt to move things on a stage.
More than a sexy trial a *Trauerspiel*
needs make-believe to launch the sordid fact.
Does this miscast us as a tragic chorus?
Can't answer that, I'm working on my rôle.
Shyster's from a Yiddish word for shit.
It's not, you know.
This is late scaffold-humour, turn me off.

4

On vision as a mode of neural tort:
and I could find myself becoming
overseer for rehabilitation,
imprinting with due licence the late-cancelled
stanzas that hymn roulette. Everything mortal
has to give from life. When we're exhausted
by ill-willing, the fictions of our joys,
violin, pleach-toned harp, and grand piano
melodize; the contessa's niece
glitters her gift three lengths of the salon.
Symbol burns off reality: take *The Red Shoes*—

since I'm to show beholden—how for instance
those awkward, svelte, death-struck, life enhancers
labour their immortality proclaimed.

5

Gold, silver, to gel-blaze the dark places.
Black has its own gleam. Pascal's
name is a blank to many people (blank
being blanc); so too are yours and mine.
There must be unnamed stars but all are numbered
*de profundis*. Check these on the web
spun by their own light. And does such knowledge
firm up allegiance to the stoic heavens?
And is the question real or rhetorical
when finally the all-or-nothing man
presses his wager? Such extravagance
here to expand on, to elect chaos
where there's a vacancy and peradventure
if chaos is the word.

6

The work of mourning—the *Trauerarbeit*—
bugles dead achievements. Regardless
and in spite of, what a memory
topped out by glittering breakage. Bitter stabs
at the long jump (juniors) from a greased run up,
off a rain-swathed board. Five seconds' freedom
I nominate to be the normal freedom
of the mob-ruled. Subsequent fables,
men of stale will nursing their secret wounds,
the token of the scarecrow as sufferer,
seem done for. Death fancies us but finally
leaves us alone. Metaphysics remain
in common language something of a joke.
Mourning my meaning is what I meant to say.

*Nominated by Literary Imagination*

# BENEDICTION: ON BEING BOSWELL'S BOSWELL

by DAVID GESSNER

from THE GEORGIA REVIEW

I SAT IN THE FRONT ROW like a rock groupie, straining forward so that I could catch every word. He sometimes spoke in a plaintive whisper and, never having quite mastered the use of the clip-on microphone, presented no more than a dramatic mime show to those seated in the back of the class. He was frail with wispy tufts of white hair floating out above his large ears and thin bones canopied in oversized clothes, a mismatched plaid jacket and striped pants. Occasionally his lectures, like his appearance, were haphazard, dissolving into wistful monologue.

"Let's skip some of this stuff," he'd say, waving it off.

Once, I remember, he looked down at his watch and, startled by the amount of time left in the class, exhaled a loud *woof*. His comments could be dreamlike: "I may have mentioned this to you earlier—or was that years ago?" Or halfway through the lecture, he'd apologize: "I'm sorry that this wasn't better."

The transition of English literature from neoclassicism to romanticism was our stated theme, but a leitmotif of old age and melancholy ran through the lectures. Aging and Loneliness 104. "Don't let anyone tell you about how wonderful it is to grow old," he sighed. "The only value of getting older is that you care less about what other people think of you." He looked down from the podium with his elastic face, twisting and pulling at it as if it were made of putty. It was a great comic face, a gentle clown's face that had led a studious and difficult life. Introducing Keats's *Endymion*, he took off his glasses and stared out with blue eyes. He referred to the biography of Keats he'd written "in my greener, happier days."

Those were the moments that made me love the man, but there were other moments, too, when an idea would catch his fancy, and he would spark alive. Then his hands slid from their resting place below his chin. First, the right hand would pulse to life, slowly rising up from the podium in a circling flight. It opened and closed steadily, then began fluttering and darting, dipping and rising as if barely within his control. When his point was made, the hand would fall gently, a leaf dropping in slow, unpredictable swoops, back and forth, never twice along the same path, finally landing on the podium, or nestling back into the folds of his face and resting for its next flight. Then, just as the room was calming, the other hand would take off, dipping and flying out toward the class.

"We must look to the past's great examples," he exhorted, and it took all my will not to shout "Amen!" He spoke of Samuel Johnson and as he did his left arm flew up so violently that it looked as if it might pull him off the ground. He stood there—strict, masterful, and commanding, his white fingers balled up into a fist. But then, abruptly, a second later, they broke into an undulating dance. With this same light pulse, he removed his thick black glasses and, with that, underwent another miraculous change: glasses off, hand and voice in unison again, he calmed. Rubbing the creases arcing below his eyes, he looked out with an expression watery and kind. The transformation was complete. There again stood the most gentle man in the world.

I was drunk, in one way or another, the better part of my time at Harvard. Like a lot of people, I felt I had no right to be there in the first place—this was a place for geniuses and Thurston Howells after all—and so I threw myself into a bacchanalian frenzy: drinking, skipping classes, smoking pot from the hookah I bought at the Leavit and Pierce tobacco shop, sleeping late, spending afternoons playing Ultimate Frisbee by the stadium. I didn't take Harvard too seriously, or maybe I took it too seriously and so, as a defense, I acted in very silly ways. During my freshman year I tore a sink off the wall of our communal bathroom in a fit of drunken fury, and the next year, hoping to impress a girl, I leapt out of the second floor window of her dorm after bidding her goodbye. I thought I would catch a branch and swing, Erroll Flynn-like, to the ground in a dazzling exit. Instead the branch snapped. I fell fifteen feet backward and fractured my skull on the concrete. It was a pattern that would repeat itself throughout my twenties: grandiose visions, impulsive decisions, disastrous results.

For me the campus was less an ivory tower than a territory which I prowled at night like an animal, full of beer and lust. I remember a particular oak tree in the quadrangle in front of Eliot House where I liked to mark my territory. Often I roamed until morning, when the garbage trucks came rumbling and roaring like dinosaurs down the Cambridge streets. I grew my hair long and did countless push-ups, the latter my only concession to discipline. Feigning a deep lack of ambition, I was secretly, intensely ambitious. Though I had no definite idea what it was yet, I knew deep down that I would do something great. This secret vision, coupled with my profligate behavior, caused me no small amount of self-loathing.

My one saving grace in college was that I loved to read. Under my brutish exterior, I was bookish. I discovered Rabelais and then Montaigne, whose earthiness and constant self-examination struck a chord; Dostoevski, taught by a brilliant gnomelike Russian professor; and, of course, Thomas Wolfe, who stoked my delusions. It was after reading Wolfe that my previously vague and inchoate ambitions began to coalesce into clarity. I became more interested in Wolfe's biography than in his actual writing, which bored me after a while. What I loved was the myth, the idea of being a famous writer, and of also being, not incidentally, a giant (he was six feet seven inches), bigger than other men—though I, not quite six feet, could only imagine. I loved reading about his life: the fame, the intensity, the anguish, its oh-so-exciting wrought-upness.

I learned that Wolfe had gone to Harvard for graduate school and had reacted to his new surroundings with characteristic volatility. He was, as always, overwhelmed by the "pity, terror, strangeness, and magnificence of it all." But he was also lonely. "He felt more lost at Harvard than ever before," wrote Elizabeth Norwell, an early Wolfe biographer. I understood: after the leaves fell that first autumn in Cambridge, the cold winds whipped down the brick streets between the buildings and I felt lost.

Partly in response to his loneliness, Wolfe spent hours prowling the deep stacks of Widener library. My first encounter with those book-lined catacombs was not quite so literary: I was playing a stoned game of tag with my five roommates, running through the underground corridors and catacombs. But later I went back on my own. I descended three floors below the ground into the darkness (you had to flick on the lights in each row) of acres and acres of books. I loved the smell of the place and the sense of possibility. There was an added layer of self-consciousness to my explorations, of course, since I had just recently read about Wolfe's own monumental assault on the Widener stacks. Unlike me, he gorged systematically, timing his reading with a stopwatch. He records that rapacity in the autobiographical novel *Of Time and the River*:

> To prowl the stacks of an enormous library at night, to tear the books out of the shelves. . . . The thought of these vast stacks of books drove him mad. . . . He pictured himself tearing the entrails from a book as from a fowl. . . .

Prowling the same stacks sixty years later, I pictured Wolfe and then pictured myself picturing him while ripping through books of my own.

But if reading Thomas Wolfe was like the lighting of a fuse for what would become my incipient megalomania, then by far the most important event of my college life was my discovery of Walter Jackson Bate. Bate, who had recently won the second of his two Pulitzers, was one of Harvard's fabled great men, a lineage that extended back to Alfred North Whitehead (whom he'd heard lecture in the thirties) and beyond. I blew off many of my classes but I never missed the Age of Johnson.

The thrill of Bate's lectures came first—his malleable face, trembling voice, and hand floating above the podium—but soon his ideas began to infect me. I took long walks by the Charles River muttering to myself, mulling over the notion that literature must retreat from modern games and return to essentialism, whatever that was. I did poorly in the rest of my courses; this was the only class that mattered. Back in my room I hunched over his biographies of Johnson and Keats, and his little book *The Burden of the Past and the English Poet*, ripping deep furrows beneath the sentences with my ballpoint, feverishly scrawling notes and quotations.

By my sophomore year Walter Jackson Bate—the great man himself—lived only a few doors down from me and I often saw him eating in the dining hall, not ten feet away. There he was, taking his breakfast or lunch, wearing mismatched plaids or what looked like pajamas, often eating alone, absorbed in his Salisbury steak and profound thoughts. At least a hundred times I picked up my tray and started across the room to sit with him, but I always chickened out. Though I was taking another of his lecture courses, I'd never encountered him in person outside of class. I could have gone to see him during office hours, but by then he meant—he symbolized—too much to me, and I didn't have the courage to approach him.

That was left to Jon, my bolder and less self-conscious roommate. Jon and I had become good friends and it was in Jon that I confided my growing hope that I might one day become a writer. I also confided how much Bate meant to me. "Why don't you just go over and talk?" Jon asked, logically enough. Finally one day, fed up with my equivocations, Jon, with my halting blessing, marched over to Bate.

Jon introduced himself and soon the two were friends. Three months later, when Bate invited him up to his New Hampshire farmhouse, it was a crushing blow. I hated hearing the stories from that weekend, but of course I asked Jon to tell them again and again until I knew them by heart. I heard about Bate and Jon spending the day pitching horseshoes and walking through the woods, then drinking hot cider and rum that evening in front of the fire with Bate reading out loud the poetry of his "old friend Archie MacLeish."

I was devastated.

But if Jon knew the actual man, I still believed that I alone understood his ideas. I'd entered college flirting with the notion of going to law school, but Bate's lectures permanently derailed that course. "The boldness desired involves directly facing up to what we admire and then trying to be like it," I read. "It is like the habit of Keats of beginning each new effort by rereading Lear and keeping close at hand the engraving of Shakespeare." And so I tacked pictures of Keats and Johnson, and yes, of Bate, too, above my desk. In his biographies—his stories, as I saw them—great writers always struggled and eventually perservered.

"The hunger of youth is for greatness," was a line from Longinus that Bate often quoted. By my senior year my own hunger was a gnawing one. Near the end of that year I finally got up the nerve to visit Walter Jackson Bate during office hours. There he was in person, white hair disheveled, sitting behind a large desk and slamming his empty pipe on a glass ashtray. I stared into his watery blue eyes and wondered what to say. I knew I needed to make an impression, to become his friend the way Jon had. We had just begun to talk when he managed to shatter the ashtray with a particularly sharp whack from his pipe. He called in his secretary and the three of us got down on our knees, sweeping up ash and gathering broken shards.

When we resumed talking I tried to explain how much his courses and books had meant to me. I admitted that I wasn't a very good student overall but that I'd spent the better part of the last four years prowling Widener and reading, as Samuel Johnson had put it, "by inclination."

He studied me closely, brushing ash off his pants.

"It sounds like you've given yourself quite a self-education," he said.

That was as close as I would come to a blessing that day. We had a nice chat, but there were no invitations up to the old New Hampshire farmhouse, no special advice conferred. I left his office happy to have finally spoken to him, but disappointed that I hadn't performed better or garnered more pearls of wisdom. "There are a series of answers available in man's long and groping quest," he had said in class, "answers that can shed some light on our problems now, can teach us what might work, and what not to do." That was what I really wanted, some of those answers.

It didn't matter, though, not really. Unbeknownst to him, Bate had already given me his blessing almost a year before. It had been during a survey class called "From Classic to Romantic" in the spring of my junior year. In a lecture during that course I heard him speak about the possibility of a "new romanticism," a return to the essential tenets of romanticism that might rise out of the compost heap of postmodernism. He described how the romantic movement itself grew out of neoclassicism, in part born of a rebellion against neoclassicism's "worst excesses": the eighteenth century's increasingly rigid emphasis on unity of form, order, decorum—that is, "the rules." Then he suggested the parallels to our current situation, comparing the worst excesses of postmodernism and deconstruction to those of neoclassicism: a dry emphasis on reason, on mind; a focus on games, a literature that had moved away from essentialism, from a direct connection to life. "What is literature if it isn't relevant to how we live?" he asked the class. Though a scholar and not a prophet, Bate speculated that the next logical movement in the arts would be toward a kind of new romanticism.

It was just a theory, of course, maybe even an offhand remark, but in my fervid young brain it quickly became much more than that. In my mind's eye I saw Walter Jackson Bate floating above the stage, clad in a tunic, reaching over with a blazing sword which he placed on my shoulders. In my head his new romanticism became the *New Romanticism*. Was there any doubt who the first great New Romantic writer would be?

I graduated from college in 1983. For the next seven years I tried to write my *New Romantic* novel. I wrote it in every conceivable fashion from every conceivable point of view. I had many titles, but I might have aptly called the book "Quagmire." I never found an angle into my material or, more to the point, I found too many angles. Too much freedom, I was beginning to learn, could be just as deadly as too much restraint.

My classmates grew rich as I labored at my intangible, and possibly insane, project. During the years I actually did my taxes, the profession I wrote insistently down on the forms was "writer." What that meant, for practical purposes, was that I worked in bookstores, substituted at high schools, framed houses, and once did a stint as a security guard at a phone store.

At the time I thought these jobs the gravest injustice on the planet. With a wild sense of entitlement I once asked my girlfriend what Shakespeare's fate would have been had he been forced to labor as I did. I said this in anger and without irony. I thought my situation unique, not understanding that I was just a type. The type I was was an *apprentice writer*, and the side effects of that vocation—the bitterness, the occasional megalomania, the sense of injustice and impotence, the envy and frustration and rage—were as much a part of the job as carpal tunnel or tennis elbow were part of my work as a framing carpenter.

I felt a growing sense of panic and failure, but deep inside I was sure that if I finally completed my book it would change everything. Then I'd be hailed as the great artist I secretly dreamed I was. I saw myself creating a Wolfean tome that I would someday bring to Bate and drop on his doorstep, just as Thomas Wolfe had brought his manuscript to Max Perkins. Samuel Johnson spoke of the "epidemical conspiracy for the destruction of paper," and during those years I did my part. I created new drafts, destroyed them, created dozens more. The trouble was that while I had a romantic vision of a great writer writing a great book, I had little else.

But it wasn't only delusion that Bate spurred. Looking back it seems that the important thing was to continue writing, to get the bad out and get to the good, and Bate's books helped keep me going.

There's a profound impotence to apprenticeship. Beginning is terrifying business, and chaos is inherent in beginning. Most of us are unable to see that beginnings will ever end. "I spit on the grave of my twenties," wrote Mencken. I can't quite build up that much anger for the character I was; he was silly and immature, but I don't hate him. If anything I feel a little sorry for him, and, at times, even feel gently admiring. I like the fact that when the whole world was saying "Pick door A and you'll be a success," he picked door B. And I like the fact that, when everyone was saying that the most important thing in the world was to make money, he tried, however clumsily, to make art.

It isn't just how to write that a writer learns during his or her apprenticeship. Looking back, I can't help but feel that there's something healthy about spending years banging one's head against a wall. One gains, among other things, the luxury of failure, a necessary luxury for an artist. Working long and hard at things that others consider ridiculous builds the muscles of nonconformity. And perhaps delusion is a necessary tool. "Without hope there is no endeavor" was a line of Samuel Johnson's that Bate was fond of quoting. I wonder if any young writer would ever finish a book if he knew just how long and hard the effort would be, and how little the end result would impact the world. Without the drunkenness of excitement, would we ever even start anything? I admire the grit of that character I was, but I also know that much of his energy sprang from his delusions. He would never get the fame and glory he so craved, but in its stead he would get regular habits and pleasure and the sanity of work—not such a bad trade in the end. I'm glad it wasn't easy for him. Our failures are our strengths; our calluses define us.

My extended adolescence showed no signs of abating as I approached my thirtieth birthday. It was only through the good fortune of a life-threatening illness that I finally stopped my obsessive scribbling. Had I not gotten sick, I'm sure I'd be sinking in my "Quagmire" to this day.

I learned I had testicular cancer. For a month or two the prognosis was uncertain and I wasn't sure if I would live or die. When it became clear I would survive, I felt like a snake that had shed its old skin. I secretly hoped the surgeon had cut the old book away with the tumor. I began to make a story out of what was happening to me as soon as I got sick; I understood that now I finally had something to say. But during the enervation of the radiation treatments, I couldn't yet muster the energy to begin to say it.

In April, in the midst of radiation, I received some good news. I had been accepted into a writing program in Colorado and would move west in September. But before I left the East, I had some unfinished business. Perhaps freed by the desperation of sickness, I finally had the courage to contact Walter Jackson Bate. I wrote him a long, honest letter, telling him how much he and his books had meant to me over the years, how I had struggled to begin to write, and how I would like to visit him. He responded by inviting me to his home in Cambridge.

A few weeks later he was greeting me at his door, wearing a light blue flannel shirt with blue suspenders and blue pinstriped pants. His hair was whiter now, and I noticed, as we shook hands, that his fingers were smaller than I recalled, not the elongated flesh spiders they had grown into in my imagination.

We retired to the living room where he reclined in a brown La-Z-Boy. I sat on the edge of the couch across the room, leaning forward again like the old days, eager to catch every word. Tobacco spilled out over his side table; he pinched up a fingerful and jammed it into his pipe.

I sat silent and waited, with no thought of starting the conversation. Older, a little wiser maybe, I was still deeply intimidated by the sleepy-looking septuagenarian with blue smoke swirling up and around his face. What could I possibly say that would be significant to such a man?

Around his waist Bate wore a white cummerbund, or girdle, that I now realized was a brace. He leaned back farther in his La-Z-Boy.

"I can't sit up for long," he sighed.

"Your back's bad?" I asked quickly.

He studied me. His eyes were a soft blue, weighed down at their ends by the slight droop of age.

"Oh, it's not good, I'm afraid," he said.

I had mentioned my own health problems in my letter, and now I saw an opening, a way to at once change the subject and sound literary.

"I'm thinking of moving out to Colorado," I said. "Like Hans Castrop going to the mountains to recover."

"Oh, yes, Thomas Mann, *The Magic Mountain*," he smiled. "I'm afraid I could never bring myself to reread it. Every time I started it would bring out my hypochondriacal tendencies."

His pipe had gone out and he began to distractedly bang it on the ashtray, dislodging old tobacco, but then he blinked once, and looked up at me, his blue eyes shining alert.

"But your health," he said. "You are feeling well again?"

Up until that moment he had sounded weary, but now he was wide awake. I like to think that it was empathy—the quality that so distinguishes and enlivens his work—that woke him up that day. In his books he had always become those he wrote about. The legend in college was that he had grown sick and developed a nearly tubercular cough as he neared the end of his life of Keats, and in the same way my sickness seemed to draw him out of himself. Worried about my health, he leaped to his feet to cook us a lunch of broccoli soup and grilled cheese. During the meal, of course, I was on my best behavior, as if my literary future were being judged by my table manners, but I couldn't help smiling when he put down his spoon and his right hand began to flutter above our sandwiches.

I listened as he railed against former Harvard presidents and deconstructionists and the excesses of modern art.

"Perhaps I'm lost in the past," he said, "but I have a preference for the nineteenth-century straight narrative novel. Since Joyce, it seems that fiction has become a puzzle built for academics to figure out."

I reminded him of a comment he'd made in class once. "You were talking about that Henry Moore statue in front of Lamont. You said it looked like a giant pretzel left out in the rain."

He laughed. "That might have been a little harsh."

For the rest of the afternoon his mind tendriled into different subjects, crawling out into them, exploring one idea, moving on to explore the next. I drove him to the Mt. Auburn cemetery where we walked for over an hour. Anything seemed capable of sparking new thoughts.

He pricked his finger on a rosebush and swore. Immediately the subject turned to the derivation of common curses. He began a discourse on the word *shit*.

374

"It comes from the Latin, you see. It means to shoot—to expel."

He shot his arm out quickly as he said the last word.

"And what about *fuck*?" I heard myself asking.

He laughed.

"Quite a direct word, isn't it?"

Directness led to indirectness which led to Samuel Johnson's disdain for periphrasis. He pointed at me.

"Johnson wouldn't have liked the way you called the toilet a *washroom* after lunch. He had no patience for roundabout talk. Like calling fish the *scaly breed*."

I asked him if he still lectured.

"Oh, no, no. They've put me out to pasture, you see. This retirement age is a relatively new thing, but they're quite steadfast about it. Even John Kenneth Galbraith couldn't fight it. When I was an undergraduate it was different. I remember listening to Alfred North Whitehead lecture in a course called Cosmology. His voice was thin and frail by then, and you had to lean forward to catch his words, but what he said was fascinating."

He sighed.

"Yes, they let people carry on a good deal longer back then."

It was a good day. Afterward we wrote letters and spoke on the phone a few times. Then later that summer, right before I left for Colorado, Walter Jackson Bate called and invited me up to the mythic farmhouse in New Hampshire. It had taken over ten years, but I had finally achieved the same status as my roommate Jon.

In early August I made the trip to New Hampshire. On the first afternoon we toured the property in his old jeep, just as he and Jon had. I had to bite my tongue to keep from crying out as we bombed down dirt paths, through briars, and across farmland. Here was my old professor wearing a pair of flip-up sunglasses and smiling with delight at the speed and rushing wind. I'd heard stories about his charging round campus on a motorcycle as a young man, but I'd never before been able to imagine Walter Jackson Bate as daredevil. This was a new twist.

After dinner that night, he poured us drinks. We drank several "Italian kisses," a mixture of red and white vermouth, then small glasses of Madeira, or "old Maumsby" as he called it—"The liquor that Richard the Third had his brother drowned in," he muttered. I nodded as if I knew the allusion.

That night, as usual, his talk was varied, ranging from cattle to religion. The first subject came up because it turned out he'd owned a small dairy farm "after the war"; the second when I, emboldened by liquor, asked him if he believed in God.

"Oh, yes, I suppose," he said. He pointed out through the plate glass window. Rain poured down hard on the flowerbeds and mist rose above the rolling hills. "I have to believe that there is something behind such a miraculous world."

I was surprised by his statement, even more surprised by the adamancy of my response.

"I can't believe in Heaven," I said. "Heaven seems the worst case of wishful thinking. Like believing in Santa Claus."

He studied me.

"I said I believed in a God who created the universe," he said. "I never said I believed in an afterlife."

He stood up and excused himself, and I wondered if I had committed a grave faux pas. But he returned a moment later with a book in his hands.

He sat down and, without introduction, began to read from T. S. Eliot's "East Coker." He began in a near monotone, but then his voice began to quaver, becoming more dramatic, and his hand—the wonderful right hand—fluttered and rose off his lap. Throughout the poem he held his hand up by the side of his head. It trembled slightly like a dry leaf as he read:

> Home is where one starts from. As we grow older
> The world becomes stranger, the pattern more complicated
> Of dead and living. Not the intense moment
> Isolated, with no before and after,
> But a lifetime burning in every moment
> And not the lifetime of one man only
> But of old stones that cannot be deciphered.
> There is a time for the evening under starlight,
> A time for the evening under lamplight
> (The evening with the photograph album).
> Love is most nearly itself
> When here and now cease to matter.
> Old men ought to be explorers
> Here and there does not matter
> We must be still and still moving

Into another intensity
For a further union, a deeper communion
Through the dark cold and empty desolation,
The wave cry, the wind cry, the vast waters
Of the petrel and the porpoise. In my end is my beginning.

He sighed as he finished, cupped wrinkles drooping below his eyes. At that point in my life his reading was the most dramatic thing I'd ever heard. I had no idea what to say.

"Thank you," I managed.

"Thank *you*," he said. "It's been years since I read poetry out loud. The last time I read this piece was at Eliot's memorial service."

If I had not already been transported to some other mythical literary stratosphere, this last bit of casual name-dropping sent me there. The poetry, the liquor—"Old Maumsby"; here even the booze was poetic!—and Bate's presence intoxicated me. Of course I should have let the moment settle, should have savored it, but that wasn't my style. Before I could stop myself my lips began to flap and words spilled out of my mouth.

"I don't really know how to tell you this, or even if I should," I blurted, "but I feel I have to. Since I first heard your lectures I've tried to write the book I mentioned in my letter. For seven years now I've been writing it and rewriting it, but I can't stop. No matter how I try I can't get it right. You see, I want it to be a great book but . . ."

I carried on in this vein for a good ten minutes, my words becoming more and more tangled. I tried to explain how I had begun a new story, about my cancer, but I didn't feel it would be right to start the new book until the old was finished. Wasn't it logical to kill off the old and put it to rest before starting the new?

When I finally finished my confession, I stared down at the floor. I had no idea what to expect, but wouldn't have been too surprised if he'd walked across the room and slapped me.

"A tar baby."

I heard the words and looked up. His chin rested in one hand while the other rubbed his eyes.

"What?" I asked.

"A tar baby. That's what we used to call it before the word became unfashionable. A tar baby. You put your hands on it, get stuck to it, caught on it, never get away from it. I've seen the same thing happen to friends and colleagues. Seen it ruin careers."

377

He paused to sip his drink.

"They say that knowing too much about a historical period makes it impossible to write historical novels. Maybe you know too much about your book. Maybe it's time to stop for a while, to put it aside and work on other things."

"But I feel I have to finish it. If I don't, the last decade will be a failure."

"Of course you feel that way," he said sharply. "If you didn't it wouldn't be a tar baby. But despite how you feel, you must put it aside. Keats had the right idea when he refused to further revise *Endymion*. He wrote: 'Let this youngster die away.'"

The next two days passed quietly. We read, walked, talked, and toured the property in his jeep. I took notes in my journal, a Boswell to his Boswell. During those days Bate spoke of many things but never mentioned my outburst over my writing or his response, and I thought perhaps he'd forgotten about it since we'd both been a little drunk. Our conversations grew less literary, often revolving around domestic affairs.

"The one rule is we don't let the cat out at night. If we do a fox might get her. You've got to be careful. She waits by the door and then—zip!" With the last word he shot his finger and whole arm forward with amazing speed.

Another day passed and I imagined that I was perhaps overstaying my welcome. I decided to leave a day early. The night before my departure Bate left me in his study as he headed up to do his nightly reading.

"The TV is set on channel three for the VCR," he said as he left. "You just call me if you want to turn it on. It's easier to do than to explain, like so many things in life."

I had no interest in watching TV. Instead I sat quietly at the plain oak desk without drawers where he'd composed the Johnson and Keats biographies. He had written them, he'd told me, while teaching full time.

"The teaching is the pleasure," he said. "The writing the work."

I began to examine his bookcase, the classics and the Agatha Christies and *The History of Hand Cut Nails in America*. I came across an old, particularly tattered book, an Avon Classic that had cost thirty-five cents: *The Aims of Education* by Alfred North Whitehead. The pages were working their way free of the spine, and I delicately picked up each one, turning them over one by one. It wouldn't be going too far to say there was an air of religious discovery about my enterprise. I couldn't tell what was more exciting—Whitehead's own words or Bate's notes scribbled excitedly in the margins. "Knowledge does not keep any better than fish" had a checkmark next to it, and "Above all the art of reading aloud should be cultivated" was underscored twice. "Interest is the sine qua non for attention and apprehension," Whitehead had written. Next to that, scrawled in the margin, was Bate's response: "So literature, when it is taught, must be tied up with a student's concerns. It must be shown as projecting or dramatizing the problems of life with which he is familiar." At times Bate argued with his old professor. "The second-handedness of the learned world is the secret of its mediocrity," Whitehead wrote. Bate took exception: "But the second-handedness can be supplemental. Also it depends on how the feeling is felt. If felt directly, it is not second-hand."

I was lost in his books when Bate himself called down goodnight. Jamming Whitehead back into the case, I returned to my bedroom. But I was far too excited to sleep and soon was back in the study. I took a volume of Johnson's *Rambler* off the shelf, copying down in my notebook the sections Bate had underlined. Among the passages was one from *Rambler #60* on biography. I'd heard Bate quote it often before; it would become a guide for me in my future work. "There are many who think it an act of piety to hide the faults or failings of their friends," I read, but "If we owe regard to the memory of the dead, there is yet more respect to be paid to knowledge, to virtue, and to truth."

Next I took Bate's own biography of Johnson down and, on a whim, skimmed forward to the front pages. According to the title page, Bate had been born in 1918. I checked that date against the date of publication of his various books. Despite being obsessed with Johnson, Bate had not published his first book about him until 1955, at the age of thirty-six. He published the Keats biography eight years later at forty-four, and hadn't produced his great life of Johnson until 1975, at the age of fifty-six.

There was something comforting about those numbers.

I hadn't yet experienced the exhilarating feeling of rebirth and regeneration I'd feel the next year while living and writing my new book in a cabin in the Rockies, but perhaps it was then, in Bate's study, that I got my first hint of it. I remembered Johnson's phrase,

"Without hope there is no endeavor." I put the books aside and turned off the light. That night, for the first time in many nights, I fell asleep comforted by a feeling of hope.

Before I left New Hampshire, I already knew that I would follow my Boswellian impulse and write an essay about the experience. Of course I would. That weekend had been one of the most thrilling occasions in my life. I would do what almost any writer would do: I would record it. What I didn't know was that Bate would react with indignation to that essay, which I thought a tribute, ending its chances at publication along with our friendship.

As any sophisticated reader knows, these mentor/disciple stories rarely have happy endings; they follow a fairly standard arc of infatuation to worship to disillusionment. My story is no exception. I wrote my essay a couple of years after my visit, having by then abandoned my tar baby. I wrote about Bate well, I think, and sent it out to a prestigious review where it was accepted, my very first acceptance as a writer. To be polite I also sent the piece to Bate, sure that he would appreciate the admiring, even loving, spirit in which it had been conceived. What he saw instead was a caricature of an enfeebled, senile old man. He called the editor of the review and raged, and the editor promised not to run the piece.

Due to the miracle of modern technology, I got the news of my first acceptance and subsequent rejection within seconds of each other, both singing out to me from my answering machine. I had been away for a weekend of cross-country skiing and had come back home, my face flushed from the outdoors and from the beer I'd drunk driving down the mountain. My fine mood got better as I listened to the first message on the machine, accepting my essay. I was in the middle of a celebratory dance when I heard—and was crushed by—the second.

Bate wrote me a scathing letter, along with a marked-up version of the essay. He particularly objected to my description of his overactive hands, saying they made him look crazy, like something from "Hogarth's pictures of Bedlam." The essay's pages were filled with his scrawled notes: "Too much fluttering of hands!" "Hands again!" "Do you have a mania for hands?"

Reading the old piece today I agree with him up to a point. The essay verges on caricature, but my admiration for my subject—why call him anything other than my hero?—comes through. At the time

I was decimated. Wasn't this the man who embodied magnanimity and empathy? I sent a letter of apology, but Bate refused to respond either to it or to my phone calls. I wrote again, promising never to publish the piece.

I'm now breaking that promise. I do so with Bate dead five years and with the Johnson quote about the salutary effect of honesty in biography in mind. Though I blamed myself for the incident, I later heard stories of Bate's occasional irrational rages, how he once threw his ashtray against an English department wall, for instance. At first it didn't sit well with my image of the kindly, wise professor, but later I was a little more inclined to believe it.

Of course it isn't big news that heroes have faults. For all that we pained each other, Bate remains my greatest teacher, an inspiring guide whose voice I still hear and who helped me define who I am. What I choose to remember about him is that he was heroic in the Johnsonian sense, struggling to manage his own imagination, disciplining it toward empathy and the creation of art. That that imagination might have been a bit more unruly and irrational than I first believed is no longer cause for despair or bitterness, but hope and reassurance.

At Bate's New Hampshire farmhouse, of course, I knew nothing of the feud to come and still regarded the idea that I might one day publish an actual book the way a dying skeptic regards the possibility of a miracle cure, hoping but unbelieving. My infatuation with Bate was still in full bloom: I saw him as my Merlin, my Obi-Wan Kenobi. If this sounds mythic and overdone, it was. But also somewhat fitting. Recovering from cancer, coming back from the dead as it were, I was about to move to the West into a new life. And, now, how could I fail? I had the benediction of a wizard.

We took one final jeep ride around the property on that last day—the last day I would ever see Jack Bate, as it turned out. I had spent the better part of the morning thanking him, but before stepping into my car, I extended my hand for one final "thank you." To my surprise he clasped my hand tightly and then laid his other hand on top of mine. His voice was gentle.

"I've been thinking about your book," he said. "The more I think of it, the more I think you must be done with it."

He let go of my hand.

"You understand?" he asked as I climbed into the car.

I nodded.

"There are plenty of other things to write. You can always go back to it. But for now be done with it. Let it die away."

I nodded again, and he turned and began to walk the cobbled path back to the house, the cat running in front of him. He didn't turn around as I pulled out of the driveway, but threw his right hand straight up above his head in a final backward wave.

*Nominated by The Georgia Review*

# THE FEEDER

## by ELLEN BRYANT VOIGT

from BLACKBIRD

*For Michael Collier*

1.

Bright blossom on the shrub's green lapel—
within hours after we hang the feeder
beside the wild viburnum, a goldfinch lights there.

And then, next day, a rose-breasted grosbeak
posing for us, making us proud as though
we'd painted ourselves, on the puffed white chest,
its bloody bib: our first failing.
                             Our second:
disappointment with the chickadees—
common and local—despite the sleek black cap,
clean white cheeks, acrobatic body.

But weren't the early gifts a promise?
We've hung fat meat from a nearby branch, wanting
*large, crested, rare, rapturous,*
redbird fixed on the bush like a ripe fruit.

2.

Whenever the grosbeak comes, he comes
with his harem, lumps plain as sparrows,

and doesn't merely eat but preens,
never to be mistaken for some other.

The goldfinch "likes to travel in flocks"—
several indelible males, jostling,

careening up to the feeder, then away,
each a child on a stick, galloping;

and females, less spectacular,
shades of green and brown mixed into the yellow,

better to subside into the foliage.


3.

It struts on the grass, like a crow but smaller,
or, the grackle, whose green head shines,
or starling, aiming its golden eye,

or Red-Winged with its gaudy flags,
but this bird, this bird crosses the grass
white stripe tucked, the orange locked up.

*Blackbird, blackbird, fly away.*
*Take sorrow with you when you go.*
*Raven, starling, grackle, crow.*

Tricolored Blackbird, my favorite, my signature:
nobody knows for sure what it is
till it flies away.

4.

O poor little bird, little dull peewee
with your condescending name—

is it enough merely to sing
with such a transparent song?


5.

Some: thistle; some: sunflower, cracked, already shelled.
But it's grease that wooed these out of the woods,
a pair, Hairy not Downy, we know this
from their size and not their call.

Why are they squeaking? Bigger
than the rest, not bullied by jays, seizing the stash,
swinging on it, drilling into it, one at a time
as the other clings to the trunk of the nearest pine
and waits its turn,
                              even the one with the red
slash on his head.


6.

Today: one wild turkey, more a meal than a bird,

refusing to stay with the others out in the field
bobbing for apples—
                              bobbing *up*, from a crouch
on the crusted snowpack, olympic leaps.
They also fly,
improbable and brutally efficient, low to the ground;

and the tree they roost in
trembles.

7.

Late March: glazed over, here,
don't go near Virginia—

that stab of forsythia, cherry weeping,
redbud smeared on the hill,

and perched in my sister's dogwood,
seven elegant cardinals, each

wearing a crown like something
it had earned, and trumpeting.


8.

Suddenly there suddenly gone.
                              Do they count
if they come not to the back yard but the front,
not to the feeder but the crabapple tree,
its ornaments dulled
by winter?
              Multiple, tufted,
pulled forward by the blunt beak
like dancers propelled by the head:
                              Cedar Waxwings:
I almost missed them, looking the other way.


9.

Nothing at the feeder. Nothing at the bush.
It takes awhile before I see the shadow.


10.

So: she's found me here:
chief bird of my childhood,

gray, pillow-breasted,
only needed asking—
no, only the crumbs
of other's invitations.
She waddles beneath the feeder,
retrieving what she can
from the hulls, the debris dropped
to the grass by the glamorous birds,
thrusting her undersized head
forward and back, forward
and back again. And her call,
*alto, cello, tremolo,*
makes the life I've made
melt away.

*Nominated by C. E. Poverman, Marianne Boruch, Debra Spark, Rachel Hadas, Blackbird*

# ELEVENS

## by STANLEY PLUMLY

from THE KENYON REVIEW

1.

The sun flatlining the horizon, the wind
off the Atlantic hard enough to swallow—
arctic, manic and first thing—
the morning beach walk north lasting less
than half an hour, while you've stood
in the middle of the room that long
trying to get your breath back to normal.
It seems to take all the time there is,
as if a flake of ash burning off the sun
had entered at the mouth, turned ice,
and had, in slow-borne seconds, grown

2.

glacial, granite, dark. The summer
in the mountains there was snow, new snow,
you could walk in fifteen minutes down
the narrow gravel road and there'd be
ghostweed, spiraea, and stunted laurel trees
blossoming their own snow-on-the-mountain.
Ten, eleven thousand feet, and the water,
with a spirit of its own, moving over rock

without once touching, flying toward the world.
The thin fresh air too spiritual as well.
Down below, with lights, Durango, Colorado.


3.


City snow, especially, transforms backwards—
antique, baroque, medieval, hand-to-mouth.
Karel Čapek, in a book called *Intimate
Things*, says Prague can go back one, two
hundred years just overnight in a three-
or four-inch snowfall, as in the stillness
of a postcard of the Charles, looking from
the square in Mala Strana toward the sad-faced
saints along the high sides of the bridge,
snow-capped, blessed and even fouled with
the Old World and other-worldly, since Prague


4.


is a winter city, night city, streetlights
blurred in mist, the centuries-looming
buildings basic gothic under the glow.
Čapek adds "that you are startled at the
darkness deep within you" standing in
the history and cold beauty of the place.
Kundera, too, clarifies the quality of light,
as if among the weight of intimate things
you were lifted, and the face in the water
looking up from the river were not yours,
and those weren't your footprints in the snow.


5.


Water filling a void created by a glacier—
hundreds of these lakes healing over wounds.
And when you choose you must be silent.

So we'd row out slowly, barely lifting up
our oars, in order to fool the fish, who'd
rise to see what foolish fish we were, then
go back down. Fresh water, black water deep.
You had the sense, at dusk, of dreaming,
of floating in a light now almost gone—
the anchor tied to a ladder, oars like wings,
but nowhere to go but drifting until morning.


6.


At a height above Punto Spartivento,
the point at which the northern wind divides,
Como and Lecco assume their separate waters,
deep enough they've drained the deepest sky.
The lift from the lakes' sun surfaces is
swallows, terns, and Mediterranean gulls,
green hills and granite mountains, white
tourist boats and seaplanes circling in, then
steps beyond the timed arrivals and departures,
terraces and gardens of terra cotta towns
that look like, from here, no one lives there.


7.


Eliot says that home is where you start from,
memory and body so confused they are the same.
In London, in Holland Park, in late October
on a Sunday, in an after-rain late afternoon,
I stood under the great horse chestnut
I'd stood under in the spring when it lit
its candelabra into flame. The chestnuts,
like the eyes of deer, were gone—buckeyes
if you'd grown up in Ohio, conkers if you
played them or fed them to the horses.
And half the leaves were gone. Yet through

8.

the intricate yellow lattice of what was left
the changing sky took on a shape less random.
Eliot, in "East Coker," also says that as we
grow older the world becomes stranger, the sky,
the painter's sky, transformative as earth—
Constable's wool-gathering, towering clouds,
Turner's visceral, annihilating sunsets.
I went to this tree every season for a year.
In winter it was purity, in summer full green
fire. The sky's huge island canopy felt focused
through its branching, the ground more certain.


9.

The way a child might hide. I remember walking
into the sharp high grass of a hayfield, lying
down, closing my eyes. If you were patient
with the insects and the papercuts of blades
you could, after awhile, hear the Moloch
under the earth, and in your mind, if you tried,
ascend into the afterlife of air hovering
just above you. It had to be that falling
time of day the sun is level with the dead last
word. Levitation was the first word you thought
of down on a knee in the hospital, kissed . . .


10.

When I saw my heart lit up on the screen,
the arteries, veins and ventricles
all functioning, pictured, as if removed,
in picture-space, I knew that this is
what is meant by distance, the way, flying
once at forty thousand feet, the needle nose
of the needle flashing in the sun, traveling
alone, and nothing but clarity under us,

I felt like a visitor inside my own body.
I could see myself invisible on the ground
following the threadbare vapor trail. We

11.

claim the body as a temple or cathedral,
meaning the house in which I am that I am,
breath and bone, water, mortar, earth.
Brunelleschi, bricking up the eggshell
of his dome, understood the soul must live
in space constructed out of nature.
He could see within his double-vaulted,
self-supporting ceiling a sky "higher
than the sky itself." When I was there,
in the Duomo, looking up, the terror of
a bird took all the heart out of the air.

*Nominated by William Olsen, Michael Collier, Arthur Smith*

# SAMANTHA

fiction by ROBERT BOYERS

from ONTARIO REVIEW

SHE WAS ANGRY. No one had told her to be, not in so many words, but she felt the rush of indignation, heard her voice tremble when she told the man to keep his explanations to himself. She had asked him a simple question, made a simple request, and he had refused her. That is all she needed to know and all she wanted to hear from him. His song and dance about inadequate staff and poor equipment, his complaints about having to put up with endless hassles—none of this seemed to her to have anything to do with her. She had asked him—a flunkey in the college's audiovisual department—to arrange for her a private screening of Hitchcock's *Shadow of a Doubt*, a film she was supposed to have seen with her class on Monday night, when she was just too tired to go out.

Now the charmless little man had turned her down, said it was impossible, and she was required to listen to him justify himself to her. He had stringy, probably unwashed red hair and an ugly little pointed beard. He wore, beneath a v-neck sweater, a button-down white shirt and an impeccably knotted silk necktie which she thought pretentious and ridiculous. He called her "Miss" and she thought the best thing she could do for him was to tell him to keep his reasons to himself. But she let him go on and finally said only that she didn't like the tone of his voice and did he know that he was rude? For a moment she liked the nervous shifting of his beady eyes after that, the way he sort of retreated, asked her to let him apologize for his rudeness—though he had not intended to be rude—but then almost at once she felt again the surge of raw anger and asked him to write

393

for her his name and his extension number. Nor did she explain to him why she needed his name, or agree to let him apologize. When she grabbed the ragged scrap of paper from his twitchy hands she told him only that he should be more careful, jack, and that he'd be hearing from her. He didn't seem happy.

She had been feeling angry all week. Her roommate Sulema had told her she had a scowl on her face, and once or twice in class the other day she had heard herself raise her voice when she disagreed with something her history teacher had said. But the encounter with the guy at audiovisual had left her feeling even more agitated than usual. She walked out of the building and moved quickly across the green, failing to acknowledge the wave of a suite mate, not quite knowing what she was going to do. Someone has got to talk to that boy, she repeated to herself as she entered the college center and went down the stairs to the office of minority affairs. The walls in the corridor were as always plastered with notices announcing multicultural dinners, dances and discussions. Grievance meetings were scheduled on Wednesday at 7. A specialist in English as a second language would be on campus every Monday. A fund-raiser for a new multicultural resource center was planned for late November.

She hated all this multicultural bullshit. They were building their own little world, she thought, and she was supposed to be grateful. More than once in the past she had wanted to tear down every one of these notices, to sit in one of the uncomfortable plastic chairs at the far end of the corridor and look at the expressions on the faces of the brothers and sisters when they arrived for work in the morning and saw the clean white walls, stripped of all that irrelevance. You'd have to be more than a little brain-washed, she thought, to buy into this stuff, into this pathetic little world with its Afro-American pride and its Latino heritage and its Asian-American feel-good fantasies. She had come down here not, she assured herself, because she had anything but contempt for all of this, but because she had a simple question to ask. If a sister could give her an answer, she'd just say thank you very much and depart. She wouldn't need to do more than that.

The sister at the desk, in fact, offered her a cup of coffee and insisted that Samantha sit down, though she said she was in kind of a hurry. She was in no mood to trade niceties with this flunkey, and she bristled when the sister noted that she'd never seen her "down here" before. And just why would she be expected to put in an appearance down here? she asked. Was this a requirement? Did every other black girl come in for a "periodic" chat? She had thought that might be the case, and that was why she'd stayed away for the two years she'd been at the school. Did the sister understand that? Whatever the problems students had, it was not a good thing for every black girl to take her ass on down to the same place to be handed the same kind of social worker jive. None of that, no way, not at the Concord Academy—you know it?—where she'd spent four years of high school without once being forced into some poor little black girl office. She had thought, having stayed away from this basement office for two whole years, and handled her own problems in her own way, that she might just come down to ask a simple question. But now she was sorry she had bothered, and she would bring her question to someone else, who didn't expect her to come in, and who wouldn't get all moist and excited about adding another name to their inventory of needy cases. Know what I mean? This ain't no affirmative action baby you got here.

The woman watched her with what looked like amazement. She was a big woman, with fleshy forearms and a wide nose. She leaned forward and gripped the ends of her desk with thick, angry hands. Samantha could see that she had hit a nerve, and for a moment she thought the woman might just ask her to get the hell out. But of course, Samantha thought, these sisters never got that excited. She knew their kind. They were into control, soothing and control. Samantha was not surprised when the woman asked her to just state the problem, then, and to spare her all the anger. She did have a problem, didn't she, or did she just come down to insult a sister? Samantha repeated that she should never have come, but took a chair and said, quietly, that a guy in audiovisual had been rude to her. Did he call her a name? the sister asked. No, he didn't call her a damn name. Did he make some reference to her race? No, of course he didn't. The sucker didn't have the balls to say anything like that straight out. And was there something in his tone she could identify? It was there, Samantha assured her, but she didn't think she could identify it, not exactly. And did she, perhaps, not speak first to the man with a certain obvious hostility of her own?

Samantha didn't like this question, and asked the sister what she meant. But the sister just stared silently at her for several seconds and then said she didn't think Samantha had much of a story. She asked for the name of the man in AV, wrote it down and reported that no one had ever complained to her about him before. Did

Samantha want to file a formal complaint and have the man brought in? Or did she want to tell her more about it? Samantha said she'd think about it and let the sister know. Would a week be alright? The sister nodded. And would the sister drop the FM radio voice and stop treating the student sisters like helpless children? "You get the fuck out of here" was all Samantha heard before the woman heaved her large body out of the ample desk chair and left Samantha sitting by herself in the office.

Samantha heard the woman slam the door to the adjacent room and looked up at the poster-size photograph of Nelson Mandela garbed in a colorful dashiki. As she rose to leave she caught a glimpse of her own twisted scowl and neatly ironed white button-down shirt in the fake eight-by-ten Victorian mirror propped on the sister's desk. She turned the glass face down and scrawled on the sister's appointment calendar "Samantha Bailey, extension 2465."

A few minutes later she left the campus and crossed the wide thoroughfare towards the familiar shop fronts. She headed for the Barnes and Noble superstore, a pained, weary expression on her face as she elbowed past the browsers massed at the remainder tables in the entranceway. Inside, she paused and put on a look of ferocious incredulity as she studied the titles arrayed on the wide shelves below the information counter. Stray fragments caught her eye, assailed her. They Can Kill You . . . How to Survive the Loss of Love . . . Race Matters . . . Cruel and Unusual . . . Good Boys . . . To the Friend Who Did Not Save . . . Again and again she looked over the "Staff Selections" titles. It seemed to her pathetic that anyone would take seriously these selections. Did anyone actually care what some bookstore flunkey recommended?

She looked around and saw a couple sit down heavily on the carpeted floor a few feet away and spread out in front of them what looked like a computer printout. The guy adjusted the glasses on the bridge of his nose while the girlfriend ran a finger down the long sheet. She wanted to ask them if they'd considered what the other customers were supposed to do with them blocking up the aisle. Was she supposed to fly over them? Or did the cozy pair think that no one would possibly be interested in the biographies shelved just past them, in a place no one could reach now that two fools were blocking the way? She didn't ask, of course. The two little darlings wouldn't know what hit them if she so much as breathed in their direction.

396

Probably they'd smile nervously at her and quickly gather up their stupid mess. Then she'd want to hit them.

Not ten minutes later she stood in line at the counter waiting to buy a book of interviews with film directors. Her teacher had read excerpts from the book in class, and she found herself talking about the directors and their films more than anything else these days. Sulema couldn't understand what spoke to her so powerfully in those films, with their subtitles and their depressing melancholy. What was worse, far worse, Sulema complained, all but two of the directors they studied in their film class were white and male. At the register a clerk asked her if she had read the book of interviews with Scorsese, and Samantha asked him, "You ever read *The Magic Lantern?*" She didn't like the way the sissy-ass boy looked at her, but when she took her change she couldn't help telling him they should do a better job with the film books. For a big store they let their stock run down too damn fast. The boy muttered something about telling a manager, and she was out the door before he could say anything stupid.

She had moved up the sidewalk only eight or ten steps when she found herself face to face with slick Professor Rothstein. He smiled at her and held out his hand. This boy had all the moves. He asked her if she had found what she was looking for, and she said "apparently" as she held up the Barnes and Noble bag and waved it at him. Was she in a hurry? he wanted to know, and within a few seconds she had agreed to go back with him into the little café at the front end of the bookstore.

She looked around quickly to be sure no one she knew was watching. Inside they stood briefly together until they spotted an open table and moved to occupy the chairs. He bought her a cappuccino and a slice of zucchini bread and sat grinning across from her at the bright red table. She thanked him for the "treat" and stared at the long silver hair in his fine moustache. He wore his standard herringbone tweed jacket over a plaid flannel shirt open at the collar. He seemed comfortable, she noted, not overfriendly but wanting to connect. She had no idea what he thought he was doing, taking a student to a café, but she wasn't shy, and she just had to find out what this boy had on his mind. He was old enough to be her father, and in class often mentioned his wife and his daughter. Once he even said he'd seen the Bergman films when they first opened in New York twenty, thirty years earlier. With his shoulder-length hair and unruly beard he didn't much look like somebody's idea of a father, but he was more than starting to go gray, and his eyes seemed to her older than the rest of him. She noticed that he didn't in the least seem nervous with her, that he invited small talk, and that he drank his own cappuccino with undisguised pleasure. She was only momentarily surprised when he asked her "by the way" what he'd been meaning to ask her, whether she went to "a special place" to have her hair done "like that." It occurred to her that this might have been offensive, and that she might have ended their little chat before it even got started, but she told him calmly that she liked doing her dreadlocks for herself, and that it had taken her a long time to learn how to do them right. He said he could only faintly imagine how hard it was, and how much trouble it had to be to undo it all and give it a good wash. Was that part hardest of all? he asked.

"You're asking," she said, "do I wash my hair and undo all my hard work?"

"I mean," he said, betraying no sign of discomfort, "that people tell me you can't just routinely wash your hair if you want your hair like that."

"What kind of people tell you?" she demanded.

"I don't know," he replied. "More than one person."

"You talk a lot about girls with dreadlocks?" she asked.

"Not a lot," he said. "But it does seem to come up."

"They excite you?" she asked. "Maybe the fact you figure they're kind of dirty, unwashed and all, maybe that gives you a kind of thrill or something."

"I'm not talking about thrills," he said. "I think I'm able to like something without becoming excited, not that way. There is something to be said for disinterested liking."

"More or less disinterested," she corrected him. "We're not sitting together here in a café talking about the hair on the head of a Roman princess in some wall painting. We're talking about the hair on the head of an actual black girl in your own class."

"You have me there," he said, smoothing his beard. "Fair enough. Not altogether disinterested. But almost."

They went back and forth this way for almost a half hour, the professor only a bit more cautious, Samantha clearly delighted with her ability to tease him. "Seriously now," she said to him at one point, "how many times you talk about my locks?"

"If you want to know," he said, "I've mentioned them more than once to my daughter, Jennie, who's twelve. She thinks that's the way to do her own hair, which is kind of unruly, like a bird's nest that's seen a lot of action."

"You tell your daughter my name? You tell her I have a gold tooth in my mouth, up near the front?"

"I believe I've stuck to the dreadlocks."

"That's better," she said, "safer. Best not even to think about the tooth. Am I right?"

Here he looked briefly reluctant, stretched his legs out, moving slightly away from the table, from her, and she figured she'd hit a nerve, or something, threw him off, who could tell. And this boy thought he knew everything, thought there was nothing could surprise him, or not really.

But then he said, "Actually I have thought about the tooth. More than your hair, I mean. It's so, you know, surprising, in you. When you open your mouth and those tremendously sophisticated sentences roll out I find myself just staring at the tooth, not so you'd notice, but I do stare, so that it puzzles me afterwards. I mean, it doesn't exactly fit with the button-down white shirts and the, you know, expensive-looking shoes."

"Didn't figure I'd bring up the tooth, did you?" she asked.

"I wouldn't have wanted you to," he said. "Too hard a subject for either of us."

"Not hard for me," she said, "and so not really hard for you. Not if you're brave and all."

"I'm not brave actually," he said, "but now that you've opened it up, I can't very well run away, can I? And so I'll ask you right out, what the hell is going on with that tooth of yours?"

"You don't like it," she said. "I can hear it in your voice. It makes you a little sick just to think of it, doesn't it?"

"I never said I hated it," the professor replied. "On the contrary. It just seems to me so strange for a girl like you. I mean, I would have thought the family that sent you to, you know, Concord Academy and such places, and then to a place like this, that the family would just have said no, that tooth is out of the question."

"Well they did try to talk me out of it," Samantha said. "But I was defiant, and I'm nobody's sweetheart when I decide to say no, no way I'm gonna give something up."

"And so," he interrupted, "you insisted on the thing mainly because you knew it would drive your parents nuts."

399

"Not so," she said, smiling brightly and wagging her finger at him. "In a way my parents were, you know, negligible in the decision I made. It was freshman year, two years ago, and I had a tooth pulled. Painful, but simple. And then I thought, why not a gold tooth? I saw them on some kids in my neighborhood, and I thought, that's weird. Now, when I imagined a gold tooth shining there in my own mouth, it came to me: nobody, but nobody's gonna know what to do with that, and so why not? Didn't take me more than five minutes to decide. You know what I'm talking about? It's something, you know, unassimilable, and don't you like that word? Unassimilable? Nobody's gonna be able to do a thing with a tooth like that, except like it, or hate it. You can't use it, can't explain it. You can take it or leave it, but you can't give any reason for it. It's a thing, you know, beyond reason, if you know what I mean. You can't look at it and say, why that girl, she's got a nigger tooth in her head, 'cause you don't see a lot of black girls walking around with a tooth like that, not right up front. And if you're a black brother, you know, the kind who's not gonna sit here with you sipping a nice hot cup of cappuccino, you sure won't say, that Samantha, she studies hard and does what she's supposed to, and all because she wants to be white. You take one look at that tooth and you're sure this is one girl who sure doesn't wish she was white. No way. And that suits me, 'cause I sure don't want to be an ordinary defensive black girl, and I sure don't want to be white, 'cause there's no way I can pass, and there's no way I'm gonna look up to most of the white people I meet. Present company excluded, if you know what I mean. And you can stop looking so amazed, with your mouth open just enough to show me there's no gold tooth out there in the middle of your pretty white mouth."

They had by then been at it for more than an hour, the professor obviously content to bring her out, Samantha not in the least reluctant to take the lead and to stun him wherever possible, now a little flirtatious, now merely teasing. I got this boy right where I want him, she thought to herself now and again, not knowing really what she wanted or whether there was some further prospect in this exchange she would soon discern. But she felt an acute sense of disappointment when at last he looked at his watch and said it was getting very late. She had an impulse then to reach out and cover his wrist with her hand, and she was—she hoped not visibly—relieved when he asked if they shouldn't order "just one more drink." But then something, she didn't know what, came over her, and she said, simply, "no more drinks" and "I think we've had enough for now, don't you?" and "don't want to make too much of a good thing, now do we?" And with that, he said, "you're right," and "thank you, Samantha," and they got up together to go out.

Through the large windows she could see that darkness had fallen, and she noted that several students stood browsing nearby among the foreign newspapers and quarterly magazines. She no longer cared, quite the contrary, that they might be noticed leaving together, but she was mildly irritated by one student who kept looking her over and maybe even straining to catch what she and Rothstein were saying to one another. Samantha wouldn't give her the satisfaction of lowering her voice, no way, and she saw that Rothstein took no notice of anyone else as he helped her on with her jacket. She liked the half smile she caught on his face, thought he licked his lips when he felt her arm slide into the jacket sleeve.

On the sidewalk outside he reached forward to shake her hand, but she laughed, a short, abrupt, nervous laugh, and held onto his fingers much longer than was usual, held onto them and said, finally, "Now that's not so bad, is it?" And then she released him, and brazenly blew him a kiss as he backed away and turned to retrieve his car.

When she played it back to herself that night, over and over again, she thought: not wise, not prudent at all, but she couldn't decide whether the words applied to Rothstein or to herself. Was there, she wondered, some drama of sexual subjugation unfolding in there, Rothstein somehow pretending to be cool and, like he said, dispassionate, or disinterested, but in fact communicating all the while his desire and counting on her to pick up the cues? Was the whole thing a seduction, Samantha herself the improbably manipulable object, swollen with pride at her own command of the situation but deceived, oh yes deceived, by the man who never doubted, not once, that he had her where he wanted her? It wasn't easy to sort this out, she thought, not with all those weird convolutions, those thickets of improbability. She had been, no doubt about it, caught up in something there, all afternoon removed from her usual sense of self, not bitter at all, not sniffing around to spy the moves she thought she'd learned to spot from a mile away. But this boy, he had the moves, had them down so well even she couldn't make them out, not till they had worked their way with her, as she now felt, reduced her to a kind of confusion she didn't at all recognize or like. She liked the man, of course, and that was a big part of the problem. She liked the way he listened to her and said she was sophisticated and all, the way not a lot of others would dare say to her face. And for that matter, who else ever would tell he couldn't stop thinking about her tooth? Who else? Though just that was a sort of sign, wasn't it, that he wanted to tell her something more, you know, dangerous, without having to put it out there in so many words?

And yet she had very abruptly put an end to their flirtatious afternoon, as if she had not at all enjoyed what was happening and wanted just to get the hell out of there. Was she, suddenly, afraid that he might go on to say something really imprudent, something she would have to count as offensive? Was she trying, without quite knowing it, to prevent him from spoiling the little thing they had managed between them, something small and, when you came right down to it, incorrigibly innocent? She liked that sort of expression when she read it in a book or when, unbidden, it crossed her mind, liked the knotted, tangled-up contradictoriness of the thing, its heading two or more ways at the same time. And that was what she was feeling at this strange juncture, that she had just participated in something heading off in several apparently irreconcilable directions, teasing and sort of affectionate, innocent and strangely seductive, ordinary and, in a way she didn't grasp at all, elemental.

Had she hoped, she wondered, or half hoped, that he would make some further move? When she put her hand out on the table right under his nose, stretched her arm out there so that he might almost have thought she was reaching for his hand, idly passing back and forth over the rim of the cup, did she hope or expect that he would in fact take hold of her hand? Now that would have been something, she thought. And would he have known that, had he done that simple thing, it would have seemed to her objectionable, even if she wanted him to do no less? Oh she could see herself—even with her revulsion at the thought that he was somehow taking advantage— could see herself going off somewhere with Rothstein if he invited her, said to hell with the fact that he was expected at home and simply proposed that they, you know, spend the evening somewhere together. It wasn't so ridiculous, not really, to imagine herself with this man. She could imagine worse things than letting him do her while they lay together somewhere watching a video of *Wings of Desire*. Sure she might have wanted, all the while, to haul his sweet improper ass into some hearing room to file a complaint against him for what would surely seem to anyone a grown man's abuse of his professorial authority. But that part, about hauling his ass into more trouble than that boy had ever seen, that part she didn't know about. Not really sure what she would have done. There was something she didn't like, never liked, about the coercive, inescapable indignation young women like herself had been made to hold at the ready, suspicious always of anyone, any man, who liked them, and suspicious too of themselves and of what had been done to them when they felt their throats tighten in expectation of some implacable sexual excitement. She was, she felt, excitable, sensual, but she didn't at all like to think of herself as a girl who could be seduced. Not certainly by an older man practiced in seduction. This boy Rothstein had that air about him, though he sure as hell didn't give too much of it away.

Later that night, impatient for her dorm mate Sulema to come in, and unable to read or write, she showered, but left the bathroom door open, expecting—it was stupid, sure—that he would maybe phone her. Had she left her number? Of course she hadn't. But he was a bright boy. He would know how to look up her number. And what would he say if he did call? That he had a question to ask her about *Chloe in the Afternoon*? That he was taking a shower and couldn't get her dreadlocks or her gold tooth out of his mind? That she should come right on over and have a friendly chat with his wife, or help his daughter with her hair?

By the time she emerged from the shower and stood squeezing a tiny, ugly gray pimple on her left cheek, she knew he couldn't call. Not if he wanted to. Not if he could read her mind. Especially not if he could read her mind. He wasn't careful, that was sure, but he wasn't stupid either. She'd read often enough that men as old as Rothstein became easily infatuated with younger women. Often they were—she liked this expression—sexually inebriated in the presence of girls young enough to be their daughters. They obsessed a lot. That Russian guy Nabokov knew about this better than anyone. Rothstein might be such a guy. Maybe he told himself he was interested in her mind. Maybe he liked what she had to say about the movies. But he'd noticed her hair, couldn't stop thinking about her tooth. He hadn't taken his hand away, had he, when she grazed his knuckles? She seemed to recall that there had been such a moment. And there was no stiffening or look of aversion on his face when she threw him that kiss—a daughterly kiss, maybe, but no, he could tell it was more intimate than that. It couldn't have been lost on a bright boy.

She wanted Sulema to come home. Possibly she would tell her nothing, or at least not more than a part of what had happened. But she wanted to make up her mind about a few things, and she couldn't decide how much to tell until Sulema stood there. She dried her hair and several times said into the mirror, shit, Sulema, where the fuck are you? She applied alcohol to her pimple with a cotton ball and put on a CD of *Bachillanas Brassilleras* she'd owned since that music teacher played it for the class that time in high school. The soprano voice always seemed to her unearthly and exalted. She tried to sit and listen but found herself restless and strangely exhilarated. She moved around the little apartment, from one corner to another, and only realized when she stood in front of the tall window in the kitchen that she hadn't dressed. She ran back to her room and took a plush white terry-cloth robe from the hook behind her door.

By 11.15, really angry now with Sulema for staying out so late, and with herself for giving a damn, she phoned Professor Rothstein and heard a woman pick up and ask in a faint husky voice who it was. Samantha said nothing, but breathed loudly enough to be sure the woman would know someone was there. The woman asked her husband to try, and when Samantha heard him say hello, who is it, is anybody there? she hung up and turned off the kitchen lights.

The next day, early, she noted with disgust that Sulema had stayed out all night, probably shacked up with some twenty-year-old half-wit. She dressed quickly and went out for breakfast at the dining hall on campus. For some reason she couldn't remember the name of the woman down at the minority affairs office, the phony sister of mercy who'd finally exploded at her, as she was bound to do. But that was no matter. She could easily find her way to the office and look up the name in a directory. No doubt the sister would remember the name of one Samantha Bailey. But there was every reason to doubt she'd know what to do with the information Samantha intended to set before her now. Would she conclude, pretty much the way she did the other time, that the behavior described was, you know, how that writer put it in his book, not sufficiently reprehensible? Samantha helped herself to a bowl of muesli and vanilla yoghurt and tried to picture the professionally concerned look on the face of that perfect hand-holding political correctness machine seated complacently down there surrounded by all those comforting icons of struggle. She searched her mind for the conscientious jargon words the sister would spread around to soothe her troubled spirit. Even if she could not find sufficient cause in anything Samantha told her to bring formal charges against the Professor, she would surely find ways to say the right things and to nurture at least the capacity for sustained indignation.

Samantha drank a second cup of less than acceptable coffee and was tickled by the observation that, as usual, she had the table all to herself, though any number of students known to her had passed nearby and failed to greet or join her. Out on the campus green she closed her parka tight against the wind and put out her tongue to taste a blowing snowflake or two. She walked on the covered walkway around the periphery of the green and made the circuit not once but three times. She was seized by a powerful desire to speak to Rothstein, to tell him something he would not be able to ignore. But first she would ask him what he meant to say the other day when he confided to her that he often thought of her gold tooth. Was that some sort of sign or message he intended her to pick up? She could excuse that, she would say, so long as he was in fact—how best to say this?—interested in her, not really or solely in the fact of her tooth, or the hair, or her curiously unstable classroom demeanor, but in her, her, in which case she would have no trouble at all saying that she understood and would try as hard as she could to reciprocate that interest. To tell the truth, she had once or twice acknowledged to herself that she was interested in him, and well before the time they had spent together in the café.

As she made her way slowly around the campus walkway it seemed to her that she was getting nowhere with her fantasies, getting nowhere with Rothstein. Why should such a man be drawn to a black girl like herself? What indication had he given, that she should construct such fantasies of reciprocal intensity? There was, she felt, though she was not at all sure how to put it to herself, something more than Rothstein himself at the bottom of the powerful attraction she was allowing herself to feel. It was not, she was certain, a father-thing she was feeling, a displaced affect of the kind she'd read about in a psych class. No, it was something more powerful, more openly sexual. And it had, she was sure, something also to do with the sister waiting ever so patiently, massively, down in that unspeakably virtuous basement office. To go to Rothstein, she felt, would be to do something good and necessary, whether he was glad to see her or not, afraid of her or willing to have a dangerous fire lit under him. Not to seek out Rothstein, to go instead to see the sister, would be to betray something in herself. That she knew, though there was, just as surely—she could taste it—the usually surging, corrosive indignation she knew so well and, until very recently, fully trusted. She was, it seemed, in the grip of something new, some urge to say no, no to the big sister, no to some idea of propriety and to the settled suspicion of malfeasance. This suspicion she knew to be somehow alien to her, though she had not the words to say exactly how, not alien or corrosive merely but stupid and shallow.

Was she a confused young black girl with ideas too big for her to handle? She said to herself again and again that yes, she was young and confused and in over her head. And then, having repeated this to herself, and completed a final circuit of the campus green, she went to Rothstein's office and, seeing that he wasn't expected in at all on this day, she sat in the department secretary's office and wrote him a short note. It said: "Samantha Bailey is very grateful for the interest you have shown her and patiently awaits your call (evenings, extension 2465). At your leisure, at your discretion."

She slid the note under Rothstein's office door, then, standing outside the door in the dark corridor, wrote another note, this one addressed to "Director, Office of Minority Affairs." It read: "Samantha Bailey of the Junior class wishes to inform you that she is presently involved with a white Professor, and if you don't believe that is at all appropriate, you can either kiss my perfect black ass or offer me an explanation that doesn't condescend or repeat the standard stupefying bullshit. I may be reached most evenings at extension 2465. You can leave me a message if you must, but it had better be damn good if you expect me to answer it. And no, I am definitely not yours very truly, SB."

*Nominated by Joyce Carol Oates, Ontario Review*

# THE DARKNESS TOGETHER

fiction by STEVE ALMOND

from THE SOUTHERN REVIEW

MICHAEL'S MOTHER WALKED INTO HIS ROOM and announced that she was going to supervise packing. "Let me get dressed," Michael said. He was in his underwear. "We've got plenty of time." She made little fluttering motions with her hands and backed out of the room. They were the first couple to board the train.

His mother made a great show of inspecting the compartments, which were identical. She was a creature of habit, and dealt with travel anxiety by aggrandizing the minor dividends and setbacks of the journey. She seated herself by the window and patted the place beside her. "How peaceful this is," she said. "Don't these look new? These seats?" And so on. Her nose, small like her face and dusted in foundation, kept to its schedule of wrinkling and unwrinkling.

The train filled up. "You'd think the airlines were on strike," Michael's mother said. She placed a magazine on the seat across from her and gestured for Michael to do the same. Michael watched the other passengers file past and thought that it might not be bad to have some company. A couple of teenage girls came and went, and as he often did, Michael glanced at them and quickly imagined them stripped of their baggy clothing: pale, smoothly lumped, awaiting trespass.

"But it is *hot* in here," his mother said. She pulled her sweater off and the elaborate cups and bindings of her brassiere pressed against her peach turtleneck. Though demure in public, privately Michael's mother spoke with a certain tender urgency about the state of her breasts. When he was a bit younger, she would face the mirror in her bedroom, disrobed to the waist, a glass of sherry in one hand. "They used to be so beautiful," she would announce. "And now look at them—fallen." For a brief time, Michael enjoyed a certain mysterious cachet among the older boys in his apartment complex, who dropped by after dinner and draped themselves on the couch facing her room.

"Aren't you hot, Mikey? Take that ridiculous sweater off."

"I'm fine."

"Won't Nana be pleased to see you? I try to tell her how big you've gotten, but it's no good. She'll have to see for herself." She took his shoulders, one in each hand, and squared them. "And soon you'll be off to college, won't you? Two more years. What will we do then?" Michael felt her fingers begin to massage, and he gently shrugged away from her and picked up his magazine.

"Will they bring us tea do you think, Mikey? No. What am I saying? This isn't Europe." His mother pouted over this idea for a moment then leaned back into her seat.

From time to time, a passenger would pause in front of their compartment. Michael's mother managed to marshal them along with a shrug of apology. When the train eased forward, she sighed lavishly. Down below, the brownish grime of the Maumee River steamed and distant girders knit themselves in buildings. She sat beside him, smelling faintly of talc, the purse on her lap ticking with the train's motion, the ball of her shoulder leaning against his with an unstated expectation of contact. Michael shifted and felt a damp layer of heat around his skin. His breathing seemed not quite the way it should be, too forced. He gazed at magazine rock stars and movie stars and wondered how long the trip to Gary would last.

The compartment door slid open and a chubby conductor appeared. The collar of his blue uniform pinched his neck to such a degree that his face was a rich, creamy pink. He doffed his small cap and held it before him. "Where you folks headed today?" Michael's mother presented their tickets. "Gary? Fine city. Just you and your brother, ma'am?"

Michael listened to her keening giggle. She got this way around men of an official capacity—daffy, girlish. "What a nice man." She slipped her shoes off and rested her stockinged feet on the seat across from her.

"What a fat man," Michael said.

"Don't say that now, Michael. You know very well that people store fat in their bodies at different rates. He can't help the way he looks."

"Look at his pants." A view was afforded of the conductor's backside as he attended to the riders in the next compartment.

"Maybe they gave him only that one uniform," she said. But Michael knew from her tone that she wasn't angry, or even disappointed, was instead secretly approving of his hauteur. The world was often a nasty place. A fine sense of discrimination affirmed this, and it was nice to have someone with whom to share a quiet intolerance or two.

Only a few passengers boarded in Angola and the teenage girls departed, giggling as they rushed past. "We'll get to spend some time, won't we? Not like at home." Michael's mother rested her head on his shoulder. "I don't know what you do with the hours. When shall we eat, Michael? Let's eat now. I *am* hungry. Will you get the pastries?" He stood and turned to grab the paper bag in the rack above her. As he rose onto his tippy toes, she set her hands on his hips to steady him. There was about the action a practiced intimacy. "Look how much you've grown," she said.

But then the train lurched and Michael stumbled against her and she let out a happy shriek and as all this happened—Michael drawing his knee into and away from his mother's soft belly, she clinging to his belt loops, laughing, her forehead brushing his thigh—a third figure slipped into the compartment.

"Don't let me interrupt," he said.

Michael felt a thrilling, complicated dread and jerked the bag free and twirled away from his mother. He wondered how long the stranger had been in the dark corridor, and whether he'd been watching. "Excuse me." Michael made a gesture, hoping to slide past him, back into his seat.

But the man was busy fumbling with one of several zippers on his jacket and his eyes were fixed on Michael's mother. He had a large head of red hair and gave off a strong scent of cigarettes and sweated-over cologne. Moving with a deliberation that suggested slow-wittedness, he seated himself across from Michael's mother.

She made quite a show of the pastries, jabbering on about the bakery and its blind proprietor, but did not acknowledge the man across from her, though their knees were an inch apart. "Have a bear claw, Michael," she said. "This man, Gitlitz, told me they were the specialty. What a sweet little fellow. He had a special cane. With a hook for opening the ovens. Isn't that clever?" For a time, the only sounds were the rustle of waxed paper and moist chewing. "They are good, aren't they?" Michael's mother reached out with a moistened finger and dabbed a flake of pastry from the fine hairs of his moustache and brought this to her own mouth.

As if in response to this action, which Michael found humiliating, the stranger placed a hand on her knee. "Please allow me to say hello. My name is Chaleaux. William Chaleaux. I hope you'll feel comfortable calling me Billy."

"Hello," Michael's mother said. She glanced at his hand.

"Where are you folks headed to this evening?"

She said nothing, her face reddening, and shifted her knee away.

"Gary," Michael said.

The man sat back and nodded and drew a pack of cigarettes from one of his pockets. He looked disarmingly content, swaggering in stillness. His coat was thin vinyl disguised as leather—that's what all the zippers were about—and his pants were of a style that had passed out of fashion a few years ago, absurdly baggy but drawn at the waist and decorated with signs intended to radiate the dull glow of neon, each reading MIAMI BEACH . . . NEVER GETS DARK.

Michael had never been to Miami Beach, but knew his mother and father had met there on some long-ago vacation. He could re-member his father saying, "How 'bout you give me the Miami Beach treatment tonight, Marj," or words to that effect, and his mother laughing in the way she did when embarrassed, little tiffs of air, and shoving him away.

The stranger lit up. Owing to the light, or perhaps the vigorous way in which he inhaled, the smoke swirled with a milky thickness.

Michael's mother coughed.

"Not much of a city, Gary. You all have family there?"

His mother coughed again.

"Oh, I get you," the stranger said. "Smoke's bothering you. Smoke gets in your eyes, right? You know Sinatra? All right, I'll take it out-side." He turned to Michael. "Save my place, would you kid?"

His mother batted the air with her arms. "What a repulsive man."

"You want to move?"

"Of all the compartments on this train. Repulsive."

Billy Chaleaux *was* repulsive. His cheeks were tracked with scars, and the heavy folds over his eyes made him look sleepy, primitive.

410

Sharp gray teeth showed between his lips. He looked untended to, beyond tending. "We can move," Michael said, knowing they would not.

"I'll bet he doesn't even have a ticket." His mother began stuffing papery remains into the pastry box.

The stranger slid open the door. "We were talking about your family," he said, seating himself. "Can't imagine why you'd want to go to Gary otherwise, with all the niggers they got there. They don't know how to handle them in the Midwest."

Michael's mother said, "That is in no way appropriate—"

"Oh sure. I know, I know." The stranger made his eyes round with remorse. "It's terrible to speak like that, to have those thoughts about another human being. You're right. But the truth is I was the victim of a crime and it's made me bitter, I suppose. Where are you from, folks? Akron? Toledo? Toledo it is. Well, what about that downtown you got there? Full of them. The Adam and Eve, you know that place? Sure you do. Your son's probably seen it a thousand times, all them drunken jigs hanging around outside like the sidewalk was built to hold them up."

Michael wondered if the stranger had ever been inside the Adam and Eve, a place he pictured as full of red light and beery mist and shiny black tits. His mother turned to him and said, "Shall we do a crossword?"

"I got you," the stranger said. "No offense intended. Not to a nice-looking woman like yourself. Nor to your son. Fine-looking boy. He got your lovely green eyes. Off to see family, I'm guessing. Grandma, is that it? A real family tableau." He traced the air with his index fingers, framing them, and flashed his little gray dagger of a smile.

Though he said nothing for some time, the stranger looked at Michael's mother intently. While this caused her a great and obvious discomfort—she angled herself away and began jabbering about the lakes of the Upper Peninsula—Michael pondered what he might be seeing: an attractive woman in her midthirties, hair bound into a bun, conservatively dressed, but not so conservatively as to lose the contours of her figure. She looked like a naughty librarian of the sort encountered in pornography, a woman of compressed desires. The stranger's inspection seemed to bear this out, linked them somehow. Michael felt his perspective tested, pulled out toward the brotherhood of men, then drawn back to his mother: delicate, broken-hinged, now hidden behind a magazine.

411

"Thing about Gary, ma'am, is that it's a dry county. You can't buy the hard stuff there. Not that you'd have an immediate interest in such things. But with any family gathering, I've found, it's never a bad idea to have the option. You've got to head down to St. John or Crown Point. Did you know that Capone once had his world headquarters right there on Jersey Street? Over a Chinese laundry. Used to have guys rubbed out by drowning them in washers. Clean-corpsing, they called it. Then he headed down to Miami, of course."

"Where is that crossword book?" Michael's mother rose from her seat and began rummaging in the shopping bag overhead. Billy Chaleaux surveyed the length of her inseam and whistled softly and raised his eyebrows at Michael.

She turned and glowered at him and stammered, "I don't know who exactly you think you are, sir—"

"I'm William Chaleaux," he said. "I wish you'd call me Billy. Now please don't get angry. Please. There's no need for that. You can't really blame me, can you? To admire a woman of your beauty, you can't blame a man for that. Your son knows. See, he forgives me. He's a lucky kid. Lucky. You must do some sort of exercise to keep in the shape you do. No question about it. Not that you'd look any worse with a little more, not at all. But you must do something. Do you run? Or those aerobics classes?"

"She swims," Michael said quietly.

His mother fixed him with a murderous look.

"Swimming. Even better. Exercises the heart and the muscles. Lengthens the muscles. None of that shaking up the internal organs."

She took a deep breath. "We'd like to enjoy our ride in peace, Mr. Chaleaux. I hope you can understand that."

"OK, ma'am. I get you. Sure. Trains are peaceful. They move us like when we were inside our mamas, that same motion, what you want to call amniotic motion. Lots of folks feel that way. They get on a train and they like to enjoy some peace and quiet." His tone was patient but oddly displaced, as if he were reciting a script. "But you know, for me, it's just the opposite. I get kind of jumpy. Perhaps this is on account of my own upbringing and the way my mother moved us around all the time. You can never be sure, can you?"

Michael's mother offered a wan smile. "I'm glad you understand."

"I'll maybe just toodle off and get myself something in the dining car. Either of you folks want anything? My treat."

412

Michael had given plenty of thought to the dining car on previous trips. His mother, however, insisted the food was overpriced. He imagined sandwiches, steaming slices of pie, hearty stew. "Thank you, no," his mother said, tucking a loose strand of hair behind her ear.

"All right, then. Your son doesn't look so pleased about that. But you're the boss on these things, aren't you?"

Michael's mother waited for the door to slide shut. "Why do you speak to a man like that, Michael? Just to provoke me?"

"It slipped out. Look, I asked if you wanted to move. We can just move."

"Don't be silly."

"You could speak to the conductor."

"And say what?"

"You know, whatever. That there's some creep who's bothering you. Find that fat guy. He seemed to like you."

A familiar and flattering bloom rose on her cheeks. "Where do you get such ideas? OK, I'm going to the little girl's room. I'll check. Honestly, Michael." She returned with a fresh coat of lipstick, her bun reknotted.

They were past Sturgis and headed into Elkhart when Billy Chaleaux returned. He moved loosely, his great head bobbing, his zippers tinkling. The seat across from Michael's mother was layered with magazines. These he stacked neatly and removed to the seat beside Michael. He then withdrew a brown bag from his coat and set it down atop the magazines. "Picked up a slice of apple pie for the kid, if he's so inclined. It's a bit gluey. But tasty. Good crust."

"Thank you," Michael's mother said. "That was kind."

"Sure. No problem. I didn't want you to suppose that I wasn't thinking about you. I sure was. A nice mother and son like yourselves, a good-looking pair. But it is hot in here, isn't it?" Billy Chaleaux shucked his coat and sat in the place he had made for himself. He wore a combed cotton T-shirt—what the kids at Michael's school called a "wifebeater"—and his freckled biceps bunched when he curled his arms. He had the look of a boxer gone slightly slack. On one forearm was a monstrous tattoo. Michael stared at this straggled design, bluish, nearly purple, and Billy Chaleaux held it out for him to inspect. What on first glance appeared an octopus was in fact a woman whose eight arms held a man in a distorted posture of sexual congress. His mouth was a tiny circle and his hair flowed in all directions, as if he were being electrocuted. The legend beneath read

Love Me Eight Times in crude blue letters. "Can't tell you where I got that," Billy Chaleaux whispered. "But it's a place your mother might know."

She looked at him sharply, her lips tensed.

He held up his huge palms and grinned sheepishly. "I just mean that it was a place over in Toledo. I forget the name. Down by the river, behind the Sheraton. All the sailors used to hang out down there. Now don't get yourself in a tizzy. It's just a figure of speech. I only mean it's a place for adults, for the things adults do." He picked up a magazine from the seat and began thumbing through it. "Would you get a load of all this," he said and whistled again. "What sort of youth culture magazine is this? I don't remember there being all this kind of skin in *Rolling Stone*." Chaleaux held up a picture of a thick-lipped young woman in a bra and panties. "Is this how girls at your school dress? Lord help us."

Michael's mother cleared her throat. "I really would appreciate it if you held your opinions to yourself." She turned her head and settled into a feigned sleep against the window.

"Sure," Billy Chaleaux whispered. "I got you." He flicked at the picture with bony, yellowish fingers. "You suppose they're real, kid?"

Michael shrugged.

"You ever seen a fake pair? I'll bet you have. Nice-looking kid like you. More and more girls get that operation, don't they? With this new stuff, the saline. It's become like a regular part of the growing up process."

Michael's mother opened her eyes and looked at Billy Chaleaux. "I'm not sure what point you're trying to make, but my son and I didn't ask for you to join us or to make those kinds of statements."

"What kind of statements?" Billy Chaleaux touched his chest. He was back to the script. "Your son and I are talking a bit, that's all. These are things that have to do with being a guy. Guy things."

"I don't hear him talking. You're the only one talking."

"Well now, I can't argue with that, mom. All right. Now don't get angry at Billy Chaleaux. I mean no exact harm here. Maybe I had one or two beers there on the dining car, just to loosen up. I've been under a lot of pressure lately. That's not your fault, but just the same." He bowed his head and his eyes disappeared behind the prominent lids. "I hope you won't take offense."

Outside, the tire plants of Niles pumped black smoke against the low skyline.

414

"It was nice of you to get that pie," Michael's mother said, as a kind of compromise. "That was kind."

"It's important to be kind, I think," Billy Chaleaux said. "I like to take care of the people I'm fond of. That's the truth. A man who's been through what I have learns about the value of kindness."

Michael's mother said, "I see."

"Those comments about that girl in the magazine, the little girl with her dressed-up bosoms, those were just a between-men thing. I'm sorry if they offended you or kept you from sleeping. A woman as beautiful as yourself needs sleep. I hope you won't mind my saying this." Billy Chaleaux flicked off the light on the door of the compartment and sat again. The pattern on his trousers fluoresced slightly so that words appeared in the loose-hanging folds. NEVER. DARK. "I only point to a picture like that because a boy of your son's age has certain thoughts, certain preoccupations. Pretending otherwise is really no solution. That creates all kinds of pressure, which could result in things like juvenile delinquency. Not that Michael, a boy like Michael, would be involved in that. It's only the motives I'm speaking about. Denying certain kinds of thoughts. I think we all know what those would be, and there's nothing unnatural in them. Not at all."

Michael expected his mother to say something, perhaps to get up and leave the compartment. But Billy Chaleaux continued to speak, growing more serene, conveying a smooth inevitability. The sorts of words he used changed, and his inflection flattened out, as if he were studied in the art of disguising his voice. "Nothing unnatural at all. Not at all. Even if he didn't think these thoughts during the day, they would come to him at night. He would think those thoughts that young men think. Who knows exactly what he thinks about? The specific images and so forth. That's just his business, in the end. I know what I'd be thinking about, mom. With just the two of you in that house."

Michael's mother said, "Stop."

"But you can't hide a child forever, can you? A boy's desires are perfectly natural. We all have desires." Billy Chaleaux was chuckling and shaking his head. "Even you've got some in there, mom, underneath all those long skirts and hairpins. A woman like yourself."

She issued a distressed sound, and Michael said: "She wants you to shut up. Shut up."

"Oh sure, I know. I need to shut up. And you two need to get on

415

with this family vacation of yours. Sure, Mike, you're just defending what belongs to you. There's no harm in that. Your mom sounds pretty upset and maybe kind of worried too. She has every right to worry, Mike. Every right in the world. She doesn't know what I might do. She's seen enough in her life, more than you might imagine, and she can't help but worry. She's probably thinking about when the conductor might come by. But she knows he's not going to come by on this train, the red-eye out of Detroit. He's supposed to. Says so right in his regulations. But we're a good thirty miles out of Gary and there's no more stops on this line. He's in that warm little room they have for conductors, shooting the shit with the others, talking about what he's going to do for the holiday. He might have some coffee, or cocoa maybe. Your mom could get up and try to find him, but I think she's a bit too spooked, Mike. She doesn't want to leave me alone with you, and she doesn't want to drag you and all that luggage to some other crowded compartment. She doesn't know what I might do, I think. When you live a certain kind of way for a long time—any kind of way—it gets hard to adjust, to do things differently. What I mean is this: when you live in fear, fear becomes anything you look at."

"Such a philosopher," Michael's mother said. Her jaw muscles bunched. "We didn't realize you were such a philosopher."

Billy Chaleaux smiled and dipped his head, undoing her irony. "I'll tell you what your mom's really afraid of: she's afraid that you'll try to do something to save her, that you'll attack me or something, Mike. She'd like that, really, a certain part of her. But another part of her is scared to death. Her mind tells her she's just being a good mama, worrying about her boy tangling with some loudmouth stranger on a train. It's more than that, though. She's not really afraid you'll get hurt. She's afraid you'll do just fine, and afraid of what would happen afterwards. Because then, I think, it would be obvious what you deserved."

Michael sat, clenching and unclenching his fists. He considered his options—fetching the conductor, attacking the man, yelling threats at him—but all these seemed absurd. Billy Chaleaux wasn't really *doing* anything. He was just talking.

And the more he spoke, the more relaxed he became, the movements of his throat slow and elaborate, his eyes looking hooded and ancient in greenish shadow. "She's sort of trapped, Mike. Both of you are. I think I might recognize that. There might have been some-

416

thing in the way you two conducted yourselves. Getting onto this train in a town like Toledo, first ones on, can't afford to fly, car in the shop, taking this late train because it's the cheapest ticket, and making sure you're the first ones on so you can choose a place and protect it, so you can ride along with your shoulders brushing in the dark. Setting out all these things to make the place look full, a full house. It's a certain kind of mentality."

Michael's mother said something under her breath, which Michael did not catch. Billy Chaleaux said, "Yes, I know, mom. I've heard all those words before, filled my mouth and released them into the air. You need to cash some of that anger. I understand. You're in the right, mom. That young man who did so much wrong to you so long ago: how do you forgive a man like that, who won't stay put or do what he's told? How long has that man deserved punishment? And you—you're still a young woman. Vibrant. Alive. There are things you deserve. Not just money or comfort, but things in the way of flesh."

"If you so much as lift a hand—"

"No, no," Billy Chaleaux said. He spoke as if his words were plucked from a dream. "That's not what this is about, mom. You know that. Violence does none of us any good. It's just a place you move towards or away from. There's nothing in it that lasts. Mike knows that. We have a lot in common, Mike and me. I look at him and I see a younger version of myself. I hear you make that noise, mom, as if you find that ridiculous. But we have more in common than you'd like to think. We have our thoughts about you, for instance, and we have the night, and we have whatever might happen in the night. These are not small things and time will only make them larger. Mike can't stay around forever, after all, dressing and undressing in that room next to yours, taking showers, walking around in his summer tank tops, both of you struggling to lift that large, unnameable need onto the other. How do we undo need, mom? Loosen its hold? I'm asking a question here, a serious question."

Billy Chaleaux pulled a cigarette out from the zippered coat on the seat beside him and put it between his lips. He flexed his arms, and the muscles ran along them like small animals. "He'll have to leave. You know that. It's just something that men do to you. And once he's gone, he'll never come back. He'll visit, of course, and bring you flowers and gifts and some insufficient bride. But he'll never really be back, like it was before, just the two of you. And that need."

417

Michael's mother was gazing out the window. The distant lights of Gary shone on her small face. She was not weeping. From what Michael could determine, she was trying instead to assume a posture of boredom or disinterest, which he tried to mimic.

"Now listen," Billy Chaleaux said. "I need to smoke this cigarette, because I'm addicted to the damn things. This is one of *my* needs. And I know you don't like to have smoke all over your clothing and hair and skin—because there are things you would like to touch your skin, but smoke, my smoke, isn't one of them—so I'm going to head down to the dining car. But before I do that, I want to take another look at the two of you so I can sort of save a picture in my head. I'm sure I don't look like a man who would go in for that kind of thing. I doubt someone like you, mom, would give me that much credit. But it's not difficult to make a picture in my mind." Chaleaux closed his eyes and let the cigarette dangle from his lips as he spoke. "I can see the both of you together on this train, leaning into each other in a darkened compartment, feeling the motion of the cars and the heat of one another's bodies, that heat that merges after a time. You're looking away, mom, out the window. But not in this picture I have in my mind. In this picture I'm thinking of, you're looking at your son, your only son, your firm, handsome, sweet-smelling son. And I almost know what you're thinking, what your exact thoughts are, how you would like certain moments of your life to never end."

Billy Chaleaux rose slowly, his hands raised in deference, and, with a curious formality, folded his jacket over his arm. He opened the door to the compartment and slipped through.

Michael thought about how best to dismiss the man, with a curt comment, maybe, or a murmured curse. He thought about apologizing to his mother for not throwing Chaleaux out of the compartment. He tried to envision himself comforting her.

She was still staring out the window, at snakes of smoke and low-slung black shapes, factories filled with sooty men.

"He was crazy, Mom. Drunk and crazy."

His mother only shook her head. She slumped in her seat, her mouth hanging slightly open, her eyes smudgy, unfocused.

The train was slowing, pulling into the steel berth of the Gary station, where Michael's grandmother would meet them, swallowed up by her shabby coat and smelling of rosewater. For three days she would fret over them, in the yellow, knotted warmth of the apartment she could no longer quite manage. And then she would hail

418

them a taxi and hug them a bit too long and they would get back on the train and return home.

Michael stood and began to lift the luggage down from the overhead rack. "We're here," he said.

"Yes."

"We should get going. She'll be waiting."

His mother nodded and extended her hand, bent primly at the wrist. Michael felt her fingers on his palm. He lifted her to her feet and she weighed nothing at all. The skin around her mouth, which she moisturized each night with ardent little dabs of cream, had grown thin and papery. He could see the pale slashes of scalp where her hair was pulled tight. Her eyes were delicate cups of ink.

She stood and now Michael could feel her buckle against him, and certain pictures came into his mind—of his mother at a different age, swollen and pink with her desire—and his body stiffened and she pressed against this stiffness, her soft belly pressed, and her hands searched for a place on his body and settled on the small of his back. He wanted to pull away from the heat of her. But she was holding him there and his body was responding and he knew then that Billy Chaleaux was watching them from outside the compartment, that he had been watching them all along.

"Don't grow up to be a man like that," she whispered. "Michael. Promise me."

Michael felt his mother shudder against him and his body responded with a fierce happy motion. She gasped a little. He thought about the arms of Billy Chaleaux: thick veins and muscle, threaded ink. His mother wanted to step back, but Michael held her—held her easily—and their bodies were together in the darkness. He bent down and the soft whiskers of his mustache brushed against her cheek, which was damp, and he squeezed her body one final time and waited until her breath was shallow and urgent and hot on his ear before answering, "Yes. I promise."

*Nominated by Elizabeth Graver, Joyce Carol Oates*

# IT IS THE NATURE OF THE WING

by FRANK GASPAR

from ALICE JAMES BOOKS

The problem is being a fragment trying to live out a whole life.
From this, everything follows. Or the problem is being
fractured and preoccupied with one's own mending, which
lasts as long as you do and comes with its legion of distractions.
Just now, when a lovely-throated motor comes gliding up
the street to one driveway or another, I can tell you
there is a certain kind of safety in a fact like that. It is so
solid you can lean on it in your bad hours. It can lift you, too,
from your despair, which is of no consequence, which can
be measured against the dropping flowers of the wisteria,
which fall because of their nature and essence, and stain
the redwood planks of the small deck in the back of the house.
That doesn't mean those used-up blossoms feel at home
under everyone's feet or at the mercy of my stiffened broom.
Didn't Plato say it is the nature of the wing to lift what is heavy?
He was speaking of love again, I can remember that much, and
then love was a ladder, too, but lifting again, always upward.
Then it is possible to love Plato for his faith, which is so strong
he becomes difficult and obdurate in the late nights. He is
hardly distracted by a passing car. He is fixed on something
beautiful, and why not? When I step out onto the porch, there
is nothing shining in the sky. Oh, and the wisteria blooms have
fallen some more and are like a sad carpet. And some small

insects are dancing in the garage's yellow lamp. They don't hear
the little bats squeaking. It's all right. You could even say they
look happy, they look joyful. Surely they are beautiful in their
ignorance and danger. See how they hold your head and command
your eye? Looking upward? Looking toward that homely light?

*Nominated by Jane Hirschfield, Dorianne Laux*

# A HAZE ON THE HILLS

## by PAMELA STEWART

from TRIQUARTERLY

Let love—to my bones in.
Let love—from my bones out.

It is awful to sit down to eat among the ashes.
Even dogs wander away.

But if you ask me in I will take one step at least
though I am greatly unsure
and sometimes walking hurts.

Listen—the black swan calls.
Two-toned, it sounds like "Come here!"

It is awful when ashes fill up the mouth.
There is helplessness
in having too full a mouth, too many words at once.

If only love filled up those words. . . .

A dog runs silently through tall grasses
as though all four feet were on fire.

*Nominated by Colette Inez*

# CHEST X-RAY

## by AMY BARTLETT

from TIN HOUSE

The pic line was threaded
up a vein in my arm, like an elastic
through a pants waist

In the x-ray room
against the light box
it showed up a pale white
shepherd's crook above
my heart. I saw the looming cliffs
where my death may begin;
the gate of my ribs;
and the two metal valves
that replaced my nipples
when they cut the cancer away.
The clavicles above
were like the bonnet tops of gates
to heaven or a cemetery

I saw the dark, unspecified shapes
of organs, blurred like a fish in a tank.
I saw the column of spools
that is my spin—the keel of the boat—
the long bones of my arms,
oars pulled in to rest,
the ark of my ribs
the vessel I will climb into
to bear me out of life.

*Nominated by Henry Carlile, Tin House*

# MANHATTANS

fiction by FREDERICK BUSCH

from FIVE POINTS

H E DROVE THOUGH HE WASN'T SUPPOSED TO. According to the tiny print of the pamphlet that came with his medications, he must not operate heavy machinery or drive a car. He steered in the passing lane before his courage failed and he wobbled back to the right and slowed to forty-five.

"I'll get better," he had promised his wife, sick with his conviction that his sickness was the only truth and health was a lie.

"But I might not," she'd said. She had said it flatly and evenly, as if she was telling the time.

He understood her anger, he thought. She had spoken to him, before leaving, in the sorrow of her understanding that nothing was left for her but leaving him. If she didn't, she would have to face him during all the hours of every day of the weeks of his medical leave of absence—it would never be long enough—and even Green himself knew the bleakness of the prospect of living with him. He found it impossible to live with himself, he thought, speeding up, then slowing down, blinking in the bright, watery light that poured around trees and over the face of an iron-stained high, white cliff at the side of Route 17, a hundred miles from his city, New York. Was that thought, about not being able to live with himself, a thought about not living at all? Was he talking to himself about suicide? He didn't much care, he thought, and he knew that such considerations might be called ominous, though disguised in something like *unpleasant*, or *a warning shot, let's call it*, by Marcy Bellochio, his therapist. Dr.

Xin, who wrote his prescriptions, didn't speak English well enough to suggest synonyms. He would call a suicide just that.

Bess, his wife, was angry at his disorderly disease—angry at him for giving in to the illness and angry at herself for failing to understand that he hadn't chosen to suffer it. And she knew it, he knew. Still, something in her fury at him, which left her trembling at times as hard as he always did, suggested to him that maybe a broken segment of his character had made him get sick, or had kept him entangled in what he thought of as its thousands of tiny branches that grew through his body and couldn't be torn away unless the body were torn apart.

They'd been right to marry, he thought, speeding up. They'd always understood each other, even now, while her energy for sustaining the knowledge, the plain bad news, ran out.

Tearing the body apart to root it out would be classified by Marcy Bellochio, he knew, as a suicidal ideation.

"We'll have none of that," he instructed the car, slowing it at an exit that he thought he remembered and driving, according to the rental-car dashboard compass, due north. "Let's really try and have none of that."

He passed a diner and thought of hot coffee with a lot of sugar and milk. He saw his hands shake as he gripped the cup with both of them. He saw the coffee spill, the mess of sugar crystals and milk drops and dark tan coffee stains on the napkins he would wetly wad as he scrubbed at his paper placemat.

He said, "Let's try having none."

At first, Bess called them The Shakes. Then, when she understood that calling it A Case of The Shakes suggested that sometimes he didn't suffer them, she stopped referring to them at all. "It's a side effect," he'd told her, although she knew it was, and he knew that she did. "Pharmacological side effects may include sexual dysfunction, palsied trembling, and being unable to gauge the distance between the self and the world or the pain inflicted on the world by the presence of the self. It's the price one pays for ingesting psychotropics in what I think we could call large quantities."

"I think we could call them frighteningly large quantities," she said. "It's part of the treatment, though. I say treatment because I suppose we shouldn't call it the cure, there apparently not being one."

"My trembles and the little dysfunction business and your tears."

"Never mind my tears, thank you."

"And never mind my trembles or the other," he said.

She smiled a broad, false smile that made her lean, patrician face look cruel, and she said, "There. Haven't we managed our little crisis?"

He remembered that while they parried, he had very powerfully felt that he might start to cry. It wasn't until she had left the room, turning to walk away as if she'd suddenly been frightened, that he wiped at his cheeks and felt the moisture of his tears.

It would be best to be strong and resolute and comforting by the time he got there, he thought. Jerry and Nancy Stradling were old people in a cul-de-sac of distress, whereas Green was only middle-aged, merely rocked breathless, from time to time, by sorrow. Everyone in the world gets sorrow, he knew. You hadn't a right to complain when you did. But distress, he thought, was another matter. Distress was a complaint of a higher order. The Stradlings were very old people alone in the world except for others like themselves in their circle. By now, it had to be the smallest of circles. He imagined drawing it on the sand of a hot Rhode Island beach, or in chalk on the cloudy, gray board of a Fordham Law School classroom, or with a brush dipped in whitewash on the liver-colored stone of a three-story town house around the corner from lower Fifth Avenue. It would be closer to a big dot than a circle. The old couple's son lived in Europe, and he flew from Brussels to New York and drove this same route up to them in a rented car whenever he could. Jerry Stradling's partners were dead, and his remaining associates in the Syracuse firm conducted a cold, lucrative legal practice that had nothing to do with his former clients or him; at Christmastime, the firm sent a basket of cheeses out in a van, Nancy had told him. She had also told him that her sister sometimes visited, but she was as old as Nancy and Jerry, and she had to be driven from Concord, Massachusetts by her daughter, who seemed not to have too much time for her mother, much less her ancient uncle and aunt.

That apparently left Green as the one to call, and as he drove under the dwindling flare of dusk he imagined a little circle inside of which was a doodle resembling his face. He had been a summer intern for Jerome Stradling several decades before, and then for nearly six years he had practiced law as a junior colleague while learning what Jerry could teach him about pleading in the Second District of the federal bench and the New York State Supreme Court. Jerry was a gent, a cordial maverick, a slick litigator, and an accomplished scholar of the law. In the office, he'd worn excellent Donegal tweed sport coats with slacks of bright primary colors such as golfers wore on the links. In court, he wore rich sharkskin suits with muted stripes and neckties that cost a hundred dollars each. His little moustache had sat heavily on a mouth that frowned more often than it smiled, and that rarely was still. His nose was hawkish, his forehead high, his body broad. He was a decorated naval officer who had served on destroyers in World War II, and in the long winters so common to this part of the state, he liked to talk about some weather making, and how they might see a little action on the deck. Now, backed into the last available corner of his old age, Jerry was alone with Nancy, once a great giver of dinner parties and cocktail parties and even high teas—cucumber sandwiches on homemade bread, Green remembered, and slices of salty Southern ham, and real scones, buttercream layer cakes. She had been rumored to have been a debutante in Rochester, New York. She had been a fine skier, trained by professionals after World War II. She could sit much of the day without complaint in a duck blind and bring down more than most of the men who shot with her. It was Nancy who had telephoned after so many years of silence between them to say, "Can you come for a weekend visit, Jim? Well. It's actually—could you come up here and lend us a hand?"

The Stradlings' house was 200 miles from New York City. He felt as if he'd come a thousand. He was probably the fifth or even tenth she had called, Green thought. He could imagine her sitting with their very old book of telephone numbers and addresses, many of them perhaps crossed out. He couldn't bring himself to efface the names and numbers of the dead who had begun to accumulate in his life. He saw it as a coming on, a kind of dusk, an ashen light that would grow dull and then dim and then dark. As if he were not giving in to the failing light, he kept the names of friends and acquaintances who had died. Their telephone numbers were there to consult among the numbers of those who had greeted him with pleasure when he called. But he didn't call them anymore, and he suspected that they wouldn't be smiling at the sound of his voice if he did. And Nancy, hearing reason after reason for the failure of their past to assist them, had at last come upon his name and had called him for help.

They had exchanged holiday greetings every year. They hadn't spoken since he'd left to practice in New York City. But you have to say yes when they call, Green thought, because when you stop responding to something like that, you're controlled by the darkness. It owns you. All you have a right to expect, after not saying yes when they call, is the purchase of a newspaper every day, and a meal if you can keep it down, and the medication, and then television with everyone laughing, and nights of not sleeping followed by what is sometimes called the light of day but which Green and others knew was darkness with its name changed.

Although it was spring, the low-ceilinged Colonial house was cold. Nancy Stradling wore a man's bulky gray cardigan over a dark blue polka-dotted dress. She greeted him with a smile that appeared to raise each crease of her seamed, small face. Her hair was thick and silky, purely white and twisted into a bun. He remembered it as a shade of light chestnut, or maybe even a honey blond. She was proud of it, he could tell, because she drew the eye to it with a filigreed silver pin bearing small garnets that protruded from the bun and caught the light. As soon as she let go of his hands, he stuck them in his trouser pockets and followed her to the kitchen, where she insisted on his drinking a cup of coffee.

"I forget how you take your coffee," she said. "Of course, some days, I forget how I take *mine*."

"It's been a good many years, Mrs. Stradling."

"Oh, you call me *Nancy*, for heaven's sake, Bill."

"It's Jim."

"Jim. God. Jim! Of course. Forgive me. Tell me the truth, now. Do you think the house has grown shabby after all these years?"

"Well, no, actually. No. It's always been lovely. I remember wanting to live in a house like yours—when I was working for Jerry, in the early days. I even insisted that we buy a table like this one. Curly maple, right? I remember you telling me it was curly maple at, I think it was, one of your parties. Maybe at some Christmastime."

"And did your wife agree when you insisted? She's called—"

"Bess."

"Perhaps next time she can come with you."

He smiled. He had to look away from what her face did when he tried to smile. "Maybe so," he said. "Jerry's pretty low these days?"

"If he were any lower," she said, carrying the coffee to him in the dim chilliness of the narrow kitchen with its unlighted wood stove and windows with crazed panes that made the daylight look smeared, "he'd be flat on his back." She set the coffee before him. "Of course, he *is* on his back. Oh, he's very pleased that you're coming. He'll be up and about later. I wouldn't be able to keep him from dressing smartly and greeting you. Later on, he'll be out."

"Nancy, you said you needed a hand."

"I did?"

"Over the phone. You asked if I could come here and give you a hand. Is there a specific problem? You know, something concrete I could tackle for you?"

Sitting in the junction made by the side of the table and the kitchen wall, she opened her hand to reveal some small silver spoons that were tarnished nearly black. "You must remember these," she said.

He didn't. He nodded and smiled, and Nancy looked away.

"Would you like the one celebrating the Erie Canal, the lovely Stuttgart, the—ah!—the Cipriani in Venice, and this is Mexico, this is Taos, and here's Niagara-by-the-Lake. We've collected dozens. Pick whichever one you want."

Suddenly, he did remember them, from an evening's cocktails, with Jerry very carefully measuring out small shots of bourbon for what he called highballs, though he served them in low glasses, and excessive portions of vermouth for weak martinis on the rocks. He recalled candles scented with vanilla and someone playing *Moonlight in Vermont* on the huge, Victorian upright piano in the front sitting room, as he now remembered their calling it. He remembered his broad pleasure, Green recalled, as he'd thought that night of the woman who was flying in to wait for him at the Hotel Syracuse: Bess, he said to himself as his stomach twisted and his face felt filled by a surging of blood. It had been their first hotel together at the start of what was a very short courtship and a marriage that had lasted at least a year too long for her. And he had come to the senior partner's party without her because her plane was arriving late and because he knew how little she would want to be among the braided rugs and old, dark furniture inherited by Jerry from his mother in Kansas, and the worried junior lawyers, and of course the polished commemorative spoons arrayed beside the glasses for stirring drinks. He remembered how Stradling and his wife had made them select a souvenir spoon that then was served protruding from their drink. Perhaps he was inventing it, he thought, his recollection of the young lawyers standing and sipping with one hand while holding with the other a purposeless, shiny, small spoon.

He paddled tiny circles through his coffee with Niagara-by-the-Lake and lifted his cup with both hands. She had the grace to turn her attention to her cup while he tried to drink from his.

"The firm frowned on our living here, you know."

"No, I never did. Of course, the junior associates only speculated about the senior partners. We called them The Gods."

"I had heard that," she said. "Look at us. Some gods."

"But why? The frowning, I mean."

"They wanted all of him they could get, and that included time spent in commuting. The partners found it difficult to understand that it was his therapy—the cars, I mean, and the drive. It cleared his mind."

"Good cars," he said. "I remember that now: excellent machines."

"The Studebaker Silver Hawk," she said. "And the little Spitfire. And the Jaguar, of course. He always complained about the carbure-tion in the Jag. But he adored the Hawk. And now we aren't allowed to drive. We can't. But we kept a little white Ford, very bland, and I can get us around by going slowly. It's not so easy in winter, you re-member our icy roads. I'm not supposed to operate a car. But you have to live."

He felt himself about to argue with the proposition that living was imperative, and he said, "But Jerry would let himself relax when he drove, you're saying? It would clear his mind?"

"Exactly. He remembered you as being sympathetic, he said. And there you are. You can put yourself in the other fellow's shoes."

"Shoes are easy," he said. "But about my being useful to Jerry and you. . . ."

She cocked her head and took a noisy breath. She said, "It gets *very* hard."

"Yes."

"Aging. Illness. He's quite ill."

"Yes."

"And that gets hard."

"Yes, it must."

"I'm as healthy as a dray horse," she said, laughing without any ap-parent pleasure. "I have normal cholesterol and my blood pressure's rather good for someone my age. All my tests are always rather good. And poor Jerry, the military hero. He's the one who crossed the

North Atlantic four times on a World War I-vintage tin can. He's the one who was always splitting wood and mowing the lawn, for gosh sakes, with a hand-powered mower. He's the one people used to call on to help them take up tree stumps in the town, or put together a pipework scaffolding to lay down a roof. He hasn't barely got a pulse some days, Jim. His blood pressure's so low. It's affecting the—well—"

She turned away as if to look at someone seated beside her. She shook her head, then faced him again.

"All that's left is indignity," she said. "The best of it's frustrating, or embarrassing, and the worst of it's as bad a humiliation—an affliction, I'm tempted to call it—as you could imagine. He can't see very much at all. He can't read anymore. It affects his brain, I think. I don't mean the memory. That's gone most days, or going, though he still remembers events from the office or the court room. So that's that. But his *reasoning*. He was the most sensible man, wasn't he?"

"A good lawyer's as analytic as a chemist—as an accountant. Even his feelings have to be mostly cold thought. Or so his wife would say." He barked a laugh too loudly, and she recoiled.

She moved her cup away and clasped her hands on the table before her. She said, "He isn't thinking well. I wondered if someone from the old days, coming into the house, into his mind, I suppose I mean, might jolt him. Do you know? That kind of *jolt* you sometimes can get from the past? Even when you might not be remembering well? Do you and your Bess have children, Jim? I should have asked you right away."

"We have a son and a daughter, yes."

"And where are they?"

"One's in the Army and the other is either a partner in a dot-com in Eugene, Oregon, or he's on unemployment, we aren't sure which because neither is he."

"So your *girl's* the soldier. It's a new world."

"Sarabeth is a captain. She flies helicopters in frightening places. Like her mother, she is very brave."

"How wonderful for you."

"Yes," he said, "it's wonderful."

"And do you think I was right to ask you all the way up here from Manhattan?"

"Right?"

"The jolt," she said. "Like the—you know. Oh, what's it called?

Electric shock, for crazy people? It's supposed to bring them to their senses, or something. Do you know?"

"Electroconvulsive therapy," he said. "It's called ECT."

"The little jolt," she said.

"The little jolt. I believe it's thought of as the last resort for certain patients."

"Is it really? I'm afraid I know nothing about it."

He said, "I know about the jolt is all."

"Yes," she said. "And do you think we might try that with Jerry?"

He saw himself leaping from behind a curtain with his arms outspread, providing the sudden little jolt. He saw Jerry, in liver-colored Donegal tweed jacket paired up with lime green golf slacks, standing still, paralyzed with terror, then going pale, then falling to the hardwood floor with his heart stopped.

"Maybe telling him first that I'm here."

"Yes," she said. "Of course. He knows that already."

"Then maybe a gentle, small prod more than a jolt."

"I knew you'd know what's best," she said.

"You did?"

"Well, of course, Jim." They nodded like the little figures on an old German clock who spring out to chase each other when the hour tolls. "That's why I called you up," she said. And then, as if it had been the topic of conversation all along, Nancy asked him, "Do you have photographs of you and your Bess at your wedding?"

"I think we do," he said. "Yes. I think we have a scrapbook's-worth, a lot of them. We never look at them," he said. "Like most people, I suppose."

"Not us," she said in a flat, hard voice. "Not us. We were married by one of Jerry's professors, a philosophy teacher at Lehigh. He was a Lutheran pastor and because I was Catholic and Jerry was a rather exotic species of Baptist, the teacher was our way of bridging the gap. A Christian, but not a sectarian, marriage, I suppose you would call it. We were very independent, and no one in his family knew about marriages. That is, the planning, you know, and catering and all of that. My people, if we'd have let them, they'd have taken it over and staged a quiet little affair with the Rockettes and the Notre Dame marching band. So we just drove out to the professor's farmhouse, near Easton, and we got married. Well, we had set the *date*, mind you. We had an appointment with the professor, we didn't just show up. But it was more or less 'Hello, let's have the wedding, now you're married, congratulations, goodbye.' His wife was very un-happy. She was our witness. I mean, I think they were unhappy to-gether. At first, I was frightened that it was an omen for us. But we did pretty well for a very long time. I can't complain about that. It's the pictures."

"Pictures of you and Jerry at your wedding."

"We don't have any. The unhappy wife never thought to take them. I never thought to ask for them. Maybe she enjoyed knowing that some day we'd want them and there wouldn't be any. Maybe that was the omen part of the ominousness that I felt. She was all pale and doughy and slope-shouldered and quiet, and she frightened me. She had a wen or some sort of thick, fleshy protrusion under her lower lip. She never said a word. She didn't even say 'Congratula-tions.' She never hugged either of us. She shook my hand. Her hand was as cold as a stone from the river. And now there isn't a picture of us from the day we were married. It's as if the day didn't happen. Of course, it did, and I know it. But I would love a little proof. You and Jerry understand proof. It's what you deal in."

"You make me want to drive home and look at our photos and feel lucky," he lied.

"You do that. Don't rush off, of course. But count your blessings."

"I will," he said. "I do."

"Good," she said, "because you've a sad expression etched into your face, Jim."

"That's what my mother always warned me," he said.

She laughed, and she was a little bit of a pretty girl. " 'Make that face too much, and your face will freeze that way.' God. Didn't they all tell all of us that?"

"And all of them were right," he said.

She nodded, and he nodded back. He thought again of the dark, high wooden clocks in Europe when, as the hour was struck, the fig-ures chased other figures in jerky motions across the base of the broad, white dial. It was often someone wielding a scythe in pursuit of maidens, he thought he recalled.

While Nancy went in to Jerry, Green walked, on his toes, like an intruder, through the front of the house—the living room that led to the foyer that led to the sitting room with its piano and its broad bu-reau that they used as the sideboard for drinks. The living room was furnished with comfortable chairs and deep sofas, and the walls were dressed with paintings by artists Green had never heard of. The pictures were mostly of snowy scenes, although there was one portrait that bore a likeness to what Jerry looked like thirty years before. In the sitting room the furniture was dense, more black than brown, heavily worked—the worst of proud Victorian decoration—and the walls were hung with murky prints. On the sideboard were bottles and glasses and, of course, more small commemorative spoons. In the back of the sitting room on the wall was hung a plaque that celebrated Jerome Stradling for his selfless service to the Bar Association of Central New York. Beside it was a photo, in a hardware-store frame, of a smiling, athletic young Nancy Stradling in a strapless gown who held the arm of Jerry, in his late 20s, who was wearing a dress shirt and cummerbund with his tie undone, his eyes a little glazed with drink, Green assumed, and the two of them about to take possession of a lot of the known world.

He went quietly back to the kitchen to drink cooled coffee. He slopped some over the side of the cup and onto the floor. He was mopping it with a paper napkin when she brought Jerry in. He had shrunk in height and breadth and had become her size, Green thought, and he wobbled a little from side to side as he moved forward. His face was bony and pale, and his nose seemed all the more like a beak. It was naked-looking, and Green took a minute to understand that the bristly moustache was gone. The waxy skin around the nose was blooming small suppurations, some of which had formed red-and-white scabs. His light blue eyes looked clear, though his vision was nearly gone. He gripped Nancy's upper arm and appeared, at first, to be looking directly at Green. But he didn't see much, Green thought, because he focused on the space between them, no matter how close he came, until they were nearly toe-to-toe.

Jerry stuck his small hand before him and said, in a slightly hoarse voice that had little of the baritone resonance Green remembered, "Bill!"

"It's Jim," Nancy said.

Stradling leaned his head back, as if trying to remember something. Then he said, "Of course. Of course, it's Jim. You must forgive me."

"I'm happy to see you, Jerry. Any name you want to use is fine."

"You're as elegant as ever," Stradling said, smiling uncertainly.

He looked like an ancient child who made an appearance at the grownups' party. He was dressed in pale yellow golf slacks tightened high on the waist by a brown leather belt. The pants hung loosely

434

about his legs and broke in a puddle over his black-and-red checked cloth bedroom slippers. His corduroy shirt was a dark olive green worn with a loosely-knotted golden silk tie such as Jerry might have worn to court 40 years before. Green felt a surge of affection for her effort to dress Jerry as he might have dressed himself.

They sat in the kitchen, Jerry at the head of the maple table, where Nancy served him Postum while she reheated their coffee. "Perhaps you'd care to tell us about your practice," Jerry said, looking to Green's left. Green moved in that direction and Jerry said, "My eyes, as you can tell, have suffered. I'm not blind. I *am* debilitated. But of course you can see just fine, so you see that for yourself. Jim, why is it that I am tempted, steadily, to call you Bill?"

Green knew. It was because Nancy must have told him that she was phoning up Billy Grossman, who overlapped with Green for three or four years before Green left to work at the firm on Pine Street in lower Manhattan.

"A lot of people have told me I look like a Bill."

Nancy said, "But not a counterfeit bill. Nor a two-dollar bill. Nor a bill of lading?"

"You do crossword puzzles," Green said.

"I do," she said with pleasure. "You're a canny lawyer, aren't you?"

"I do them too," he said. "On the subway, coming down from our apartment, going to work."

" 'Six-letter word for a sixteenth-century lunatic Spanish ruler?' " she said, giggling. "Joanna. She was known as Joanna the Mad. I love any kind of game."

"It's the word part that I like," Green said, or would have, when Jerry cut in by saying angrily, "I enjoyed the billing letters. I itemized everything to the tenth of an hour. I included the sharpening of pencils, the steeping of a pot of tea. I dared them to object. And there was somebody, always, who did. Those were the conversations I enjoyed. 'I just kept you from a whopping fine for tortious interference, you maladroit boat jumper, and you quibble with me over *tea* leaves?' I used to have the girl make them with an infuser. We brewed first-rate tea that I sent her to buy over on Townsend Avenue. She had to scald the pot and use a cozy that Nancy purchased in Harrod's. And they paid for the leaves, for the water to pour on them, and for the breath the girl expelled when she poured it into good china cups."

They sat in silence.

435

"That was an outburst, I'd say," Nancy announced. "What got into *you*, Jerome Stradling?"

"Some things need to be said," he told her.

She looked at Green. "But what I really want to know," she said, "is what in heaven's name is a—what was it? A boat jumper. What's that?"

Jerry raised the fingers of each hand, one after the other, and held them against the table. "What's that? Ten? A ten-letter word for an illegal immigrant," he said. "You're welcome to make whatever use of it you wish."

Green noted how steady Stradling's hands and fingers seemed, and how he did not spill his Postum when he sipped it. The table in front of Green was spotted with sugar and coffee and milk. He saw Nancy notice it and he placed his hands in his lap.

"His wife's name is Bess," Nancy said to Jerry. "Did you ever meet her?"

"I regret that I did not," he said. "Not having met Bill, I could hardly have encountered his wife, given the unfolding of circumstances."

"Jim," she reminded him.

Stradling nodded and stared off. Green suspected that Nancy would be thinking that now, as Jerry wore out after a few minutes of conversation, now Green ought to deliver the little jolt for which she had made him responsible. It was almost five o'clock, and he thought of taking his medication while they watched and then excusing himself to go upstairs to nap. He hadn't slept for many hours of the past three days. When you've spent a good number of hours of the night in not sleeping, and you walk without purpose through your apartment to pause, finally, at a window, and you look at the city at night from eight stories up, and you wait—you're waiting, by then, for anything at all to approach through the thick nothing that wraps you— you begin to feel the pressure one remove from you in the air above New York. You sense the chill, you hear engine noises thinned to tinny rattles, and you see the lighted windows of office suites and apartments, the dampered intensity of distant lives nearby.

Then, let's say, you lie down again to close your eyes again and try. Your head is filled with the lights you saw against the nighttime sky, but now it's a different New York City that's inside you. After a while, instead of seeing bright, rectangular windows pulsing on the dark buildings framed against the dark sky, you're teeming with fragments of conversation and scraps of ideas and small shreds of image you can barely identify before they leave your head to be replaced by frightening pictures, whole sentences spoken to you years before by forgotten speakers. For people who cannot sleep at night for many nights, this other city is what you have instead of nightmares.

Even now, at this table in the kitchen lit by smeared, declining light, he heard his wife say as he had heard her say during so many of his hours of not sleeping, "Sure, it could be your mother's death. It could be your father dying eight years before her. It could be *my* father, or because we never got a dog and the—the *undogginess* just hit home. Maybe it's our daughter living like a man and our son is living like some over-privileged boy. Just because you give it a name, just because you *name* something, doesn't mean you know it. I don't *care* what it is. Call it whatever you want to, you know? But how selfish can I be? How unfeeling can I *be* after you've been living in hell for a year, for more than a year? Right? I am so sorry. I am. I really am. But I want you to just not *be* like this. Jimmy, get us back our *life!*"

"Jim," Stradling said.

"Sir?" he said.

"You argued the Oneida Board of Education matter, didn't you? Before the state appellate?"

"What an excellent memory you have," Green said. "Yes. I did. I won."

"I remember the victory. The head of the board actually kissed me on the cheek. He was that relieved. He smelled, I remember, of cheap deodorant. I ordered in chilled champagne from Liquor Square. It cost us a pretty penny. But then we delivered the bill. And they paid, of course. And we had our pretty penny back. So you can see that my mind is unaffected by the advance of—what would you call it?"

"I wouldn't," he said, waiting for Nancy to rescue him.

"Your complaint," she said.

"My complaint," Stradling said. "My broken-down heart. The heart isn't sad," he said, "but it doesn't pound away as sturdily as it used to. And of course there's the eyesight problem."

"But he sees well in his *mind*," Nancy said to Green.

"Try a—" Stradling counted his fingers. "Try a nine-letter word for hectoring blabbermouth," he said.

"Jerry!"

"Termagant," he said. "Seeing well in the mind, my Irish ass."

And so much for the little jolt, Green thought.

"I'm going to put the stew on," said Nancy. "It's a *daube*, actually, a stew of lamb that's been flavored with white wine, although one would drink some light-bodied red with the meal. We'll have to see what bottles are out in the pantry. I always prepare this meal in advance to let the flavors marry. It's a jolly springtime dish. I'm going to add some green peas, and it already has pearl onions and carrots. So I'll get to that, Jim, if you'll make us our highballs? Do you remember where the liquor is?"

Stradling said, "How many guests did you *invite*?" His nostrils were white and flared. The eruptions around his nose seemed to darken. His bony face seemed even more drawn. He said, "Gatherings and gatherings, with our backs still against the wall from the *last* time you invited so many strangers in."

"Jerry Stradling, you will lie down before dinner, even if it's only for a minute or two," Nancy said.

"I suppose I ought to. I suppose I will. Otherwise she'll knock me down is what she'll be telling me next. You remember." Then he said to Nancy, "Does he remember what drinks we want?"

She said, "I'm sure he does. He *knows* us, Jerry."

She looked at Green as if now, at last, he could deliver the necessary jolt. But then she turned to Stradling and moved him out of the kitchen. He went obediently, wobbling. Green took a tray of ice cubes from the freezer compartment of the refrigerator and went along to the sitting room to make them their drinks.

He remembered the care, the miserliness, with which Stradling at that party given so many years before had measured the shot of liquor he'd put in each drink. As if retaliating, Green dropped ice cubes into heavy, cut-crystal glasses and carelessly poured plenty of bar-whisky bourbon into cheap sweet vermouth that looked and smelled like Mercurochrome. Green doubted that Jerry Stradling was supposed to drink liquor any more than he was. He used the same spoon—from a hotel in British Columbia—to stir each drink. Then he worked at opening a crusted, small bottle of maraschino cherries. He used the British Columbia spoon to place a cherry in every drink. He had to use his fingers to pick up two that his shaking spoon had let fall to the surface of the sideboard. He ate them both and then found purple-and-gold paper cocktail napkins in the first drawer he opened. He used a napkin to wipe his fingers and then to scrub the cherry syrup from the sideboard. He wanted to telephone his wife. He knew he made her sad. But he wondered whether she was as miserable without him as she'd been in their life together. He was afraid that she felt too much better away from him. He had a real malady, he knew, but to his wife he *was* the disease. He would have loved her to tell him otherwise, but he wouldn't ask. Even he, because he loved her and sometimes could remember that he did, would prescribe for her a life without him. He sucked at his sticky fingers like a child.

"Ladies and gentlemen," Jerry Stradling said.

He stood in the doorway of the sitting room. He moved his head as if surveying a crowd of guests. He smiled with the taut confidence of a capable attorney about to deliver his opening argument. "I want to thank you very much for coming tonight, and I apologize for the delay. If you will be patient a moment longer, my junior colleague will see to your drinks. And I will return to join you shortly." He smiled with no sincerity and said, "If you'll take over from here, Bill?"

Stradling nodded to no one with great courtesy, then turned in the doorway and, pushing at the door frame as if to launch himself, he lurched lightly down the corridor and out of sight.

Green looked at the empty doorway for a while. Then he took a small oval metal tray from the sideboard. It was decorated with the faded head of a terrier, painted in white and black on a red background. He put the Manhattans on the tray, and then he selected for each drink a spoon that was a forgotten commemoration—the British Columbia for one, an Allentown Fair for another, and a Red Lion in Salisbury, England for the last. Two of the tarnished spoons were stubby and broad, and the third was longer, slimmer, with a narrow, dull brass band around the handle, souvenirs stolen by a healthy, confident young couple who were starting to take their ease in the world. He folded three napkins and set them on the tray, and then he squeezed his trembling fingers around and under its edge. He lifted and wheeled and set off to follow Jerry Stradling down the dark corridor. He knew that he must not spill a drop.

*Nominated by Andrea H. Budy, Melanie Rae Thon, Five Points*

# OUR SPRING CATALOG

fiction by JACK PENDARVIS

from CHELSEA

*As Goes the Zephyr*

LURLEEN BIVANT

This luminous and engaging first novel takes place in a suburbia unlike any suburbia you have ever encountered. Marchie Whitaker's days as a self-recriminating soccer mom and nights as an unsexed sounding board to her workaholic husband are interrupted by the surprising appearance of a rather libidinous manticore. That's just the beginning of the whimsical visitations! When workers come to dig the new swimming pool—a symbol of middle class status quo that should, *should*, answer all of Marchie's dreams—the most wonderful thing begins to happen. Goblins, trolls, witches, and other inhabitants of the underworld skitter upwards through the broken soil—including the great god Pan himself! Anyway, everybody wants to lock up Marchie as a crazy person because they can't understand her magical shit. It kind of tapers off at the end, like she ran out of ideas.

*I Couldn't Eat Another Thing*

ANGELA BIRD

In this luminous collection of sparkling stories, former newspaper columnist Bird makes a stunning fictional debut with a wry look at the state of modern commitment. A lot of the time I'd get to the end of one of the stories and turn a page like, "Huh?" Like, "Where's the end of it?" Like, "What happened next?" But nothing happened next. You know, those kind of stories. Luminous.

## Low Town

Karl Harper

This is one of those finely wrought first novels of surprising tenderness and depth where a cool teenager is stifled by the closeminded assholes in his small town. He has sex with a lot of beautiful girls and then he makes it big as a painter and says, "So long, losers!" There's a tragedy that makes him rethink everything and pretty soon he comes of age. At the end he's headed off for fame and fortune and all the losers are sorry they didn't suck his dick when they had the chance. But in a funny kind of a way Boy Wonder will always carry a piece of Loserville with him wherever he goes. Blah blah blah. If you look at the guy's picture on the dust jacket, you'll see that he made up the part about having sex.

## The Sighing of the Stones

Louis Delmonte

A boy and girl grope innocently toward first love against the backdrop of an Oklahoma farming community where a lot of cattle mutilations are taking place. Who cares?

## The Little Dog Laughed

Harry Parks

Seriously, what am I doing with my life? Is this it? What am I supposed to say about this book that will make you buy it? Look at the cover. Look at the title. If you like books with covers and titles like that, go for it. It won't kill you. I keep meaning to get around to *The Naked and the Dead*. That's supposed to be awesome. If you have to know, this particular piece of shit is about a guy who's haunted by the

441

death of so-and-so and he takes a trip in a hot air balloon to forget all his problems. But then he finds out you can't run away from your problems. Big fucking deal.


## A Good Family

BECKINSALE CRUTHERS

Delia Moon had it all: riches, glamour, wit and erudition. But suddenly her Park Avenue world came crashing down around her ears. I bet you never read a book like this before! It's about the horrible pain and turmoil of being rich and white. The Moon family has a shitload of dramatic tragedies and problems. I think there's some incest in there. That makes the title ironic! *Kirkus Reviews* is going to eat this shit up.


## The Enormous Swan

M. A. McCORQUEDALE

Set against the colorful backdrop of some historical period nobody gives a rat's ass about, *The Enormous Swan* tells the story of a humble craftsman who comes into contact with an emperor or some shit. To tell you the truth I didn't make it past page 10 or so. It's one of those books where the author spent half his life in a library looking up facts about medieval culinary techniques and galley slaves and shit, and now he thinks we're supposed to care.


## Eat the Lotus

MARIE OVERSTREET

I swear to God I'm going to cut my own throat. I just don't give a shit. Husband and wife reach a crossroads in their relationship against the colorful backdrop of blah blah blah. They're haunted by the suicide of their only son or some shit. Pull yourself together, you pussies! God I'm sick of this shit. I'd rather work at fucking McDonald's, I swear to God. You know what? It's not even about my career goals anymore. "Come on, Annie, this job will be good experience. You'll make a lot of contacts. I want to read your novel, Annie. When am I going to get to see this novel of yours, Annie?" You can bite my ass, you creepy old fuck. One day you're going to get what's coming to you.

*Nominated by Chelsea*

# DNA

## by LINDA BIERDS

from VIRGINIA QUARTERLY REVIEW

At hand: the rounded shapes, cloud white, the scissors, sharp,
two dozen toothpick pegs, a vial of amber glue.
It's February, Cambridge, 1953,
and he's at play, James Watson: the cardboard shapes,

two dozen toothpick pegs, a vial of amber glue.
White hexagons, pentagons, peg-pierced at the corners—
he's at play, James Watson, turning cardboard shapes
this way, that. And where is the star-shot elegance

when hexagons, pentagons, peg-pierced at the corners,
slip into their pliant, spiral-flung alignments?
Where is that star-shot elegance? This way? That?
He slips together lines of slender pegs that quickly

split in two. (Pliant, spiral-flung, one line meant
solitude. But one to one? Pristine redundancy.)
He slips. Together, lines of slender pegs quickly
conjugate. White hexagons, white pentagons:

not solitude but—one, two, one—pristine redundancy.
So close the spiral shape, now. Salt and sugar atoms
congregate: white hexagons, white pentagons.
So close the bud, the egg, the laboratory lamb,
the salt and sugar atoms' spiral shape. So close—

444

it's February, Cambridge, 1953—
the blossom, egg, the salutary lamb. So close
at hand, the rounded shapes—cloud white—the scissors—sharp.

*Nominated by Ted Genoways, Carl Phillips, Kathy Fagan,
William Olsen, Bruce Beasley, Virginia Quarterly Review*

# PICTURE

## by ATSURO RILEY

from POETRY

Tᴴɪѕ ɪѕ ᴛʜᴇ ʜᴏᴜѕᴇ (and jungle-strangled yard) I come from and carry.

The air out here is supper-singed (and bruise-tingeing) and close.

From where I'm hid (a perfect Y-crotch perch of medicine-smelling sweet-gum), I can belly-worry this (welted) branch and watch for swells (and coming squalls) along our elbow-curve of river, or I can hunker-turn and brace my trunk and limbs—and face my home.

Our roof is crimp-ribbed (and buckling) tin, and tar.

Our (in-warped) wooden porch-door is kick-scarred and splintering. The hinges of it rust-cry and -rasp in time with every Tailspin-wind, and jamb-slap (and after-slap), and shudder.

Our steps are slabs of cinder-crush and -temper, tamped and cooled.

See that funnel-blur of color in the red-gold glass?—Mama, mainly: boiling jelly. She's the apron-yellow (rickracked) plaid in there, and stove-coil coral; the quick silver blade-flash, plus the (magma-brimming) ladle-splash; that's her behind the bramble-berry purple, sieved and stored.

Out here, crickets are cricking their legs. Turtlets are cringing in their bunker-shells and burrows. Once-bedded nightcrawling worms are nerving up through beanvine-roots (and moonvines),—and dew-shining now, and cursive:

*Mama will pressure-cook and scald and pan-scorch and frizzle.*

*Daddy will river-drift down to the (falling-down) dock.*

*I myself will monkey-shinny so high no bark-burns (or tree-rats, or tides) or lava-spit can reach me.*

*I will hunt for after-scraps (and sparks) and eat them all.*

*Nominated by Kay Ryan, Richard Garcia*

# GLACIOLOGY

## by LIA PURPURA

from AGNI

*Plan*

WHEN THE SNOW BEGAN TO MELT, the drifts left behind a sur-prising collection of junk—paper cups, socks, Matchbox trucks, a snarl of CAUTION—POLICE—CAUTION tape, pinkly wrapped tampons, oil-rag T-shirts, banana peels: intimacies of toy box, bathroom, and garage amid the lumps of sand and salt we threw down for traction. It was as if after the big event of snowfall we'd forgotten there was more, still, to be said. A cache of loose details below to attend. A trove poised. A stealth gathering.

Deposition below the singular-seeming white cover.

I shall make my own study of snow and time. I will learn from that which has built the very ground I'm now slipping around on: glaciers. Their formative act: deposition, for example: *fine-grained rock debris, rock flour, and coarse rock fragments picked up or entrained within the base of a glacier and then transported and deposited from either active or stagnant ice. This product of glacial deposition, known as till, consists of particles that follow complicated routes, being deposited on the top or along the sides of the glacier bed, entrained again, and finally dropped. As a sediment, till has certain distinctive features: it exhibits poor sorting, is usually massive, and consists of large stones in a fine matrix of minerals and rock types.*

Poor sorting: I like that: that it all gets dropped, the big stuff enmeshed with the grainy soft stuff. The indiscriminate mess. That it forms a long train, so that seeing it all, one can trail events back.

Guess at them. View time. And by way of the whole scattered and shifting pattern, by the gathering eye, make something of these loose details, collecting.

## DEPOSITION ON THAW

I will note, though its impetus was warmth, the sharpness of the thaw. During the thaw we were given to see the way snow melted into vertebrae, whole bodies of bone inclined toward one another. Bones stacked and bent in the attitude of prayer, the edges honed and precarious. Forms arced over the sewer grates and curbs as the gutter streamed with bubbly melt. What remained were not yet remains. It was clear how the warmth would eat everything down, but where some parts were colder than the rest, that core kept the figure upright. The shapes were knife-edged, hunched, easing a pain; they grayed and were everywhere pocked with dirt, and unlikely in their strength.

A few days later, just sheering, frayed patches covered the ground, and the elbows of everything poked through. White remained where the ground must have been colder, or wind blew and packed the snow hard.

How to read a land?

There were thicknesses, white places layered in smears that others were trained to read. *Densities* amid the rivulets of veins. *Occlusions. Artifacts.*

I remember, about the X-ray, thinking *Artifacts? That sounds harmless.* Evidence of some action past—a little shard, small bit taken out of my body and sent off for further study. Vase, mirror, tile. Lip of a cup. A thing that remained to be found and told. An image that sings about time.

## DEPOSITION ON THE SHAPES OF TASKS

Waiting all that long week—for test results, the snow to stop, dough to rise, nightfall—small tasks turned into days. Days unfolded into tasks. The inside-out arms of clothes pulled right, made whole and unwrinkled, took lovely hours. Tasks filled like balloons and rounded with breath; they floated and bumped around the day: some popcorn, some dishes, some mending. And though dressing for sledding, undressing and draping everything wet over radiators was deliberate, a stitch ran through, jagged and taut, cinching the gestures tight with uncertainty. Everything coming down—snow, sleet, threat, delicacy—twined through like a rivulet (the cut water makes in its persistence, its pressure carving) so the bank grows a dangerous, fragile lip. The work of glaciers changes a landscape: old stream valleys are gouged and deepened, filled with till and outwash. *Filled*, of course, over millions of years. In sand-grain, fist-sized increments.

This kind of time illuminated tasks that one would hardly be given to see otherwise. Titled them, even: the scraping of old wax from candlesticks, the tightening of loosened doorknobs. Oil-soaping the piano keys.

## DEPOSITION ON FEVERS AND STILL LIFES

That week time was ample, broad as a boulevard, a stroll, a meander. Not a tour. Not a map or a path to be found. School was canceled. Scents fully unfolded: coffee, chocolate, and milk marbling together on the stove, thinnest skin across to touch and lift and eat. And like a concentrate of heat itself, my bounded sight burned holes in the things most fixed upon: the ceiling's old butterfly water stain. One rough, gritty chip in the rim of a favorite cup.

It was in this way that joy and severity flared everywhere: along the banks of steep places I went to quickly, glanced, then ran from. They burned together in cornmeal in a pour, the yellow dust that rose and stuck to my hands as I folded in the unbeaten eggs, cold suns to poke and dim with flour—as outside, too, the cold sun dimmed, and the sky sifted and shushed down.

Yes, that week passed with a fever's disheveled clarity. That time, its atmosphere, moved the way fevers by turn dilute and intensify moments, so by evening one cannot reconstitute the day and calls it "lost," calls it "flown," says after a night's sleep "what happened to the day?" Things that week were touched in sweaty uncertainty and weakly released. There were intimacies akin to falling back to a pillow after water, soup, and tea were brought, gratitude unspoken; the night table's terrain, the book, the book's binding, glue at the binding and the word for each sewn section, *folio*, surfacing from far off. The sheet's silk piping to idly slip a finger under for coolness.

In its riotous stillness, that week was a study: Dutch, seventeenth century, with its controlled and ordered high flare and shine. Days held the light and feverish presence of a bowl of lemons in pocked disarray. Always one lemon pared in a spiral of undress, its inner skin gone a flushed, sweet-cream rose. Always the starry, cut sections browning, and the darkness, just beyond the laden table, held almost successfully off. I, with my props—mixing bowl, dough—tilted toward, soaked in late afternoon light, while time raged all around in shadow, the dark stroking cup, quartered fig, plate of brilliant silver sardines left on the counter from lunch.

## DEPOSITION ON MILLENNIA/EFFLUVIA

To say "a glacier formed this land" sanctifies the blink of an eye.

To see, from the air, glacial streams and think *like a snake* or *ribboning*, and of the land on either side *accordion* or *fan* colludes against awe. Neatens up the work of time. Makes of time a graven thing, hand-sculpted, carved, and held. Time should seize, should haul us back, then let go, wind-sheared into *now*, breathlessly into the moment's hard strata. Each morning in Rome, my old friend runs in a park along the aqueduct, which breaks and restarts in yellowed fields, its arches sprouting wild grasses, its arches collapsing, the houses, apartments, roads of his neighborhood visible through it, as they have been for nearly 2,000 years. You can sit on rocks in Central Park, soft outcrops undulant as sleeping bodies, formed tens of thousands of years ago, and look up at the city skyline knowing the North American ice sheet flowed exactly that far south. Or hold in your hand a striated stone from Mauritania, abraded at the base of a glacier 650 million years ago, and touch the markings, those simple scratches so easily picked up and put down again on the touch-me table at the museum. Kick any stone beneath your foot, here, in Baltimore, and you're scuffing 300 million, even a billion years of work.

I cast back for any one thing I did on any one day that week: how unencumbered the brushing of my hair, the perfect scrolls of carrot peel I lowered like a proclamation into the hamsters' cage; careless grace of understatement, luxury of simple gesture after gesture (fork to mouth, mouth to glass, fork and glass rinsed in the sink, and— linger here, see the heat pulling fog up the glass, atilt and cooling in the drainboard). I'm calling up the tongue-and-groove gestures, the hook-and-eye moments of the day, so they might again spend themselves freely, mark the layers of events en route, classify the waiting.

451

Cajoled from somewhere back in the morning, the peeling of that tangerine (cut thumb plunged into the yielding core, stinging and wet and red) comes forth.

I am recalling such occasions for attention offered in a day I was free to ignore. And now, am not free at all (for this *is* a deposition): cutting burnt crust away; snagging a sock on a rough stair plank; digging a sliver of dirt from a nail under running water. I am tied to the sight of the world, to things burnished and scoured by use, and by their diminution loved—as I so loved and saved my grandmother's wooden cooking spoon, older than me, smooth as driftwood, when to relieve her boredom, her aide used it to plant and prop a geranium on the balcony. The spoon has folded into its profile, has tucked within it, englaciated, the rim of the aluminum roasting pan (why *that* of all the nicked sauce pans and ceramic bowls of creamy batters tapped and tapped and tapped against?). I took and washed (as my grandmother no longer can wash) its singed rack burns, its smooth neck, thinned from lifting huge roasts by their taut white lacings.

One idly picks up pinecones, rocks, shells to mark a moment, to commemorate time. One picks them up because they shine out from their mud, or water lapping brightens their veins and shorn faces, or there they are, wedged inexplicably whole in a jetty, and a spiral tip beckons, though the center be partial and broken.

## DEPOSITION ON WATCHES

That week my watch broke, so I borrowed my son's digital Monsters, Inc. strap-on. But I missed the clean, white face of my old one, its celestial circular sweep. The digital time that came to replace it dosed its minutes, shifted its numbers too economically one into the next, the angular 2 and angular 5 simple mirror images, a single bar across the middle making the 0 an 8. Then, as the days without schooltime unwound and were lashed together instead by flares of fear, spots of love, solemn noon bell at the cathedral, all the morning's held breath, all the whites piling, like suds, their calm expanse up, it was easy to wear no watch at all. But I have not become a person divested of watches. I miss the circle's perpetuity, dawn and dusk sharing the same space, if only for minutes. The hour pinning itself to the changing light of seasons.

The watch I want now—I saw a picture of it yesterday—posits a looker at the center, who to properly see the numbers would have to turn and face each one: already by 2 the numbers start to tilt so that the 6 is a 9 if you're outside looking in. But a 6 if you're in the middle. I like to think of standing in the center, arms reaching out and brushing all the minutes and hours.

I like the idea of turning to face the hour, having the hours arrayed around me. From a still point, having to face the increments of a day.

## DEPOSITION ON FAILURE

Last May, I remember, on this very sidewalk: a fly's soap-bubble, gasoline colors; taut grimace on the face of a baby bird, that hatched and unliving, ancient, pimpled bud on the grass; corms of daylilies, and "corm" itself that most perfect union of "corn" and "worm," meaning exactly the thick, stubborn grub I hacked to separate. I remember the ripe, raw, shivery scents.

But during this thaw, come on so fast now—just for a day, just for caprice, it was 60 degrees.

And when I went out walking and the sun was so soft—an assertion, bravura. Where warmth thawed the planes of bone like a high bank, my face was a running stream again. I took off my mittens and left them in the crook of a tree; it always takes a few days to believe the warmth.

The snow receded, the warmth returned, and I was fine. I was negative. *Negative, negative*, I was thinking, buoyant. The hard winter lifted all at once, the sun came, dewy and beading, the air was sweet and I was fine—oh burgeoning cliché I entertained, cannot believe I entertained: spring bearing its blood-tide and life all abloom, all's well ending well in a spate, a thrall of undulant weather, et cetera. Rising, on cue, such music as dripping icicles conduct, such shine and promise, oh window of light on the nibbled Red Delicious little Sam just dropped. And the neighbors' voices carrying, the out-of-doors voices lofting, reconfiguring again the space between our houses: it was New World Symphony, English horn-solo-fresh. I was a turning season, a spit of land at low tide, a window thrown open. Would you believe it if I told you (told *unto* you, lo! for real) I saw a butterfly—and it was corn-yellow? I resisted the easy convergence—*spring, warmth, I'm fine*—not a bit, and I knew that to be an indulgence, a failure, partial sight. As if I had come to the brightness of that day wholly—wholly—from dark.

But I cannot forget, for this is a deposition, that all that dark week

453

there was this, too: the diamond-blue light at each drift's core. My husband's abundant embrace. Sanctum of my child under quilts. In candlelight, sewing the ghost. Folding a swan. With books, in the folds of a story. Our son, himself, that most beloved unfolding.

And the color of the sky: workshirt-turned-inside-out, and the gray of our house against it, a darker inner seam, revealed. Our house an object that light chose for lavishing, a river stone eddied into calm. The tender crack in a baking loaf, its creamy rift rough at the edges and going gold. Of all the names for snow considered, of all the shifts in tone it made, I found clamshell, bone, and pearl. That week I found lead in the white, mouse in it, and refracted granite. Talc with pepper. Layers of dried mud, zinc, and iron. Blown milkweed and ashy cinder. Silvered cornfield. Uncooked biscuit. Mummy, oatmeal, sand, and linen. Some morning glory. Some roadside aster.

*Nominated by Agni*

# GLOSE

## by MARILYN HACKER

from BLOOM

> *Blood's risks, its hollows, its flames*
> *Exchanged for the pull of that song*
> *Bone-colored road, bone-colored sky*
> *Through the white days of the storm*
> Claire Malroux "Storm"
> (translated by Marilyn Hacker)

Once out of the grip of desire,
or, if you prefer, its embrace,
free to do nothing more than admire
the sculptural planes of a face
(are you gay, straight or bi, are you *queer?*)
you still tell your old chaplet of names
which were numinous once, you replace
them with adjectives: witty, severe,
trilingual; abstracting blood's claims,
blood's risks, its hollows, its flames.

No craving, no yearning, no doubt,
no repulsion that follows release,
no presence you can't do without,
no absence an hour can't erase:
the conviction no reason could rout
of being essentially wrong
is dispelled. What feels oddly like peace

now fills space you had blathered about
where the nights were too short or too long,
exchanged for the pull of that song.

But peace requires more than one creature
released from the habit of craving
on a planet that's mortgaged its future
to the lot who are plotting and raving.
There are rifts which no surgeon can suture
overhead, in the street, undersea.
The bleak plain from which you are waving,
mapped by no wise, benevolent teacher
is not a delight to the eye:
bone-colored road, bone-colored sky.

You know that the weather has changed,
yet do not know what to expect,
with relevant figures expunged
and predictions at best incorrect.
Who knows on what line you'll be ranged
and who, in what cause, you will harm?
What cabal or junta or sect
has doctored the headlines, arranged
for perpetual cries of alarm
through the white days of the storm?

*Nominated by Maureen Seaton, Grace Schulman, Reginald Shepherd*

# PURSUIT OF THE YELLOW HOUSE

## by ROBIN BEHN

from TRIQUARTERLY

The way the body builds a house
          around a grain in its own sight,
objecting to the object, mulling

       and mouthing it, washing and rubbing it,
          making a little gem of pain
the body soothes and swaddles in a small red

       pearl it sets upon the outer grasslands
          of the eye—
did the house arise around you

       because of something *other*, the barren
          possible, a tender, trembling mux
that flowed from you and cooled?

       Or did it first appear
          in the distance—
note-on-a-staff, hand-shaped bird,

       flickerings' ledger, cornice-of-a-cure—
          so that you,
Manger-Monger, Dank-

Hankerer, Daffodil-Whisperer, Termite-
                    Diviner and Would-Be Curator
of the Secret Stair where you did and you

            did and you wept and you
                    lay down and
no more than usual did the sun refuse you,

            pursued—
                    with wood with wooing with words—
this casket of sun this what-you-hath-done this

            deckled abyss this claw-colored *is*.
                    Mute vial.
Tear-on-a-string

            the color of use.
                    Amber ampul
to contain our space—all.

            To set us loose.


*Nominated by Molly Bendall, Edward Hirsch, Ralph Angel*

# THE BROTHERS

fiction by LYSLEY TENORIO

from MĀNOA

M̲Y BROTHER WENT ON NATIONAL TV to prove he was a woman. I don't know which talk show it was, but these words kept flashing at the bottom of the television screen: IS SHE A HE? IS HE A SHE? YOU DECIDE! The show went like this: a guest would come out onstage, and the audience would vote on whether or not she was the real thing.

They came out one at a time, these big-haired and bright-lipped women, most of them taller than most men. They worked the stage like strippers, bumping and grinding to the techno beat of the studio music. The audience rose to its feet, whistling and hooting, cheering them on.

Then came Eric.

My brother was different from the others. He was shorter, the only Filipino among them. He wore a denim skirt and a T-shirt, a pair of Doc Martens. His hair, a few strands streaked blonde, fell to his bony shoulders. He was slow across the stage, wooing the audience with a shy girl's face, flirtatious, sweet. But he wasn't woman enough for them: they booed my brother, gave him the thumbs down. So Eric fought back. He stood at the edge of the stage, pounded his chest like he was challenging them to a talkshow brawl. "Dare me?" he said, and I saw his hands move down to the bottom of his T-shirt. "You dare me?"

They did, and up it went. The audience went wild.

He put his shirt down, lifted his arms in triumph, blew kisses to the audience, and then took a chair with the other guests. He told the audience that his name was Erica.

I glanced at Ma. She looked as if someone had hit her in the face.

Eric had left a message the night before, telling me to watch Channel 4 at 7 P.M. He said it would be important, that Ma should see it, too. When I told Ma, she looked hopeful. "Maybe he's singing," she said. "Playing the piano?" She was thinking of the Eric of long ago, when he took music lessons and sang in the high-school choir.

I reached for the remote, thinking, *That bastard set us up.* I turned the TV off.

That was the last time I saw him. Now he's lying on a table, a sheet pulled to his shoulders, dead. The coroner doesn't hurry me, but I answer him fast. "Yes," I say. "That's him. My brother."

Eric's life was no secret, though we often wished it was: we knew about the boyfriends, the makeup and dresses. He told me about his job at HoozHoo, a bar in downtown San Francisco where the waitresses were drag queens or transsexuals. But a year and a half ago, when Eric announced on Thanksgiving night that he was going to proceed with a sex change ("Starting here," he said, patting his chest with his right hand), Ma left the table and told him that he was dead to her.

It's 6:22 P.M. He's been dead for six hours.

"We need to call people," I tell Ma. But she sits there at the kitchen table, still in her waitress uniform, whispering things to herself, rubbing her thumb along the curve of Eric's baby spoon. Next week she turns sixty-one. For the first time, she looks older than she is. "We have to tell people what's happened."

She puts down the spoon, finally looks at me. "What will I say? How can I explain it?"

"Tell them what the coroner told me. That's all." He had an asthma attack, rare and fatal. He was sitting on a bench in Golden Gate Park when his airways swelled so quickly, so completely, that no air could get in or out. When he was a kid, Eric's asthma was a problem; I can still hear the squeal of his panic. *Can't breathe, can't breathe,* he'd say, and I'd rub his back and chest like I was giving him life. But when he became an adult, the attacks were less frequent, easier to manage, and he called his inhaler a thing of the past. "The severity of this attack was unusual," the coroner explained. "There was no way he could have prepared for it." He was dead by the time a pair of ten-year-olds on Rollerblades found him.

460

The look on Ma's face makes me feel like a liar. "He couldn't breathe," I say. "It's the truth." I go through cupboards, open drawers, not sure what I'm looking for, so I settle for a mug and fill it with water, and though I'm not thirsty, I drink it all down. "He couldn't breathe. And then he died. When people ask, that's what you say."

Ma picks up the spoon again, and now I understand. "Ang bunso ko," she's been saying. *My baby boy,* over and over, as if Eric died as a child and she realized it only now.

The morning after the show, my brother called me at work. When I picked up the phone, he said, "Well . . . ?" as if we were already in the middle of a conversation, though we hadn't spoken in months, maybe half a year.

"You grew your hair out," I said. "It's blonde now."

"Extensions," he said.

"They look real."

"They're not." He took a deep breath. "But the rest of me is."

It was a little after seven. I was the only one in the office. Not even the tech guys were in yet. I turned and looked out the window, watched an old, bent man unlock the door to his newspaper kiosk, get ready to set up shop.

"Come on, Edmond," my brother said, "say something."

I didn't, so he did. He went on about being on TV, about flashing the audience and everyone at home. He said he was sorry if it hurt Ma and me, but this was a once-in-a-lifetime opportunity. "I showed the world what I'm made of," he said slowly, as if it was a line he'd been rehearsing for months. "What do you think of that?"

"I saw nothing," I said.

"What?"

"I saw nothing." It was the truth. When Eric lifted his shirt, they didn't use a black rectangle the way they sometimes do on TV to protect a person's identity. They didn't cut to a commercial or pan shocked faces in the audience. Instead, they blurred him out: just below his shoulders was a strip of scrambled air. It looked like he was disintegrating, molecule by molecule. "They blurred you out," I said.

I could hear him pace his apartment. I never went there, but I knew he was living in the Tenderloin in downtown San Francisco. The few times he called, things were always happening on his end: cars honking, sirens, people laughing or screaming each other's name. But that morning, there was just the sound of us breathing, first one

461

and then the other, as if we were taking turns. I imagined a pair of divers at the bottom of the ocean, sharing the same supply of air.

"You there?" I thought we'd been disconnected. "Eric, are you there?"

"No." Then he hung up.

And that was it for Eric and me.

I go to my apartment to get clothes, and I stay the night at Ma's. My old bed is still in my old room upstairs, but I take the living-room couch. I don't sleep, not for a minute. Before light comes, I call Delia in Chicago; her fiancé picks up. I ask for my wife, which irritates him. Technically, I'm right: the divorce isn't final, not yet. I'm still a husband, and I won't let that go, not until I have to.

He says she's not there.

"No message," I tell him, then hang up.

I'm still wide awake in the morning. Driving to the funeral home in North Oakland, I don't even yawn.

Loomis, the man who handled Dad's funeral eleven years ago, waits for us in a small square of shade outside the main office. He's heavier now, his hair thinner, all white. Back then he walked with a limp; today he uses a cane.

"Do you remember me?" It's the first thing Ma says to him. "And my husband?" She pulls a picture from her wallet, an old black-and-white of Dad in his navy days. He's wearing fatigues, looking cocky. His arms hang at his sides, but his fists are clenched as if he's ready for a fight. "Dominguez. First name Teodoro."

Loomis takes the photo, holds it at eye level, squints. "I do remember him," he says, though he only saw my father as a dead man. "And I remember you, too." He looks at me, shakes my hand. "The boy who never left his mother's side."

That was Eric. Ma knows it, too. We don't correct him.

The funeral doesn't take long to plan: Ma makes it the same as Dad's, ordering the same floral arrangements, the same prayer cards, the same music. Only the casket is different. Dad's was bronze, which best preserves the body. Eric's will be mahogany, a more economical choice. "It's all we can afford," Ma says.

Later, Loomis drives us through the cemetery to find a plot for Eric. We head to the west end, stop at the bottom of a small hill. "There," Ma says, walking uphill toward a small eucalyptus. She puts her hand on a low, thin branch, rubs a budding leaf between her fin-

462

gers. "It's growing." She quickly surveys the area, decides this is the place.

"But your knee." I point out the steepness of the hill, warn her that years from now, when she's older, getting to Eric will be difficult.

"Then you help me," Ma says, starting toward the car. "You help me get to him."

Back home, Ma calls the people we couldn't reach the night before, and each conversation is the same: she greets the person warmly and pauses, but can't catch herself before she gives in to tears. Meanwhile, I get the house ready, vacuuming upstairs and down, wiping dirty window screens with wet rags, rearranging furniture to accommodate all the guests who will pray for my brother's soul. We'll have nine nights of this.

"I hate the way Filipinos die," Eric once said. It was the week of Dad's funeral. "Nine nights of praying on our knees, lousy Chinese food, and hundred-year-old women asking me where my girlfriend is." The businessmen were worse. On the last night of Dad's novena, one guy—he said he was related to us but couldn't explain how—tried selling life insurance to Eric and me. He quoted figures on what we could get for injury, dismemberment, and death, and even took out a pocket calculator to prove how valuable our lives were. "Promise me, Edmond," Eric had said, "when I die, take one night to remember me. That's all. No kung pao chicken. No old people. No assholes telling you how much you'll get for my severed leg." He came close to crying, but then he managed a smile. "And make sure Village People is playing in the background."

" 'YMCA'?"

" 'Macho Man,' " he said. "Play it twice."

He started laughing. I started laughing. The house was full of mourners, but we kept to ourselves in one corner of the room, wearing matching two-piece suits from Sears and joking around like the closest of brothers. But now I know that we were wrong to talk as though I would outlive him. I was five years older than Eric, and he was only twenty-six when he died.

Brothers are supposed to die in the correct order. I keep thinking, *Tonight should be for me.*

By six, the house fills with visitors. A dozen or so at first. Soon it's fifty. I stop counting at seventy-five.

463

Strangers tell me they're family. They try to simplify the intricate ways we're related: suddenly they're cousins, aunts and uncles, the godchildren of my grandparents. Not one of these people has seen my brother in years, has any idea of the ways he's changed. All they know about him is that he's dead.

Twice, an elderly woman calls me Eric by mistake.

When an old neighbor asks, "Where's Delia?" Ma answers before I can. She's embarrassed by the idea of divorce, so she says that Delia is on the East Coast for business, but will be here as soon as possible. I wish it was true: I keep checking the door, thinking that Delia might walk in any moment, that somehow she found out what happened and took the next flight out to be with me. Eric's death could have been our breakthrough, the turn she said our life needed. I try not to think of tonight as a lost opportunity for Delia and me.

At seven, we get to our knees, pray before the religious shrine Ma's set up on top of the TV—a few porcelain figurines of Jesus Christ and the Virgin Mary, laminated prayer cards in wood frames, plastic rosaries. In front of the TV screen, an arm's reach from me, stands an infant-sized ceramic statuette of Santo Niño, the baby Jesus Christ. All good Filipino Catholic families have one, but I haven't seen ours in years. He still looks weird to me, with his red velvet cape trimmed with gold thread and a crown to match, silver robes, brown corn-silk hair falling past his shoulders, the plastic flower in his hand.

When Eric was small, he thought Santo Niño was a girl: I caught him in his bedroom, kneeling on the floor, and Santo Niño was naked, his cape, robes, and crown in a small, neat pile by Eric's foot. For the first time, I saw how he was made: only the hands and face had been painted to look like skin; everyplace else was unglazed and white, chipped in spots. "See," Eric said, his finger in the empty space between Santo Niño's legs, "he's a girl." I called him an idiot, tried to get it through his head that he was just a statue, a ceramic body that meant nothing. "Santo Niño is a boy," I said, "say it." He wouldn't, so I took Santo Niño from Eric, held him above my head. Eric jumped, reaching to get him back, then knocked him out of my hands.

Ma heard the crash, ran upstairs, and found pieces of Santo Niño scattered at our feet. Before she could speak, I pointed at the pile of clothes on the floor and told her what Eric had done and said.

I tried putting Santo Niño back together in my room as I listened to Eric getting hit.

But my brother had a point. At eye level and an arm's reach away,

464

this second Santo Niño—the one Ma bought to replace the one we broke—does look like a girl: glass-blue eyes, long black lashes, a red-lipped smile, a rose in one hand. While everyone's eyes are shut tight in prayer, I reach out and try to take the flower. It's glued to his fist.

What started as prayer is now a dinner party, and Ma is on top of everything. She makes sure the egg rolls stay warm, that there's enough soy sauce in the chow mein. I hear her gossip with neighbors who moved away long ago, watch her hold the babies of women who grew up on our street. In the Philippines, my parents threw three to four parties a year, and Ma boasted how her wedding was the grandest her province had ever seen. She promised equally grand weddings for us. But I was twenty-one when Delia and I eloped, and she gave up on Eric long ago. Funerals and novenas, I think, are all Ma has left.

People keep coming. I try to stay close to familiar faces: I comfort Mrs. Gonzalez, Eric's second-grade teacher, who's brought the crayon portraits he drew on paper sacks. I talk with Isaac Chavez, Eric's best friend from grade school and the first boy, Eric confessed to me later, he ever loved. He never told Isaac. Maybe I should. But when Isaac introduces me to his new wife, I know it's best not to complicate the night.

When the Agbayani brothers walk in, I stay away. At a Fourth-of-July picnic long ago, they found Eric under a slide, making daisy chains and singing love songs at the top of his lungs. I watched as they called him a girl, a sissy, a faggot. "That's what you get for playing with flowers," I told him later.

Ma catches me in the kitchen. "We're out of ice," she says. Beside her is a Filipino woman rattling ice cubes in her plastic cup. She looks like she came to dance instead of pray: her black hair falls in waves past her shoulders, and her tight, black dress ends above the knee. In her high-heeled boots, she's as tall as I am.

"No problem." I lift the cooler, step outside. The freezer is in the backyard, and its low hum is the only sign of life out there. The lawn is nothing but weeds. Ma's roses are gone. And the four stalks of sugar cane Dad planted when he bought the house—one for each of us—have been dried sticks for years.

I take out a blue bag of ice from the freezer, then pound it against the concrete, breaking it up. Behind me the glass door slides open: it's the woman who wanted ice. "This OK?" she asks, indicating the cigarette between her fingers.

465

I slide the door shut. "It is now."

"I'm Raquel."

"Edmond." We shake hands.

"The brother." She lets go. "Cold."

Icy flakes stick to my fingers. I wipe them on my pants. "You're friends with Eric?"

"Sisters. That's what we call ourselves, anyway." She lights the cigarette, takes a drag, then lets out a long breath of smoke. "I have no family here. They're all back in Manila, pissed at me for leaving. So she became my sister. Sweet, huh?"

*Sisters. She.* It's like this woman is testing me to see what I know and don't know about my brother.

"Eric always wanted a sister," I say.

"Well, if we're sisters, then that makes you my Kuya Edmond, right?"

"*Kuya?*" My Tagalog is more rusty than I thought.

"Big brother." She unfolds a lawn chair and sits down. She crosses her legs, rests an elbow on her knee, places her chin on her hand, and looks at me closely. "How are you?"

Not even the coroner asked me that when I saw the body. "Fine." I squat down, smash more ice. "Holding up."

"Not me. Last night, when you left that message at the bar, I wanted to erase it. I was thinking, 'I don't know anyone named Eric, and I don't know an "Eric's brother." ' But I knew who you meant."

She describes the rest of the night: how they closed the HoozHoo early, gathered the waitresses and the regulars together, drank and wept and sang songs until morning. Before everyone went home, they stood in a circle on the dance floor, held hands, and said a prayer. The music was off, but the lights were on, a disco ball spinning above them. "It looked like heaven," she says. "All the girls wanted to come tonight, but I told them no. It should just be me. Out of respect for your mother."

It's like the start of a joke: *A dozen drag queens walk in on eighty Filipinos on their knees praying* . . . I can picture the rest of it: six-foot-tall women in six-inch heels, glittering in a crowd of people dressed in black. I can see the stares, hear the whispers, Ma in the middle of it all, wishing them away. But maybe everyone would have been fooled, taken them as the very girlfriends that old ladies pestered Eric about. I knew from the start what Raquel was, but so much of her looks real, like she was born into the body she made.

466

"You're staring at my tits, hon."

The ice slips from my hand, slides across the cement and onto the dirt.

She manages a smile, shrugs her shoulders. "People look all the time." She looks at them herself. "Four years ago, when I came to the States"—she puts her hand over her heart—"there's nothing here. Empty. So now, if people want to look, I let them. They're mine, right?" She puts out her cigarette, lights another. "It's the same thing with Erica. Hers turned out really nice, really—"

"More ice?" I point to the freezer. "There's ice."

She reaches out, puts her hand on my shoulder. "I've embarrassed you. Sorry. That wasn't Coke in my cup." Raquel pulls a silver flask from her purse, unscrews the top, and turns it upside down. "All gone," she sighs. "I should be gone, too." She gets up, but she's off balance. I catch her in time. "Walk me to the door?" Her hands are tight on my wrist. I don't know that I have a choice.

We step inside, work our way through the crowds in the kitchen, the living room. People look but don't stare, and I think we can slip out quietly. But when Raquel remembers her coat and walks to the closet by the stairs, I think of leaving her to rejoin the crowd. The Agbayani brothers are on the couch, eyeing Raquel and smirking at one another. My guess is that they've gone from being childhood bullies to the kind of men who would follow a girl to her car with whistles and catcalls.

I help Raquel with her coat. "Let me walk you to your car."

She smiles as if it's the nicest thing anyone has said to her all day. "I'm at the end of the street." We step outside, walk down the driveway. Beyond tipsy, Raquel takes my arm again.

"Maybe you should've had Coke after all," I say.

"No," she says, "I need to be this way tonight."

We get to her car, a Honda covered with scratches and dents. Where a back window should be are plastic and duct tape. "Time for you to go back home," she says to me while leaning against the door. She searches her purse for her keys, not realizing she's holding them in her left hand.

Then she says, "Oh, shit."

On the corner, seven tall women empty out of a minivan and head toward Ma's house, their heels clicking loudly against the sidewalk. They look like a kind of sorority, all of them made up the same way to let the world know who they are. "I told them they shouldn't," Raquel

467

says. "I told them." She rubs her forehead, starts toward them, but I don't let her go. "Let them pay their respects," I say. "It's fine." I take her arm, slip the keys from between her fingers, and walk her to the passenger's door. Then I help her in and return to the driver's side.

"What about your guests?" Raquel asks.

"I don't have any." I start the car, watch the women enter Ma's house one by one. "Where to?"

"San Francisco."

I drive down Telegraph Avenue, head for the bridge.

"You're a nice man, Kuya Edmond." Raquel reclines her seat, turns to the window as if she's watching the moon. "Can I call you that? *Kuya*?"

"Why not." No one else will, and Eric never did.

It's less than ten minutes from Ma's house to the bridge, and yet I never cross it. Yesterday, when I drove to ID the body, it was the first time in nine years that I'd been to San Francisco.

The time before that was when Ma kicked Eric out. He was seventeen. She found him in his bedroom, made up as a girl and in bed with a guy. She told them to leave and warned Eric not to come back. "For good this time," he said on the phone. "But there's nowhere for me to go." He was breathing fast and heavy, fighting tears.

"Find a place," I said, "and I'll drive you there."

When I got to the house, he was sitting on the curb, a duffel bag and a yellow beanbag at his feet. He looked up at me, and what I thought were bruises was just smeared makeup. "She tried wiping it off with a dishrag," he said. "Couldn't she have just slapped me instead?"

"Get in the car." I went inside to check on Ma. She was sitting at the top of the stairs, still in her Denny's uniform, Dad's terry-cloth robe draped over her lap. She had just gotten home from a late shift when she found Eric. "I brought home a sandwich for him," she said. "He doesn't want to take it. If you're hungry . . ."

"I'm not," I said.

She nodded, went to her room. I heard her lock the door.

I went back outside, got in the car. Eric was in the passenger's seat, putting on lipstick. I grabbed his wrist, squeezing so hard that he dropped it. "Didn't I tell you," I was shouting now, "you don't do this here! You want to play dress-up, that's fine. But not in Ma's house. You keep it to yourself."

"I'm not playing dress-up."

I started driving. "Just tell me where to go."

He gave directions, and before I realized it, I was on the Bay Bridge, bound for the city. He had a friend with a spare couch who lived in the Mission District. I headed down South Van Ness, turned in to a dark street that got darker the further down we went. "Stop here," he said, and I pulled up in front of an old peeling Victorian.

"Take this," I said, and I put four twenty-dollar bills in his hand. He looked at the money like it was more than a person deserved, then took one bill and gave the rest back. "Mother's Day is coming up," he reminded me. He asked if I could buy Ma flowers, if they could be from the both of us. I nodded.

He got out of the car, but before he closed the door, he leaned in and said, "It was the first perfect night I ever had. Know what I mean?"

I didn't. "Call me in a few days," I said.

Eric walked toward the front door, dragging his things behind him. At the top of the driveway, he turned around. We looked at each other as though neither of us knew who should be the first to go.

What I wished then I'm wishing now: that I'd reached over and opened the passenger door. Maybe then we could have made our way back home, or someplace else. An all-night diner. A road that dead-ended with a view of the city. If we'd had more time, maybe things could have stayed the same.

It took me hours to find my way back to Oakland.

Ma spoke to Eric again a year later, just in time for his high-school graduation. But she never asked him back, and he never asked to come back. Eric's room is storage space now, but mine is as I left it: my childhood bed against the window, my blue, square desk beside it, Dad's wood-and-wicker rocking chair in the corner. It's like she knew that Eric was never coming back and that I always would.

I tap Raquel on her shoulder. "Wake up," I say. "We're here. Tell me where to go."

For now, Raquel is homeless; a pipe burst in her apartment building three weeks before, flooding every unit. She'd been staying with Eric ever since. Had she said this before I got in her car, I'm not sure what I would have done.

It takes over thirty minutes to find parking, and when we do, it's blocks away. Walking, we pass drunken college boys flirting with prostitutes, homeless kids sharing a bottle, cops who seem oblivious to everything around them. "I get scared at night," Raquel says. I let her hold my arm.

Eric's building is on Polk Street. Two teenaged girls sit on the front steps, smoking cigarettes. "New boyfriend, Miss Raquel?" one says.

"Ask me again in the morning and I'll tell you." Raquel laughs, highfives both girls.

We take the stairs to the third floor, head down a narrow hallway lit by fading fluorescent lights. Eric's apartment number is 310. The door is white, like all the rest. "I'd meant to visit," I say. Raquel says nothing.

She takes the keys, opens the door. "After you, Kuya." I don't know how I'm getting home.

Those times I spoke to Eric on the phone, I imagined him sitting on his windowsill and pictured what his apartment might look like: wigs and dresses piled on a red leather couch and scattered on the floor, Christmas lights framing every window and wall or hanging from the ceiling. It was a place where I would stand in the middle with my arms folded against my chest, careful not to touch anything; I'd keep an eye on the door, ready to escape at any moment. But when I step inside the apartment, everything is muted: metal desk, cream-colored futon, cinderblock shelf with a stack of books. On the windowsill are two framed pictures: one of Ma and Dad in Long Beach, when they first came to the States; and the other of me, from a time I don't remember. I'm just a kid, four or five, looking unbelievably happy. I don't know why or how. It seems impossible that anyone could be that pleased with life.

Raquel offers tissue. I tell her I'm fine.

She opens the tiny refrigerator beneath the desk, takes out a Mountain Dew and a small bottle of vodka. She mixes them in a paper cup, stirs it with her finger.

Then she takes out a bottle of pills from her purse.

"Headache?" I ask.

"Nothing's wrong with my head." She pops a pill in her mouth, sips her drink, makes a face when she swallows, as if it hurts. "Hormones," she says. "No pain, no gain." She takes another sip.

"There's pain?"

"Figure of speech, Kuya. It goes down easy."

"There must be pain. There has to be." I think of Eric on a table, surgeons cutting into his body, needles vanishing into his skin. I think

470

of that studio audience, giving him the thumbs down, like a jury deciding his life. I think of Ma telling Eric he's dead. "The things you do. To prove yourself. We loved him as he was. That should have been enough."

Raquel walks over, stands in front of me, eye to eye. "You think that's why we do this? To prove a point to you? Listen, Kuya Edmond. All of this"—she unfolds her arms, takes my hand by the wrist, and puts it on the center of her chest—"I did for me." She presses my hand into herself as if she wants me to feel her heartbeat, then lets me go before I can feel anything.

I tug at my watch. "I should go home."

"I'll walk you out."

As we go down the stairs, I make a tentative plan to stop by the following week and pick up some of Eric's things, though I'm not sure what I can rightfully claim. Raquel says yes, of course, anytime, like she doesn't believe that I will ever come this way again.

Outside we stand on the corner. Raquel flags down a cab for me. Before I get in, she hands me forty dollars for the ride back to Oakland and refuses when I tell her to take it back. "You brought me home," she says. "If you didn't, I could be dead, too." She starts crying, then puts her hand on my face. I don't come closer, but I don't pull away either. "She loves you," she whispers, "believe me." Then she holds me, her body pressing against mine. I wonder if this is how Eric felt after he changed, if the new flesh made him feel closer to the person he held. I won't ever know, but I wish I could stay this way a little longer and listen to Raquel whisper about Eric the way she just did, in the present tense, like he's still going on.

The next morning, Ma is sitting at the bottom of the stairs, a vinyl garment bag over her lap. Eric's body is being prepared for the viewing, and we need to deliver his clothes. She says nothing about the girls from HoozHoo, doesn't ask me where I was the night before. But on the way to the funeral home, I can feel her staring at me, like she's waiting for me to confess something.

Loomis is waiting in the lobby. "We've set up a room, Mrs. Dominguez," he says. We follow him through the lobby, pass his office, and continue down the hallway. "There's a phone right by the door, if you need anything." We stop in front of a metal door. He looks serious, like he's worried for us. "It's not too late to change your mind."

Ma shakes her head.

Loomis takes a breath, nods. "All right then." He turns to me. "It's good that you're here," he says, then leaves.

Ma opens the door. I close it behind us. Eric lies on a metal table with wheels, a gray sheet covering him from the neck down. Hanging over the edge is a single strand of hair, the darkest thing in this white room. I can see the incision on his neck, the thread keeping his lips shut.

Ma takes the garment bag from my hands. She goes to Eric. I stay by the door. "They have staff who can do this," I tell her.

She hangs the bag on a hook on the wall, unzips it. It's a suit. One of Dad's. "We have to change him." The sheet between them, Ma puts her hand on Eric's right arm and rubs it up and down. She bends over, whispers, "Ang bunso ko," between kisses to his cheek, his forehead, his cheek again, weeping. For a moment I mistake this for tenderness, her gesture of amends, a last chance to dress him the way she did when he was a boy.

Then she wipes her eyes, stands up straight, takes a long, deep breath, and pulls several rolls of Ace bandages out of her purse. Now I understand.

She lifts the sheet, folds it neatly down to his abdomen. For the first time, we see them, his breasts. They look cold and hard and dead as the rest of him, like they have always been part of his body. If this was how he wanted to live, then this was how he wanted to die.

"Lift his arms," Ma says.

I don't move.

"This will work. I saw it on TV. Women who try to look like men. This is what they do."

"You can't."

"Everyone will see him tonight," Ma says. She unrolls the bandage, fingers trembling.

I tell her to forget tradition and custom, to keep the casket closed, locked up for good. "You picked out a nice casket for him. Beautiful flowers." I keep my voice calm and move toward her slowly, as if I'm trying to stop her from jumping off the ledge of a skyscraper. "Just let him be this way. They won't see," I say, "they won't know."

"I will," she says.

I reach for her arm, but she pulls back. She steps around, stands behind Eric's head, slips her hands beneath his shoulders, and manages to raise him a few inches off the table, but he slips from her hands. She tries again, her arms shaking from the weight of him.

472

"Please," she says, looking at me. One way or another, she means to do this, and I know she'll hurt herself if I don't help.

I walk over to the body. The light in here is different from that in the morgue. Yesterday, the room seemed filled with a gray haze, and it took me only a second to identify my brother. Today, the light makes shadows on his face, and I notice the sharpness of his cheekbones, the thin arch of his eyebrows. His lips are fuller than I remember, his neck more narrow. "It's still him," I say, but Ma ignores me.

His body hard from the embalming fluid inside him, he is heavier than I expect. To lift him up, I have to slip my arms beneath his, fold them across his chest. I hold him and I don't care how we look: we are together and we should stay this way, for all the moments we can. We have been apart for so long; soon he'll be gone for good. "Leave him alone," I say, but Ma doesn't listen. Her hands separate me from my brother as she works the bandage round and round his breasts. I kiss the back of his neck once, in love and in apology.

Ma continues, bandage after bandage, rolling so tightly the breasts vanish back into him like they never existed. If my brother was alive, he wouldn't be able to breathe.

I say nothing to Ma on the way back to her house. When I let her off at the bottom of the driveway, I don't wait until she makes it to the door. I just drive away, refrain from looking in the rearview mirror, in case she's still there.

Before I know it, I'm on Telegraph Avenue, heading for the bridge. Once I'm past the tollgate, I have to force myself not to speed. I take slow, deep breaths as I get closer to the city.

I make my way to the Tenderloin and, as if I was meant to, find a parking spot right in front of Eric's building. I hurry inside, pass the two girls on the doorstep who were there last night, run up the three flights of stairs and down the hall to the end. I knock on the door, hunched over, out of breath.

"Who is it?" Raquel says.

"Edmond," I say. "The brother."

And she opens to me.

*Nominated by Eric Puchner, Mānoa*

# THE INVENTION OF STREETLIGHTS

## by COLE SWENSEN

from GOEST (ALICE JAMES BOOKS)

> *noctes illustratas*
> (the night has houses)
>                          and the shadow of the fabulous
>                 broken into handfuls—these
> can be placed at regular intervals,
>                          candles
> walking down streets at times eclipsed by trees.

Certain cells, it's said, can generate light on their own.

There are organisms that could fit on the head of a pin
and light entire rooms.

Throughout the Middle Ages, you could hire a man
on any corner with a torch to light you home

                          were lamps made of horn
and from above a loom of moving flares, we watched
Notre Dame seem small.
Now the streets stand still.

By 1890, it took a pound of powdered magnesium
to photograph a midnight ball.

While as early as 50 BCE, riotous soldiers leaving a Roman bath
sliced through the ropes that hung the lamps from tree to tree
                        and aloft us this
                        new and larger room
*Flambeaux the arboreal*
                        was the life of Julius Caesar
        in whose streets
        in which a single step could be heard.
We opened all our windows
and looked out on a listening world laced here and there with points
    of light,
                        *Notre Dame of the Unfinished Sky,*
oil slicks burning on the river; someone down on the corner
striking a match to read by.

Some claim Paris was the first modern city to light its streets.
        The inhabitants were ordered
        in 1524 to place a taper
        in every window in the dark there were 912 streets
                walked into this arc until by stars
                makes steps sharp, you are
        and are not alone
by public decree
October 1558: the lanterns were similar to those used in mines:
"Once
we were kings"
                        and down into the spiral of our riches
still reign: *falots* or great vases of pitch lit
at the crossroads
                —and thus were we followed
                        through a city of thieves—which,
but a few weeks later, were replaced by chandeliers.

While others claim all London was alight by 1414.
                In utter vigil ordered:
*Out of every window, come a wrist with a lanthorn*
                                        and were told
                                        hold it there
                and be on time
and not before

475

and watched below
the faces lit, and watched the faces pass.     And turned back in
(the face goes on) and watched the lights go out.
Here the numbers are instructive:
                    In the early 18th century,
London hung some 15,000 lamps.
And now we find (1786) they've turned to crystal, placed precisely
and each its own distance, small in islands,
large in the time it would take to run.


                    And Venice started in 1687 with a bell


                    upon the hearing of which, we all in unison
exit,
match in hand, and together strike them against an upper tooth and
touch the tiny flame to anything, and when times get rough (crime
up, etc.) all we have to do is throw oil out upon the canals to make
the lighting uncommonly extensive. Sometimes we do it just to shock
the rest of Europe, and at other times because we find it beautiful.

Says Libanius
                    Night differs us
                              Without us
                              *noctes illustratas*
                                        Though in times of public grief
when the streets were left unlit, on we went, just
dark marks in the markets and voices in the cafes,
in the crowded squares, a single touch,
                                        the living, a lantern
swinging above the door
any time a child is born, be it
                              Antioch, Syria, or Edessa—
and then there were the festivals,
                    the *festum encaeniorum*, and others in which
                    they call idolatrous, these torches
                                        half a city wide
                                                  be your houses.


*Nominated by Reginald Shepherd, Alice James Books*

# SPECIAL MENTION

(The editors also wish to mention the following important works published by small presses last year. Listings are in no particular order.)

## POETRY

Dog Gospel—Brian Barker (Poetry)
Lenten Stanzas—Robert Cording (Southern Review)
Facts About The Moon—Dorianne Laux (Speakeasy)
The Good Newes From Plimoth—David Roderick (Missouri Review)
The Art of the Nature Poem—Robert Wrigley (Georgia Review)
Things Chinese—Adrienne Su (Prairie Schooner)
Wound Man: Apologie and Tretise—Beckian Fritz Goldberg (TriQuarterly)
Aquarium Fire—Joy Katz (Cincinnati Review)
Dear Lacuna, Dear Lard—Paisley Rekdal (Poetry)
Tonight—Mark Kraushaar (Gettysburg Review)
Mortogenesis—Bruce Beasley (Shenandoah)
The words I did not say . . .—Killarney Clary (Xantippe)
Zeus—Laura Kasischke (Iowa Review)
Early Snow—James Richardson (Boulevard)
I Think Satan Done It—David Kirby (Shenandoah)
Ode To W. E. Diemer—Barbara Hamby (Yale Review)
Torn—C. Dale Young (Virginia Quarterly Review)
Lions Are Interesting—Joel Brouwer (Poetry)
Names We Sing In Sleep and Anger—Amaud Jamaul Johnson (New England Review)
Before You Leave—Holly Henke (Seattle Review)
Marriage In Canaan—D. Nurkse (Kenyon Review)

Taxidermy—Jo McDougall (*Satisfied With Havoc*, Autumn House)

Blue Crab—Carol Frost (9th Letter)

Not Only Parallel Lines Extend to the Infinite—Jane Hirshfield (Atlanta Review)

To The Green Man—Mark Jarman (*To The Green Man*, Sarabande Books)

Summertime—R.T. Smith (Georgia Review)

Techno—Dana Levin (Kenyon Review)

A Grave—Elizabeth Spires (Iowa Review)

Just-So Story—Eleanor Wilner (*The Girl With Bees In Her Hair*, Copper Canyon)

Arkansas Good Friday—Franz Wright (Image)

The Trent Lott McNamara Blues—Gerald Stern (5 a.m.)

Evening Walk As The School Year Starts—Sydney Lea (Hudson Review)

Bad Intelligence—Tony Hoagland (TriQuarterly)

Echocardiogram—Suzanne Cleary (Connecticut Review)

Winter Solstice: Newgrange, Ireland—Richard Foerster (TriQuarterly)

It Happens—Donna Masini (MS.)

## NONFICTION

The Mirror Diary—Garrett Hongo (Georgia Review)

A Pick To The Heart—Floyd Skloot (Boulevard)

Song For My Father—Sebastian Matthews (Virginia Quarterly Review)

Gone West: Farmers, Pirates, And Suitcase Ranchers—Douglas Unger (Colorado Review)

Reflections from A Concrete Shore—Donna Seaman (TriQuarterly)

Aquariums—Todd Newberry (Threepenny Review)

William Metts, American Poet—Paul Zimmer (New Letters)

Desire Distilled—Susan Straight (Speakeasy)

The Writing Life: Envy and Editing—Daniel Harris (Antioch Review)

Bodies Swayed to Music—Willard Spiegelman (Yale Review)

Last Making—Brad Comann (Raritan)

My Paris—Edmund White (Boulevard)

The Rat Pack—Barrie Jean Borich (Speakeasy)

The Bioterrorism Scare—Philip Alcabes (American Scholar)

Engagement—Terry Tempest Williams (Orion)

Toward The Black Interior—Elizabeth Alexander (*The Black Interior*, Graywolf Press)

Same, Same But Different—Lee Minh McGuire (Michigan Quarterly Review)

Dogs: A Moscow Triptych—Martha Cooley (Agni)

Letter To A German Friend—C. K. Williams (Salmagundi)

On Leaving Normal Behind—Laura S. Distelheim (Iowa Review)

Love In A Box—Andrew Hudgins (American Scholar)

Faith And The Impossible: The Gay Sublime—Linda Gregerson (Georgia Review)

Footnote On Metaphor—Alyce Miller (Fouth Genre)

From Baghdad To Brooklyn—Jack Marshall (ZYZZYVA)

Poor Dick—Blake Bailey (Harvard Review)

Shock And Awe: Anthologies And The Nortonization of Poetry—David Wojahn (Shenandoah)

The Fence—Jonis Agee (Colorado Review)

The Sky Is Falling, the Sky Is Falling:—Art Spiegelman (Virginia Quarterly Review)

On Being Text—Sallie Tisdale (Fourth Genre)

FICTION

Wonder—Derek Nikitas (Ontario Review)

Unkindness of Ravens—Maureen Farr (Eggemoggin Reach Review)

The Peacock—Tom Annese (Quick Fiction)

Faith—Aimee Liu (Other Voices)

Industries of the Blind—Ethan Hauser (Witness)

Uncle Simon and Gene—Richard Burgin (Witness)

The Arabian Nights Shift—Jorge Saralegui (ZYZZYVA)

Peter Lorre In The Afterlife—Howard Norman (Conjunctions)

Ordination—Scott Kaukonen (Third Coast)

The Convert—Bruce Jay Friedman (Antioch Review)

The Women Were Leaving The Men—Andy Mozina (Tin House)

Executors of Important Energies—Wells Tower (McSweeney's)

The Guide—Robin Black (Indiana Review)

The Drought—Miles Harvey (Ploughshares)

Intimacy and the Feast—Leslie Daniels (Ploughshares)

Dream Boy—David Michael Kaplan (TriQuarterly)

The Fifth Wall—Malinda McCollum (Paris Review)

The Boucherie—Stephanie Soileau (StoryQuarterly)

481

ICU—Dennis Lehane (Beloit Fiction)
Small Mercies—Tim Winton (At Length)
The Identity Club—Richard Burgin (TriQuarterly)
Wolves—Susan Fromberg Schaeffer (Prairie Schooner)
Future House—Alice Mattison (Glimmer Train)
The Taste of Dirt—Allen Wier (Five Points)
The Wamsutter Wolf—Annie Proulx (Paris Review)
Appearance of Scandal—Erin McGraw (Daedalus)
The Secret Life of Margaret Dumont—Lorraine Mavis Lupo (New England Review)
The Bridge—Cary Holladay (Hudson Review)
My Father, The Perfect Man—Vivek Narayanan (Agni)
Five Forgotten Instincts—Dan Chaon (Other Voices)
The Matinee—Jack Pulaski (Agni)
Quick—T.M. McNally (Crazyhorse)
The Exclusive Interview—Kate Braverman (ZYZZYVA)
Life Drawing—Suzanne Pivecca (Another Chicago Magazine)
Wandering Boy—James Gish Jr. (Phoebe)
Ghost Town—Elizabeth Parrish (Antietam Review)
Self-Portrait in Camouflage—Marjorie Hudson (West Branch)
Grips—L. Button (Passages North)
Scoldings—Rebekah Bloyd (Sou'wester)
The Romona Tomorrow Story—Gary Gildner (Contemporary West)
Across From The Shannonso—Joanna Scott (Cincinnati Review)
From The Personal Record Collection of Beniamino Gigli—Shelley Costa (Georgia Review)
Savasana—Rick Moody (Paris Review)
Cana II—Starkey Flythe, Jr. (Inkwell)
The Physicist—Alexander Blackburn (War, Literature and The Arts)
Bête Noire—Rick DeMarinis (Antioch Review)
The Weight of the World—Yelizaveta P. Renfro (Alaska Quarterly Review)
Smokestack Polka—Patrick Michael Finn (Third Coast)
Angel Moreno—Jeff Percifield (Caribbean Writer)
The Penance Practicum—Erin McGraw (Kenyon Review)
The Prize—Edwidge Danticat (Caribbean Writer)
Our Lady of the Artichokes—Katherine Vaz (Pleiades)
Chicken Bus Girl—Stephanie Dickinson (Tiferet)
Fallout—Jacob M. Appel (Colorado Review)

The Behavior of Sea Creatures—Bradford Tice (Alaska Quarterly Review)
Brief Lives of the Trainmen—Alyson Hagy (Idaho Review)
The Skull Hunter—Robert Day (New Letters)
The Offering—Jean McGarry (Boulevard)
Poor Cousins—Sheila M. Schwartz (Hunger Mountain)
Number One Tuna—Amber Dermont (Open City)
From Farrow To Fork—Rita Welty Bourke (North American Review)
Scorched Earth—Deirdra McAfee (Paper Street)
The Gateway—T.M. McNally (Conjunctions)
Private Dance—Donald Hays (Southern Review)
Bashi Ja-lut—Dev Hathaway (Gettysburg Review)
Disquisition on Tears—Stephanie Reents (Epoch)
Black Box—Michael Martone (Mid-American Review)
Ice—Kim Addonizio (Mississippi Review)
Beach Ball—Christopher Torockio (Gettysburg Review)

# PRESSES FEATURED IN THE PUSHCART PRIZE EDITIONS SINCE 1976

Acts

Agni

Ahsahta Press

Ailanthus Press

Alaska Quarterly Review

Alcheringa/Ethnopoetics

Alice James Books

Ambergris

Amelia

American Letters and Commentary

American Literature

American PEN

American Poetry Review

American Scholar

American Short Fiction

The American Voice

Amicus Journal

Amnesty International

Anaesthesia Review

Another Chicago Magazine

Antaeus

Antietam Review

Antioch Review

Apalachee Quarterly

Aphra

Aralia Press

The Ark

Art and Understanding

Arts and Letters

Artword Quarterly

Ascensius Press

Ascent

Aspen Leaves

Aspen Poetry Anthology

Assembling

Atlanta Review

Autonomedia

Avocet Press

The Baffler

Bakunin

Bamboo Ridge

Barlenmir House

Barnwood Press

Barrow Street

Bellevue Literary Review

The Bellingham Review

Bellowing Ark

Beloit Poetry Journal

Bennington Review

Bilingual Review

Black American Literature Forum

Blackbird

Black Rooster

Black Scholar

Black Sparrow
Black Warrior Review
Blackwells Press
Bloom
Bloomsbury Review
Blue Cloud Quarterly
Blue Unicorn
Blue Wind Press
Bluefish
BOA Editions
Bomb
Bookslinger Editions
Boston Review
Boulevard
Boxspring
Bridge
Bridges
Brown Journal of Arts
Burning Deck Press
Caliban
California Quarterly
Callaloo
Calliope
Calliopea Press
Calyx
Canto
Capra Press
Caribbean Writer
Carolina Quarterly
Cedar Rock
Center
Chariton Review
Charnel House
Chattahoochee Review
Chautauqua Literary Journal
Chelsea
Chicago Review
Chouteau Review
Chowder Review
Cimarron Review
Cincinnati Poetry Review
City Lights Books
Cleveland State Univ. Poetry Ctr.

Clown War
CoEvolution Quarterly
Cold Mountain Press
Colorado Review
Columbia: A Magazine of Poetry and
    Prose
Confluence Press
Confrontation
Conjunctions
Connecticut Review
Copper Canyon Press
Cosmic Information Agency
Countermeasures
Counterpoint
Crawl Out Your Window
Crazyhorse
Crescent Review
Cross Cultural Communications
Cross Currents
Crosstown Books
Cumberland Poetry Review
Curbstone Press
Cutbank
Dacotah Territory
Daedalus
Dalkey Archive Press
Decatur House
December
Denver Quarterly
Desperation Press
Dogwood
Domestic Crude
Doubletake
Dragon Gate Inc.
Dreamworks
Dryad Press
Duck Down Press
Durak
East River Anthology
Eastern Washington University Press
Ellis Press
Empty Bowl
Epoch

Ergo!
Evansville Review
Exquisite Corpse
Faultline
Fence
Fiction
Fiction Collective
Fiction International
Field
Fine Madness
Firebrand Books
Firelands Art Review
First Intensity
Five Fingers Review
Five Points Press
Five Trees Press
The Formalist
Fourth Genre
Frontiers: A Journal of Women Studies
Fugue
Gallimaufry
Genre
The Georgia Review
Gettysburg Review
Ghost Dance
Gibbs-Smith
Glimmer Train
Goddard Journal
David Godine, Publisher
Graham House Press
Grand Street
Granta
Graywolf Press
Great River Review
Green Mountains Review
Greenfield Review
Greensboro Review
Guardian Press
Gulf Coast
Hanging Loose
Hard Pressed
Harvard Review
Hayden's Ferry Review

Hermitage Press
Heyday
Hills
Holmgangers Press
Holy Cow!
Home Planet News
Hudson Review
Hungry Mind Review
Icarus
Icon
Idaho Review
Iguana Press
Image
Indiana Review
Indiana Writes
Intermedia
Intro
Invisible City
Inwood Press
Iowa Review
Ironwood
Jam To-day
The Journal
Jubilat
The Kanchenjuga Press
Kansas Quarterly
Kayak
Kelsey Street Press
Kenyon Review
Kestrel
Latitudes Press
Laughing Waters Press
Laurel Review
L'Epervier Press
Liberation
Linquis
Literal Latté
Literary Imagination
The Literary Review
The Little Magazine
Living Hand Press
Living Poets Press
Logbridge-Rhodes

Louisville Review
Lowlands Review
Lucille
Lynx House Press
Lyric
The MacGuffin
Magic Circle Press
Malahat Review
Mānoa
Manroot
Many Mountains Moving
Marlboro Review
Massachusetts Review
McSweeney's
Meridian
Mho & Mho Works
Micah Publications
Michigan Quarterly
Mid-American Review
Milkweed Editions
Milkweed Quarterly
The Minnesota Review
Mississippi Review
Mississippi Valley Review
Missouri Review
Montana Gothic
Montana Review
Montemora
Moon Pony Press
Mount Voices
Mr. Cogito Press
MSS
Mudfish
Mulch Press
Nada Press
National Poetry Review
Nebraska Review
New America
New American Review
New American Writing
The New Criterion
New Delta Review
New Directions

New England Review
New England Review and Bread Loaf
    Quarterly
New Letters
New Orleans Review
New Virginia Review
New York Quarterly
New York University Press
News from The Republic of Letters
Nimrod
9 × 9 Industries
Noon
North American Review
North Atlantic Books
North Dakota Quarterly
North Point Press
Northeastern University Press
Northern Lights
Northwest Review
Notre Dame Review
O. ARS
O. Blēk
Obsidian
Obsidian II
Oconee Review
October
Ohio Review
Old Crow Review
Ontario Review
Open City
Open Places
Orca Press
Orchises Press
Orion
Other Voices
Oxford American
Oxford Press
Oyez Press
Oyster Boy Review
Painted Bride Quarterly
Painted Hills Review
Palo Alto Review
Paris Press

Paris Review
Parkett
Parnassus: Poetry in Review
Partisan Review
Passages North
Penca Books
Pentagram
Penumbra Press
Pequod
Persea: An International Review
Perugià Press
Pipedream Press
Pitcairn Press
Pitt Magazine
Pleiades
Ploughshares
Poet and Critic
Poet Lore
Poetry
Poetry East
Poetry Ireland Review
Poetry Northwest
Poetry Now
Post Road
Prairie Schooner
Prescott Street Press
Press
Promise of Learnings
Provincetown Arts
Puerto Del Sol
Quaderni Di Yip
Quarry West
The Quarterly
Quarterly West
Raccoon
Rainbow Press
Raritan: A Quarterly Review
Red Cedar Review
Red Clay Books
Red Dust Press
Red Earth Press
Red Hen Press
Release Press

Review of Contemporary Fiction
Revista Chicano-Riquena
Rhetoric Review
Rivendell
River Styx
River Teeth
Rowan Tree Press
Russian *Samizdat*
Salmagundi
San Marcos Press
Sarabande Books
Sea Pen Press and Paper Mill
Seal Press
Seamark Press
Seattle Review
Second Coming Press
Semiotext(e)
Seneca Review
Seven Days
The Seventies Press
Sewanee Review
Shankpainter
Shantih
Shearsman
Sheep Meadow Press
Shenandoah
A Shout In the Street
Sibyl-Child Press
Side Show
Small Moon
The Smith
Solo
Solo 2
Some
The Sonora Review
Southern Poetry Review
Southern Review
Southwest Review
Speakeasy
Spectrum
Spillway
The Spirit That Moves Us
St. Andrews Press

Story
Story Quarterly
Streetfare Journal
Stuart Wright, Publisher
Sulfur
The Sun
Sun & Moon Press
Sun Press
Sunstone
Sycamore Review
Tamagwa
Tar River Poetry
Teal Press
Telephone Books
Telescope
Temblor
The Temple
Tendril
Texas Slough
Third Coast
13th Moon
THIS
Thorp Springs Press
Three Rivers Press
Threepenny Review
Thunder City Press
Thunder's Mouth Press
Tia Chucha Press
Tikkun
Tin House
Tombouctou Books
Toothpaste Press
Transatlantic Review
Triplopia
TriQuarterly
Truck Press
Turnrow
Undine
Unicorn Press

University of Georgia Press
University of Illinois Press
University of Iowa Press
University of Massachusetts Press
University of North Texas Press
University of Pittsburgh Press
University of Wisconsin Press
University Press of New England
Unmuzzled Ox
Unspeakable Visions of the Individual
Vagabond
Verse
Vignette
Virginia Quarterly
Volt
Wampeter Press
Washington Writers Workshop
Water-Stone
Water Table
Western Humanities Review
Westigan Review
White Pine Press
Wickwire Press
Willow Springs
Wilmore City
Witness
Word Beat Press
Word-Smith
Wormwood Review
Writers Forum
Xanadu
Yale Review
Yardbird Reader
Yarrow
Y'Bird
Zeitgeist Press
Zoetrope: All-Story
ZYZZYVA

# CONTRIBUTING SMALL PRESSES FOR THIS EDITION

(These presses made or received nominations for this edition of *The Pushcart Prize*. See the *International Directory of Little Magazines and Small Presses*, Dustbooks, P.O. Paradise, CA 95697, for subscription rates, manuscript requirements and a complete international listing of small presses.)

## A

Adept Press, P.O. Box 391, Long Valley, NJ 07853
The Adirondack Review, 305 Keyes Ave., Watertown, NY 13601
Agni, Boston Univ., 236 Bay State Rd., Boston, MA 02215
Alaska Quarterly Review, Univ. of Alaska, 3211 Providence Dr., Anchorage, AK 99508
Alice James Books, 238 Main St., Farmington, ME 04938
Alligator Juniper, 220 Grove Ave., Prescott, AZ 86301
Amarillo Bay, 131 Parkview Dr., Amarillo, TX 79106
Amaze: The Cinquain Journal, 10529 Olive St., Temple City, CA 91780
American Letters & Commentary, 850 Park Ave., Ste. 5B, New York, NY 10021
American Poetry Journal, P.O. Box 4041, Felton, CA 95018
American Poetry Review, 117 S. 17th St., Ste. 910, Philadelphia, PA 19103
The American Scholar, 106 New Hampshire Ave., NW, Washington, DC 20009
&, Journal for the Arts, P.O. Box 150398, Brooklyn, NY 11215
Ancient Paths, P.O. Box 7505, Fairfax Station, VA 22039
Another Chicago Magazine, 3709 N. Kenmore, Chicago, IL 60613
Antietam Review, 41 S. Potomac St., Hagerstown, MD 21740
The Antioch Review, P.O. Box 148, Yellow Springs, OH 45387
Apogee Press, P.O. Box 8177, Berkeley, CA 94707
Architecture Boston, 52 Broad St., Boston, MA 02109
Arkansas Review, P.O. Box 1890, Arkansas State Univ., State University, AR 72467
Arsenic Lobster, 1800 Schodde Ave., Burley, ID 83318
Artful Dodge, College of Wooster, Wooster, OH 44691
Arts & Letters, Georgia College & State Univ., Milledgeville, GA 31061

At Length, P.O. Box 594, New York, NY 10185
Atlanta Review, P.O. Box 3248, Atlanta, GA 31106
Aypress, 3546 Steubenville Rd., SE, Amsterdam, OH 43903

# B

The Baltimore Review, P.O. Box 36418, Towson, MD 21286
Banyan Review, P.O. Box 921, Smithville, TX 78957
Barbaric Yawp, 3700 County Rte. 24, Russell, NY 13684
Barnwood, P.O. Box 146, Selma, IN 47383
Bayou, Creative Writing Workshop, Univ. of New Orleans, New Orleans, LA 70148
Bellevue Literary Review, NYU School of Medicine, 550 First Ave., OBN-612 New York, NY 10016
Bellowing Ark Press, P.O. Box 55564, Shoreline, WA 98155
Beloit Fiction Journal, Beloit College, Beloit, WI 53511
Beloit Poetry Journal, P.O. Box 151, Farmington, ME 04938
Better Non Sequitur, 776 Scranton St., El Cajon, CA 92020
Birch Brook Press, P.O. Box 81, Delhi, NY 13753
The Bitter Oleander Press, 4983 Tall Oaks Dr., Fayetteville, NY 13066
BkMk Press, Univ. of Missouri, 5101 Rockhill Rd., Kansas City, MO 64110
Black Warrior Review, P.O. Box 862936, Tuscaloosa, AL 35486
Blackbird, P.O. Box 843082, Richmond, VA 23284
Blink, Greenlaw Hall, Univ. of North Carolina, Chapel Hill, NC 27599
Blue Cubicle Press, P.O. Box 250382, Plano, TX 75025
Blue Fifth Review, 264 Lark Meadow Ct., Bluff City, TN 37618
Boise Journal, 1109 W. Main St., Boise, ID 83702
Borderlands, P.O. Box 33096, Austin, TX 78764
Boulevard, 7545 Cromwell Dr., #21V, St. Louis, MO 63105
Brain, Child, P.O. Box 5566, Charlottesville, VA 22905
Branches Quarterly, P.O. Box 85394, Seattle, WA 98145
Briar Cliff Review, P.O. Box 2100, Sioux City, IA 51104
Brick, Box 537, Stn. Q, Toronto, Ont. M4T 2M5, *CANADA*
Brilliant Corners, Wyoming College, Williamsport, PA 17702
Broken Watch Press, P.O. Box 3336, Silver Spring, MD 20918
Geoff Butler, P.O. Box 29, Granville Ferry, *Nova Scotia* BOS 1KO, Canada
Bullfight, P.O. Box 362, Walnut Creek, CA 94597
Byline, P.O. Box 5240, Edmond, OK 73083

# C

Calyx, P.O. Box B, 216 SW Madison, Corvallis, OR 97339
The Canary, 512 Clear Lake Rd., Kemah, TX 77565
Canio's Books, Main St., Sag Harbor, NY 11963
Cape Cod Literary Press, P.O. Box 720, North Eastham, Cape Cod, MA 02651
The Caribbean Writer, Univ. of the Virgin Islands, RR2-10000 Kingshill, St. Croix, U.S. Virgin Islands 00850
Carve Magazine, P.O. Box 1573, Tallahassee, FL 32302
Center, 107 Tate Hall, Columbia, MO 65211
Central Ave. Press, 2132-A Central S.E. #144, Albuquerque, NM 87106
Chaffin Journal, Eastern Kentucky Univ., 521 Lancaster Ave., Richmond, KY 40475
The Chariton Review, English Dept., Brigham Young Univ., Provo, UT 84602
Chautauqua Literary Journal, P.O. Box 2039, York Beach, ME 03910
Chelsea, Box 773, Cooper Sta., New York, NY 10276
Chicory Blue Press, Inc., 795 East St., N, Goshen, CT 06756
Cider Press Review, 777 Braddock La., Halifax, PA 17032

Cimarron Review, Oklahoma State Univ., Stillwater, OK 74078
The Cincinnati Review, English Dept., Univ. of Cincinnati, Cincinnati, OH 45221
The Citizen, 96 Suffolk Rd., Island Park, NY 11558
City Lights Books, 261 Columbus Ave., San Francisco, CA 94133
Clean Sheets Magazine, 5082 E. Hampden, #159, Denver, CO 80222
Cleveland State University Poetry Center, 2121 Euclid Ave., Cleveland, OH 44115
Cogno Press, P.O. Box 1431, Portage, MI 49081
Colere, Coe College, 1220 First Ave., NE, Cedar Rapids, IA 52402
Colorado Review, English Dept., Colorado State Univ., Ft. Collns, CO 80523
Conjunctions, Bard College, Annandale-on-Hudson, NY 12504
Connecticut Review, Southern Connecticut State Univ., New Haven, CT 06515
Cottonwood, 3102 Wescoe, Univ. of Kansas, Lawrence, KS 66045
Cranky Literary Journal, 322 10th Ave. E, C-5, Seattle, WA 98102
Crazyhorse, College of Charleston, 66 George St., Charleston, SC 29424
Cream City Review, P.O. Box 413, Milwaukee, WI 53201
Cross-Cultural Communications, 239 Wynsum, Marrick NY 11566
Crowd, 487 Union St., #3, Brooklyn, NY 11231
Curbstone Press, 321 Jackson St., Willimantic, CT 06226
Cynic Press, P.O. Box 40691, Philadelphia, PA 19107

# D

Daedalus, Five Cambridge Center, Cambridge, MA 02142
Dana Literary Society, P.O. Box 3362, Dana Point, CA 92629
John Daniel & Co., P.O. Box 2790, McKinleyville, CA 95519
Diagram, 628 Crescent NE, Grand Rapids, MI 49503
Dirty Swamp Poets, 145 Whittington Dr., Lafayette, LA 70503
Divide, Univ. of Colorado, UCB 317, Boulder, CO 80309
The DMQ Review, 16393 Bonnie La., Los Gatos, CA 95032
Dogwood, Fairfield Univ., 1073 N. Benson Rd., Fairfield, CT 06824
Drum Voices Revue, Southern Illinois Univ., Edwardsville, IL 62026
Drunken Boat, 1615 Stanley St., New Britain, CT 06050
Dunhill Publishing, see Warwick Associates

# E

Edgar Literary Magazine, P.O. Box 5776, San Leon, TX 77539
EDGE Publications, P.O. Box 799, Ocean Park, WA 98640
Eggemoggin Reach Review, P.O. Box 376, Deer Isle, ME 04627
Ekphrasis, see Frith Press
Emerson Review, Emerson College, 120 Boylston St., Boston, MA 02116
Emerson's Eye Press, 637 S. Broadway, #B334, Boulder, CO 80305
Epiphany, 311 East Third St., #33, New York, NY 10009
Epoch, 251 Goldwin Smith Hall, Cornell Univ., Ithaca, NY 14853
Erosha, P.O. Box 185, Falls Church, VA 22040
Eureka Literary Magazine, 300 E. College Ave., Box 146, Eureka, IL 61530
Evansville Review, Univ. of Evansville, 1800 Lincoln Ave., Evansville, IN 47722
Event, Douglas College, Box 2503, New Westminster, B.C., *CANADA* V3L 5B2

# F

Facets, P.O. Box 380915, Cambridge, MA 02238
Failbetter, 40 Montgomery Pl., #2, Brooklyn, NY 11215
Fandango Virtuel, 4C Burnbrae St., Fairley-Clydebank, *UNITED KINGDOM* G81 5BT
Fence, 303 East 8th St., #B1, New York, NY 10009
Fiction International, San Diego State Univ., San Diego, CA 92182
Field, 50 N. Professor St., Oberlin, OH 44074
Fine Madness, P.O. Box 31138, Seattle, WA 98103
Firefly Books, Ltd, 66 Leek Crescent, Richmond Hill, Ont., *CANADA* L4B 1H1
Fithian Press, P.O. Box 2790, McKinleyville, CA 95519
5 AM, Box 205, Spring Church, PA 15686
580 Split, P.O. Box 9982, Mills College, OAkland, CA 94613
Five Points, Georgia State Univ., Univ. Plaza, Atlanta, GA 30303
Flashquake, P.O. Box 2154, Albany, NY 12220
Floating Bridge Press, 1634 Eleventh Ave., Seattle, WA 98122
Florida Review, English Dept., Univ. of Central Florida, Orlando, FL 32816
Flume, California State Univ.; Chico, CA 95929
FMAM: Futures Mysterious Magazine, 3039 38th Ave., S, Minneapolis, MN 55406
Folio: A Literary Journal, Dept. of Literature, American Univ., Washington, DC 20016
The Formalist, 1800 Lincoln Ave., Evansville, IN 47722
42 Opus, 214 E. Portland St., Phoenix, AZ 85004
14 Hills, Creative Writing Dept., 1600 Holloway Ave., San Francisco, CA 94132
Fourth Genre, Michigan State Univ., East Lansing, MI 48825
Free Lunch, P.O. Box 717, Glenview, IL 60025
Free Verse, see Marsh River Editions
Fresh Yarn, 11350 Ventura Blvd., #205, Studio City, CA 91604
Frith Press, P.O. Box 161236, Sacramento, CA 95816
Frostproof Review, P.O. Box 21013, Columbus, OH 43221
Fugue, Univ. of Idaho, Moscow, ID 83844
Futurepoem Books, P.O. Box 34, New York, NY 10014

# G

The Georgia Review, Univ. of Georgia, Athens, GA 30602
The Gettysburg Review, Gettysburg College, Gettysburg, PA 17325
Gin Bender Poetry Review, P.O. Box 150932, Lufkin, TX 75915
Gival Press, P.O. Box 3812, Arlington, VA 22203
Glass Tesseract, 795 Via Colinas, Thousand Oaks, CA 91362
Gloucester Spoken Arts, 2066 Kings Grove Cres., Gloucester, Ont. *CANADA* K1J 6G1
Gobshite Quarterly, P.O. Box 11346, Portland, OR 97211
Graywolf Press, 2402 Univ. Ave., Ste. 203, St. Paul, MN 55114
Green Hills Literary Lantern, 100 E. Normal, Truman State Univ., Kirksville, MO 63501
The Greensboro Review, English Dept., UNCG, Greensboro, NC 27402
The Grove Review, 1631 NE Broadway, PMB #137, Portland, OR 97232
Gulf Coast, English Dept., Univ. of Houston, Houston, TX 77204
Gulf Stream Magazine, 3000 NE 151st St., North Miami, FL 33181

# H

Hanging Loose Press, 231 Wyckoff St., Brooklyn, NY 11217
Harp Strings Poetry Journal, Box 640387, Beverly Hills, FL 34464
Harpur Pilate, English Dept., State Univ. of New York, Binghamton, NY 13903
Hayden's Ferry Review. Arizona State Univ., P.O. Box 875002, Tempe, AZ 85287
The Healing Muse, 725 Irving Ave., Ste. 406, Syracuse, NY 13210
Heat City Review, 62 Windsor Rd., Wabon, MA 02468
Heyday Books, P.O. Box 9145, Berkeley, CA 94709
H-NGM-N, 715 College Ave., Natchitoches, LA 71457
Hobart, 394 Waymarket, Ann Arbor, MI 48103
Hogtown Creek Review, Marathonweg 84, 1076 TM, Amsterdam, *NETHERLANDS*
Hotel Amerika, Ohio Univ., Ellis Hall, Athens, OH 45701
The Hudson Review, 684 Park Ave., New York, NY 10021
Hunger Mountain, Vermont College, 36 College St., Montpelier, VT 05602

# I

Ibbetson Street Press, 25 School St., Somerville, MA 02143
The Iconoclast, 1675 Amazon Rd., Mohegan Lake, NY 10547
Iguana Publications, 1239 W. Farwell, #3B, Chicago, IL 60626
Illya's Honey, P.O. Box 700865, Dallas, TX 75370
Image, 3307 Third Ave., W, Seattle, WA 98119
In Posse Review, 3735 N. 161 Dr., Goodyear, AZ 85338
Indiana Review, 1020 E. Kirkland Ave., Bloomington, IN 47405
Inkwell, 2900 Purchase St., Purchase, NY 10577
Invisible Insurrection, 925 NW Hoyt St., #231, Portland, OR 97209
Iowa Review, Univ. of Iowa, Iowa City, IA 52242
Iron Horse Literary Review, Texas Tech. Univ., Lubbock, TX 79409

# J

Jabberwock Review, English Dept., Drawer E, Mississippi State, MS 39762
The Journal, English Dept., Ohio State Univ., Columbus, OH 43210
Journal of New Jersey Poets, Co. College of Morris, 214 Center Grove Rd., Randolph, NJ 07869
Jubilat, 452 Bartlett Hall, Univ. of Massachusetts, Amherst, MA 01003
July Literary Press, 294 Hunters Lane, Williamsville, NY 14221

# K

Kansas City Voices, P.O. Box 428, Liberty, MO 64069
The Kelsey Review, P.O. Box B, Trenton, NJ 08690
The Kenyon Review, Kenyon College, Gambier, OH 43022
The King's English, c/oB. Chambers, 3114 NE 47th Ave., Portland, OR 97213
Kitchen Sink Magazine, 5245 College, #301, Oakland, CA 94618
Konundrum Engine Literary Review, 30-74 32nd St., #21, Astoria, NY 11102
Kyoto Journal, Minamigoshomachi, Okazaki Sakyo-Ku, Kyoto 606-8334, *JAPAN*

494

# L

Lake Effect, 501 Station Rd., Erie, PA 16563
Land-Grant College Review, P.O. Box 1164, New York, NY 10159
Laurel Poetry Collective, 1168 Laurel Ave., St. Paul, MN 55104
The Ledge, 40 Maple Ave., Bellport, NY 11713
Licking River Review, Northern Kentucky Univ., Highland Heights, KY 41099
Light of New Orleans Publishing, 828 Royal St., New Orleans, LA 70116
Lilies & Cannonballs, P.O. Box 702, Bowling Green Sta., New York, NY 10274
Lily Literary Review, P.O. Box 76, Nucla, CO 81424
LIT, New School Univ., 66 W. 12th St., Rm. 214, New York, NY 10011
Lit Pot Press, Inc., 3909 Reche Rd., Ste. 96, Fallbrook, CA 92028
Literary Imagination, Classics Dept., Univ. of Georgia, Athens, GA 30602
The Literary Review, 285 Madison Ave., Madison, NJ 07940
Little Poem Press, P.O. Box 185, Falls Church, VA 22040
Livingston Press, Univ. of Western Alabama, Livingston, AL 35470
LOS, 150 N. Catalina St., #2, Los Angeles, CA 90004
Louisiana Literature, Southeastern Louisiana Univ., SLU 792, Hammond, LA 70402
Louisville Review, 151 S. Fourth St., Louisville, KY 40203
Lynx Eye, 581 Woodland Dr., Los Osos, CA 93402
Lyric, P.O. Box 980814, Houston, TX 77098

# M

The MacGuffin, Schoolcraft College, 18600 Haggerty Rd, Livonia, MI 48152
The MAG Press, 4630 Leathers St., San Diego, CA 92117
The Magazine of Speculative Poetry, P.O. Box 564, Beloit, WI 53512
The Malahat Review, P.O. Box 1700 Stn CSC, Victoria, B.C. V8W 2Y2 CANADA
The Manhattan Review, 440 Riverside Dr., #38, New York, NY 10027
Manic D Press, P.O. Box 410804, San Francisco, CA 94141
Many Mountains Moving, 627 Lafarge, Louisville, CO 80027
Margie, P.O. Box 250, Chesterfield, MO 63006
Margin, 321 High School Rd., NE, Bainbridge Island, WA 98110
Marsh Hawk Press, P.O. Box 206, E. Rockaway, NY 11518
Marsh River Editions, M233 Marsh Rd., Marshfield, WI 54449
The Massachusetts Review, South College, Univ. of Massachusetts, Amherst, MA 01003
McSweeney's, 826 Valencia St., San Francisco, CA 94110
The Merton Seasonal, 109 Univ, Square, Erie, PA 16541
Michigan Quarterly Review, 3032 Radcham Bldg. Univ., Michigan, Ann Arbor, MI 48109
Michigan State University Press, 1405 S. Harrison Rd., Ste. 25, East Lansing, MI 48823
Mid-American Review, English Dept., Bowling Green State Univ., Bowling Green, OH 43403
Mindfire Renewed, 2518 Fruitland, Bremerton, WA 98310
Mindprints, 800 S. College Dr., Santa Maria, CA 93454
Minnesota Review, Carnegie Mellon Univ., Pittsburgh, PA 15217
MIPO Magazine, 4601 SW 94 Ct., Miami, FL 33165
Mississippi Review, Univ. of Southern Mississippi, Box 5144, Hattiesburg, MS 39406
The Missouri Review, 1507 Hillcrest Hall, Univ. of Missouri, Columbia, MO 65211
Monkey Bicycle, 23-55 38th St., Astoria, NY 11105
Moondance, P.O. Box 92-3713, Sylmar, CA 91392
Mot Juste, 1915 Brown Place, Murphysboro, IL 62966
Mud Rock Press, P.O. Box 31688, Dayton, OH 45437
Mythic Delirium, P.O. Box 13511, Roanoke, VA 24034
MZIP, 4416 Fairview Ave., Newtown Square, PA 19073

# N

Nanny Fanny, 2524 Stockbridge Dr., #15, Indianapolis, IN 46268
National Poetry Review, P.O. Box 640625, San Jose, CA 95164
Natural Bridge, English Dept., Univ. of Missouri, St. Louis, MO 63121
New England Review, Middlebury College, Middlebury, VT 05753
New Letters, Univ. of Missouri, 5101 Rockhill Rd., Kansas City, MO 64110
New Orleans Review. Loyola Univ., New Orleans, LA 70118
The New Orphic Review, 706 Mill St., Nelson, B.C., V1L 4S5 *CANADA*
The New Renaissance, 26 Heath Rd., #11, Arlington, MA 02474
The New Yinzer, 277 Main St., Pittsburgh, PA 15201
New York Stories, La Guardia CUNY, 31-10 Thomson Ave., Long Island City, NY 11101
Nexus Press, 535 Means St., NW, Atlanta, GA 30318
NFG Magazine, Sheppard Centre, P.O. Box 43112, Toronto, Ont. *CANADA* M2N 6N1
Night Train, P.O. Box 6250, Boston, MA 02114
Ninth Letter, Univ. of Illinois, 608 S. Wright St., Urbana, IL 61801
No Tell Motel, 11436 Fairway Dr., Reston, VA 20190
North American Review, Univ. of Northern Iowa, Cedar Falls, IA 50614
Northwest Florida Review, 21 Kathleen Dr., Mary Esther, FL 32569
Northwest Review, Univ. of Oregon, Eugene, OR 97403
Not One of Us, 12 Curtis Rd., Narick, MA 01760
Notre Dame Review, English Dept., Univ. of Notre Dame, Notre Dame, IN 46556

# O

Octopus, 2215 Remington Way, #305, Bozeman, MT 59718
Off the Coast, P.O. Box 205, Bristol, ME 04539
On Earth, 40 West 20th St., New York, NY 10011
One Story, P.O. Box 1326, New York, NY 10156
Ontario Review, 9 Honey Brook Dr., Princeton, NJ 08540
OP, P.O. Box 106, Eureka, CA 95502
Open Spaces Publications, Inc., 6327-C SW Capitol Hwy., Portland, OR 97239
Orchid, 3096 Williamsburg, Ann Arbor, MI 48108
Osiris, P.O. Box 297, Deerfield, MA 01342
Other Voices, English Dept., Univ. of Illinois, 601 S. Morgan, Chicago, IL 60607
Oyez Review, Roosevelt University, 430 S. Michigan Ave., Chicago, IL 60605

# P

Painted Bride Quarterly, 39-82 52nd St., 2F, Woodside, NY 11377
Palo Alto Review, 1400 W. Villaret Blvd., San Antonio, TX 78224
Pangolin Papers, P.O. Box 241. Nordland, WA 98358
Panther Creek Press, 116 Tree Crest, Spring, TX 77381
Parakeet, 115 Roosevelt Ave., Syracuse, NY 13210
Passages, Univ. of Baltimore, Baltimore, MD 21201
Passages North, English Dept., 1401 Presque Isle Ave., Marquette, MI 49855
Paterson Literary Review, One College Blvd., Paterson, NJ 07505
Pathwise Press, P.O. Box 2392, Bloomington, IN 47402
The Paumanok Review, 254 Dogwood Dr., Hershey, PA 17033
Pearl, 3030 E. Second St., Long Beach, CA 90803
Pebble Lake Review, 15318 Pebble Lake Dr., Houston, TX 77095

Perugia Press, P.O. Box 60364, Florence, MA 01062

Phantasmagoria, English Dept., Century College, White Bear Lake, MN 55110

Philograph Press, 1085 Commonwealth Ave., pmb 253, Boston, MA 02215

Phoebe, George Mason Univ., 4400 Univ. Dr., Fairfax, VA 22030

Pine Island Journal, P.O. Box 317, West Springfield, MA 01089

Pleasure Boat Studio: A Literary Press, 201 W. 89th St., New York, NY 10024

Pleiades, English Dept., Central Missouri State Univ., Warrensburg, MO 64093

Ploughshares, Emerson College, 120 Boylston St., Boston, MA 02116

PMS, English Dept., Univ. of Alabama, Birmingham, AL 35294

Poems Against War, 2720 St. Paul St., #2F, Baltimore, MD 21218

Poems & Plays, English Dept., Middle Tennessee State Univ., Murfreesboro, TN 37132

Poetic Matrix Press, P.O. Box 1223, Madera, CA 93639

Poetica Magazine, P.O. Box 11014, Norfolk, VA 23513

Poetry, 1030 N. Clark St., Ste. 420, Chicago, IL 60610

Poetry Miscellany, Univ. of Tennessee, Chattanooga, TN 37403

Poetry West, P.O. Box 2413, Colorado Springs, CO 80901

Pool, P.O. Box 49738, Los Angeles, CA 90049

Portland Review, P.O. Box 347, Portland, OR 92207

Post Road Magazine, P.O. Box 400951, Cambridge, MA 02140

Prairie Schooner, 201 Andrews Hall, Univ. of Nebraska, Lincoln, NE 68588

Prism International, Univ. of British Columbia, 1866 Main Mall, Vancouver, B.C., *CANADA* V6T 1Z1

Prose Ax, P.O. Box 22643, Honolulu, HI 96823

Puerto del Sol, New Mexico State Univ., Las Cruces, NM 88003

# Q

Quadrangle Magazine, Canisius College, 2001 Main St., Buffalo, NY 14208

Quick Fiction, 50 Evergreen St., #25, Jamaica Plain, MA 02130

# R

Raritan, 31 Mine St., New Brunswick, NJ 08903

Red River Review, 2108 Stein Way, Carrollton, TX 75007

Redactions: Poetry & Poetics, 1322 S. Jefferson, Spokane, WA 99204

Rhapsoidia Press, 939 Hough Ave., #3, Lafayette, CA 94549

Rhino, P.O. Box 591, Evanston, IL 60204

Rivendell, P.O. Box 9594, Asheville, NC 28815

River City, Univ. of Memphis, 467 Patterson Hall, Memphis, TN 38152

River King, P.O. Box 122, Freeburg, IL 62243

River Teeth, 401 College Ave., Ashland Univ., Ashland, OH 44805

River Walk Journal, 641 Chestnut St., Irwin, PA 15642

Rock Salt Plum Review, PSC 3, Box 258, APO-AE 09021

The Rose and Thorn, 3 Diamond Ct., Montebello, NY 10901

Runes, P.O. Box 401, Sausalito, CA 94966

# S

Saint Ann's Review, 129 Pierrepont St., Brooklyn Heights, NY 11201

Salmagundi, Skidmore College, Saratoga Springs, NY 12866

Sandstar Publications, P.O. Box 181, Rockport, MA 01966

Santa Monica Review, Santa Monica College, 1900 Pico Blvd, Santa Monica, CA 90405
Sarabande Books, 2234 Dundee Rd., Ste. 200, Louisville, KY 40205
Schuylkill Valley Journal, 240 Golf Hills Rd., Havertown, PA 19083
Seattle Review, Univ. of Washington, Box 354330, Seattle, WA 98195
Seems, Lakeland College, P.O. Box 359, Sheboygan, WI 53082
Semiotext(e), Columbia Univ., New York, NY 10027
Sensations Magazine, P.O. Box 90, Glen Ridge, NJ 07028
Sentence, 181 White St., Danbury, CT 06810
Skidrow Penthouse, 44 Four Corners Rd., Blairstown, NJ 07825
Skyline Publications, P.O. Box 295, Stormville, NY 12582
Slipstream, P.O. Box 2071, Niagara Falls, NY 14301
Slope Editions, 77 Lyman St., Holyoke, MA 01040
Slow Trains Literary Journal, P.O. Box 4741, Denver, CO 80155
Small Spiral Notebook, 248 W. 7th St., #307, New York, NY 10011
Soft Skull Press, 71 Bond St., Brooklyn, NY 11217
Solo Press, P.O. Box 954, Ventura, CA 93002
Southern Poetry Review, Armstrong Atlantic State Univ., Savannah, GA 31419
The Southern Review, 43 Allen Hall, LSU, Baton Rouge, LA 70805
Southwest Review, Southern Methodist Univ., P.O. Box 750374, Dallas, TX 75275
Sou'wester, English Dept., Southern Illinois Univ., Edwardsville, IL 62026
Speakeasy, 1011 Washington Ave. S, Minneapolis, MN 55415
Spite Press, 532 LaGuardia Pl., Ste. 298, New York, NY 10012
Spoon River Poetry Review, Campus Box 4241, Normal, IL 61790
Square Lake, 6041 Palatine Ave., N., Seattle, WA 98103
Star Cloud Press, 6137 E. Mescal St., Scottsdale, AZ 85254
Starcherone Books, P.O. Box 303, Buffalo, NY 14201
Stirring: A Literary Collection, 1406 N. McKinley Ave., Apt. 1, Champaign, IL 61821
Story Quarterly, 431 Sheridan Rd., Kenilworth, IL 60043
Storyglossia, P.O. Box 19804, Seattle, WA 98109
StorySouth, 898 Chelsea Ave., Bexley, OH 43209
The Storyteller, 2441 Washington Rd., Maynard, AR 72444
Streetlight, P.O. Box 259, Charlottesville, VA 22902
Subtle Tea, 444 Hoodridge Dr., B-6, Pittsburgh, PA 15234
The Summerset Review, 25 Summerset Dr., Smithtown, NY 11787
The Sun, 107 N. Roberson St., Chapel Hill, NC 27516
The Sun Rising Poetry Press, 724 Felix St., St. Joseph, MO 64501
Swan Scythe Press, 2052 Calaveras Ave., Davis, CA 95616
The Swannigan & Wright Literary Matter, 3429 Bellevue Ave., #410, Los Angeles, CA 90026
Sweet Annie Press, 7750 Hwy F-24W, Baxter, IA 50028
Swink Magazine, 244 Fifth Ave., #2722, New York, NY 10001
Swivel, PO Box 17958, Seattle, WA 98107

# T

Tallfellow Press, 1180 S. Beverly Dr., Ste. 320, Los Angeles, CA 90035
Tampa Review, 401 W. Kennedy Blvd., Tampa, FL 33606
Terminus Magazine, 1034 Hill St., SE, Atlanta, GA 30315
Terra Incognita, P.O. Box 150585, Brooklyn, NY 11215
Thema Literary Society, Box 8747, Metairie, LA 70011
Third Coast, Western Michigan Univ., Kalamazoo, MI 49008
32 Poems Magazine, P.O. Box 5824, Hyattsville, MD 20782
Three Candles, 5470 132nd Lane, Savage, MN 55378
The Threepenny Review, P.O. Box 9131, Berkeley, CA 94709
Tiferet, P.O. Box 654, Peapack, NJ 07977
Timber Creek Review, 8969 UNCG Sta., Greensboro, NC 27413

Tin House, 2601 NW Thurman St., Portland, OR 97210
Triple Tree Publishing, P.O. Box 5684, Eugene, OR 97405
Triplopia, 6816 Mt. Vernon Ave., Salisbury, MD 21804
TriQuarterly, Northwestern University Press, 629 Noyes St., Evanston, IL 60208
Tupela Press, P.O. Box 539, Dorset, VT 05251
Twenty Pounds of Headlights, 17410 Guernewood Lane, Guerneville, CA 95446
Twisted Spoon Press, P.O. Box 21, Preslova 12, 150 00 Prague 5, *CZECH REP.*
219 Press, P.O. Box 352, Perry, KS 66073
Typo, 1206 N. Maxwell, Fayetteville, AR 72703


# U


Ugly Duckling Press, 106 Ferris St., Brooklyn, NY 11231
Unicorn Press, 201 N. Coulter Dr., Bryon, TX 77803
University of Georgia Press, 330 Research Dr., Athens, GA 30602
University of Nebraska Press, 233 N. 8th St., Lincoln, NE 68588
University of New Mexico Press, Univ. of New Mexico, Albuquerque, NM 87131
Unsaid, 123 7th Ave., PMB #172, Brooklyn, NY 11215


# V


Vallum Magazine, P.O. Box 48003, Montreal, Que. H2V 4S8 *CANADA*
Verse Press, 221 Pine St., 258, Florence, MA 01062
Vestal Review, 2609 Dartmouth Dr., Vestal, NY 13850
Via Dolorosa Press, 701 E. Schaaf Rd., Cleveland, OH 44131
Virginia Quarterly Review, One West Range, P.O. Box 400223, Charlottesville, VA 22704


# W


War, Literature & the Arts, English Dept., USAF Acad, 2354 Fairchild Dr., USAF Acad., CO 80840
Warwick Associates, 18340 Sonoma Hwy., Sonoma, CA 95476
Watchword Press, P.O. Box 5756, Berkeley, CA 94706
Water-Stone Review, Hamline Univ., 1536 Hewitt Ave., St. Paul, MN 55104
Wayne State University Press, 4809 Woodward Ave., Detroit, MI 48201
Weber Studies, 1214 Univ. Circle, Ogden, UT 84408
West Branch, Bucknell Univ., Lewisburg, PA 17837
West Wind Review, 1250 Siskiyou Blvd., Ashland, OR 97520
Western Humanities Review, English Dept., Univ. of Utah, Salt Lake City, UT 84112
Whistling Shade, P.O. Box 7084, St. Paul, MN 55107
White Pelican Review, P.O. Box 7833, Lakeland, FL 33813
White Pine Press, P.O. Box 236, Buffalo, NY 14201
Wild Berries Press, 1000 Bourbon St., #219, New Orleans, LA 70116
Wild Plum, P.O. Box 49019, Austin, TX 78765
Willow Review, College of Lake Co., Grayslake, IL 60030
Willow Springs, 705 West 1st Ave., Spokane, WA 99201
Wings Press, 627 E. Guenther, San Antonio, TX 78210
Witness, Oakland Community College, Farmington Hills, MI 48334
Women in the Arts, P.O. Box 2907, Decatur, IL 62524
Word Tech Editions, P.O. Box 541106, Cincinnati, OH 45254
Words, School of Visual Arts, 209 E. 23rd St., New York, NY 10010

Words of Wisdom, 8969 UNCG Sta., Greensboro, NC 27413
Words on Walls, 3408 Whitfield Hwy., Cincinnati, OH 45270
Writer's Hood, 2518 Fruitland, Bremerton, WA 98310
Writers Notes Magazine, P.O. Box 11, Titusville, NJ 08560

# X

Xantippe, P.O. Box 20997, Oakland, CA 94620

# Y

The Yale Review, Yale Univ., Box 208243, New Haven, CT 06520
Yalobusha Review, P.O. Box 1848, University, MS 38677

# Z

Zoetrope, 916 Kearny St., San Francisco, CA 94133
ZYZZYVA, P.O. Box 590069, San Francisco, CA 94159

# FOUNDING MEMBERS OF THE PUSHCART PRIZE FELLOWSHIPS

501

Betty Adcock
Agni
Carolyn Alessio
Dick Allen
Henry H. Allen
Lisa Alvarez
Jan Lee Ande
Ralph Angel
Antietam Review
Ruth Appelhof
Philip Appleman
Linda Aschbrenner
Renee Ashley
Ausable Press
David Baker
Jim Barnes
Catherine Barnett
Dorothy Barresi
Barrow Street Press
Jill Bart
Ellen Bass
Judith Baumel
Ann Beattie
Madison Smartt Bell
Beloit Poetry Journal
Pinckney Benedict
Andre Bernard
Christopher Bernard
Wendell Berry
Linda Bierds
Bitter Oleander Press
Stacy Bierlein
Mark Blaeuer
Blue Lights Press
Carol Bly
BOA Editions
Deborah Bogen
Susan Bono
Anthony Brandt
James Breeden
Rosellen Brown
Jane Brox
Andrea Hollander Budy
L. S. Bumas
Richard Burgin
Skylar H. Burris
David Caliguiuri
Kathy Callaway
Janine Canan
Henry Carlile
Fran Castan
Chelsea Associates
Marianne Cherry
Phillis M. Choyke
Suzanne Cleary

Joan Connor
John Copenhaven
Dan Corrie
Tricia Currans-Sheehan
Jim Daniels
Thadious Davis
Maija Devine
Edward J. DiMaio
Sharon Dilworth
Kent Dixon
John Duncklee
Elaine Edelman
Renee Edison & Don Kaplan
Nancy Edwards
M.D. Elevitch
Failbetter.com
Irvin Faust
Tom Filer
Susan Firer
Nick Flynn
Stakey Flythe Jr.
Peter Fogo
Linda N. Foster
Fugue
Alice Fulton
Eugene K. Garber
Frank X. Gaspar
A Gathering of the Tribes
Reginald Gibbons
Emily Fox Gordon
Philip Graham
Eamon Grennan
Lee Meitzen Grue
Habit of Rainy Nights
Rachel Hadas
Susan Hahn
Meredith Hall
Harp Strings
Jeffrey Harrison
Lois Marie Harrod
Healing Muse
Lily Henderson
Daniel Henry
Neva Herington
Lou Hertz
William Heyen
Bob Hicok
R. C. Hildebrandt
Kathleen Hill
Edward Hoagland
Daniel Hoffman
Doug Holder
Richard Holinger
Rochelle L. Holt
Richard M. Huber

Brigid Hughes
Lynne Hugo
Illya's Honey
Susan Indigo
Mark Irwin
Beverly A. Jackson
Richard Jackson
David Jauss
Marilyn Johnston
Alice Jones
Journal of New Jersey Poets
Robert Kalich
Julia Kasdorf
Miriam Poli Katsikis
Meg Kearney
Celine Keating
Brigit Kelly
John Kistner
Judith Kitchen
Stephen Kopel
David Kresh
Maxine Kumin
Valerie Laken
Babs Lakey
Maxine Landis
Lane Larson
Dorianne Laux & Joseph Millar
Sydney Lea
Donald Lev
Dana Levin
Gerald Locklin
Rachel Lodin
Radomir Luza, Jr.
Annette Lynch
Elzabeth MacKierman
Elizabeth Macklin
Leah Maines
Mark Manalang
Norma Marder
Jack Marshall
Michael Martone
Tara L. Masih
Dan Masterson
Peter Matthiessen
Alice Mattison
Tracy Mayor
Robert McBrearty
Jane McCafferty
Bob McCrane
Jo McDougall
Sandy McIntosh
James McKean
Roberta Mendel
Didi Menendez
Barbara Milton
Alexander Mindt
Mississippi Review

Martin Mitchell
Roger Mitchell
Jewell Mogan
Patricia Monaghan
Jim Moore
James Morse
William Mulvihill
Carol Muske-Dukes
Edward Mycue
W. Dale Nelson
Daniel Orozco
Other Voices
Pamela Painter
Paris Review
Alan Michael Parker
Ellen Parker
Veronica Patterson
David Pearce
Robert Phillips
Donald Platt
Valerie Polichar
Pool
Jeffrey & Priscilla Potter
Marcia Preston
Eric Puchner
Barbara Quinn
Belle Randall
Martha Rhodes
Nancy Richard
Stacey Richter
Katrina Roberts
Judith R. Robinson
Jessica Roeder
Martin Rosner
Kay Ryan
Sy Safransky
Brian Salchert
James Salter
Sherod Santos
R.A. Sasaki
Valerie Sayers
Alice Schell
Helen Schulman
Philip Schultz
Dennis & Loretta Schmitz
Shenandoah
Peggy Shinner
Vivian Shipley
Joan Silver
John E. Smelcer
Raymond J. Smith
Philip St. Clair
Lorraine Standish
Michael Steinberg
Barbara Stone
Storyteller Magazine
Bill & Pat Strachan

*The Pushcart Prize Fellowships Inc., a 501 (c) (3) nonprofit corporation, is the endowment for The Pushcart Prize. We also make grants to promising new writers. "Members" donated up to $249 each, "Sponsors" gave between $250 and $999. "Benefactors" donated from $1000 to $4,999. "Patrons" donated $5,000 and more. We are very grateful for these donations. Gifts of any amount are welcome. For information write to the Fellowships at PO Box 380, Wainscott, NY 11975.*

# CONTRIBUTORS' NOTES

STEVE ALMOND is the author of *My Life in Heavy Metal* (Grove, 2002), *Candy Freak* (Algonquin, 2004) and *The Evil B. B. Chow* (Algonquin, 2005)

DANIEL ANDERSON's first collection of poems, *January Rain*, was published in 1997; his latest collection, *Drunk In Sunlight*, was published in 2004. He is the editor of *The Selected Poems of Howard Nemerov*.

CHARLES BARBER is the author of *Songs from the Black Chair: A Memoir of Mental Interiors* about his work in homeless shelters and his personal experience with obsessive-compulsive disorder. He is currently at work on *Zoloft at the Super Bowl: How Biological Psychiatry Medicated A Nation* for Random House.

AMY BARTLETT was the poetry editor for *Tin House* until her death. Tom Sleigh remembers her and her poems "so clear, so free of verbal affectation . . . a sense of balance . . . her habitual modesty . . . a mind realizing itself with integrity, resourcefulness, and preternatual cool."

RICK BASS is the author of 21 books of fiction and non-fiction including most recently a novel, *The Diezmo*. He lives in northwest Montana where he is active with several local environmental organizations.

ROBIN BEHN is the author of three poetry books, most recently *Horizon Note*, winner of the Brittingham Prize from the University of Wisconsin Press. She teaches in the MFA program at the universities of Alabama and Vermont.

AIMEE BENDER is the author of two books, *The Girl In the Flammable Skirt*, a New York *Times* Notable Book of 1998, and *An Invisible Sign of My Own*, Los Angeles *Times* pick of 2000.

LINDA BIERDS's sixth book of poetry is *The Seconds* (Putnam, 2001). She is the recipient of a fellowship from the MacAuthur Foundation and teaches at the University of Washington.

ROBERT BOYERS' recent publications include a story in *Harvard Review* and a piece on Norman Manea's memoir, *The Hooligan's Return* for *The New Republic*. He edits *Salmagundi* from Skidmore College.

ROSELLEN BROWN's novels include: *Civil Wars, Before and After*, and *Half a Heart*.

FREDERICK BUSCH's most recent book is *North*. He lives in upstate New York.

ROBERT OLEN BUTLER has published ten novels and three collections of stories, one of which, *A Good Scent from a Strange Mountain*, won the 1993 Pulitzer Prize. "Christmas 1910" is part of his new book of fiction, *Had A Good Time: Stories from American Postcards*, based on his collection of antique postcards.

E. L. DOCTOROW's numerous books include *Ragtime* (1975) and *Billy Bathgate* (1989), both of which received a National Book Critics Circle award, and the National Book Award-winning *World's Fair* (1986). His latest book is *Sweet Land Stories* (Random House).

BRIAN DOYLE is the editor of *Portland Magazine* and the author of five collections of essays. His new book is *The Wet Engine*.

ANGIE ESTES's most recent book is *Chez Nous* (Oberlin College Press, 2005). Her second book, *Voice-Over* (2002), was awarded the Alice Fay di Castagnola Prize from the Poetry Society of America.

ANDREW FELD's first collection of poems, *Citizen* (HarperCollins), was a National Poetry Series selection in 2004. He is Associate Professor and Writer-in-Residence at Carthage College and lives in Kenosha, Wisconsin.

DIANE GILLIAM FISHER's book *Kettle Bottom* (Perugia Press, 2004), a collection of poems written in the voices of people living in the coal camps at the time of the 1920–21 West Virginia mine wars, was selected by the ABA as one of the Top Ten Poetry Books of 2004.

DAISY FRIED is the author of two books of poems, *My Brother Is Getting Arrested Again* (2006) and *She Didn't Mean To Do It* (2000) both published by the University of Pittsburgh. She is currently a Writer-in-Residence at Smith College.

505

JOHN FULTON is a professor of creative writing at the University of Massachusetts, Boston and the author of two books: *Retribution*, winner of the 2001 *Southern Review* Short Fiction Award and the novel *More Than Enough*.

TESS GALLAGHER's new collection of poetry, *Dear Ghosts*, is forthcoming from Graywolf in 2006. She is a past poetry co-editor of this series.

FRANK GASPAR lives in Long Beach, California. His latest collection is *Night of a Thousand Blossoms* (Alice Jones)

GEORGE GESSERT is an artist and occasional writer living in Oregon. He has exhibited widely in the United States, Canada, Europe and Australia and published in many anthologies and periodicals.

DAVID GESSNER's most recent book is *Sick of Nature* and before that *Return of the Ospreys*. He teaches at the University of North Carolina.

MARILYN HACKER is a National Book Award winning poet whose most recent book is *Desesperanto* (W.W. Norton, 2003). Her *Selected Poems* received the Poet's Prize in 1996.

DONALD HALL lives in Wilmont, New Hampshire. He has published many books of poetry and prose and is the former Poet Laureate of New Hampshire..

DONALD HAYS is the author of two novels, *The Dixie Association* and *The Hangman's Children*, and of the recently published *Dying Light and Other Stories*. He teaches at the University of Arkansas in Fayetteville.

GEOFFREY HILL is the author of more than a dozen volumes of poetry, most recently *Scenes from Comus* (2005), and *A Treatise of Civil Power* (2005). His new collection of poems, *Without Title*, will be published by Penguin (UK) in 2006.

EDWARD HIRSCH's most recent book of poems is *Lay Back the Darkness* (Knopf, 2003). He is co-editor of *A William Maxwell Portrait* (W.W. Norton, 2005) and serves as president of the John Simon Guggenheim Memorial Foundation.

ANN HOOD is the author of seven novels. Among them, *Three-Legged Horse*, *Something Blue*, *Places to Stay the Night*, and *Ruby*. Her newest short-story collection was published by W.W. Norton in 2004.

A. VAN JORDAN's first book, *Rise*, won the PEN/Oakland Award and his second book, *M-A-G-N-O-L-I-A* (W.W. Norton & Co.) won a Whiting Award.

BRIGIT PEGEEN KELLY's most recent book is *The Orchard*, published by BOA Editions. She teaches creative writing at the University of Illinois.

TED KOOSER is Poet Laureate Consultant in Poetry to the Library of Congress. His book from Copper Canyon Press, *Delights & Shadows*, was awarded the 2005 Pulitzer Prize.

PHILIP LEVINE won the National Book Award in 1991 with *What Work Is* and the Pulitzer Prize in 1995 with *The Simple Truth*. His most recent book is *Breath* (Knopf, 2004)

DAVID MAMET is a playwright, screenwriter and movie director. His works include *Glengarry Glen Ross*, and *Wag the Dog*.

JAMES McKEAN played basketball for the Washington State Cougars as an undergraduate and later published a book of essays *Home Stand: Growing Up In Sports* (Michigan State University Press). His poetry books include: *Headlong* (University of Utah Press) and *Tree of Heaven* (University of Iowa Press).

JOSHUA MEHIGAN's first book, *The Optimist* (Ohio University Press), was named by *ForeWord* magazine one of the ten top university press books of 2004. His poems have appeared in The New York *Times*, *Ploughshares* and other periodicals.

ALEX MINDT is both a playwright and story writer. His plays have been produced in Seattle and Los Angeles and his stories have been published in numerous periodicals including *Fiction*, *The Literary Review* and the *Missouri Review*.

JACK PENDARVIS comes from Bayou La Batr, Alabama. The story "Our Spring Catalogue" will soon appear in his book *The Mysterious Secret of the Valuable Treasure* (MacAdam/Cage).

LUCIA PERILLO's most recent books are *Luck Is Luck* (2005) and *The Oldest Map with the Name America* (1999), both from Random House.

CARL PHILLIPS' new book, *Riding Westward*, will be published by Farrar, Straus, and Giroux in the spring of 2006. *The Rest of Love* (FSG, 2004) was a National Book Award finalist.

STANLEY PLUMLY is a Distinguished University Professor at the University of Maryland. His two most recent books are *Now that My Father Lies Down Beside Me: New & Selected Poems 1970–2000* and *Argument & Song: Sources of Silence In Poetry* (2003).

LIA PURPURA has published a collection of essays, *Increase*, and a poetry collection, *Stone Sky Lifting*. She was awarded a 2004 NEA Fellowship in Prose and is Writer-in-Residence at Loyola College.

ATSURO RILEY lives in Menlo Park, California, and appears in this series for the first time.

DAVID RIVARD's new collection, *Sugartown*, is forthcoming in early 2006 from Graywolf. His previous

506

books, also from Graywolf, include *Bewitched Playground* and *Wise Poison* for which he won the James Laughlin Prize from the Academy of American Poets in 1996.

VALERIE SAYERS, who teaches Creative Writing at the University of Notre Dame, is the author of five novels including *Brain Fever* and *Due East*.

CYNTHIA SHEARER is the author of the novels *The Celestial Jukebox* and *The Wonder Book of the Air*.

JIM SHEPARD is the author of six novels, most recently *Project X*, and two story collections, most recently *Love and Hydrogen*. He is a film columnist for *The Believer*, and teaches at Williams College where he lives with his wife, three children and "a harried and unreliable dog."

TOM SLEIGH's books include *After One*, *The Chain*, *The Dreamhouse*, and a translation of Euripidies' *Herakles*. His new book of poems, *Far Side of the Earth*, was published by Houghton Mifflin (2003).

GREGORY BLAKE SMITH has published two novels, *The Devil in the Dooryard* and *The Divine Comedy of John Venner*, a Notable Books selection from the New York *Times*. A new novel, *The Pope's Daughter* (Crown), appears in 2005.

R. T. SMITH's stories have appeared in numerous publications including *Southern Review*, *Virginia Quarterly Review*, and *Best American Short Stories*. He edits *Shenandoah*.

PAMELA STEWART's most recent book is *The Red Window* (University of Georgia Press, 1997). She lives and works on a fiber farm in western Massachusetts.

COLE SWENSEN's ninth book, *Goest*, was a finalist for the National Book Award. Her translation of Jean Frémon's *Island of the Dead* won the PEN/USA Award for literary translation in 2004.

LYSLEY TENORIO has published stories in *Atlantic Monthly*, *Ploughshares* and elsewhere. He is a winner of the Nelson Algren Short Story Award and teaches Creative Writing at St. Mary's College in San Francisco.

MELANIE RAE THON's most recent book is the novel *Sweet Hearts* (Washington Square Press, 2002). She is also the author of *Meteors in August* and *Iona Moon* and story collections, *First*, *Body* and *Girls in the Grass*.

NEISHA TWEED lives in Snellville, Georgia. This is her first appearance in this series.

ROSANNA WARREN lives in Vermont. Her most recent collection is *Departure* (WW Norton).

CYNTHIA WEINER's work has appeared in *Open City* and *5Trope*. She teaches at the Writers Studio in New York City and is working on a collection of short stories.

NANCE VAN WINCKEL's fourth collection of poetry is *Beside Ourselves* (Miami University Press, 2003). She received the Christopher Isherwood Fellowship in 2005.

ELLEN BRYANT VOIGT is the author of six books of poetry, most recently *Shadow of Heaven* which was a finalist for the National Book Award in 2002. She has just completed a term as the Vermont State Poet.

DEAN YOUNG lives in Berkeley, California. His most recent book is *First Course in Turbulence*.

PAUL ZIMMER is the author of eight collections of poetry and a volume of memoirs and essays, *After the Fire: A Writer Finds His Place* (U. Minnesota Press, 2001).

507

# INDEX

The following is a listing in alphabetical order by author's last name of works reprinted in the *Pushcart Prize* editions since 1976.

510

512

513

514

515

516

519

520

521

523

525

526

527

529

530

531

533

535

539

**DATE DUE**

DEMCO, INC. 38-2971